Dionisios Metaxas-Iacovatos

Othonas Metaxas
b. 1830–1900?

Countess Maria Zthrin
b. 1844–1914

Panagis Vergotis
b. 1842–1916

m. Eleni Tsitselis
b. 1853–1953

Yiannikostas Metaxas *b. 1878–1938*
Sisters: Penelope, Stamatina, Olga

m. Regina Metaxas, née Vergotis *b. 1896–1970*
Twin Sister: Angeliki Vergotis b. 1896–1976

Panagis Metaxas
b. 1918–1988

Nicholas Metaxas
(My Father)
b. 1927

Othonas Metaxas
b. 1922–1992

Praise for

Fish Out of Water

"In this portrait of Metaxas as a young man, deeply serious matters exist most comfortably with great wit and maximum humor. As enjoyable as it is to follow him from birth through the fog of his twenties and into the sunlight at their end, you will see that you have also painlessly embraced a wonderful complexity. Even the title represents multiple meanings woven throughout the book that are, as in the solution to a mystery, unified and made clear at its end. I read it in the sunshine, which was entirely appropriate."

— **MARK HELPRIN**, *New York Times* bestselling author of many books, including *Winter's Tale* and *A Soldier of the Great War*

"Eric Metaxas [is] one of our nation's most brilliant and morally serious public intellectuals."

— **ROBERT P. GEORGE**, McCormick Professor of Jurisprudence and director of the James Madison Program in American Ideals and Institutions at Princeton University

"Metaxas is a major writer. Not to be missed."

— **DICK CAVETT**, legendary American television personality

"This memoir of one of our best writers' coming of age is a beautiful thing: deeply intelligent, spiritually acute, and laugh-out-loud funny."

— **BRET LOTT**, bestselling author of fourteen books, including *Jewel*, an Oprah's Book Club selection

"A wonderful story wonderfully told. Eric Metaxas knows how to tell complex things simply and serious things with lively wit. He is that rare and delightful being: a terrific writer with something important to say."

— **ANDREW KLAVAN**, international bestselling author and two-time Edgar Award winner

"The story rolls along and carries us with it, hilarious and heartbreaking by turns, vivid and contemplative, and regularly touched with poetry. Eric Metaxas is a brilliant communicator."

—**FREDERICA MATHEWES-GREEN**, Orthodox Christian author and speaker

"According to Dostoevsky, when Russian boys meet, they talk about God. Reading the book by Eric Metaxas, I felt the author and myself as such Russian boys. His youth was spent in the U.S.A., mine in the U.S.S.R.—countries, to put it mildly, that are very different. Despite this, we are remarkably similar. This concerns our first literary impressions (special thanks to 'Werther'!), our first own discoveries, and most importantly, what are commonly called 'universal values.' Only good books create unity between author and reader—wherever each of them may live. *Fish Out of Water* is such a book. It sparkles with wonderful humor. This only happens with the most serious books."

—**EUGENE VODOLAZKIN**, author of *Laurus*

"Truth really is stranger than fiction—stranger, less predictable, often (though not always) funnier, and weirder. Reality is not fastidious and doesn't pay any attention to opinion polls. Hence the appeal of this memoir by Eric Metaxas, an account of his formative years: a zany tale of literary aspirations...."

—**JOHN WILSON**, former *Books & Culture* editor (1995–2016), contributing editor for the *Englewood Review of Books*, and senior editor at the *Marginalia Review of Books*

"With his inimitable intelligence and wit, Eric Metaxas recounts his formative years as a first-generation immigrant, the crucial development of his ability to think for himself rather than following the herd, and the process of learning to follow his heart and mind wherever the truth leads...."

—**JILL LAMAR**, former editor-in-chief of Henry Holt and Company and curator of new titles for Barnes & Noble

"A delight! Eric Metaxas has crafted for each discerning reader a personal gift: A richly detailed, lovingly remembered American story that faces squarely serious issues to which every one of us should attend. From the struggles of immigrant families to bullying in school, from the trauma that victims of war and totalitarianism carry to the hunger for meaning that postmodern students face in college, Eric uses his own experience to illumine enduring, important questions. He does so with humor [and] moral insight...."

—**JOHN ZMIRAK**, editor at The Stream

"How do brave men advance through adversity with courage and then summon courage from the rest of us? Read Eric Metaxas's artfully scrappy memoir to cultivate courage and meet the public intellectual behind the books that we love. This memoir stands as a beacon to a world lost to us, and casts a tractor beam to a future which demands virtue, bravery, courage, and personal sacrifice...."

—**ROSARIA BUTTERFIELD**, author of *The Secret Thoughts of an Unlikely Convert*

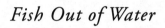

Fish Out of Water

ERIC METAXAS

#1 *New York Times* bestselling author

Fish Out of Water

A Search for the Meaning of Life

A Memoir

✴

SALEM
BOOKS

an imprint of Regnery Publishing
Washington, D.C.

Cover photo by Annerose Kraegen.

Salem Books™ is a trademark of Salem Communications Holding Corporation
Regnery® is a registered trademark of Salem Communications Holding Corporation

ISBN: 978-1-68451-172-3
eISBN: 978-1-68451-174-7

Library of Congress Control Number: 2020945141

Published in the United States by
Salem Books
An Imprint of Regnery Publishing
A Division of Salem Media Group
Washington, D.C.
www.SalemBooks.com

Manufactured in the United States of America

10 9 8 7 6 5 4 3 2 1

Books are available in quantity for promotional or premium use. For information on discounts and terms, please visit our website: www.SalemBooks.com.

This book is for my father and mother,

and for Charis Conn, who swan-dove into the
period at the end of the sentence God wrote for her
and emerged in His presence in Heaven

Contents

Author's Note

One night in the summer of 1988 I had a dream. It was so powerful that it changed my life utterly and forever. Although I'm essentially the same person I was before the dream, it was so unprecedented and otherworldly that it's perfectly fair to say I'm also not at all the same person I was before. Please understand that this was an actual dream; it happened while I was sleeping and unconscious. And I think that what the dream really did—and did astonishingly exquisitely and brilliantly—was make sense of my life up until that point. But in doing that, it has also made sense of my life going forward; it has lent deep meaning and purpose to my life ever since. There is no hyperbole here. Eternity broke into my life while I was sleeping and worked its ways backwards and forwards, making sense of the past and the future. I'm afraid that for you to appreciate what I'm trying to say you need to know the story of my life until the dream happened. This is that story.

Introduction

It was February 2, 2012, and I was at the podium at the National Prayer Breakfast in Washington, D.C., eight feet away from President Barack Obama, who was politely giving me his rapt attention in that monstrously vast Hilton Hotel ballroom outside of which President Ronald Reagan was shot by a man[1] inspired to his assassination attempt by a woman with whom I once danced at Yale.

Next to the president on the dais was the first lady. Near me was Nancy Pelosi, and right next to me was Vice President Joe Biden, with whom I had been chit-chatting uncomfortably, seriously tongue-tied by a combination of three hours' sleep and a knowledge of him unfairly compromised by the hysterical articles about him in the parodic *The Onion*, in one of which, shirtless, he washes his "awesome" Camaro in the White House driveway, horrifying the president yet again.

I had previously backstage-kidded with the Speaker of the House. It was my wife's birthday, and she had begged me not to point her out in the audience. In fact, she shyly chose to sit not with me on the dais, but with my

---

[1] President Reagan's would-be assassin, John Hinckley Jr., had a copy of *The Catcher in the Rye* in his hotel room.

parents and daughter in the crowd. Yet I thought I might have her cake and eat it too by pretending that the Speaker—who was on the dais—was my wife. I would mention my wife's birthday and point to the Speaker, and she would stand and acknowledge the crowd as though she were my wife, and it would of course be comedy gold. I tried to make the joke clear to the Speaker backstage so she would know how to play along when the killer moment presented itself, but when at the podium I said it was my wife's birthday, gestured to the Speaker and said, "Please stand up, sweetie," she only smiled confusedly as though we had never spoken. And the historic moment passed. Directly in front of me as I gave my speech about twenty feet away was Hillary Clinton, whose gaze made me think she felt compelled to be there and had spent her life doing dutiful things like this, and I felt sorry for her and hoped and prayed something I said might break through and touch her somehow.

When in my speech I jokingly and shamelessly handed the president a copy of my biography of the German pastor and martyr Dietrich Bonhoeffer—and then, larding on the goofball shamelessness, did the same with my William Wilberforce biography, saying I knew he had a lot of time on his hands on long plane rides and was probably looking for something to read—the president dutifully held *Bonhoeffer* up for the cameras, and nearly instantly the wire services sent that photo around the world.

I thought it might be appropriate to close my peroration by leading the crowd and president in singing the first verse of "Amazing Grace" *a capella*, since most people know the lyrics. I was inspired in this by Garrison Keillor, who had moved me greatly when he did this at the Boston Opera House in 1985, as I explain in this book. And so we sang that happy verse—and to my great joy it was nearly as magical as I had remembered it being all those years before, with the a capella harmonies of that sweet melody being as transcendent as harmonies sometimes can be, as though they are harmonizing the very souls of the singers themselves, uniting us with each other on that frequency where truth and beauty and goodness live, and doing more than we can see or feel as we join in singing them—and then I sat down, and then the president spoke, and then it was over.

But as the president was leaving, I realized the White House photographer had not taken any pictures of me with the president—which I certainly had hoped for—so when the president came down from the dais to say goodbye to each of us I pulled out my phone, planning to take a selfie. But before I could do this the eternally avuncular vice president forcefully and graciously intervened, taking my camera and himself taking the picture of me and the president, which picture I cannot help but treasure, though I treasure even more the picture I found some weeks later, which the White House photographer had indeed troubled himself to take. It was of the vice president taking my picture with the president.

Of course the question *becomes* how I had gotten onto that stage in the first place, and this book means among other things to be an answer to that question. I might say I had gotten there by writing my biography of Dietrich Bonhoeffer, which unexpectedly became a bestseller the previous year, drawing me to the attention of those who invited me. But one might still wonder how I came to write that book. And I could answer *that* by saying I had a dramatic experience in the summer of 1988, around when my friend Ed Tuttle gave me a copy of Bonhoeffer's *The Cost of Discipleship*. But one must still wonder how I came to that place in 1988 where I was open to reading that book and thinking about what Bonhoeffer writes in it regarding what we might call the meaning of life.[2]

---

[2] Who has not at some point longed for meaning? Can such a person exist? By meaning I of course mean meaning in our own lives personally, but also the meaning of life in general, or the question of whether there is such a thing. This does not mean every one of us is aware of such longings or questions, but I do know that I myself became aware of such longings at some point much as someone becomes aware of being awake after having slept. I suppose the circumstances of my life conspired in such a way that I was obliged to attend to this question, perhaps against my own wishes. So this book is really the story of those unfolding circumstances; and you will of course judge for yourself what to make of it, if anything. If my own life is any indication, many of us prefer to drift along without paying much attention to these longings, feeling it's emotionally or socially safer to bat them away and keep moving. Perhaps we fear these questions have no good and satisfying answers, or may even have horrifying answers, so to ask them too insistently is to look for trouble. And who hasn't known people who seem to have all the answers to such questions—and are often especially

In any event, I think I must begin the story before the beginning, before I began to exist in the darkness of my dear mother's womb, and before I was banished therefrom into the bright brokenness of our mysterious and meaning-haunted world.

annoying, if not plainly nutso? So is it really surprising that we might prefer to avoid these questions?

In any event, it happened that I was eventually unsuccessful in avoiding these questions, or was even shoved along toward them. But to my deepest surprise—and certainly to my own shock, which remains perpetual—I discovered certain answers I was previously sure could never be found, even if they existed, which I suspected they did not. So it is precisely and only because I know I cannot take credit for this that I am able to tell my story, and to tell it as much as possible precisely as it happened. I have also become convinced that my story unfolded less for me than for some others who dare now and again to wonder whether we might ask questions about—or even of—the universe in which we never asked to exist, but nonetheless discover ourselves existing.

In other words, I believe my story unspooled as it did so that I might tell it, so that whoever wishes to might come along for the ride and themselves see what I am sure I didn't deserve to see, but nonetheless saw. I further believe that in relating these events as honestly as I can the perfect specificity and parochialness of it may open onto a universal, perhaps as a black hole may open onto another universe—or at least onto something that, if not quite universal, is nonetheless large enough to include others such as those who are reading this. So I believe that in surrendering to the naked subjectivity of my own story I may be able via the art of art to overcome the perennial divide between us, and magically by it lend both of our stories something not invaluable. So although the telling may be mine, I believe the story itself is actually for you.

So this book is the answer to that final question more than any other. In some ways it is a *bildungsroman,* and in another a picaresque novel, although the characters are real and the events are as written.

Omphalos

I AM AN AMERICAN, the son of immigrants. My parents came to these golden shores separately in the great American 1950s, after the war that had ravaged their continent had spent its wrath.

My father came here from Greece in August 1955, aged twenty-eight. His family had lived on the Ionian Island of Cephalonia since 1453, when Constantinople fell to the Turks. In the 1670s our ancestor Iakomos Metaxas settled on the land that is still ours, though what belongs to us has dramatically diminished, this being due—at least in part—to my great-grandfather, Othon Metaxas, leaving his wife and four children in the late 1880s. His three daughters were teenagers and his son—my grandfather Yiannikostas—was ten. His mother, the countess Maria Metaxas (née Zthrin), sold off parts of the land so he and the three girls could continue with their education and have dowries sufficient to marry within their class, a goal in which all succeeded. But my grandfather was obliged to help by going to sea as a cabin boy when he turned twelve. That was in 1890, and for the next forty-two years he circumnavigated the watery part of the world innumerable times, eventually rising to become the captain of his own ship. He only returned home periodically, during which episodes he married my grandmother Regina (née Vergotis) and fathered their sons: Panagis—called Takis—in 1919; Othon in 1922; and my father, Nikolaos, in 1927.

My grandfather, Yiannikostas Metaxas, circa 1910

As the story goes, Yiannikostas (my grandfather) became engaged to a woman rumored to have been seen with another man while Yiannikostas—who had already purchased their marriage bed—was at sea. When the news reached him, he ended the engagement and soon afterward was visiting friends in Argostoli who urged him to find another bride when, just across the street, staring from their window, he saw identically attractive twenty-one-year-olds. The twins were of a good family and had been raised in the "proper" way, with English, French, and piano lessons. And their father, who had died that year, was the renowned author and educator Panagis Vergotis.

My dashing thirty-eight-year-old grandfather said that "the one on the left" appealed to him. Her name was Angeliki, and she was called "Kikí." But his friends knew Kikí was then corresponding with a devotee of her father's work; the budding relationship seemed promising. "Then I'll take the other one," he replied. And so it was that he and Regina—called "Renee"—were soon engaged and married.

When my father was born in 1927—on what thirty-six years thence would become my own birthday—he was unable to digest his mother's milk. The only solution to this potentially fatal problem was to locate a lactating donkey; and so Yiannikostas searched far and wide before finding one, and it was that particular ass's milk that enabled my father to survive and my own life to become possible.

Because he suffered from asthma, which the sea air was thought to exacerbate, Yiannikostas retired from his captaincy in 1932. My grandmother Renee lived with their three children in the capacious villa in Argostoli from whose window she and Kikí had looked out nineteen years before, and which had been the Vergotis family home throughout the previous century. But now when Yiannikostas returned from the sea for good, he and Renee would live apart, though the reasons for this are unclear. She would remain at her family's villa with Takis and Othon, then in school—and with her unmarried sister Kikí and their mother, Eleni—while Yiannikostas would settle in the distant village of Mavrata, where the Metaxas family had been for two and a half centuries in their own impressive villa. For company he would take my father, then five, who recalls those years with his own father as the happiest of his life.

When he went into the village *kafeneion* to play cards, Yiannikostas always took my father along, who remembers that the cards were so worn they no longer had corners, and whenever Yiannikostas won he celebrated by rewarding my father with a *demitasse* of cooked chickpeas—*stragalia*, as they were called. One summer afternoon Yiannikostas was taking a typical Cephalonia siesta, but my father could not sleep. So he slipped into the yard, where he climbed enough trees to catch five or six cicadas with his little hands, imprisoning them in a cardboard cigarette package. After his labors he lay down again with his father—having put the package inside his buttoned shirt for safekeeping—and fell asleep. But when he awoke, he realized that the clever insects had escaped to every unknown corner of the house, from which they broadcast their punishing prehistoric racket for many days. But my grandfather was not angry. He obviously took delight in his Nikolaki.[1] Once when they visited relatives in nearby Katelios, Yiannikostas asked his son to sing something, and when my father proved too shy to do so, suggested he simply sing from the next room, where no one could see him. So my father went to the other room. But when the adults heard no singing for some time, my grandfather went into the room himself and discovered an open window, from which the disinclined songbird had cleverly flown the coop.

---

[1] The Greeks often add the suffix "aki" to names to create an endearing diminutive. The standard diminutive of my Uncle Takis's name "Panagis" is therefore "Panagakis," but his "Takis" is taken from the yet further endearing "Panagiotakis."

Takis, Nikos, and Othon, 1929

Traveling from Mavrata to Argostoli in the thirties meant boarding a run-down but roomy 1923 Chevrolet, which passed for a bus and made the thirty-two-mile roundtrip each weekday. The roads were unpaved, so everyone could see this car coming from a very great distance because of the tremendous cloud of dust it kicked up. Most of its battered exterior was eventually replaced with scraps of lumber, and children might be forgiven for thinking that the whole thing—engine and all—had been carved from a single block of wood. Young passengers were sometimes obliged to ride standing on the running boards, although the old motor's power was such that when they came to the long hill on the return journey, just before St. George's Castle, everyone had to get off and walk.

One day in January 1938, my grandfather made the trip into Argostoli alone, leaving my father in the care of a neighbor. Late that afternoon, while playing in the street, my father heard the discordant and warped-sounding *dang … dang … dang …* that is the dirge of church bells in that part of the world. As the ominous sound cast its vulture's shadow over his head, my father looked up and saw a woman in a window calling to her neighbor across the way, asking in what he still imitates today as a plaintive and ghostlike voice: *"Pios pethane?"*, meaning "Who died?"

And then the unforgettable response: *"O Yiannikostas! O Yiannikostas pethane!"* This was how my ten-year-old father learned that his own father had left the world.

My father, 1938

So my father returned to Argostoli now, to live again with his mother and two teenaged brothers. But when war came to Greece in October 1940, he again returned to the rural environs of Mavrata, this time to live with his grandmother Eleni and his Aunt Kikí. The following May they looked up to see descending out of their own Greek blue sky a frightening host of Italian paratroopers, come to occupy the island.

Days later, one knocked at the door. He was visiting every house in the village to see that no one was hiding weapons. But on spying a small Greek flag in a vase in the entrance hall, he demanded in Italian to know whose it was. My father—then a skinny thirteen-year-old—answered in Italian: "*Mio.*" The soldier slapped him across the face, knocking him to the ground, then grabbed the flag, broke it in two, and threw it to the floor. My great-grandmother—in the Italian she had herself learned seventy years earlier from her brothers who had gone to the universities there—brusquely spoke to the soldier. "Were you not taught to love your country's flag when you were a boy?" she asked. The soldier turned on his heel and left.

This extraordinary woman—Eleni Vergotis (née Tsitselis)—was the principal influence on my father's life. She was born in 1853 and lived to one hundred, dying just months after the 1953 earthquake. My father says the village children often gathered to hear her stories and recalls that at the end of her life, possessing but a single tooth, she ate only boiled greens such as Swiss chard or dandelion greens—or amaranth, which they call *vlita*.

Eleni had been married in the 1870s to the scion of the wealthy Charetatos family who lived in Lixouri, across Argostoli Bay. She became pregnant three times, but each of these ended in a miscarriage. Desperate for an heir, she and her husband then traveled to the capitals of Europe in search of a cure—and at last having found one, gratefully returned to Cephalonia, where Eleni became pregnant a fourth time. But during this fourth pregnancy her husband died unexpectedly. It was a terrible blow, but at least according to the laws of that time Eleni was entitled—as the mother of her late husband's heir—to remain in the Charetatos home and be financially secure throughout her life. In the eighth month of the pregnancy, however, while at the top of a staircase, she happened to trip on the hem of her long skirt and fell down the stairs. A doctor was summoned and the child was soon delivered, stillborn. My father has often said that if the child had drawn a single breath outside the womb, as determined by the doctor, it would legally have been considered an heir, and Eleni would have been allowed to stay. She convalesced in Lixouri for a time, but after a month, knowing she must go, packed her things and returned alone to her parents' home in Argostoli.

Her brother, the historian and scholar Ilias Tsitselis (1850–1927), had a good friend named Panagis, whom she came to know and eventually married. And then, many years after her fourth ill-fated pregnancy, she unexpectedly became pregnant for a fifth time, and in her forty-third year bore a pair of healthy twins, Regina and Angeliki.[2]

My father was not nearly as close to his mother as he was to his Aunt Kikí, with whom he spent the five years in Mavrata during the war, missing all of high school and having to make it up afterward. Even after the war, the Greeks continued fighting, this time in their own civil war against the Communists. In the early fifties my father served in the Greek navy and then briefly lived with his mother in Athens. But in August of 1953 a series of extraordinarily destructive earthquakes struck the island, killing almost a thousand people and leveling nearly every building. My father quickly traveled there to salvage what he could from the destroyed home in Argostoli, but most of it was lost. He recalled stepping off a navy ship to see the unspeakable chaos and destruction, and to meet his best friend Tassos Grigorakis as if for the first time, obviously undone by what he had witnessed, looking "wild" and permanently distracted. Others who knew him saw him stepping off the boat and greeted him almost as a "messiah" come to save them in their darkest hour. He carried a canvas tent that he had bought in Athens to give to Kikí and his centenarian grandmother, who were sleeping on cots outside. They slept in this tent until November, where his grandmother finally slipped into the next world. As it happened, it was because of this earthquake that the United States agreed to

---

[2] My father said that his mother and aunt—as was the custom with other women of their generation—guarded the actual year of their birth utterly, but if pressed hard enough by the right person might with tremendous reluctance allow that it had been "1900." It was not until 1975, after his mother's death and not long before Kiki's, that my father received a letter from his aunt, confessing the actual date as 1896.

receive a number of Cephalonian refugees, enabling my father to come to New York in August 1955, where his elder brother Takis was already living.

MY MOTHER came to New York from Germany in 1954, aged twenty. Her mother's family had lived in the village of Großstoebnitz—south of Leipzig—for centuries. My grandmother Gertrud was the thirteenth of seventeen children born to Minna Grosse (née Krug), and often told me that they were so poor that all the children worked, no matter how young. Before and after school the youngest took in what she called "piece work," which entailed simple tasks, like putting the bristles in toothbrushes, while the older girls worked as maids for nearby land-owning farmers. My grandmother's father, Otto, was in charge of just such a farmer's horses. But during the winter of 1912, when my grandmother was seven, he died. "How I cried!" she said to me, so many times, recalling how the village's volunteer fire brigade beautifully played their brass instruments behind the horse-drawn bier carrying her *Papa* through the snow to the old church. A few years later two of her four brothers were killed in the First War, and two decades later a third was killed in the Second, which would also claim her husband, Erich.

My grandfather—for whom I am named—was killed while riding on a train to the Russian front on April 4, 1944. It was blown up by partisans near Lviv in Ukraine, where his bones lie still. He had an older brother, Charles, but his parents divorced when he was two, and we know little of them, but we know that his paternal grandfather was Emil Phillip Kraegen, a pianist and music teacher at court in Dresden, who there met and in 1849 married Mathilda Fenton of Berwick-upon-Tweed, Scotland, who was governess to three young Russian princesses.[3] Emil's father, Karl Phillip Heinrich Kraegen (1797–1879), a music teacher and celebrated pianist and composer, was close friends with Robert Schumann, whose wife, Clara, taught piano to Dietrich Bonhoeffer's maternal grandmother, the Countess Kalkreuth.

---

[3] These were Maria Sidonia (b. 1834), Anna Maria (b. 1836), and Margarete (b. 1840).

My mother in New York, 1954

My mother often recalled the horror of her mother's shrieking when she received the unthinkable news. My grandfather had been quietly opposed to the Nazi regime and even dared to listen to the BBC, pressing his ear against the radio speaker, lest he be discovered and sent to a concentration camp. A close family friend under whom he worked at the Altenburg sewing machine factory had managed to keep my grandfathe out of the war until 1943, an extraordinary feat. But at last he had to go. My grandmother recalled that he wept the night before leaving and a year later, aged thirty-one, he was killed. My mother was nine.

The years after the war were far harder for my family than the war years themselves. My mother recalls once returning from school to see her mother weeping because she had no food to give her girls; and if not for the care packages sent by our Tante Ella—who had gone to New York in 1930—they might not have survived. That my mother and father both experienced the war and real hunger, and the childhood deaths of their fathers, would forever bond them to each other, and each had innumerable tales of the horrors and privations of those times. My mother said that for a time her best friend Brigitte shared a pair of shoes with her mother, such that only one of them could leave the house at a time.

When the Russians had fully occupied what became East Germany, my mother found the Communist propaganda in school unbearable—so much so that in 1951, at age seventeen, she and a friend took the great risk of leaving their families to attempt crossing the border into the West. She succeeded, but not without some trials, and two years later was joined by my grandmother

From left: My Aunt Eleonore, my grandmother Gertrud, my mother, and my grandfather Erich

and aunt. When in 1953 Tante Ella visited West Germany, she asked my mother whether she wanted to come to New York. And months later my mother did just that, boarding the MS *Stockholm* in August 1954.[4] Upon arriving in New York she stayed with Tante Ella and days later joined the ranks of the immigrant domestic help, taking a kitchen job in the magnificent townhouse of the Whiteman family on East 65th Street.

My father also lived in Manhattan in the fifties, working as a busboy at Neptune's Corner on Broadway, and then as a waiter at Howard Johnson's near Radio City while also taking English classes. If this weren't enough, he was also for two and a half years enrolled at RCA Institutes, taking classes in the mornings and hoping for a job in the burgeoning field of electronics. He often told us of his struggle to get ahead, sometimes carrying home huge jars of cold coffee from the restaurant so he could stay up through the night to study for a morning exam. And he recalled with laughter the small humiliations of being new to the language, as when—at Howard Johnson's—he delivered a Scotch on the rocks to the perplexed customer who had ordered a

---

[4] Two years later it collided with the *Andrea Doria*, which sank off Nantucket, killing forty-six passengers in one of the worst maritime disasters of the twentieth century.

butterscotch sundae. He also said it was his duty to return the live lobsters displayed on ice in the window at Neptune's Corner to their tank at the end of the night, placing them on a vast tray that he carried at shoulder level, and recalled that one Houdini among them one night, having slipped its rubberized bonds, promptly seized his nearby ear, causing such pain that he dropped the entire tray.[5]

It was in the fall of 1956 that these two fatherless immigrants met in an evening English class on First Avenue, in what was then the Julia Richman High School. And that December they had their first date, visiting Teddy Roosevelt's birthplace on East 20th Street, which patriotic fact I will always treasure, the star-spangled specific that swathes the first happy moments of my origins.

---

[5] Only during the writing of this book did he reveal to me the existence of the permanent scar from this epsiode, sustained some sixty-five years earlier.

I Am Born, Etc.

The evening before I was born, my parents[1] took a walk to Astoria Park; and as they began the journey home my mother felt her water beginning to break. They quickly hailed a cab, but not quickly enough, so that her water broke in the back seat, embarrassingly flooding the taxi. Once home they grabbed her overnight bag and walked the three blocks to Astoria General Hospital where at 8:08 the following morning—my father's thirty-sixth birthday—I took my first breath.

Our apartment was two blocks from the "El"[2] and a block from St. Demetrios Greek Orthodox Church, where months later I was fully immersed in

---

[1] My parents were married on the memorably hot and humid afternoon of August 22, 1959, in the Greek Orthodox Cathedral on East 74th Street. My father has often said that their reception guests were so squeezed in the small room at Ricardo's in Astoria that to reach your food with your utensils you had to ask one of the people next to you to move. Though in their first months together they lived with my grandmother in Woodside, they soon found an affordable—but dramatically dreary—apartment in Astoria. My mother was then working as an IBM keypuncher at its Madison Avenue headquarters, and the following year my father earned his RCA diploma and traded waiting tables for a job with the Bulova Watch Company. In the summer of 1962 my parents went to Greece so my mother could meet her new relatives, and that fall she discovered they were expecting a child.

[2] Elevated "subway" train

the waters of baptism contained in the ornate golden font used for this ceremony. Across the alley lived a woman named Mrs. Smith, to whom I have an earliest memory of waving when my mother or father held me to the window. The other memories from these months are of being weighed on the pediatrician's horizontal scale, and of two black knobs on each side of my carriage, and of the oversized pastel-colored plastic keys hanging overhead.

My father often said our apartment was depressing, that "just to see a piece of sky" you had to stick your head out the window into the alley and look straight up. Seventeen months after my birth my brother, John, came into the world, after which we happily moved to 91st Street and Northern Boulevard in Jackson Heights. For twenty-eight hundred dollars my parents bought a small two-bedroom on the fifth floor of a six-story high-rise in a three-block development of identical red brick buildings, three per block for three blocks, with benches and trees and playgrounds between them.

My father took the El to work, returning precisely at five, when we ate dinner, after which he played with me and my brother in the living room. Sometimes he smoked a cigarette, but this would end soon. But as is typical of most children's earliest years, my main memories are of my mother, whose love for me was a palpable undergirding presence.

She and I often looked together out of the window in the bedroom I shared with my brother. Once, as we did this she held my hand and said, "Eric, do you feel that?" And I could feel the blood pulsing in our clasped hands. And because I knew our blood came from our hearts, I accepted it when she said: "That's the love you're feeling, between us." I inherited most of my romantic nature from my mother, and the need to hug and kiss—which I now do to everyone for whom I feel affection. It was not the peasant Saxon German side, but the more patrician Greek side of my family that was more reserved.

My mother often sang German songs to me, one of which—a nineteenth-century carol—we sang whenever it snowed.

Kling, Glöckchen! Kling-eling-eling!
Kling, Glöckchen, kling!
Laßt mich ein, ihr Kinder,

ist so kalt der Winter!
Öffnet mir die Türen,
laßt mich nicht erfrieren!
Kling, Glöckchen! Kling-elin-geling!
Kling, Glöckchen, kling!

One afternoon as we daydreamed together at the window, it suddenly began snowing. Each of us—entirely unaware the other was going to sing anything—began singing this at exactly the same time. We were each looking straight ahead at the falling snow and separately began the song in such perfect unison we both knew neither of us had prompted the other. It was a mystical moment, the first I can remember, with the snow floating from the overcast sky, down between the brick-colored buildings and each of us singing and knowing we had begun this song together in a way that somehow confirmed our love for each other.

Often I walked with my mother through the tree-lined streets of Jackson Heights, usually with my brother in his stroller. When we were both old enough, she took us to story time at the library a few blocks north, and by the time I was four she had taught me to read, although she implausibly maintains that I somehow taught myself. Before that, whenever my brother was asleep, my mother sometimes took short naps on the living room couch while I lay on the carpeted floor near her and flipped through copies of *LIFE*, mesmerized by the photos.

We often walked across Northern Boulevard to the Key Foods store, and once I took along a Playskool toy that

The author recovering from pneumonia, December 1964

was pushed along like a lawnmower. It had a yellow wooden pole and handle, and down at the end of it was a clear plastic bubble containing what looked like brightly colored gum balls that *pop-popped* around as you pushed it. On the sidewalk in front of the store my curiosity so overtook me that I smashed the plastic bubble onto the concrete, only to learn they were not gum balls after all. That Christmas, I was given a drum and curiosity again compelled me to find out what was inside, such that I violently punctured the top with the drumsticks and was again bitterly disappointed.

When I was four I noticed the flag pole in the neighborhood schoolyard at half-mast and asked about it. My mother said it commemorated a man who had been shot and killed. Seeing the same thing two months later I asked again and learned that another man had been shot and killed. The first was Martin Luther King Jr., the second Robert Kennedy.

Our building was almost exclusively Jewish. Down the hall lived Mrs. Weingarten, then in her seventies, to whom my mother spoke German and who once showed me the tattoo on her arm from when she had been in one of the Nazi camps. We also knew the Ungers, whose son Wayne sometimes came over to play with me. Mr. Unger generously invited my father to join the group of Jewish men who played poker in the basement every Friday night. Many weekends my father made extra money installing "hi-fis" with his friend Jack Seligman and recalled installing a deluxe system in the author Philip Roth's house in Westchester, where drilling holes behind a wall they discovered a box containing the handwritten manuscript of *Portnoy's Complaint*.

We often drove to Flushing Meadows Park, the site of the 1939 and 1965 World Fairs, the latter of which we visited, though I only remember being in a rowboat and passing the "It's a Small World" exhibit and singing along to the music. Every Easter thereafter we drove to Flushing Meadow and parked near a stand of young pine trees, and my mother would disappear to see if the Easter Bunny had left anything under them. He always had, so my brother and I grabbed our baskets and ran to find colored eggs and chocolate atop the light brown pine needles. After we found what my mother said was everything, we took a long walk, though I kept looking under every bush and tree as we did, hoping I might find just one more.

My mother sometimes took us into Manhattan via subway, usually to the Central Park Zoo, with its Monkey House that stank and the Reptile House and another building with a huge hippo tank of opaque jade-green water. The Children's Zoo had a Three Little Pigs exhibit of real pigs, and a Noah's Ark you boarded via a gangway, featuring cages with small animals that inevitably hid. There was also a whale into whose open mouth and across whose pink rubber tongue you dared to walk to see the dirty goldfish tank lodged in his gullet, which always somehow confused me. We sometimes waited to see the bronze animals come to life on the Delacorte clock atop the brick archway: a kangaroo, a hippo, a bear, a goat, and an elephant, who went round and round on a track holding instruments, and above them a large bell that two monkeys struck with mallets.

My grandmother lived with her sister, Tante Ella, in Sunnyside, a few El stops away, and because she worked in Loft's Candy Company in Long Island City, she always smelled of chocolate. She came for dinner every Tuesday and when I hugged her the magical aroma was overpowering. She usually worked on the assembly line, wrapping "parlay bars" in foil, and sometimes brought us a huge five-pound box of chocolates that employees could buy for a dollar fifty. She loved her job and was a strikingly joyful person, though never cloyingly so. Despite what she had suffered, there was a childlike innocence to her.

My Theo Taki and Aunt Mary and my older cousin John lived in Manhattan, where on Saturdays my father often took my brother and me. Once, getting on the subway, I saw rattan seats and ceiling fans overhead and my father explained it was a very old car. I never entered another, but have since spotted them in movies from the thirties. Theo Takis owned a coffeeshop on 76th and Third, which we always visited. I marveled at the autographed photos of JFK and Barbra Streisand and other celebrities who had visited. After visiting him we sometimes went to Lyric HiFi on 83rd, where my father had worked, and across the avenue to see Mr. Phillis and his nephew Speros at the Lexington Candy Shop Luncheonette. Speros was one of my father's closest friends and like an uncle to us. They too had met in an English class and lived together in a run-down four-flight walk-up on East 75th. Like my father, Speros married a northern European and eventually would convince my staid father to leave the city. In my father's estimation, the only downside to New York was the mayor, John Lindsay, a rising star in liberal politics who would later run for president. My father said if he became president we would move to Greece. So it was not really until Lindsay's drubbing in the 1972 primaries that we knew for sure we were in America to stay.

My first impression, aged seventeen months

Actually it was not until we moved to Connecticut that year that I myself felt truly American, because before then Europe and WWII were our inescapable cultural lodestones. From when I was sixteen months old, my father often asked me to imitate Benito Mussolini, which I instantly did, shooting out my chin and lower lip and looking imperious, to his great delight. As long as I can remember, my father always ranked European powers in how they had acquitted

themselves in the War, though this never affected how he related to individual members of those countries. Of course, the Germans were militarily without peer, and deserved respect for that, despite all else. The Greeks were a close second, being famously courageous in standing up to Mussolini's Italians.[3] And down the line it went. The Poles were great heroes, as were the Norwegians. The Swiss were rightly despised for their craven "neutrality." The Italians were generally regarded as a cheerful joke. But ignobly at the bottom of the martial totem pole were the French, whose speedy capitulation to the Wehrmacht stood without peer in the annals of modern warfare. My father often explained how they had welcomed the Germans by doing his best Greek-accented impression of a French maître d' holding an

---

[3] The Greeks then fought the Germans, too, who had to rescue the Italians from the Greeks in the fall of 1940. In fact it was this unyielding fight on the part of the Greeks in spite of overwhelming opposition that slowed Hitler's march to Russia, such that the "Barbarossa" campaign was delayed six fatal weeks, placing the Germans there too late to escape the Russian winter, and greatly contributing to their eventual defeat.

invisible towel over his left hand and gesturing with his right, saying, "Mees-ter Heet-ler, right this way ..."

Uncle Takis was eight years my father's senior, and my father's love for him could never compete with the closeness between my mother and her sister Eleonore, who were seventeen months apart, minus one day.[4] Their fierce bond included my grandmother, who was more like a third sister. They had together suffered the loss of "*der Papa*," as they called him, and endured the painful years after the war. So most of our family time on weekends was spent with my Tante Eleonore and her family in Astoria.

Just as my parents had created a home that was Greek and German, Tante Eleonore and Uncle Joe, whose surname was Sarrantonio and who was Italian—had a similarly mixed home. But just as marrying a Greek essentially meant becoming Greek, marrying an Italian from Astoria essentially meant becoming Italian. My aunt and uncle—and our two cousins Eleanor and Marion—lived in the apartment above Uncle Joe's parents, "Nanny" and "Pop," and just across the alley from my uncle's brother's family. So the world in which they lived seemed a hermetically sealed Italo-American universe in which all the pasta and wine were homemade and most of the boys were named Joe or Frank. The atmosphere was something out of *Goodfellas*, with beehive hairdos and Jerry Vale on the stereo singing "Non Dimenticar." My Tante Eleonore swooned over him and—sounding remarkably like Marlene Dietrich—often said: "I love Jeh-wee Vale!"

Uncle Joe was a New York City fireman with tattoos and impressive biceps. It seemed Uncle Joe could do almost anything, including build a whole house, which he soon did. When I was five he put me on a kitchen chair and with one hand holding one of its legs raised it to the ceiling with me on it. He

---

[4] My brother and I were seventeen months apart, minus one day, too. In fact, my mother's birthday was just three days earlier than my father's and mine, and my aunt's birthday and my brother's were a day apart, which doesn't mean anything in particular, but nonetheless seems a vague confirmation of something positive, and as far as that goes, must mean something after all, though we can hardly say what.

loved doing things like that and always joked around with us, and my brother and I idolized him. In part because he was born in America, he always seemed "cooler" than our father, so when we were with him we felt more American and more "normal." For example, my father drove a decidedly square 1960 gray Dodge Valiant with tail fins, but Uncle Joe—and my Tante Eleonore and cousins—drove a gleaming white Pontiac Bonneville with a black roof and much bigger tail fins. And our Valiant's speedometer only went up to 110, while theirs went up to 120, which we kids took as hard evidence of how fast each actually could go.[5]

Many Sundays after church we drove to the Sarrantonios' in Astoria for Sunday dinner with their whole family, which included my uncle's father "Pop," a forbidding figure whom I never heard speak, but who was famously strong and had helped build the Hell Gate Bridge in 1917, just before fighting in the First World War. That's probably how Uncle Joe learned the song he taught us:

> *The first Marine bought the bean, Parlez-vous!*
> *The second Marine cooked the bean, Parlez-vous!*
> *The third Marine, he ate the bean—*
> *And PFFFFTT! all over the submarine!*
> *Inky stinky! Parlez-vous!*

My brother and I begged him to sing it with us, principally because the full volume of his ripping raspberry in the climactic fourth line undid us.

---

[5] Until I was two we didn't own a car, but when I threw up in the backseat of another couple's car my parents were so embarrassed they finally decided it was time. The Valiant was advertised in the paper for $350 and my father went to see it in a distant part of Queens. But when he knocked on the door of the house a woman greeted him whom he knew from Mavrata! She was the maid for the couple that owned the car! Another time at the dentist's—another Greek named Dr. Costonas—my father was staggered to see a man he remembered from the village next to Mavrata. That man had stabbed a friend of my father's to death in 1946, and in the tumultuous political atmosphere of that time had beat the rap and fled to America. And now here he was in a dentist's waiting room. Neither said a word.

Eleanor and Marion were like our older sisters, and my fastidious Tante Eleonore always dressed them beautifully in Brady Bunch–style dresses and white knee socks, with their long hair in braids or beribboned ponytails. We often got things they had outgrown, including a Beatles lunchbox, which they gave me when I began first grade in 1969. Nanny and Pop had a color TV set, and some Sunday evenings we watched Ed Sullivan with them, or *The Wonderful World of Disney* or Johnny Cash, before driving in our Valiant back to Jackson Heights.

Cutchogue

The Sarrantonios had a "bungalow" out in Smithtown on Long Island, where we sometimes visited,[6] eager to escape the city. But in the summer of 1966 we began renting an old house in a hamlet among the potato fields of Long Island's North Fork. It was on Skunk Lane in Cutchogue, and all of us—my cousins and aunt and grandmother too—were there together for the whole month every year. On the weekends my father and Uncle Joe joined us. If childhood's innocence is a picture of Heaven, my memories of Cutchogue are childhood innocence distilled, like a pearl of dew from Eden. And in a way it seemed that we were all children there together, as though my grandmother and my mother and aunt and even my uncle and my father during those times had tumbled backwards through the air to their own childhoods to join us in ours.

One evening after supper my father and grandmother and us four kids kicked a big beachball all around the yard like a soccer ball, my father and grandmother both sometimes drop-kicking it so high I couldn't believe it. My father's kicks disappeared like rockets into the clouds, and finally one of his kicks landed the ball all the way up into the impossibly high boughs of a tall

---

[6] I was there that Friday in November 1963 when late in the afternoon my mother—pushing me in my carriage—heard that the president had been killed.

pine tree. We tried and tried to get it down, but how? So eventually we gave up and all went to bed. But all that night the wind blew, and in the morning we found it again, orange and blue and white, lying in the sunshine on the wet green lawn. Why do I feel so strongly now that during those summers I was already in Heaven somehow, but just didn't know it, that I was then breathing the otherworldly air of Paradise?

I remember that Uncle Joe sometimes wore a T-shirt whose bright orange color seemed from another world, such that it almost pierced me through, and even remembering it now gives me a palpable pang, as though if you could somehow only inhale that color you would enter summer forever and never die.

One afternoon my mother and aunt arrived from shopping, excitedly telling us they had seen a giant prehistoric turtle in the middle of the road. We know now that it could only have been a snapping turtle, which looks prehistoric and does not exist in Germany, so my mother had never seen anything like it. But I remember her saying that it *had* to be prehistoric, and seemed to believe it herself, and at the time I devoutly hoped that it was, thinking it quite possible that the antediluvian past could enter our world as it did in movies and TV shows, and especially out there in Cutchogue, during those summers.

Most days we spent at the Peconic Bay beaches, where my father, who was a strong swimmer, always invited me to hold onto his back as he swam. I marveled at his size and strength as I held onto him and am now most amazed that he held conversations with me as he swam. It was even more impressive to me because Uncle Joe couldn't swim at all, which seemed a shocking flaw in the otherwise perfect image of manhood that he was for me, and yet it made me deeply glad that there was something in which my father was clearly the better. Those rides were my only experience in deep water until one day when I was seven my father decided it was time for me to swim on my own and succeeded in teaching me by holding my hands in deep water and pulling me along and then letting go and telling me to swim to him, just a few feet away, slyly backing up as I did so, and laughing with delight when I discovered it, knowing that despite my protestations it was working. He always told me to keep my fingers closed "and kick!"[7]

---

[7] I wrote a poem about it in 2007. See Appendix.

Every summer the Sarrantonios brought their three cats along. Marion's cat Pixie was the friendliest, but one afternoon he appeared at the back door with a baby rabbit in his mouth. We all screamed and called our parents, who quickly rescued it and put it in a grocery box with water and lettuce. We went to the farmer's fruit stand on Route 25 for some "real" carrots, smaller than the ones from the supermarket and with the greens still connected to them, which I'd never seen before. We put one inside the box with the rabbit and named him "Chipper" and began to imagine how amazing it would be for us to have this tiny pet rabbit, although Marion said that because Pixie was her cat, Chipper would really have to be hers too.

But in the morning Chipper was dead, saddening all of us. We decided to have a funeral at the top of the hill by the house, at the edge of a potato field, and spelled Chipper's name with white pebbles from the beach, as though he had been named this for years. Then we four cousins and my grandmother held hands around the grave and by way of ceremony sang "My Country, 'Tis of Thee" which we all knew. It is a golden memory, the five of us holding hands around the little grave and singing, but the intermingling sadness and beauty of it all was too much for Marion, who was always the most sensitive, and just as the song ended, she burst into tears and ran down the hill and into the house, and we all went in to console her.

After dinner we sometimes drove to a beach on the Sound where we got Italian ices and saw the lights of Connecticut across the water. There were swings there too, with chains much longer than the ones at the playground at home, and my grandmother delighted in pushing us higher and higher, until our mothers saw it. Grandma was by far the most like one of us, being four-foot-eleven and ninety pounds, and bursting with endless energy and fun, constantly doing handstands like a ten-year-old.

One summer in Cutchogue it rained for a week. After a few days of being cooped up, Tante Eleonore drove us to Greenport, where there was a post office and an old five-and-dime, where we bought a balsa-wood plane for fifteen cents and marveled at everything as though we had never been in a store before. We bought a balsa-wood plane for fifteen cents. The day it finally stopped raining we four kids went out onto the road and played in the deep puddles, amazed at the water's warmth, and the next day my father arrived and helped us fly the plane, with its red plastic propeller and wheels on thin wire struts and rubber-band "motor." He saw that it needed a smooth surface to run on before it would take off, so we launched it over and over and over from the roof of our Valiant.

The central appeal for me about Ditola's was how old it was. It even smelled old, as though the past were somehow still preserved there. At the top of the hill there was an old shed that was locked, but through big cracks in the rough gray wood you could barely see an old sleigh, the kind pulled by horses in the days before roads were plowed. I asked my mother how old it was and she said she didn't know, but that it was definitely an "antique." But I wanted to know how old "an antique" was, and she said she thought it was at least a hundred years, which seemed forever.

At the end of Skunk Lane there was an old general store at the end of Skunk Lane, run by a woman then ninety, who seemed so ancient to us—my grandmother was sixty-three—that talking to her was like talking to someone from the Old West. She was born in the 1870s, and the store was unchanged from then, with wide floorboards and a potbellied stove in the middle. My father would walk the mile roundtrip there with whoever was up—usually my brother—and get the newspaper and some peppermint patties. At that hour you always heard the doves—the *tri-go-nes* my father called them—cooing on the telephone lines, and sometimes heard an owl.

In the center of town was something called "The Old House of Cutchogue." My mother said it was one of the oldest houses in America, from even before we *were* America—which confused me. She explained that it was from when we "were still English," which I also didn't understand. A plaque said it was from 1649 and it had the look of something from the Middle Ages, with leaded glass windows with small panes in a diamond pattern—called "quarrels"—and a massive chimney with a cluster of flues, and a door decoratively studded with nails. The stairs inside were exquisitely narrow and made my mother remark on how much smaller people were back then, which made me wonder:

Did this trend continue backward forever, so that people got smaller and smaller the further back one went? Were tininess and oldness somehow connected?

I still wonder what it is about oldness and tininess both that has always so strongly appealed to me. Do we long to be back in our mothers' wombs? And for what exactly are we longing? And is that longing innate or is it a product of the Fall and our desire to go back to Eden? And what would tininess have to do with Eden? Or is it simply the vulnerability and preciousness of small things that captivate us? Is there something in us that instinctively wants to protect what is vulnerable and tiny? In any case, I always loved anything especially old or tiny; and when on my fifth birthday I got a tiny Matchbox 1912 Model T that combined these characteristics I could hardly contain myself for joy.

Once, walking with my mother in Central Park, we passed the towering half-million-pound obelisk she said was called "Cleopatra's Needle." I had heard of Cleopatra, and already had some sense of time and history, so I asked how old it was? "Oh, thousands of years old," she said, "From the time of ancient Egypt." I was again confused. Could the past in America go back that far? How was it possible for something in America to be as old as something in ancient Egypt?[8] The same confusion happened while visiting the Cloisters. When I asked how old it was my mother said "from the Middle Ages," but I didn't understand how something medieval could be in America.[9]

I remember coloring images of Old Testament characters in Sunday school, thinking these people lived a long, long time ago and I was in awe of this, because they lived when the world was still young and everything was possible, because God still spoke to people back then. I remember

---

[8] "Cleopatra's Needle" was built in Heliopolis in the fifteenth century BC and was almost certainly gazed upon by the Egyptian prince named Moses. It took nearly four months and sixteen pairs of horses to haul it from the Hudson River to where it now stands.

[9] The buildings of the Cloisters are indeed of medieval European provenance, purchased, dismantled, and reconstructed on the cliff overlooking the Hudson by the Rockefellers in the 1930s.

wondering what it must have been like living then, so close to the beginning and to God himself, so that you could actually hear his voice and see angels and witness miracles.

CHAPTER TWO

School

I was three and a half in late March of 1967 when one Sunday we drove to our Greek Orthodox church in Corona. There had been a winter storm, and looking for parking amidst the snow and ice, I saw a vast hole across the street. My parents said the church was building a school that would open in September and the following year I would go there. The cement and rebar were coated with white snow and rime, and it amazed me that that huge hole would soon be a school; but sure enough, eighteen months later I was on the third floor of it, attending kindergarten.

The first days of school were such a departure from what I knew that I didn't realize the change was essentially permanent. My mother walked me to school the whole first week, and on the third day I asked how often we would need to do this. She said after that day we had two days left. The next morning she said after *that* day I only had one day left. So on Friday I realized this was the last day, but had no idea that after the weekend I would have to go back for another week and another, and that there would be an infinity of similar weeks extending into the distant future. It came as a terrible surprise.

The second week I began taking the bus, and we walked to the bus stop on 34th Avenue. But after it came and I took my seat and waved to my mother as it pulled away, I cried and cried, so much so that a girl in fifth grade—who seemed to me an adult—came to console me. Though I don't remember her name, I remember her kind, wide face and how sweet and cheerful she was.

Each morning when the bus arrived at school we were ushered into the "playground," which was just a paved lot edged with weeds and high chain-link fencing. Before I knew anyone else I would hold hands with a sweet freckled girl named Dorothy, and we would walk around together. I don't remember our conversations or whether we spoke at all. But I soon became "best friends" with Harry and Noumi from my class, both of whom were rascals, but in a good way. That fall Richard Nixon and Hubert Humphrey squared off against each other and principally because of his deep hatred of Communism, my father supported Nixon. One day Harry and Noumi and I put our arms over each other's shoulders and marched three-abreast around the playground shouting "Nixon's the One! Humphrey's the Bum!"

That fall my parents invited my kindergarten teacher, Miss Papayannis, to dinner, but the conflation of school and home confused me. My brother and I were sent to bed at seven o'clock, so after dinner as always we brushed our teeth, put on our pajamas, and went to the living room to kiss our father goodnight, saying in Greek, "*Kali nichta, Patera mou*"—meaning "Goodnight, my father." But that evening I followed this by going to Miss Papayannis and saying, "*Kali nichta*, Miss Papayannis." My brother wasn't yet four, and after saying "*Kali nichta, Patera mou*" to our father, he went over to Miss Papayannis and declared *precisely* the same—"*Kali nichta, Patera mou*"—making us all howl. At the end of the year we had an official kindergarten "graduation" with caps and gowns, and even got framed diplomas on the stage as our families watched. Because Miss Papayannis knew I could read, I was given the honor of being the graduation "speaker," which became a curious pattern in my life.

During the summer weekends we were not in Cutchogue we often drove to closer beaches such as Rockaway Beach or Far Rockaway in Brooklyn, or to Fire Island—usually with our closest friends, the Drogaris family, whose son Anthony was my brother's age, but who was a genius and would soon skip *two* grades. My father met Nick Drogaris in an English Class at NYU in 1955, and from the moment Nick said he was dating a Cephalonian named Effie, they were fast friends. Although they didn't go to church, my parents made them my godparents anyway, so I always called them by the corresponding Greek titles, Nou-*no* and Nou-*na*.

Sometimes my father took me and my brother to College Point Park, overlooking the East River.[1] I remember sometimes seeing rats scurrying between the rocks by the water. Though my father knew nothing about baseball or football, he knew his way around a soccer ball and literally kicked circles around my brother and me as we tried to get it away from him. Once, after we had collapsed onto the green army blanket we always had along, I heard the plinky metallic strains of the Mister Softee truck. The music was a powerful talisman we couldn't resist any more than the children of Hamelin could resist the Pied Piper, or Odysseus—had he not been bound by his sailors to the mast—could have resisted the song of the Sirens. My brother and I promptly went crazy, begging our father for some change. But money was always tight and it was very rare we bought anything from a street vendor. For us, food was something cooked and eaten at home. But once in a blue moon my father might relent and give us the dimes and nickels for an ice cream, and I always got the orange-and-white creamsicles whose colors even now I remember against the blue summer sky, along with the shining silver of the bright dimes we held up to the man in the truck.

With my father and brother John, 1967

But on this particular day this happy ending was not to be, for as we begged my father—literally trying to pull him up from the blanket with our skinny arms—he with perfect equanimity suggested a better alternative. "No, no, no," he said calmly, in his Greek accent. "It's not necessary." But what in the world

---

[1] Actually the East River, which is the waterway between Manhattan's east side and Queens, is not a river at all, despite its official name. Rather it is a saltwater estuary.

could make ice cream on a hot day at the park unnecessary? For my father the answer was quite simple: "I have some V-8s in the back of the car!" My dear father really had no idea this wouldn't appeal to us. For him it was a simple engineering "fix": why squander hard-earned money on ice cream when in the pizza oven of our Valiant's trunk sat several cans of the popular tomatoey drink? What small boys could resist the tempting offer of some gaggy warm vegetable juice? My father made his suggestion brightly, confident that we would share his enthusiasm and having no idea that if it had been served ice-cold, we wouldn't have been able to take a single swallow, because it repulsed us *that much*. Nonetheless, not wanting to hurt our father's feelings, we probably didn't communicate this sufficiently, and after Mr. Softee left we went to our car and my dad opened the trunk. He found the six-pack, yanked a can from its plastic mooring, popped the pop top, and then cheerfully offered it to us, over and over, guzzling it himself as if to demonstrate how wonderful it was, all the while genuinely surprised we were somehow able to turn it down.

My father and Uncle Joe often talked about buying a "piece of property" someplace "out in Peconic" near Cutchogue to build on someday, and in 1968 they bought an acre between them in a wooded area in Mattituck. Now and again we went there "to inspect the property," as my father always put it. I saw no hint of the master gardener my father would become years later until then, but the moment the property was ours he employed my brother's and my help in creating a small garden of tomato plants and other things, as though every moment in the twenty-eight years since leaving Mavrata he had been desperately longing to do this, and he hasn't stopped gardening obsessively since.

My uncle began building his house almost immediately, but it was a slow process, because he really did every bit of it himself, mostly on weekends. Once he and Tante Eleonore were there alone when a thunderstorm hit and lightning struck so close to them that—as they held hands outside under the wooden deck—they could feel the electricity run through their bodies. The deck was the glory of the house, extending all the way around it, and I remember watching Uncle Joe take great care to cut a perfect circle into the deck planks around a tall oak tree so that it could stay where it was. When he put up the outer walls, he let me hammer some nails, so that I too could take some pride in the construction. He was always intentionally fatherly in that way.

In 1969 we celebrated my sixth birthday under the single tree in the middle of the yard in Cutchogue. Tante Eleonore gave me a small bound cartoon book inscribed "To My Little Professor," which is what she always called me. Three weeks later we were still there when Apollo 11 landed on the moon. Deep in the middle of that night[2] my parents woke me and set me in front of the black-and-white TV at the top of the steps where we watched the snowy image until a human being emerged from the lunar module. I could not then fathom quite how huge an event this was, nor that all of humanity was then itself squeezing through a singularity into another era from which we would never return. But I realize now that we and the rest of the world were united in watching this in a way that we had never been united before, nor since.

Gulf gas stations were offering models of the Lunar Module Eagle: two sheets of printed cardboard one cut out and assembled. My brother and I hovered over my father as he folded the infinite tabs into the various slots until the impressive replica sat in front of us. The next day we bought ten maple saplings and planted them on "the property," as we always called it, forever after calling them "the Moon Trees."

I tried to reconcile what I was hearing and seeing that week with the mythical round object in the sky, which I loved looking at, especially in the daytime, against a bright blue sky. My parents had often pointed it out, asking if I could see the Man in the Moon, which I usually did, such that he seemed a friend, somehow, like Santa Claus. So when actual men flew there in a rocket it was like hearing someone had built a tower and we could now take an

---

[2] As I never stayed up past eight, the idea of "the middle of the night" in these early years had a mythic quality for me, as though it possessed an almost infinite depth. One night I had a somewhat frightening dream where I stayed up until it was a thousand o'clock, as though I had traversed such a vast distance in time into the night that I wasn't sure I ever could get back.

elevator to the giant's castle above the clouds, where Jack had once climbed. Part of me had the sense that the Man in the Moon had been intruded upon, and a couple of weeks later when it rained for days on end, I sincerely believed it must be because the Man in the Moon was crying, and said so.

That fall I entered first grade, but because I had been reading for two years, my teacher—a Greek-American beauty named Miss Ponaris—asked my parents whether I might skip to second. Our homework those first weeks was to find three objects in magazines that began with the letter assigned and cut them out and paste them in our notebooks, writing the word next to the picture. I also remember getting my first textbook, the classic *Dick and Jane* reader, with the father in his suit and the mother in a pleated skirt, a world of book bags and fedoras and gentlemanly boys and sweet girls. I remember turning to the latter parts of the book and staring at the much longer sentences and paragraphs. What would I be like at the end of the year when we got to those parts of the book? The letters were much smaller and there were fewer pictures. It was as if I could stare into the future by looking at those pages. Of course I had no idea I would never get to those pages at all.

Because this was a Greek Orthodox parochial school, they taught Greek to us precisely as it was taught to children our ages in Greece and used the same books. Our first-grade primer was therefore quite similar to the *Dick and Jane* books, though the Greek Dick and Jane and Sally were named "Mimi"—for Demetrios—Anna, and "Nana." But the Greek primer added an old *gia-gia* grandmother wearing traditional widow's weeds, and a smiling elderly priest in black vestments, with his dignified hat and beard.

Our Greek teacher was Miss Xanthis, who was tall and wore her hair with two front pieces swooping down and then curling back up like the horns of a water buffalo. It was obviously meant to impart a regal and elegant bearing such as one might see in a Campari ad, and in her case it did just that, evoking Athena or Diana. Along with our textbook, Miss Xanthis used vocabulary flash cards that were utterly mystifying. The first three words we learned in that class are etched in my mind forever, not because they were the first three Greek words I learned—I knew other Greek words by then from my father—but because they were the strangest words one can imagine for initiating first graders into the language of Homer and Plato.

The first word was *oplo*, meaning "rifle," and pictured a hunter's single-bolt gun. The second word was *othondo-vourtsa*, meaning "toothbrush." This was at least a household item, though it certainly seemed a bit long for one's second word in a language. But the third word was so eye-poppingly weird that we would soon forget about the quirkiness of *othondo-vourtsa*. I cannot these years later fathom how it might have been chosen for American six-year-olds learning modern Greek. What was the word? The word was *Iaponezza* (pronounced *Ee-ah-poh-NEH-zah*) meaning "the Japanese woman." This perfectly baffling flash card pictured a standard geisha woman with a powdered white face and black hair, wearing a kimono and holding a fan. It was this hoary Oriental stereotype that was held up to us as we dutifully repeated the word—*Iaponezza*—as though it were as natural a first word to learn as *hat* or *dog* or *cloud*.

The Greek textbook itself was more orthodox, although this is of course saying little. The first page of the book pictured a curiously oblong-headed boy in short pants balancing a ruler on his finger and shouting "Eee! Eee!" The Greek word for this sound was simply the letter "I" or *iota*, which is pronounced as a long "e." But why exactly was the boy saying "Eee! Eee!"? I didn't get it. When I was bold enough to ask Miss Xanthis why he was saying "Eee! Eee!" she explained that he was proud of his feat and wanted everyone to look. But why didn't he just say "Look!" or whatever the Greek equivalent would have been? Only now, half a century later, does it occur to me that he was merely pronouncing the sound of the letter *iota*.

As the book progressed we learned that running water made the "r-r-r" sound, so we learned the Greek letter *roh*; and we learned that ducklings—which in Greek are called *Papakia*—always say "*Pa! Pa! Pa!*" But do they? Or was that just Greek ducklings? I also learned that Greek dogs do not say "Ruff! Ruff!" or "Woof! Woof!"—but "*ghav! ghav!*" In Greek it is written "γαυ γαυ!" And Greek cats do not say "Meow!", but "*Nee-ow!*" At first I believed these were only sounds Greek cats and dogs made, and if they spoke English, they would say "Ruff!" Or "Woof!" And "Meow!" But how did the animals know which language to speak? How did they know what country they were in?

About a month into the school year, I came upon a picture in the Greek primer that somehow captured my imagination. It was a tiny house, made of mud (*laspi*) and stones (*petres*), with a cut branch for the lintel. Oblong-headed "Mimi" had built it with Anna's help. It even had a small Greek flag and on the left and right were olive branches propped up to look like trees, and it was all surrounded by a circle of stones. The miniature-ness and cuteness of it transfixed me and created in me that longing I had felt before, though I hardly knew for what. And then I wondered, couldn't I build a tiny house like that? I couldn't, actually, and certainly not in Queens, where there were no mud or sticks to be had. But how I wanted to. What was it about that tiny house? And there was a rhyme that accompanied it:

> *Spiti mou,*
> *Spitaki mou.*
> *Spito-kalivaki mou!*

This is the Greek equivalent of "Home, Sweet Home," although it far better captures the essence of what home (*spiti*) is by also using the diminutive and affectionate form of the word (*spitaki*), and then in the third line squares sentiment by using the diminutive of the word *kalivi* which means "shack" or "cottage." In other words, it captures the "homeliness" of what a home really is, the coziness, without which even the largest house can never really be a home.

For me the rhyme sounded appropriately cute, though I didn't quite understand what a *kalivaki* was. But, as I say, it was the exquisite smallness of the mud-and-stone house that captured my fancy, and again, I wonder: What is it about smallness that speaks to us? Is it because babies are small? Is that why we have so many baby-talk words for the word "small" itself, such as *itty-bitty* and *itsy-bitsy* and *teeny-weeny* and *teensy-weensy*? It is as though we are not really talking about the relative size of things we describe, but more about their "coziness" and "cuteness." As though that is somehow the larger point or essence of tininess. But what in the world is "cuteness"? Why are the fore-shortened faces of puppies and other baby creatures "cuter" than those of their more mature counterparts? Is it simply a parental instinct bred into us over the eons, as evolutionists would surmise, or is it something else? And if it is something that evolved to make parents parent better, why would the trait appear full-blown in children, who themselves, as I did, went gaga over whatever seemed either cute or simply very, very tiny? What is that instinct?

In C.S. Lewis's book *Surprised by Joy*, he talks of how a similar feeling bloomed in him when he saw something miniature that his elder brother, Warnie, had made. It was the upside-down lid of a "biscuit tin" in which his brother had placed moss and twigs to create what he meant to be a miniature garden. Looking at it transported Lewis somehow, and called to something deep within him, something that he later called "Joy," although he also uses the German word *Sehnsucht*. He describes it as a longing for something beyond this world, like hearing Alfred Tennyson's "horns of Elfland." In fact G.K. Chesterton has a heavenly chapter titled "The Ethics of Elfland" in his little gem *Orthodoxy*. It is the call to that other side of things, through the looking glass and the wardrobe and into the painting, and beyond the horizon, and beyond the grave too, it seems, beyond that false life of temporal life into the real life of life eternal.

One day late that September my mother asked me the question Miss Ponaris had asked her—whether I wanted to "skip" first grade—and explained what that meant. Being six, I couldn't see any downside, and in mid-October transferred to Mrs. Rosner's second-grade class. I had no idea it was a decision that would affect me forever, but I was already small for my age and therefore would always be one of the shortest kids in my class, would always be behind physically and emotionally, and would forever be identified as "the smart small kid who skipped a grade," and would even in my own class always feel a bit like a fish out of water. I would graduate high school at sixteen and college at twenty, but toward what was I sprinting? What would I do when I graduated college a year early? I would flounder and float and drift, as we shall see.

It was around this time—Thursday, October 16, 1969—as all of us boarded the school bus home, that a fifth grader named Dennis with a transistor radio screamed that the Mets had won the World Series. It was 3:14 p.m. when Baltimore Oriole Davey Johnson—the future Mets manager who would guide them to their 1986 World Series—flied out to Cleon Jones to end the game, so that the previously hapless Mets really had achieved the impossible dream of these last months in which no one could stop talking about them as the "Miracles Mets," even saying that God wore a Mets uniform. Everyone on the bus instantly went bananas, jumping up and down and hugging each other. Our enthusiasm was fueled partly by the fact that we were Mets fans and partly by the fact that we were just one mile from the stadium where people were then scrambling onto the field to tear up the suddenly historic and mythic turf.

The following year Theo Takis and our cousin John took us to Shea Stadium for our first game. The great Tommie Agee blasted a home run that struck the scoreboard and we were hooked. Because Theo Taki came to America before my father and because Aunt Mary grew up in New York, they often introduced us to things our more recently arrived parents knew nothing about. For example, they brought us our first pets, a pair of goldfish in a small bowl. Two decades earlier our parents hadn't had enough to eat, so the idea of pets was as foreign as a trip to Hawaii. Nor did they seem to know how pets were typically named, so we inexplicably named them Tommy and Peter. We bought a small tank to give the fish more room, but didn't know we were supposed to cover the black bottom with gravel, and simply placed a half dozen seashells there instead. The fish weren't long for this world, but when we flushed each down the toilet I asked where the water went and my mother explained that it ultimately flowed to the sea, which made poetic sense and somehow made me feel better about the whole thing, even though they were freshwater fish and obviously already dead.

In 1970, my father left Bulova for a company called Technicon, up in Westchester County. Commuting that distance meant he now had to drive an hour each way and got home at six, so we began eating dinner at that new time. It was our friend Speros who led the way in this decision, getting a job there and convincing my father to apply. He was also steering my father to look at houses near New Fairfield, Connecticut, where he and his wife, Mona, had moved. A few weekends we visited them in their yellow house nestled amid pines and endless snow, and my brother and I romped through the waist-high drifts with their huge, friendly collie and dreamed of someday living in the country too. But it seemed that whatever we wanted, the answer was inevitably no. We knew that our parents had experienced tremendous hardships growing up, so we didn't really expect much or complain much. Sometimes life dealt you warm V-8 instead of ice cream.

So you can imagine how stunned and thrilled my brother and I were when one day at the Woolworth's we saw a tank of tiny green turtles and our mother agreed to buy two. Was this even possible? They cost ninety-nine cents each and the clear plastic oasis meant to be their home cost about the same. These adorable reptilians—called red-eared terrapins or sliders—were all the rage at the time, just before it was discovered they carried dangerous bacteria, which when coupled with their incorrigible cuteness caused kids to want to handle and kiss them, at which point they became illegal. Ours were the size of quarters and were so cute it was almost unbearable. Sometimes we filled the bathtub with water and let them swim, which they also did with an impossibly staggering cuteness.

Some months earlier a French family whose kids were named Didier and Patricia had moved in across the hall. The father, Andre, was a chef in a local restaurant and his wife, Genevieve, was the very picture of French loveliness. As far as my parents were concerned, any European immigrants were instant friends. Once Didier and Patricia saw our turtles, they got a pair too, but because their father brought home fresh raw fish, theirs grew at an almost freakish rate. In no time they were twice the size of ours, and in a few months they were monsters, five times the size or our own, who never seemed to grow a millimeter. We fed ours dry "turtle flakes," but once we saw the monsters across the hall, we offered our stunted friends bits of raw hamburger at the end of a toothpick, though they never seemed very interested.

Around this time my brother and I heard further incredible news. That summer we would be going to Germany! Our mother was taking us for six weeks to visit all our relatives and Tante Eleonore and Eleanor and Marion and our grandmother were coming too! But what about the turtles? It would fall to my father to feed them while we were away, but surely shaking out a few flakes every morning wasn't asking much. Still, when we returned, the turtles had taken a powder. But where in the world had the stunted critters gone to?

My father said he had "put them in the pond at Technicon." But what had led him to this decision? Had they asked for their freedom? We didn't understand. Had my father perhaps forgotten to feed them and they had died, and he didn't have the heart to tell us? Or perhaps someone—it was always "a guy from Technicon"—told him he ought to do this, so they would have room to swim. Although I feared they might be eaten by something larger.[3] In all these decades we have never received a satisfying answer on this subject, but for the next several years whenever we drove to Technicon, for some reason my brother and I gazed longingly at the pond, aching to see our old friends, surely by now the size of hubcaps.

---

[3] So many people who tired of caring for these once-popular creatures released them into local waters that they are today listed as one of the world's "100 Top Invasive Species." They may grow to over a foot in length and are quite aggressive, driving some native species to extinction. They constitute such a threat to other species that wildlife experts have issued a statement: "If you no longer want your terrapin, make the responsible choice and have it put down by your veterinarian."

CHAPTER THREE

Our Trip to Germany

Summer 1971

N one of us cousins had ever been out of the country or on a plane. Wasn't flying something rich people did? But the idea of entering that mythical world of the German relations about which my mother had told me my whole life seemed more amazing still. I generally felt more connected to my Greek side, going to Greek parochial school and having nearly all Greek family friends. I often observe that if you are raised by a Greek and a German, you will be raised Greek. Greeks have the stronger ethnic identity, so much so that for many of them "being Greek" is like a serious hobby, or even like a religion, and sometimes the Greek church is almost a part of that larger religion; and we weekly attended the Greek church, to which my mother "converted" before marriage.

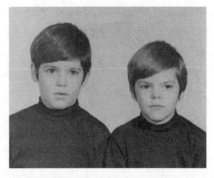

My mother always said she was raised Lutheran, but there was little church attendance or serious attention to faith in her childhood. Everyone was baptized and confirmed and

Passport photo with my brother, 1971

married in the church, but no one went on Sundays. Since the German state then required fourteen-year-olds to attend Confirmation classes, my mother did so, but only remembers the priest as "a beast" who rode a motorcycle. But her family's indifference to church didn't mean they didn't believe in the God of the Bible—only that they knew little about him.

Sometime before leaving for Germany, either at Christmas or as an early birthday present, my grandmother gave me a wooden model of Christopher Columbus's *Santa Maria* and then a model of the *Pinta,* too. But I remember that as we were walking through the John F. Kennedy International Airport to board our flight to Germany, I asked if she could get me the *Niña*, too. And of course she said yes, that after we got back from Germany she would, but somehow forgot to do so. But I've thought of it innumerable times over the decades and have longed for it every time, such that I honestly half-expect her to hand it to me when I see her again in Heaven.

I remember that after we arrived in Frankfurt at what was then for me the middle of the night, I was so tired I could barely walk, but we all made our way to the cavernous train station, built at the beginning of the century, being the largest in Europe at that time. It was right out of a film from the thirties, with innumerable platforms and a vast ironwork and dirty glass ceiling so far above us it seemed like an indoor sky. I remember groggily eating frankfurters before boarding our train, but the appropriateness of this was likely lost on me. The train would take us behind the Iron Curtain and into the Communist world, which even then I knew was essentially the largest prison in the history of the world.

When some hours later we crossed the border into *die Ostzone* I saw it all: the guard towers and barbed wire and the machine gun-toting soldiers and vicious-looking German shepherds. All to keep people from leaving. When guards came through the train to check passports and visas my mother and aunt were tense, knowing that even though they were American citizens, they had "illegally" escaped from this very place not so many years before.

From Leipzig we went to Altenburg, and then continued on the train straight into the past, to Großstöbnitz, the tiny fabled village whose paeans my mother had ever and always sung. I was sure in going there we really were returning to my mother's childhood, and because of the poverty endemic to Communism, virtually nothing had changed since my mother left. Even the train to Großstöbnitz was pulled by a black steam locomotive, like something from the 1880s. And when we arrived at the place my mother had spent most of her childhood—Tante Walli's house—we saw there was no working bathroom, just the same exotic outhouse in the barn as had been there since forever.

Our weeks there were life-changing: I was for the first time in my life connected to that world from which part of me had come. This was the soil from which my mother and family had sprung, and I soon saw that our relatives' sense of humor and outlook were so similar to my grandmother's that it was as though I had always known these people, as though part of me belonged here infinitely more than it belonged in New York.

Americans hardly expect Germans to be jokey, but those from Saxony are, the most famous Saxon of all, Martin Luther, being infamous for his jesting, often of the earthy barnyard variety.

Behind the eighteenth-century house my mother and grandmother were born in—where our relatives still live—was a stream called *die Sprotte* and that summer we played in it too, just as my grandmother and her siblings had done as kids in 1910 and her forebears had in the previous century, as though it were a mythical stream running backward through time to Eden. At the water's edge were weeping willows—and nettles (*Brenn-nesseln*) too, whose existence I discovered when I brushed against some and felt their burning sting. My mother said during the war everyone was so poor that an old man they knew used to boil them for his supper.

One day my mother took me to the village church, built in 1602, where for centuries my relatives had been baptized and married and sent into the next world. The door was locked and we couldn't go inside, which seemed fitting, given the Communist regime's brutal atheism. My brother and I liked our cousin Jürgen, two years older than I, but were surprised to hear him declare: *"Nixon ist Schlecht!"*—"Nixon is bad!"—which was something we knew was the "official" Communist view of anyone who was their enemy, which Nixon certainly was. It was odd to be among one's dearest relatives, but somehow to be at odds in this way.

I didn't know then what my grandmother would tell me over and over in later years: that she had a profound dream in 1945 that took place in that church's choir loft. She always referred to that dream as "the time I brought my husband to Heaven," as though it were an actual event that occurred in the dream. She was as guileless as anyone I have ever known and never spoke of it as anything less than utterly real. She always explained that after my grandfather was killed she dreamt of him a number of times, but a little more than a year after his death she dreamt of him for the last time, and this was that dream.

She always said that in the dream they were standing together in the choir loft of that church, and my grandfather was wearing a bright white gown, like a nightgown, with sleeves that were very wide and hung down. She usually used her hands to show me the shape of the sleeves, and said he never wore anything like it in his life. And she said there were others in the church too, and all of them were there waiting to go to Heaven. One of them was a woman who ten years earlier had borne a child out of wedlock and then drowned the child, afterward killing herself. In the dream this woman said to my grandmother, "Your husband is next. That means it will be my turn soon." With that, my grandmother turned to my grandfather. As he stood there with his hands clasped she saw him absentmindedly pushing the tips of his thumbs together, a habit he had, and then the door behind him opened ever so slightly. My grandmother always said dramatically, "And the door only opened *that much*," holding her fingers about an inch apart—and she was always transported at the memory of this. "*Und* the light!" she said. "I *ne-ver* saw a light like that! *Das war* so bright, like gold! It was *herrlich!*" The memory of this never failed to move her. And then she said her husband spoke to her with a solemnity bordering on sternness. "Now you can't come with me, Gertrud," he said. "You must stay *mit ze* girls." And soon after he said this the door opened wider and the golden white light of Heaven shone through it so powerfully that it was overwhelming—and my grandfather Erich walked into the light. And my grandmother always said, "*Und* then the door closed, *und* I never dreamt from my husband again."

My grandmother never went to church or read the Bible, but as long as I knew her, she prayed every morning and night. I don't know when she began this, but there was never any doubt to whom she was praying. It was always to the God of the Bible, whom she seemed to know. She often said she was sickly in her earliest years, and that when she was born—in April 1905—the doctor said she likely wouldn't survive the week. She was the thirteenth of seventeen born to her parents, five of whom they lost in infancy. So when her father returned from work each day during the first weeks of my grandmother's life, he would ask his wife: *"Lebt die noch?"* Meaning, "Is she still alive?"

When she was seven she again became gravely ill. She remembered one fateful night during this illness lying in bed, unable to breathe. It was so bad she didn't know what to do. Then a figure appeared next to her, whom she knew was God. Her description was of a youngish man with white hair, a white beard, and a white gown— something like Jesus in the Book of Revelation, though she would not have known this. She said that he took her hand and she arose from the bed with him and first walked and then ran with him. It was entirely real to her, and she said that as they ran together, holding hands, her ability to breathe got better and better, until she could breathe.

My German grandparents (front) at a wedding in the late 1930s

Six miles from Großstöbnitz lay Altenburg, the town of about fifty thousand where my mother grew up. We stayed there with her best friend, Brigitte, who lived with her husband and two children. Karsten was seventeen, and when we gave him a pair of American jeans it was as if we had given him Paul McCartney's comb. It was the ultimate "Western" object in a world where they were impossible to get. Brigitte's husband was a member of the Communist Party and they lived in a development of bleak modern high-rises, though Altenburg's downtown was mostly unchanged from my mother's childhood. One day we even saw a chimney sweep, black with soot and carrying his brushes and wearing a top hat, as was the old custom.

My grandfather had worked in a sewing-machine factory in Altenberg, and whenever my grandmother spoke of him, it was with great respect and admiration. If I did something sloppily, she would say "If your grandfather could see that, he would say something." She often said, "Your grandfather was a *feiner Mann*," meaning a true gentleman. My mother always said how much he loved nature, and that he ate every apple whole, core and all, leaving only the stem, and taught them that if you picked a flower in the forest an angel would die. Every Sunday after lunch he took the family for a long walk through the woods to Nobitz, or to an outdoor cafe in Wildschwitz. Once, in the deepest cold of a snowy winter, while walking through the woods he saw a beautiful red fox lying dead, perfectly preserved by the cold. He didn't draw their attention to it, but circled back later and took it to a friend who made a stole for my grandmother, which was a particular luxury.

When we stayed in Großstöbnitz, which we loved as much as my mother seemed to, we stayed at Tante Walli's. My brother and I spent much of our time with Mr. Köhler, the farmer who lived next door. He had forty cows and let us climb into his hayloft and jump down into the hay below until we sneezed. He also had a fearsome bull he led to a nearby field every morning, carrying a small sledgehammer, in case it caused trouble. When my brother once inadvertently passed behind it, Mr. Köhler instantly yanked him out of range, knowing a kick could have been fatal. My grandmother always hilariously dismissed things she thought "nonsense" as *"Mist!"*, but it wasn't until I saw Mr. Köhler's dung heap—*Misthaufen*—that summer that I understood what the word meant. She used the word *"Quatsch!"*—which simply meant "nonsense," to similar comic effect.

In Großstöbnitz we celebrated my mother's thirty-seventh birthday, and three days later my eighth. But the biggest celebration was for Tante Walli, who turned seventy-nine on July 4. Relatives came from far and wide to the old *Papiermühle* (Paper Mill) that had been a hotel and restaurant since my grandmother's childhood. I learned that my grandmother had always been the life of these parties, performing comic acts and singing. In the twenties she had competed in indoor bicycle races and dance contests there. She was especially renowned for her singing—she could sing a high C—and was invited to take lessons in Leipzig from a celebrated teacher, but her mother didn't want her to leave, and she had to let the opportunity go. That day at Tante Walli's party it seemed all the years between that past and the present had fallen away, as though we were still all together there doing what we had always been doing forever, in the same place and with the same people, only now I was somehow there too.

We also stayed in Nobitz, where my grandmother's sister Luci lived. Her husband, Uncle Rudi, had had a glass eye since the war. One day a truck dumped a huge pile of coal bricks in their yard and Uncle Rudi let my brother and me throw them down into the cellar through the small window. We beamed to be filthy with coal dust, just like the chimney sweep in Altenburg. My grandmother said just after the war, some neighbors had recruited her to climb down into a cellar window just like that one to help them steal potatoes, and with no

From left: My mother, my grandmother wearing the fox stole, and my Aunt Eleonore

husband and two girls to feed she agreed. She was small enough to do it and once lowered in simply handed the potatoes up. But just as they were finishing the job, the police pulled up and they were arrested.

We also spent a week in a village called Schönfels with my grandmother's sister Else and her husband, Uncle Paul, who spent eight years in a Russian prison camp after the war, but had never spoken of it. Tante Else had two grandsons our age who took us to a nearby stream where we built a dam and played for hours. They warned us about *"die Blut-egeln!"*—the leeches!—but we never saw any. Far up on the hill nearby was perched a little twelfth-century castle. My mother said she knew a woman who lived there, whose name was also Annerose. I had never heard of anyone with my mother's name. One day we walked up the long hill to the castle, passing through the arched entryway into the tiny courtyard and seeing a hole above our heads from which my mother said the inhabitants would pour boiling oil onto anyone attempting to invade. In an apartment giving onto the courtyard lived the other Annerose, who was heavy and had bright red cheeks—probably because her apartment was as cold as a root cellar, having walls five or six feet thick.

Afterward we climbed up to the castle chapel and then climbed the many stairs to the top of the tower's circular room with spectacular views. I took pictures with my Instamatic, but after a few minutes a bulky middle-aged man came in, out of breath. When he saw my brother leaning out one of the windows, he brusquely rebuked him—and my mother, too. My brother decided to skedaddle down the stairs, but my mother and I lingered another minute or two and then made our way back down, grumbling about the unpleasant man.

But my mischievous brother had used a stone to jam the door at the bottom of the final steps, locking us in. We had to walk back to the chapel gallery over the courtyard and beg him to release us, which he eventually did, and we all laughed. But before we left the castle, we had a wicked thought. Hoping no one could see, we put the stone where my brother had, and then giddily ran for our lives, laughing out of terror and joy both. My mother often became a child again when she was with us. "Run!" she said, laughing, "run!!!" Knowing the man would soon discover his predicament, like Jack hustling down the beanstalk we did not pause in our descent until we had safely reached our destination, out of breath from running and laughing both. A week later my grandmother, who had remained in Schönfels a day or two longer than we, said that Annerose in the castle told her that just after we left she heard a man shouting angrily from the chapel gallery, demanding to be let out.

Near the end of our stay there was yet another birthday, this time for my Tante Walli's next eldest sister, Tante Toni, visiting from Holland. My mother and Tante Eleonore never looked more beautiful than they did that day, wearing velvet chokers with a small cameo, and white blouses with long satin skirts; my mother's emerald green and my aunt's a deep pink. And it was that day that I spoke my first full German sentence: *"Bitte gib mir ein glass Milch."* ("Please give me a glass of milk."), for which I was fussed over to the point of getting my cheeks pinched.

That summer we talked of returning five years later to celebrate the thousandth anniversary of Altenburg, whose castle stood on a great precipice. When one looked at it one clearly could see two windows sealed up with plaster or concrete. As the story went, two young princes had been kidnapped from the castle in 1455 by their father's enemies, carried from those windows on a rope ladder. The kidnappers were caught and supposedly walled up in those windows forever, and merely to look at them gave me chills. Luther's close friend Georg Spalatin had lived in this castle five hundred years earlier, and Luther had visited often. Inside the castle now was an exhibit of old playing cards, for which Altenburg was famous; *Skat*—second in world popularity only to Poker and Bridge—was invented there in 1813. When we entered the castle's magnificent chapel, my mother reminded me that Johann Sebastian Bach had played on its organ, something I had included in my third-grade biographical assignment on him just months before.

CHAPTER FOUR

Transfiguration

1971–1972

That fall I began fourth grade at Transfiguration, but my mother, hoping to capitalize on my nascent German, enrolled me in a Saturday morning class in Manhattan, so each weekend we took the subway into "the City" to East 86th Street. The area still clung to some wisps of its quondam glory as New York's Germantown, which a few decades earlier had boasted numerous German dancehalls and beer halls and *konditorei*, as well as a German-language paper with eighty thousand subscribers. When my mother arrived in New York in the fifties, there was still a German-language movie theater and popular dance halls, and all through our childhoods, long after they were gone, Tante Eleonore joked with us when we were bored, saying: "Well what do you want, to go dancing on 86th Street?"

One of the last gasps of that world then was a run-down walk-up on the north side of 86th near Third, where my cousin Eleanor and I had our lessons. Financial realities dictated that only we two would take the class, but during that hour my mother and brother and Tante Eleonore and usually our grandmother too would wander around shopping—always visiting Schaller & Weber—and then we would all go the Wollman Rink in Central Park. The first time we went was the first time my brother and I put on skates, and thinking lessons too expensive, my mother enterprisingly spotted two Puerto Rican teenagers speeding around effortlessly and offered them five dollars to take us around for an hour, by which time we were indeed able to skate on our own. At the end of the school year there was an awards ceremony in distant Richmond Hill, where I was awarded first prize in the class, which was a silver medal, while my cousin Eleanor took second prize, a book, which we both reckoned "better" as it was actually useful.

But my trip to Germany and this class couldn't compete with Greek parochial school five days a week and Greek church on Sundays. If all that weren't enough, my father challenged me that year to memorize the Nicene Creed in Greek—"*To Pisteuo,*" as it is called, because it begins with "*Pisteuo eis enan theon,*" meaning "I believe in one God ..." He helped me with it most mornings and in a few weeks I had it down. When my Sunday school teacher heard about it I was asked to recite it in class, to the *oohs* and *ahhs* of everyone. Of course I hardly understood a word of it in Greek or English. Over the years I sometimes have wondered whether it verges on blasphemy to recite something so sacred without any idea what it means, as though a mynah bird were to recite the Twenty-Third Psalm. Since I still know it and now know and believe what it means, I am now glad for my father's persistence with me, though I still can't help thinking how completely the church failed in communicating the faith. It was not until decades later that I even discovered what the church's name—Transfiguration—referred to.[1]

I can only remember one instance in school of discussing the Bible or theology. My fourth-grade teacher, Mrs. Frangos, had somehow mentioned that rainbows were God's promise never again to flood the earth. But my friend Robert piped up that God was going to destroy it by fire anyway! I had no idea where he heard that, but I remember Mrs. Frangos confirming it, although she seemed embarrassed, as though it wasn't her job to tell us this

---

[1] "Transfiguration" refers to Peter, James, and John's ascent with Jesus to the top of a mountain where he essentially exits Earth and reenters eternity where he is transfigured such that the apostles behold him in his full glory, and where he speaks with Moses and Elijah. It seems to me as though the three apostles were able to look for those moments through a porthole into eternity.

unpleasant bit of news. She said we could read it for ourselves at the end of the Bible. But who owned a Bible? Besides, wasn't this the sort of thing that only priests were allowed to know?

Even though such subjects never came up, I remember that year I inadvertently turned a writing exercise on "Which came first, the chicken or the egg?" in a theological direction. I wrote that everything depended on whether one believed in evolution or in the story of Adam and Eve. If one believed God created everything, then he created chickens just as they are, and the Initial Chicken, which God created, would have laid an egg with another chicken inside it, and that egg-laying chicken would have come before the first egg. But if one believed the evolutionary account, the first chicken came out of an egg laid by a slightly less evolved—and therefore less chicken-like—chicken, in which case the egg came first.

Though our faith was mostly a cultural Christianity—no one we knew knew much more than when to cross ourselves during the liturgy and when to kneel and stand—if anyone had suggested baptism and church attendance weren't enough, we would have been offended. Most Greeks we knew were biblically ignorant, but still had a built-in respect for God and the church's authority. There was no separation of church and state in Greece. So although we weren't Bible-thumping evangelicals, neither were we blow-with-the-wind mainline Protestants—or members of what the comedian Flip Wilson once called "The Church of What's Happenin' Now."

Most Greek people's respect and love for the church came from our history of suffering under the Muslim Turks who, after overthrowing Constantinople in 1453, brutally persecuted the Greek Christians for four centuries. I had heard from my father of the *Krifo Scholeio*—the "hidden school"—where priests by night took the Greek children into caves and taught them the basics of the faith. As a result they maintained their identity through centuries of bondage and misery. I heard too how the Turks tore babies from their mothers' arms to raise them as jihadi soldiers who would eventually kill Greeks, and of how many Greek women clutched their infants and leapt from a cliff to their mutual deaths rather than surrender their children to this fate.

So while we never took following God especially seriously, and looked down on anyone who did, neither were we atheists. My father told me a story his grandmother Eleni told him from the 1880s, in which she was walking with her husband, Panagis Vergotis, who suddenly stopped, reached his hand to the ground, and returned to his full height with an ant on his finger. "Tell Mr. Newton," he said, "to make me one of these."

But I remember one day during third grade when we were informed we would all be going to confession. I had never heard of confession, nor did my teacher explain it then. But as though we had done this many times, we were each taken across the street and ushered into the office of the junior priest, Father Boyatzis, who asked us what we wished to confess. I couldn't think of anything, but because I felt an obligation to give him something for his trouble I said that sometimes I didn't listen to my parents as well as I should, which of course was true and vague enough. He asked me if I would try to do better and then said a prayer, and that was that. In all my years in the church, no one ever mentioned confession again. Had this event occurred some months later, however, I might have had something more substantive to offer.

Although I had never heard of the doctrine of the Fall, in fourth grade I got a startling picture of my own sinfulness, and the memory of it horrifies me still. Though I usually got the best grades in my class, there was a girl named Anastasia who usually managed to do better. She was extremely chubby, so much so that her cheeks bulged out dramatically, but she was always sweet and I actually liked her, though perhaps I was sometimes a bit jealous of her higher grades. One day, apropos of absolutely nothing, I turned around at my desk and did something unlike anything I had ever done before, something gratuitous and mystifying: I blurted to her that she was fat. I have no idea why I did this, but I remember doing it, almost as though I were another person. I even said it more than once, until she began to cry, which surprised me. She told our teacher about it, and Mrs. Frangos took us both out into the hallway to question us, at which point I did another thing I had never done before: I brazenly lied. Out of whole cloth and with a straight face I said the reason I said what I said was because Anastasia had made fun of me for being short. Of course she had never done anything of the kind. I remember the look on Anastasia's face when I said it, because the boldness and ugliness of my lie obviously shocked her. I had never behaved like that to anyone before, and had never been around anyone who had. What was going on? I am ashamed to recall it and still know nothing that could have incited me to behave like that. But if I ever needed proof I was not an angel, I have it.

So although we identified as Greek Orthodox, like most "Christians" we had a loopy amalgam of half-beliefs, many of which contradicted the actual tenets of our claimed faith, and resulted in what is a typical American-style "tolerance," in which one treads lightly on issues of faith and truth, and regards those who don't as odd ideologues who are best avoided. This is not to say we would have tolerated anything like outspoken atheism, nor did we have any doubt there was a spiritual world. We simply didn't know much about it, and were quite sure that no one could, since it was invisible and there was so much disagreement.

Like many Greeks my father attended church just a few times a year grow-ing up in Greece, but once in the U.S.—and with a family—it became the central community for most immigrant Greeks. Still, he and most Greeks never really departed from the standard Greek syncretistic and superstitious beliefs with which they had grown up, never hearing in church that there was any reason to do so. My father told me, for example, that whenever he and his father walked home past the cemetery at night in Mavrata, his father always lit a cigarette, saying the fire discouraged evil spirits. He also often told me a story—from the twenties or thirties—about how, following a funeral, some of the younger villagers dared one of their number to that night visit the freshly filled grave of the deceased. It was the custom to break a pitcher over the gravestone when the body was buried, and so the challenge arose: Who would go there alone to trespass upon the realm of the dead at the hour of midnight— and retrieve a shard as proof of his journey? None of them had any doubt the spirits of the dead roamed abroad at night and knew the recently interred might not look favorably upon these cocky young blades making light of his recent demise.

As the story went, one young man volunteered and just before midnight set off along the dark road. But when he neared the silent churchyard he gasped. Atop the chest-high wall encircling the necropolis he spied something so chilling he could proceed no further. It was a dark figure lying perfectly motionless in the faint moonlight, like a corpse. Only fifteen minutes earlier he had crowed of his bravery, but now, faced with this mysterious stranger, he shuddered. It could not be one of his friends, for he had moved swiftly and had listened to every sound as he traveled along the lonely road. Nor would any respectable villager be here at midnight, on the very rampart of the dead. What unholy thing lay there then, as though expecting him? He knew if he turned and fled he would for generations be the laughingstock of the village, the song of drunkards. But neither did he dare move toward the macabre form. At last, hoping to calm himself with his own boldness, he shouted: "Who are you?! Are you a man? Or are you … *the Devil?!*" The figure did not bestir itself. So he shouted the question again, desperate. At last there was movement. But who was it there, so silent upon the verge of the churchyard? It so happened that it was a trespassing shepherd from another village, pasturing his flocks in just such forbidden places where he was sure to remain undiscovered. But now the jackanapes had been caught red-handed, and he skedaddled promptly enough with his herd following, and never showed himself in the area again, lest he face a rougher justice than this midnight rebuke. So the hero returned triumphantly with the jagged potsherd, and with a further heroic tale, too, of apprehending a criminal in the act!

Although I never felt Greek enough when among the other Greek kids, my insecurity was most pronounced at lunchtime. Even though all the other kids had two Greek parents and spoke Greek at home, most mothers at least packed typically "American" lunches of baloney or peanut butter and jelly on Wonder Bread. But my mother's lunches loudly expressed our German-ness, tending toward *leberwurst* or *servelat* on thin German rye and always butter, even if mustard was also used, although my grandmother slathered her bread with bacon grease from the coffee can in which we saved it. She called it *'ne fettbemme* and if my brother and I made faces, she would wag her finger comically and sometimes cross her eyes too, saying, "You don't know what's good, *du!* You better believe it!"

Anyone who ever met her soon came to see that my grandmother was hilarious, and I can't remember her ever being serious for long. She was almost constantly laughing and mugging and entertaining us. Watching TV with her—which we did often—was an unwitting tutelage in mockery, as we poked fun at almost everything on the screen. My mother often participated in this, both of them usually likening odd-looking people to animals, and always doing so not just in German but in their dialect, and always with comic timing and intonations, as though someone had created a wacky typeface and you couldn't take anything you read in it seriously. Of course, my grandmother could sometimes be serious and thoughtful, too. Whenever an image of Nat King Cole came on the screen, she always said, "He was a good man," and said the same thing whenever Walt Disney appeared, making me think it had to do with their early deaths. Still, it was her comic derision that killed. For example, the then-octogenarian singer Maurice Chevalier was around 1971 in a frequently run commercial hawking record, and whenever he appeared my grandmother instantly dismissed him, saying *"Ach!* You old goat!" Why he rubbed her the wrong way we never asked, not that it mattered. But it was hilarious. A few years later the diminutive New York mayor Abe Beame appeared often too, at which point she would always shout, "It's the pip-squeak!" Where she got that from we never asked. And whenever a commercial came on for the Great Adventure game park in New Jersey, she reminded us that my cousin Marion had once been there with friends. "It rained!" she said, as though this was the fault of the park's proprietors. "And all they saw was one llama! *Und* he spit at them!"

Most nights we watched Merv Griffin, with his cavalcade of guests ranging from Charo to Jamie Farr to Arthur Treacher to Spiro Agnew, but one night a skinny old comedian appeared named Leonard Barr, with a face so deadpan he seemed like a corpse. He proceeded to do the funniest dance I had ever seen, so incongruous with his otherwise deathly demeanor that you couldn't help but gag for laughter. "That's Dean Martin's uncle!" my grandmother shouted. She seemed to have the inside scoop on things like that, telling us for example that Merv Griffin and Bob Hope were "millionaires," and scoffing every time we saw the Castro Convertible commercial where the four-year-old opened the sofa, saying the kid was already grown up and implying the whole thing was therefore a fraud.

Because Grandma loved Red Skelton and Jackie Gleason we did too, though we could never quite appreciate Lawrence Welk, whom she never missed and whom we sometimes endured, just to be with her. But our highlights together were Saturdays and Tuesdays. Every Saturday for years we watched Carol Burnett. One day early in 1971 my grandmother raved to us about a new show called *All in the Family,* for weeks going on about "the Meathead" until finally she showed up one Tuesday and made us tune in. We never missed it again.

The Transfiguration lunchroom was typically boisterous and Mrs. Stevens—the middle-aged non-Greek charged with maintaining order—often pulled boys by the hair to punctuate her screaming. One day she became particularly infuriated with John Kostas, who sported a crewcut I often teased him about; but on that day I was dumbstruck with respect as I watched Mrs. Stevens getting angrier and angrier as she repeatedly tried and failed to grasp his infuriatingly short hair. Corporal punishment was always part of the equation at Transfiguration, and even our otherwise mild-mannered music teacher Mr. Pappas once used it. He was trying to teach us "I'd Like to Teach the World to Sing," though we all missed the irony, and only knew the song as the jingle for a hugely popular Coke commercial. Poor Mr. Pappas was trying to teach us the emended version—without the line, *"It's the Real Thing! Coke is!"*—but his expectation that third-grade boys could resist interjecting what they found unbelievably hilarious was patently unrealistic, and even when he finally blew his cork and hauled us by our earlobes from the class-room, we could not stop laughing.

   Living in the largely Greek world in which I did then seems to me now as though I were living in an alternative universe from the rest of the kids in the country. But this sense is never more pronounced than when I recall my encounters with that forbidding and anachronistic figure known to us as *O Kyrios Siambas*—whom we may here refer to simply as Mr. Siambas. I see him now in my mind's eye wearing a gray suit and holding a cigarette, like something out of an illustrated 1940s menswear ad, looking simultane-ously authoritative and oblivious. For clarity's sake, let me simply say that Mr. Siambas was a Greek teacher in both senses of the phrase, meaning he was hired to teach Greek, but was also so freshly out of Greece that he had never really left, and he made no concession to where he now lived, nor in which decade, such that he slapped and buffeted his incorrigible charges with frighteningly unrestricted abandon. It never occurred to him that other teachers in 1970s America were not doing this anymore. As for his grooming habits, one gathers he thought the use of deodorant effeminate and French, for whenever he leaned over me to point something out in my copy book, I observed that he stank like a rutting goat. It was also then that I recoiled to see him flourishing a grotesquely long left pinkie nail, which in some bygone circles had indicated a man of leisure. One must also mention that his fear-some corpse's breath, when carelessly directed, carried the blunt force of an expertly swung truncheon.
   Nor can one do him full justice without mentioning that during his classes he hacked loudly—he was a smoker—and spat often and with great fluency into the large open trash cans lined against the wall in the lunch room where our classes were held, not neglecting almost to gargle his unhallowed ammunition before its flagrant deployment. Betimes the hell-born oyster overshot its target and struck the wall. Mr. Siambas also swore with indiscriminate abandon in front of all of us, boys and girls alike, and always in the original Greek.

But Siambas's expertly delivered clouts were his truest signature. As his student in third and fourth grade I behaved such that he never laid a hand on me, but I had the misfortune in second grade, before he was my Greek teacher, to be on the receiving end of one of these awful blows. I was then six and small for my age, but one day for an unhappy hour it had fallen to Mr. Siambas to substitute for Mrs. Rosner, then expecting and at a doctor's appointment. Siambas was there to see that we worked quietly until Mrs. Rosner returned, but when I rose to ask if I could use the bathroom, he— from his seated position—promptly slapped my face and in Greek demanded I return to my seat. I had never been slapped, so I immediately bawled awfully and slunk back to my seat. But even at six I knew that he was so out of touch with the world in which I lived that I took it no more personally than if I had been spattered by pigeon dung.

But in routinely pulling hair, yanking earlobes, and slapping impertinent young faces, Siambas was merely employing the full arsenal available to teachers since Plato, although as we have said, he was entirely unaware that in the America of my childhood these retrograde methods had been retired along with stocks and the ducking stool. At home I would sometimes imitate him for my father, who thoroughly enjoyed it, although of course my mother was disgusted. Theo Takis knew Siambas too, so when he visited us my father asked me to "make the Siambas," at which point I put my leg on a chair imperiously, as Siambas often did, swore loudly in Greek, and then very noisily pretended to summon a nasty curd—as though loading a viscous round into the chamber—and then masterfully hock-*TOO*-ed the phlegmy missile into the imagined trashcan, to the delight of my dad and Theo Takis.

We may not leave the subject of Siambas without touching on that activity for which he was best known, for by all accounts his most intimidating threat was when he would go to what for him was code red and declare, *"Th' archiso anapodes!"* which meant "I shall begin the backhands!" All the dyed-in-the-wool Greek kids instantly appreciated the import of these chilling words (pronounced *Ah-NA-poh-thes*), which meant that Siambas—having no other choice because of our wicked behavior—would proceed to the next level of corporal punishment, to wit: slapping with his full backhand. It seemed to be common knowledge among the others that the gravitational advantages of a well-delivered downward stroke, coupled with the garish rings on his fingers, would prove far more painful than the normal open-handed slaps, which they seemed to withstand with no difficulty at all, likely experiencing far worse at home. But when at last the terrible specter of *anapodes* was raised, all bets were off, and a respectful gravity fell over the room. Anything, it seemed, but *anapodes*.

In treating the subject of male teachers at Transfiguration, we may also pay homage to the curious figure of Lambros Lambrakis, who, unfortunately for hundreds of children, was the "Gym Teacher," although how he came to that position falls beyond the ken of mortal minds. His name by itself was enough to cross one's eyes, but when I think what he did with us for "gym" class, I feel we are approaching the neighborhood of what might be considered child abuse.

Each year around March 25—which is Greek Independence Day, marking our heroic and ultimately victorious 1821 uprising against the despised Ottomans—Greeks celebrate with as much or more abandon than Americans celebrate the Fourth. In New York City we even had the great boon of an annual parade down Fifth Avenue. In kindergarten in 1969 I was in the parade, sitting like an astronaut on the back of a white Pontiac convertible and waving at the crowds. My grandmother Renee had earlier sent my brother and me each a small *Tsolias* uniform, the traditional costume of the Revolutionary era soldiers, worn by the tall men guarding the Tomb of the Unknown Soldier in Athens[2] so that they function something like the cockaded busbies and frogged jackets worn by the Royal Horse Artillery in England. *Tsolias* uniforms, as I then learned, consisted of a starched and pleated white skirt—called a *fustanella*—along with white leotards, and curved slipper shoes with bright pompoms. There is also a white shirt and a beautifully brocaded blue vest, all topped with a red felt cap with a tassel. Even at five, though, I was horrified to don leotards and a skirt! But my German grandmother was visiting, and when

---

[2] *Tsolias* is the colloquial term for what are properly called Evzones. Homer first used the word, which literally means "well-girt."

she saw me, crowed her approval. *"Ach,* Eric!" she said, glowing, "You look like a little prince!" Such love from the sweetest person I knew was enough to cover a multitude of sins.

But in fourth grade, our participation in the parade was dramatically different. We would not ride like heroes in a ticker-tape parade, but rather must march with something bordering fascist precision. That's because this was the chief goal—or Aristotelian *telos*—of Mr. Lambrakis, who made us spend every single "gym" class until March 25 marching in rectangular monotony around the gymnasium. Who had charged him with this curious assignment? No one knew. Nonetheless, from September onward we weekly disported ourselves thus for forty minutes in our school uniforms. There was never a break from this to play dodgeball, which we didn't know existed, nor to do gymnastics, though we had once glimpsed some new, unused equipment under the stage. Once, however, in lieu of this monotonous prison-camp-style activity, we had the privilege of folding all the chairs in the auditorium—still there from an earlier event—and then stacking them onto rolling platforms and wheeling these under the stage. This was as close to doing leg cuts on the pommel horse as we would get.

After we had moved to Connecticut, I almost wondered whether Lambrakis had been a bad dream, but my cousin John said that he too had the privilege of serving in the man's regiment. He even recalled how Lambrakis once furiously reprimanded their misbehaving class with a memorable line that in his anger combined two imperatives with which he was equally unfamiliar, the first being "Stop trying to pull the wool over my eyes!" and the second, "Stop pulling my leg!" Thus did he irately shriek: "Stop pulling your feet over my eyes!"

The tale of marching around the gym is a fitting place to turn to the happy subject of leaving the city. My parents understood their boys needed to play outside and do whatever it was boys our age did, not that they quite knew. But thanks to our friend Speros Phillis, we finally began looking at houses in western Connecticut, near Danbury, where there was a thriving Greek community. In January 1972 we found a small yellow Cape Cod that sat on nearly two acres and was located on a dead end giving onto a huge tract of wilderness.

The house was on a hill, with a spectacular view, and when my parents first entered the living room they came in from opposite sides, meeting in the middle and seeing the view together through the huge picture window. It was settled. But my brother and I couldn't really believe it. Were we really moving to the country? So when we visited in preparation for our move, which would be when school ended, we scrambled upstairs to see the large room that would be all ours and felt we were dreaming, though we had hardly allowed ourselves even to dream along such happy lines.

But there was one strange thing now that seemed to become a pattern in my life. Although I never quite fit in at Transfiguration, I began to feel I was fitting in just as I was leaving. I was shocked to be invited to two end-of-the-year parties with some of the kids in my class and discovered they enjoyed my company. Why had they suddenly included me? The girls even suddenly thought I was "cute" and we all played "spin the bottle" and "Post Office," and when I got home I had the feeling that I would be included in their parties going forward, and that we would all grow up together. But I never saw them again. I cannot help wondering what things might have been like had we not moved; and of course that fork in the road is now a half century ago.

CHAPTER FIVE

Moving to America

1972

In 1972 Danbury, Connecticut, was a sleepy town of fifty thousand working- and middle-class families four-score miles from Manhattan, magically just beyond commuting reach and therefore free of the city's cultural gravitational pull. So living there was like being in the heartland of the country, smack dab in the middle of America. Which was why leaving the multi-ethnic stew of urban Queens and our Greek parochial school for "the country" felt like we were finally really becoming fully American—and weren't we?

The large room my brother and I would share through college was two-thirds of a finished attic whose sloping ceilings and walls were covered with wide varnished pine boards, making it feel like a tree house. There were giant pine drawers built into the pine walls, and to inadvertently complete the effect, just outside our window were pine trees. The other third of the attic, beyond the stairs, was an open sewing room, similarly pine-covered, that was my grandmother's room when she stayed with us, which was about half the time. We had a yard and would attend public school—no uniforms!—and could ride bikes and play baseball and build secret tree forts.

Danbury had been settled in 1685, but not very much had seemed to change in three centuries. Compared to New York, it felt as though American history here was recent and palpable—and we had somehow now entered it ourselves. I learned that during the Revolution the Redcoats discovered hidden magazines of weaponry in Danbury, so in April 1777 British Major General William Tryon landed ships on the coast in Westport and marched north, not only burning these stores of weapons but despicably burning every house not belonging to Tories. General David Wooster chased the British in their long retreat to the Sound and was mortally wounded in the effort,

[The following Paragraphs were taken from a *Connecticut* Paper, published by the Rebels.]

HARTFORD, May 5.

The following particulars of the late affair at Danbury we have received since our last, viz.

On Saturday the 26th of April, express came to Danbury from Brigadier General Silliman, advising that a large body of the enemy had landed the day before at sun set, at Campo, a point of land between Fairfield, and Norwalk, and were marching towards Danbury. Measures were immediately taken

but has since rightly been hailed as an American hero. Danbury's greater claim to national fame, however, came in 1802, when President Thomas Jefferson wrote his landmark letter to the Danbury Baptists, using the now-famous phrase "a wall of separation" between Church and State.

But it was indisputably for hats that my new hometown was most famous. The year Jefferson wrote his letter, Danbury led the fledgling country in hat production by a mile, manufacturing no less than twenty thousand *chapeaux*. Fifty years on the figure had soared to one and a half million annually, earning Danbury the sobriquet "Hat City," and in 1887, the city made five million hats in eighteen factories. Hat production peaked in 1900 when three-quarters of all American hats began their life in Danbury. Thus our high school sports teams were called "The Hatters" and the mascot was a bowler-wearing beaver—from whose pelts most of the hat felt was made. But the mercury used in the felt-making process was toxic—spawning the phrase "Mad as a Hatter"—and those afflicted with mercury poisoning were then said to have "the Danbury Shakes." For many decades the local rivers into which the industry's effluvium was dumped were seriously polluted. When we moved there and wandered down to the genuinely opaque Still River, a few hundred yards from our house, we never saw a single sign of life. We wouldn't have dared to swim in it.

But we often swam in Candlewood Lake, ten minutes away. Candlewood is the biggest lake in Connecticut, four times larger than its next competitor.

But it's a man-made lake, rising into existence in the late twenties, when the Connecticut Light & Power Company diverted the Housatonic River to create a body of water to power a new hydroelectric dam. Many people were forced to sell their farms and houses to the state at "market value," and anything left behind was soon underwater. Some Model T Fords and heavy farm equipment are still down there, along with a number of roads and even some covered bridges. An entire graveyard was moved, but one small village named Jerusalem was simply abandoned and forgotten. I was fascinated that families had lived their whole lives deep beneath what was now this vast happy lake, alive with boats and water skiers.

The house officially became ours in early May, but as my brother and I had to finish school we didn't move till mid-June, by which point the neglected grass in our backyard was two feet high. Our first order of business therefore was buying a lawnmower. We visited the Sears on Main Street, but in a larger store called Grandway found a non-self-propelled yellow-green model that my brother and I spent the next decade pushing and shoving around the huge and very hilly yard. At Grandway too we found my first bicycle, in Op Art yellow with a big black rear wheel, and a black banana seat. It seemed to be a two-wheeled version of the Corvette Stingrays that *vroom*-ed in and out of my daydreams, with high curved handlebars that made popping wheelies easy, this being the unspoken apotheosis of such vehicles.

In late June we celebrated my ninth birthday under the then-young maple tree at the bottom of the backyard hill, and in the decades since have celebrated so many events there that the now-crippled old tree feels like a member of the family. A bit further down the hill was the forsythia bush that bloomed yellow-green every spring, and to the left of that my father's garden, which soon became the biggest I'd ever seen. He dug it that summer and eventually planted tomatoes, peppers, string beans, zucchini, yellow squash, kohlrabi, beets, cauliflower, spinach, lettuce, corn, peas, carrots, Swiss chard, and rhubarb. There were also eventually strawberries, blueberries, blackberries, raspberries, and gooseberries, as well as watermelons, pumpkins, and gourds; and around the garden there were soon fruit trees of many kinds, and around the house itself grape vines and fig trees.

One summer, along the wall separating our property from the Wrights', my brother and I planted sunflowers, one of which grew to nearly thirteen feet. Milford and Effie Wright were old-school Yankees whose son David had gone to Yale. One day Mr. Wright gave my brother and me his old baseball equipment, which consisted of a bat with "1909" carved into it and a primitive glove that looked like it had been used by Honus Wagner. In our front yard there was a dogwood tree, two huge maples, and a line of cypress trees separating our driveway from the Nuneses' yard. The Nuneses were Portuguese and Mr. Nunes had a thriving construction business. Our house was the first one he ever built—in 1950—just prior to building his own. And at the end of our driveway stood our heavy mailbox, painted white and featuring the cheerful metal cutout of a mother robin feeding her young.

My brother and I quickly made friends with Joey Nunes, age four, and then with Peter, nine, two houses up, and Gary, seven, who lived next to Peter. The two of them often rode their bikes over, and because Gary seemed attached by the hip to Peter, my grandmother always referred to him as "the Deputy."

In late July we got our first visit from Theo Takis, Aunt Mary, and John, when everyone was talking about the Fischer versus Spassky chess championship. My dad and cousin played chess for hours. Of course the championship was a proxy battle in the Cold War, just as the Space Race had been—and as the Munich Olympics would be in a few weeks. My mother and father knew the Soviets had no qualms about lying and cheating. If there was no God, why *should* they? For them power and winning were the only virtues. Of course we now know they cheated, but the overly muscular bodies of the Soviet-bloc female swimmers made it obvious even then.

My sweet father's inability to reckon what his sons might like went beyond the infamous V-8 incident. In 1969 he took me to Radio City to see *True Grit*, with John Wayne and Glen Campbell, which was a little rough for someone not quite six, but that summer of 1972 he topped it by taking my brother and me to the local drive-in to see *The Godfather*. I was always sensitive to violence, so when Luca Brasi's hand was pinned to the bar with a knife while he was strangled, it got to me, as did the later scene, when after Barzini's men machine-gun Sonny at the toll booth one of them kicks his corpse in the head.

Finally, it was less the horse's head in the multitudinous seas incarnadine of the bed that got to me than the agonized prolonged screaming of the previously recalcitrant film director on discovering it.

Often that summer we visited Bradlees Department Store for such odds and ends as a new household required. We drove there one night after dinner, but five minutes after we fanned into the store I was paralyzed by a searing spasm. I instantly understood that this betokened a call of nature demanding the most urgent attention—but what to do? I had lost track of my parents and having never been alone in such a vast store had no inkling there might be a public bathroom. So I simply panicked, racing up and down the aisles looking for my parents, with every step fatally exacerbating the maturing problem. In my rapidly deteriorating state I now began to perspire and then concluded with climaxing anxiety that my parents must have already left the store, which was now closing. Perhaps I had lost them forever and would never find them again. So I now hobbled speedily—but with just such care as was quite mandatory—past the cashiers and then bolted for the exit.

But it was in that millisecond in which I passed the murky chrome-and-plastic gumball machines that what forcefully had been demanding egress would no longer be denied. Just then—of a sudden—the pushy fellow in the vanguard leapt forth and made his escape, with derring-do dropping from the height of my cut-off short shorts to his new position on the dirty linoleum by the vending machines. In the tenth-second after this I glanced backward and—seeing him prostrate—blanched with horror. But what could be done? Horrified to leave a man on the field and shell-shocked generally, I simply kept moving forward. But it was in these unprecedented seconds of humiliation and horror that the remaining soldiers now opportunistically made their escape too, some deploying to the field, others remaining Stateside.

I shuffled awkwardly into the hot summer air of the parking lot, wildly confused at my predicament and at the inconceivably ghastly scene in my wake which I could not address but must run from, as from a monster in a nightmare. But now, neither seeing my parents nor yet fathoming how the car ride home might present a challenge, I stood in the darkening lot. And then at last I saw them.

My parents and brother were approaching our yellow 1967 Dodge Dart. I hustled toward them—but just before they saw me or I could say a word to reveal myself or my condition, my parents suddenly burst out with joy to see some old Cuban friends, who just happened that moment to be getting into the car adjacent to ours—and whom my parents hadn't seen in a full decade. What a coincidence! Evidently the couple lived in Danbury too, with their five kids whom they now dutifully introduced, although by now I had warily skulked to the far side of our car, unable to partake in social niceties. Miraculously my parents didn't insist—in fact I wasn't sure they even knew I was there, crouching uncomfortably apart—and after ten minutes of catching up my parents bade their friends adieu. At last now I was at liberty to disclose my identity and situation, like a late-arriving figure at the end of a farce who is helping tie up loose ends. And then, after some crude prophylactic measures which my father fished out of the cornucopia of the trunk, we made our way home, windows wide. In the driveway I shed my befouled shorts and was humiliatingly hosed down as my brother stood by to mock. In the years following this episode there were very few cruel exchanges between us. Pushed to my limit, I once or twice nastily said, "Skip a grade. Then we'll talk." But from my brother there would always and ever come only one riposte, for what else was necessary? "What," he would ask, "about Bradlees?"

Beaver Brook

Our first summer in the country had been a heavenly respite, but the circulars in the local *News-Times* soon let us know it was time for school supplies. I'd never seen calculators before, but that August they were advertised everywhere, at around three hundred dollars each! My brother and I also needed clothes, but what in the world did school kids wear besides uniforms? I soon found out what they didn't, because someone in Germany had sent us a beautiful loden jacket with hunter-green piping and oak leaf accents and antler buttons. It fit my fifty-pound body perfectly and I was proud to wear it, though at the bus stop it soon dawned on me that compared to the other boys, I may as well have been dressed like Pippi Longstocking. The next day I wore something less festive.

From the first day, though, Johnny and I absolutely loved our new school. Beaver Brook was like something outside of time, a mythical American school I had dreamed up or had read about in a book by the d'Aulieres, whose heavenly picture books were always my favorites. It was made of brick in 1936, with a flagpole in front and a huge grassy area where we played at recess. My teacher was from another time, too. Mrs. Saul had begun teaching in the forties, and this marked her last academic year.

Our first assignment involved collecting and pressing wildflowers. At the end of our road there was a vast area of fields and woods called "the cow pasture," because just a few years earlier there really were cows there. It was a great place to wander, and we often rode our bikes on its trails, which went on and on into another world. So one afternoon my mother and I walked into its meadows, collecting every early September flower we could, and pressing them into old books. Once they were flat and dried, I took them to school, and Mrs. Saul identified them. Everyone mounted their flowers on lilac-colored construction paper and covered that with Saran wrap, fixed to the back with Scotch tape. According to Mrs. Saul, I had found goldenrod and buttercups and black-eyed Susans and clover and common daisies and Queen Anne's lace and purple asters. But my favorite of all to this day were the small, exquisite yellow-and-white flowers with a touch of yolk orange, called butter-and-eggs.

The change from our New York apartment to our new American paradise could hardly have been more dramatic. I had almost never done anything athletic, and that first week our gym teacher started us off with a fitness test. I never knew I was fast, but running the six hundred in two-twelve and the fifty in seven flat made me the second-best runner in the class, even though

I was a year younger. We also did pull-ups and sit-ups and jumping jacks and squat thrusts, and just days later were playing touch football and kickball. It was unspeakably exhilarating.

I had never done anything musical either, but in our first week there was an assembly in which the music teachers demonstrated various instruments. Tante Eleonore said she thought a trumpet was a nice instrument for a boy, which was good enough for me, so we drove to Eddie Kane's on White Street—a venerable Danbury institution like Meeker's Hardware or Feinson's Men's Store or JK's Texas Hot Weiners—and rented a trumpet, and I began lessons.

Behind the school there was a "Nature Center" through which ran a creek, over which an Eagle Scout had built a wooden bridge for his merit badge. I knew nothing about the outdoors and believed certain plants—like dandelions—fell into some official Linnaean "weed" category, but learned then that there was no such thing, that weeds were in the eyes of the beholder, weedhood itself being subjective. I also learned about "scouring rush," used as a pot cleaner before Brillo pads, and "jewelweed," a stalk of which our science teacher plunged into the water, moving it around until we saw the undersides of the leaves suddenly turn a dramatically shiny and bright silver; and when he pulled it out, they were dull green again.

That October Mrs. Saul announced our class would put on a short play

commemorating what happened in October 1687, when the despised Governor General of New England, Sir Edmund Andros, attempted to confiscate Connecticut's 1662 charter, which had given the colony great autonomy. But the original Nutmeggers were hardly inclined to roll over for the pompous flunky of some distant monarch; so during the ceremony in which they were to surrender the cherished document, the candles mysteriously blew out. When they were relit the charter had disappeared—having been spirited away and hidden in the yawning hollow of the gigantic and subsequently named "Charter Oak," which dated to the twelfth century.[1] I was suddenly proud to live in Connecticut and was not at all upset Mrs. Saul thought I should play the role of Andros, even though my entrance must be greeted with hisses.

But I was not so happy to have to wear one of my mother's ruffled blouses for my seventeenth-century costume, although in the end I would let verisimilitude have its way. I was also very solemnly asked whether I would wear the yellowing eighteenth-century-style wig someone had created for a play in years past. I was taken alone to another room where a box was opened and the George Washington–style wig solemnly revealed. Would I wear it? Why were they asking me? Was there something weird about wearing it? Somehow I smelled a rat, and declined. I have since seen several paintings of the poltroon Andros, who wore his hair in a typically preposterous late-seventeenth-century periwig with endless cataracts of wild curls—which one sees in images of Isaac Newton and certain 70s rock stars—so in retrospect, my decision to do what Ben Franklin had done and wear my hair *au naturel* was at least as appropriate as the anachronistic wig that day so gravely proffered.

That spring, Mrs. Saul read to us at the end of each day, first from Pearl S. Buck's *The Good Earth* and then from *The Wolves of Willoughby Chase*. It was an extraordinary treat to have a book read to us, although compared to marching around a gym or being slapped, I reckoned nearly everything a tall step up. But Mrs. Saul could be tough, too. One day during "current events" I brightly mentioned a story I had read about a two-headed baby, not realizing the *National Enquirer*—which my grandmother always bought—was not an approved newspaper. Mrs. Saul was not amused. "We do not discuss freaks in this classroom!" she said.

Mrs. Saul was also the first person to point out a problem with which I struggle yet when one day she cut me off sternly, saying: "Garrulous! Garrulous!!

---

[1] The tree stood until 1856. The governor's desk and some chairs in the state Capitol today were fashioned from its wood.

Garrulous!!!" I soon learned this was an adjective for talking too much and was made to write "I will not be garrulous." on the chalkboard twenty times, improving my vocabulary, but failing to stanch my verbosity. Another time my friend Chuck Stavola innocently interrupted Mrs. Saul, who rebuked him with another unfamiliar word. "Butt-in-ski!" she declared. "Charles! You have *got* to stop being *such* a butt-in-ski!"

There were just sixteen of us in her class, making it all the more wonderful, and we all got along, with some normal teasing here and there. One day, though, an odd thing happened. Stephen Boaz came up to me and my new friends Scott Bennett and Luke Bonacci, and out of the blue said he loved us. Because it made us uncomfortable, we made fun of it. What else would fifth-grade boys do? But then he said, "No, I'm serious. I really love you. In Jesus's name!" We still had no idea what to make of it. That sort of talk was as foreign to me, who was in church every Sunday, as it was to Scott, who said he was an atheist. So we continued making fun of him. I remember how he quickly became despondent. He looked crushed. Had a Sunday school teacher advised him to take this tack, suggesting he share God's love for others this way? And was Stephen now being rewarded for this step of faith with mockery? Doing that obviously took no small amount of courage, and I still hope we did not dissuade him forever from such sweet boldness.

But my regrets in this incident pale when compared to my feelings about how I treated a kid named Terry in the grade below mine. On the first day of school—when I sported the loden jacket—my mother had accompanied my brother and me to the bus stop, where we stood with a number of other kids and mothers. Terry was my age but in the grade below me, and his mother seemed desperately to want us to connect. She invited me over after school, and I dutifully went, but Terry and I never really hit it off.

Not long after that, though, I realized Terry was generally shunned. He had a beautiful, slightly effeminate face, and a body that was not athletic. Somehow I felt it important that in order to fit in, I should probably dislike him too. So when we were playing touch football during a combined fourth- and fifth-grade gym class I deliberately stood across from him, intending to bump him hard when the ball was hiked. As with the way I treated Anastasia a year earlier, I am now shocked I would do such a thing. But I also know that I did it. I still remember the feeling of wanting to bully him, who was probably the only one weaker than I. But asking why I did this—when my parents had never countenanced anything like that or modeled it around me—is like asking why Adam and Eve ate the apple. Was doing that my way of showing I wasn't like him? And showing whom? Myself? I did this more than once, with little real effect. Nonetheless, I must have made my wicked little point, because the final time I lined up in front of him I remember him saying pathetically with his half lisp, "Oh boy, now I'm really going to get it!" Remembering that now makes me want to weep. I think I would do almost anything to go back there now to try to undo what I did, to befriend him or show him some love or kindness. From this distance the horror of what I did is so awful I don't want to think about it, because I see I was doing what I have pointed the finger at innumerable others for doing, not just around me, but throughout history. I participated in his ostracization. I helped it along. *I.*

As I became better friends with Scott and Luke, I forgot about Terry, but at some point I realized that every day he stood alone at the bus stop between the boys and the girls, who stood in our little clots sixty feet apart and somehow pretended not to see him. He was rarely openly persecuted but just stood there day after day. His sister was popular and ignored her brother, too. But how it makes me ache now, the proverbial cruelty of children, recalling how he stood there silently for years, and how amazingly I was able to block it from my mind. We boys chatted waiting for the bus as the girls did under their tree on the corner, and Terry stood apart, staring in the same direction. That image haunts me and haunts me, but I am glad that it does, because I understand now that it should.

CHAPTER SIX

Assumption Church
& Trip to Greece

Nicely situated upon the breezy heights and running parallel to Danbury's Main Street is Farview Avenue, a broad tree-lined street along which stand the imposing Victorian houses built for the owners of the hat factories in the late nineteenth century. Most of them had by the seventies been carved into multiple dwellings and doctors' offices, but one of them had been converted into the Greek Orthodox church we would attend, though there remained little evidence of the building's previous domestic life. On the first floor was a foyer and the church hall, with a kitchen in the back; and upstairs was the narthex—with its candles and icons—through which one passed into the sanctuary, on whose right was a bay window area set off for the choir, which consisted of the Johns family. Mr. Johns directed as his wife played organ and their teenage daughters beautifully sang the Divine Liturgy.

Orthodox churches have a wall covered with icons—the *iconostasis*—that separates the sanctuary from the altar, with doors on the left and right, and in the center is an arched opening through which only the priest may venture, echoing the Holy of Holies in the Old Testament. The icons intrigued me, but were never explained. The church was called "Assumption," so I now realize the most memorable icon was a scene from the funeral of Mary, when a sword-wielding angel—with bulging calves and severe mien—severs the hands of someone spitefully intending to overturn the bier of the Theotokos. The man stands with bloody stumps, his severed hands still floating in mid-air.[1]

My Theo Takis was always up on what was happening in the archdiocese and said our priest, Father Germanos, was a tremendously intelligent, talented figure, whom we were extremely lucky to have. But soon after this news we learned he was leaving, and by the time we began attending he had already been replaced by a chubby, thirty-something man named Father Stavropoulos, who had a round face, dark eyes, and a balding pate that sweated readily amidst the myriad candles—and under the heavy, brocaded vestments—of our denomination. My mother and I thought him the very twin of Dom DeLuise, whom we loved, but soon understood that on less superficial levels they were hardly alike.

For example, there was always some element of calculation with Stavro-poulos. He smiled when necessary, but my mother wasn't fooled. "I don't trust him!" she declared, in her sometimes-blunt German way. But many Greeks shared my mother's opinion, and a few years later when he purchased a motel to run as a side business, the parish was predictably scandalized. Why would a priest run a down-at-the-heels motel just off the highway? But this was just the beginning. Soon after he bought a half share in a diner near our house and busied himself with running that too, doing less and less church business.

My brother and I attended Greek school at the church every Tuesday afternoon and hated it. Stavropoulos was our teacher—everyone called him Stavropoulos behind his back, as though neglecting his title might return to them some of the respect they lost in having him for a priest—and though I don't recall a single lesson, I remember he spent much of this time on the phone in his office, chattering in Greek, presumably about his business affairs, though at some point he would emerge, put on his forced smile and commence the lessons before usually leaving again.

Once, as we waited for him, I was chilled to my core to see him angrily explode from his office wielding a fifteen-inch ruler to chase his son—then

---

[1] As the story goes, this severely chastised troublemaker was Jerusalem's High Priest Jephonias, who instantly repented, proclaiming Mary as the Mother of God, and had his hands miraculously restored.

four—through the church foyer and into the church hall with its maze of chalkboards and dividers, finally cornering his terrified prey and with the weapon very loudly slapping the crew-cutted child about the head so that the boy squealed like a stuck pig. The screaming was deeply horrifying for me, who had never witnessed anything like this, and my opinion of Father Stavropoulos was never the same.

Most of our friends were from the Greek community, but shortly after we moved my mother discovered a German singing club called the Arion Society—whose members met weekly and competed with other German clubs around New England[2]—where she met our neighbor, Margaret Schemmel, whose three children, Monica, Cornelia, and Rolf, soon became my brother's and my good friends. Saturday mornings the Arion also offered German lessons and singing for kids, so in addition to church every Sunday and Greek school every Tuesday, my brother and I now added another embarrassing immigrant activity to our schedules.

Because we were no longer at Transfiguration, we no longer daily sang the Greek national anthem, but now every Saturday we sang the German national anthem, "Einigkeit und Recht und Freiheit" ("Unity and Right and Freedom"), to the tune of "Deutschland Über Alles."[3]

Then we sang other German songs for forty-five minutes, followed by an hour of German lessons. After class we waited to be picked up in the ancient clubhouse, with its huge ornate wooden bar and a gigantic old mirror behind it, plus all manner of taxidermy, and tall wooden-and-glass cases filled with old silver trophies with inscriptions in Old German lettering. The stout barrel-shaped barkeep—with a cigar butt affixed like a mole to his lip—was out of a thirties B-film, and in small beer glasses he wiped with his apron gave us all the free orange soda we liked.

---

[2] The word "Arion" comes from the Greek and is supposed to be the name of a kitharode—whence the Greek word kitar, from which we get "guitar"—who played the lyre, so Arion was principally a singing club. The German connection with things "Aryan" has no etymological or other connection to the word "Arion." The Arion Society was formed in 1909, decades before National Socialism.

[3] The melody was written by Joseph Haydn in 1797 to commemorate Kaiser Franz and was used by Germans as a national anthem long before National Socialism, although after the war, what became West Germany used the song, but unsurprisingly skipped immediately to the third stanza.

As in the Greek community, our fit among the Germans was hardly seamless. Just as everyone in the Greek church had two Greek parents and spoke Greek at home, almost all of the kids in the German classes came from homes with two German parents, so you could say that my brother and I almost got used to not belonging wherever we were.

Trip to Greece

That November I learned I would be going to Greece over Christmas break. I was almost as surprised as when eighteen months earlier I learned we were going to Germany. We couldn't all afford to go, though. Only my father and I would make the trip. Theo Takis had connections at Olympic Airways and at JFK got us bumped up to first. But the flight was rough, and I returned my dinner with such interest that a large plastic bag previously containing gifts was sacrificed to the situation, which we disposed of during our brief stopover at Orly. But I remember the tenderness of the stewardess, who took pity on me and brought me into the cockpit to visit the captains.

We spent our first night at our family's Athens apartment and the next morning made the three-hour bus trip to Patras, followed by the four-hour ferry to Cephalonia, that impossibly mythical island of which I had heard so much. Because it rains most of the winter, Cephalonia is by the standards of Greek islands famously verdant, and when we arrived in Argostoli it was pouring. The impressive two-story, fourteen-room Vergotis family villa featured in my father's stories was destroyed in the 1953 earthquake, and a one-story villa replaced it in 1961. Because most of Argostoli is on a hill, reaching the front door meant entering through an iron gate and climbing cement stairs. And there through the rain I saw her, standing in the open door to welcome us, my father's old aunt Kikí.

Kikí was more of a mother to my father than his own mother, and when she saw "her Niko" she embraced him and covered him with her tears, after which she marveled and gushed over me, who was like a grandchild she had never met. Kikí was so overcome that in her excitement she wanted her recently deceased twin sister to meet me too and absurdly took my grandmother's framed photo from the wall and brought it to me, saying, *"Ei yaya sou! Ei yiayia sou!"*—meaning "Your grandmother! Your grandmother!"

My grandmother Renee, 1970

There in the salon I saw the old Kaps piano which Panagis Vergotis had imported from Dresden in 1911, upon which Kikí and my grandmother learned to play as girls, and upon which my father learned to play in the thirties, and which after the '53 earthquake he had saved from destruction by dragooning six soldiers from the *Plaka* to carry it from the rubble of the house into the garden, where he covered it with a tarp. After we settled ourselves Kikí sat at the piano she had been playing for sixty-two years and played for us. And as we sat there and listened to the slightly out-of-tune music filling the room, the past returned, and my father wept.

I never dreamt Uncle Othon could be so wonderful, buoyant and joking and generous, and the only son with Yiannikostas's blue eyes. Each morning he arrived to take us someplace exciting. One day we went to Aenos, the imposing mountain at the island's center. Visible from the mainland, it is a mile high and covered with the dark firs that grow nowhere else in the world, whose species name is *Cephalieniensus,* and whose wood millennia of ship-makers have used.[4]

---

[4] Since the maritime Venetian empire for centuries included the Ionian islands, much of Venice itself is made with wood from Aenos, and the Cephalonian archaeologist Spyridon Marinatos determined that even the Minoan Palace of Knossos unearthed by Sir Arthur Evans in 1900 was made with wood from those trees. In the thirties Marinatos also discovered an altar to Zeus at the summit.

Othon, Takis, Kikí, Renee, and Nikos in front of the Kaps piano, 1931

Driving up we passed a gargantuan satellite disk, and Uncle Othon said this was a NATO outpost, so that even here atop this ancient mountain the Cold War was being fought. At the summit there was snow everywhere, and my father broke off two small fir branches which we smuggled home and have displayed in our basement ever since.

One day we visited the monastery of the island's patron saint, Agios Gerasimos, for whom a comical percentage of the island's boys are named. We entered the sanctuary where the five-hundred-year-old body is kept and revered, and my father spoke to the young, bearded priest, who glowed with joy. My father explained that Agios Gerasimos was buried twice but never decayed, after which he was declared a saint and his corpse placed in an ornate silver-and-gold-covered bier, through whose glass front one can still see him. My father often said that every August the bier is carried over the prostrate bodies of the faithful, bringing about miraculous healings and deliverances from shrieking demons.

But I grew uncomfortable when the priest brought us into proximity of the unmummified corpse, entreating us to kiss its desiccated legs. He opened the bottom part of the bier and my father stuck his head in and kissed the vestments covering the saint's withered feet. Then it was my turn. I dutifully obeyed, putting my head in—and desperately avoiding looking left, lest I glimpse the well-preserved head—and kissed the brocaded cloth and then pulled my head out and exhaled.

One evening my father went to a special dinner, leaving me with Kikí. She said she wasn't hungry but asked if I was. *"Theleis Giaourti?"* she asked. Yes, I loved yogurt. But when Kikí showed me a plastic tub of watery Greek yogurt that did not resemble the vanilla Dannon my mother bought, I embarrassingly declined. *"Theleis Augo?"* Yes, I loved eggs. While Kikí prepared my egg, she

opened a colored magazine for me to
use as my placemat. But the egg was
so slightly boiled it appeared raw, and
again, now mortified, I declined. I
don't remember what I ate, but Kikí
was so kind and gentle that I understood my father's deep love for her.
On the blue envelopes containing her
onion skin letters she sometimes
began the word "Danbury" with a tri-
angular *delta*, which I found funny
and touching—so that my brother
and I often said "*Than*-vou-ree" for
"Danbury"—and I was sad when
three years later I learned she had
died at home, alone.

Kikí and Eleni in Mavrata, circa 1943

One morning Uncle Othon
declared we must drive to Mavrata, which like my mother's village of Großstöbnitz had been so often spoken of that it seemed a distillation of childhood
itself and must be the kind of place that could not possibly exist on a map,
much less be reached by a car containing me. Nonetheless we drove the sixteen
miles there on the winding road from Argostoli, and when we arrived I was
mesmerized. Here was the fabled place of the innumerable stories my father
had told me, where he had been a little boy with his father, and a teenager
during the war, so that he missed school from age thirteen to eighteen. He was
during those years sequestered in Mavrata with his grandmother Eleni and
Kikí, and the only thing that saved him from madness, he often said, was that
his father had a cousin in nearby Theramona, an educated lawyer who had
stacked copies of the magazine *Theatis*—the *Observer*—reaching almost to
the ceiling, which my father would borrow ten at a time to read.

One story from these years involved a seance. Eleni dared to suggest
something called "table-turning," which had been in vogue in Europe in the
latter part of the previous century. Eleni's brothers—upon returning from

Italy, where they were educated in the 1870s—had introduced her to the practice.[5] So out of boredom in the winter of 1943, when she was ninety, Eleni and Kikí and my teenaged father elected to literally try their hands at this dark art.

Of course the Spiritual Movement of the nineteenth and early twentieth centuries hardly understood itself to be trafficking in anything dark. Many spirits were thought benevolent, merely the ghosts of one's own ancestors. Nonetheless, in Theramona lived a professor from Athens who had studied metaphysics and who told Eleni it was unwise to perform this exercise so close to the cemetery. Our house stood somewhat alone, just beyond the village, and five hundred feet from the churchyard. The man warned that if they succeeded in calling up a spirit so close to the cemetery they risked the real and gruesome possibility that the body itself might appear to them. Eleni herself recalled a well-known nightmare from the 1890s when university students in Corfu had inadvertently called forth "the Devil himself," whose strength nearly crushed the lot of them with the heavy table they had used.

Nonetheless late one winter afternoon, Eleni and her daughter Kikí and my father gathered to summon a spirit. They used the one table in the house that met the requirements, containing no metal and having three legs. Eleni began by solemnly asking that only a friendly spirit reveal itself, preferably someone known to them. The obvious candidates for this were her husband Panagis Vergotis, who died in 1916 and lay in Argostoli, and Yiannikostas, who had died five winters before and lay in the nearby graveyard.

Since this practice was an early version of what became the Ouija board, one asked the spirit to identify itself by tipping the table the number of times corresponding to each letter in the alphabet to spell its name. Eleni instructed Kikí and my father to place their fingertips very lightly upon the table, and as my father recalled many times, the table actually tipped: once, twice, thrice. And stopped. Corresponding to the Greek letter

---

[5] She was one of sixteen siblings from the relatively wealthy Tsitselis family in Lixouri.

gamma. The table next tipped nine times: *iota.* There followed *alpha, nu,* a second *nu,* another *iota,* and then *kappa,* at which point they knew the spirit was Yiannikostas.

Then Eleni asked the spirit a question. "Of your three sons," she asked, "Panagis (Takis), Othonas, and Nikos— whom do you love most?" Hearing this as a child I cringed, feeling the question inappropriate; but this woman, born in 1853, had other ideas, and told the spirit that for the purposes of the question she would represent Takis, Kikí Othon, and my father himself. And so they waited. Then suddenly the table tipped in rapid succession toward first Eleni, then Kikí, and then my father. It seemed Yiannikostas loved his sons equally.

Portrait of Yiannikostas

Eleni then asked a question in tones so hushed my father could not hear it. She then instructed him and Kikí to rise from their seats but to continue touching the table with their fingertips, at which point my father says the table "walked" slowly, tipping this way and that, until it made its way out of the bedroom, across the hall and into the salon, halting before the recently installed portrait of Yiannikostas, and tipped toward it. Eleni said she had asked the spirit if he wished to see his new portrait. My father firmly maintains that their fingertips rested so slightly on the table there was no way any of these movements could have come from them. Indeed, he was so taken with it that four years later— while living alone in Argostoli to make up the schooling missed during the war—he decided to ask the spirits' help with his French examination, inviting some friends from the class to the house, where they asked the spirits which chapter in their textbook to focus on. My father said nothing happened, but they persisted. As nothing continued to happen, my father's friends eventually used some nearby pillows to violently impress upon him their ire at having been drawn into this inane exercise.

The Mavrata to which I went that day was swaddled in the gray quiet of winter, so I could hardly understand that this was the place of which I had heard so much. But I stood on the property that had been in our family since the seventeenth century and stood on the millstone that had been there for centuries, with which my father and forefathers untold had pressed olives for the locals. But this big villa was destroyed in the '53 earthquake too, so all that stood there now was a small one-story building. Though it was very cold and windy, I felt thrilled to be there, having seemingly waited centuries for this privilege. I saw the fir-covered mile-high Aenos looming across the valley, precisely as my father and ancestors had seen it, and near the house was a shed and a pen in which I found an untethered young goat and hugged it.

On the way out of Mavrata we stopped at the primitive local store where my uncle persuaded a woman—who was a friend of his, as everyone seemed to be—to fry us some fresh eggs and potatoes in olive oil. The orange of the yolk was unlike anything I had ever seen and the egg was so dramatically flavorful that I was actually startled. Had there ever been another egg like it? Only now do I realize that as I ate that egg it did not disappear as they typically do, but was rather transmuted into an eternal Platonic ideal of egg-ness, an ovoid chimera I have chased ever since through the days and years of my life, and through all the kitchens and dining rooms of the world.

My Aunt Katie was elegant and sophisticated, and in her presence I became a little gentleman. She ran a boutique in Argostoli filled with beautiful objects and insisted I choose a gift for my mother. I chose a small blue glass pitcher covered with silver filigree. Another day she took me to a toy store and insisted I pick something for myself, but when I dithered between a ping-pong set and a child's tool box, she insisted on buying both, "one for work," she said, and "one for play." She once drove me to the cemetery where her father was buried and confided in me how close she had been to him, and how for years after his death she was not herself. And in our final days she brightly suggested that I should plant a tree to commemorate my visit, so we went to a nursery and bought an olive tree which I planted in the ochre mud of their yard.

My cousin Yangos was then twenty-two, doing his mandatory stint in the Greek navy, but one day he visited the island to see us and drove me in his convertible to the Argostoli lighthouse where I ordered my first soft drink. I dimly remembered him from his visit in 1965, when I was two and he was fifteen, making a tour of the United States. But now I was nine, so he asked if I wanted to drive his car, which shocked me, though of course I did. Was I able to work the stick shift and pedals, or did I just want to sit on his lap and steer? I wisely chose the latter.

At the dinner before we left, my father hosted everyone at a local taverna, at which he had me recite *"To Pisteuo,"* after which I blushed to receive their effusive accolades, although the greatest part of this was the pride I felt in being able to make my father proud among "our people." Being with figures I had heard about my whole life—and whom I now suddenly knew and loved as much as I did my American relatives—made saying goodbye overwhelming. We parted at the airport—for we were flying to Athens instead of taking the ferry— and I wept and wept. Even as I waved at them from the idling plane's window and as we took off and flew east over the water I stared out the window, weeping, and it was only thirty minutes later—when I was startled to realize we were landing in Athens—that I stopped.

CHAPTER SEVEN

My American Idyll

W hen months earlier we put on our play about Connecticut's history, it
wasn't just the history that made me feel more connected to America
than I had in New York. It was the play itself. At Transfiguration, just as we
had never had gym and had no sports, we never put on plays or musicals. To
be fair I vaguely remember a stage presentation having to do with the Greek
Revolution, but I don't remember having lines—probably because the play was
in Greek. My brother—then in first grade—wore his *Tsolias* uniform and
crouched with similarly dressed classmates at a table, where they were pretending to be contributing to the revolutionary cause by making bullets with
which to shoot Turks.

So when I got back from Greece I was thrilled that Mrs. Klebanow, the
music teacher, was planning a musical of the Frog Prince. I didn't want the
role of the frog—for most of the play he performed in an ugly crouch and wore
green leotards and green flippers—but Mrs. Klebanow gave me the role of the
king whose daughter falls in love with the frog. The queen was played by my
friend Monica Schemmel, who as a sixth grader was two years older than me
and much taller. When I gave my daughter the ball she would eventually lose
in the well, I sang my fatherly solo:

A golden ball, a golden ball
that shines just like the sun.
But no more lovely than my love
for you my little one.

Luke Bonacci hadn't wanted a major role—he was genuinely too cool to want to sing—but he was cast as one of the commoners with an important speaking line. Just before I entered, he was to step forward, point his finger "off stage," and proclaim: "Here comes the king!" But in the actual performance with all our parents watching he delivered the line five minutes early and then, seeing his error, quietly slipped back into the chorus. When he stepped out to make the proclamation at the right time a few minutes later, it got a huge laugh.

Luke and I had an adversarial relationship, principally based on his not liking me—though finally at the end of high school this would change—he always seemed too cool to want to associate with me, having the good sense to take "bass" as his musical instrument, and wearing ski tags on his winter jackets at the bus stop. But one day in fifth grade an opportunity arose that I thought could build a bridge between us. It concerned the pet we had gotten two years earlier, when we were still in New York, evidently to replace the turtles. It was an Abyssinian Guinea Pig whom we named "Lulu." She was covered with whorls of longish brown, black, and white fur, and was a far cry from the dull albino guinea pigs that looked like over-inflated white rats. When we watched TV I sat on the floor and Lulu crawled onto my lap where, surfeited with contentment, she "purred." Who knew guinea pigs purred? Once she was so content that she unleashed a torrent of hot urine into my lap; but who could be angry with Lulu? Sometimes she was uncontained in her happiness and would leap about, bucking like a little bronco and punctuating her joy with a high-pitched *wheep! wheep!* sound that always thrilled us. When we got to Danbury we sometimes let her play outside on the lawn, encircled with a makeshift fence of chicken wire, but sometimes she would escape and run under a monstrous thorny juniper bush next to our driveway and it would take forever to get her out, though she seemed to delight in our chasing her.

But one Saturday in April 1973 Lulu fell ill and died, and the next morning we buried her way down at the end of our property with a simple lath cross. That same day the Drogarises visited and it began to rain. As I stared out the living room window, crying, my sweet Nouna came over to comfort me. "Don't cry, my Eric," she said, in her wonderful accent, "because the death, it's a part of life!" I knew she meant well, but I didn't find it all that comforting. The next day on the school bus I still felt sad, and when Luke asked what I did that weekend I responded with the great solemnity warranted. "My guinea pig died," I said. I knew that my loss would force him to be civil and might even mark a new era in our relationship. But Luke did not accord Lulu's death the gravity I thought he must, and instead of retreating from his usual mockery, he served it up afresh. "Oh, your guinea pig died!" he said. "Boo hoo!"

Scott and Luke and I always sat together in the back of the bus and were usually together in school too. One day on the bus Scott excitedly told Luke and me he had discovered that his family were descended from Jesse James. But Luke, who usually reserved his venom for putting me in my place, got very serious, saying, "Jesse James was a murderer." Another time Luke said his family went to a Methodist church and I said we went to the Greek church, at which point Scott said he and his family were atheists. Luke got a smirk on his face and challenged Scott, saying, "So you think we come from monkeys?"

When I think of coming to Danbury as some kind of official introduction to America, I cannot help thinking of Scott and his family, who were as American as anyone I had ever met. Scott looked like Opie from *The Andy Griffith Show* and like illustrations of Huck Finn I had seen, complete with freckles and cowlick, and would surely grow up to look like Chuck Connors in *The Rifleman*. And his home seemed a living museum of Americana, with taxidermy and fishing tackle everywhere. In the basement Scott's older brother Doug even had a huge collection of Indian artifacts, including a display case featuring a skull and some bones from a nearby Indian burial mound he had excavated. Scott had found plenty of arrowheads himself, too, and said he found his first one sliding into first base during recess at Beaver Brook. He seemed charmed that way, and whenever we fished, he always saw fish I couldn't, and then caught them.

The Bennett home was a fecundity of live animals, too. Scott rose at five to feed the chickens, and there were cats with funny names like "Pouch" and "Elijah Jeremiah Spine the Third"; and there were two hideous dogs—a small pop-eyed mongrel named Buttons and a slavering beastie named Snoopie, who one night escaped this world when lightning struck the metal basketball pole to which he was chained. At other times they had wild turkeys and ferrets and tanks of snakes and frogs and lizards and fish and anything else you could catch. Any nine-year-old boy arriving there would surely believe he had staggered into a book, as I did. And if all this weren't enough, their back yard opened out onto an endless swamp, which we often explored. A year earlier they found an orphaned raccoon cub out there and raised it, though one day in the spring it went loco— surging on adolescent hormones, they said—and scrambled wildly around the house on a frightening rampage. When they finally wrangled the creature, it dug its ultra-sharp claws deep into Mr. Bennett's forearm, pulling up his tendons such that his fingers were cramped into a grotesque parody of the raccoon's own claw!

There was something of a distinctly American pioneer and rebellious streak about them. Their nondescript house stood virtually alone on a street half in the middle of nowhere; and they introduced me to that quintessentially American genre of goofy seventies songs like "The Streak" and "I Don't Like Spiders & Snakes" and C.W. McCall's "Convoy" and Johnny Paycheck's "Take This Job and Shove It." And who else would have introduced me to "Grandma Got Run Over by a Reindeer"? Scott and I got caught up in the Bigfoot craze of the time and at the Danbury Palace saw *The Legend of Boggy Creek* documentary. Mr. Bennett said in the fifties he saw Bigfoot when he and some friends were hunting by the Simpaug Reservoir in Bethel. They didn't know what it was, but he said it walked over a three-foot-high stone wall without breaking stride and none of the dogs would go near it.

Everyone we ever seemed to know was zero or one generation removed from their European roots—even Luke's grandfather spoke with an Italian accent—so to meet a family like Scott's, who seemed to have been here forever, seemed an impossible novelty, as though through them I could see the whole history of the country, could touch the red-white-and-blue hearts of Uncle Sam and Lady Liberty and George Washington. In fact, Mr. Bennett—whose friends called him "Corky"—said when he was our age he shook the hand of an old man who as a boy shook the hand of Abraham Lincoln. It was a mesmerizing thought, and though I desperately wanted to shake Mr. Bennett's hand, I thought the privilege too much to ask.

But if ever there was a moment when I finally felt irrevocably and officially American, it was on a morning near the end of fifth grade. That June 14, Mrs. Saul led our small class outside to stand around the flagpole in front of the school to celebrate Flag Day, something I had never heard of. We stood in a circle around the flag and my trumpet teacher, Mr. Picarello, produced from a black case a silver cornet; and as the sun shone and the flag waved above us, he played "Taps" as sweetly and beautifully as anything I had ever heard. It was a holy moment, an expression of patriotism so innocent and so beautiful I could weep remembering it. Then we sang "My Country Tis of Thee," and then it was over. But all these years later it seems to me to be the last gasp of something sacred, a living Norman Rockwell painting, but real and moving and true, and appropriate to the sacrifices of the lives given over the generations for that flag, for whom we were that morning playing "Taps," though I didn't realize it. The memory of that morning seems to grow over time, and I see now that I was being taught without words to love my country and to cherish freedom.

Great Plain School, Sixth Grade

As I said earlier, I sometimes over the course of my life have felt that finally somehow I fit in someplace, only suddenly to be yanked away to someplace else, where once again I didn't fit in. This happened in the fall of 1973, when it was time to go back to Beaver Brook, which I had truly come to love in a way I never thought possible. Even more wonderful, there were only going to be twelve kids in our sixth-grade class, and our teacher was going to be Mr. McDevitt, who taught us history the year before and whom Scott and I practically worshipped. But just as school began I learned to my horror that because there were only twelve students, the school board had decided ship us off to Great Plain School, about a mile beyond Beaver Brook, and would divide our class like Gaul into three parts. Four of us would go to each of Great Plain's three sixth-grade classes. It crushed us all to leave Beaver Brook and we argued and argued, but nothing could be done. So now each morning when the bus dropped off the kindergarten through fifth graders at Beaver Brook, we sixth graders stayed on the bus and went the extra mile to Great Plain.

All these years later, though, it seems a merciful half-step toward the madness of junior high the following year. One of my new classmates, Richie, was physically mature for his age and had a silver front tooth and made comments along suggestive lines I had never heard before. Near him sat a similarly mature girl named Rosemary, who one day sported a Mickey Mouse patch provocatively sewed onto the crotch of her jeans, causing consternation among the teachers. "Hey, Eric!" Richie asked, "You wanna go to Disneyland?"

That year we were imperiously informed we would now learn "the metric system" because this would replace the current system in six years—by 1980—and everyone in America would be using it. This was presented as "the inevitable future" and as "more scientific," both being descriptions I have grown to loathe. At the time, though, it simply seemed insane. For example, I knew the pitcher's mound was 60 feet from home and there were 90 feet between bases and our driveway was 55 feet long, and the distance to the top of the hill on our road was a tenth of a mile and there were 440 yards in a quarter mile and the moon was 240,000 miles away and the sun 92 million. Was I to forget all these things, which seemed as foundational to my world as flowers in spring? I felt similarly annoyed when later that year we were told "Eurasia" was a continent, so that now there were only six—as though suddenly deciding this was anything other than preposterous. Who had dared to make these decisions? It was as though someone had told us they were moving the equator, or declaring the letter G a vowel, or making the number seven optional.

Though in a different class now than Luke and Scott, we were still together on the bus. I never hung out with Luke outside of school, but my mother often drove my brother and me to the Bennetts', since Scott's brother Brian was my brother's age and they were in the same class too. One day Scott showed us his coin collection, which he had stashed in binders under his bed, and in seconds I was almost breathless with desire. The coins were so beautiful and each one was a literal piece of American history. Where had Scott gotten them? I was transfixed by the Indian head pennies and buffalo nickels—I'd never seen any before—and Scott said sometimes you could still find them in rolls of coins from the bank, which I tried immediately, with unimpressive results. But suddenly I realized I wanted to be a numismatist, which was of course the proper term, not "coin collector." When I told my father about my newfound passion he said he had some old coins we could have—since my brother was in on this too—and from the back of a bureau produced a box containing an 1802 British half penny and an 1837 penny and a few other treasures. We couldn't believe our luck. But it was a few weeks later that we hit the mother-lode. My cousins had moved from Astoria to Bellmore on Long Island and when we visited them I mentioned my coin-collecting passion to my grand-mother, who promptly pulled a very heavy white purse from a shelf in her bedroom closet and said we could have it. When we opened it and dumped it on the bed, we lost our minds. It was loaded with real silver: scores of old Washington quarters and Standing Liberty quarters and Franklin halves and Morgan dollars and Peace dollars. It was as though we had found sunken treasure. And we could have it all? But it was the Mercury dimes that really transported me. Who knew a dime could be so beautiful? FDR's patrician profile was no match for this ethereal lady liberty, as delicate as the thin dime itself—and wearing a headdress of silver wings! My brother and I suddenly lived to catalog these coins, stapling them with our special mini-stapler into their little cellophane-and-cardboard display envelopes, which we put into transparent vinyl sleeves that went in a three-ring binder, which we got from my father and hid under some boards in the attic.

It was during sixth grade, too, that Scott and I went through what we thought of as a "scientific" phase. Since my father's company specialized in blood-analyzing equipment, he gave me some test tubes and hemostats, and at Christmas I got a microscope. But the Bennetts always outdid us, and in Scott's pursuit of lab equipment he went through the local *Bargain News* and got his mother to drive him to some old guy's house thirty miles away where for next to nothing he got several *boxes* of vintage labware: Erlenmeyer and Florentine flasks and pipettes and graduated cylinders. Not that we had any idea what we were going to do with any of it, but still. We both immediately bought copies of *The New Field Guide of Freshwater Life* by Elsie B. Klots and pored over its illustrations. And then we proposed an "independent study project" for extra credit that year which we said would consist of a whole "limnological[1] study" of a previously "undiscovered" pond in nearby Brookfield. It was only eighty feet long, but it suited our purposes perfectly, and since it was fed by a small spring we gave it the Indian name "Mishiwum," meaning "place of the spring." We sketched the pond's dimensions on graph paper—of course—and when it froze that winter we chopped a hole in the ice to measure how deep it was. We were disappointed that it was hardly six feet deep, but there was a big bass that lived there, and whenever we went there we would watch for him. We were quite sure we could catch him whenever we wanted and then could measure his growth over time, but somehow out of respect for him, we never did. And of course a year later we had forgotten all about it.

My brother and I went through similar crazes with HO slot cars, and very briefly with weightlifting, since Scott's neighbor was a burly weightlifter who introduced us to the sport, even though we weighed between seventy and eighty pounds each at the time and could barely lift anything.

The problem we always had with any of these pursuits was that we didn't get an allowance and rarely had money to buy anything once our birthday money ran out—unless my grandmother was around, since she always slipped

---

[1] I was very excited to learn that limnology was the study of fresh water and that "*limni*" or "*limnos*" was the Greek word for "lake" and began to style myself during this period as an amateur limnologist, who almost certainly would grow up to become an actual limnologist, which was the proper term, rather than "freshwater biologist."

us a few dollars. Grandma always made everything better: for example, when we went to Stop & Shop she bought Entenmann's coffee cake and lots of chocolate—since she no longer worked at Loft's—and of course the *Enquirer*. And since I was interested in anything odd, like the Bermuda Triangle or UFOs, I couldn't wait to read it. I remember one day in November 1973 my grandmother read its headline about the tenth anniversary of Kennedy's death. *"Ach!"* she said, "Can that be ten years already?"

But one thing that was more than a mere phase or craze for us was fishing. It was Uncle Joe who pulled us into it. Being the man's man he was, he didn't fish from a boat but caught big blues and striped bass weighing up to forty pounds in the middle of the night in the dark while standing in the roaring surf of the Atlantic. Whenever we went to Bellmore he took us to tackle stores and showed us the wooden fishing plugs he made himself on the lathe in his basement. But living in inland Danbury meant we would be freshwater fishermen, and we spent much of the next years on the streams and lakes of Connecticut with Scott. I was already cuckoo for fishing in sixth grade when one afternoon in the late spring of 1974 our three classes were summoned to the lunchroom where a colorful figure named Jack Jeske presented what seemed the opportunity to live out an unimaginable dream. "Mr. Jeske," as we would call him, was a boyish man in his forties who screened films of his adventures in the wilds of Canada—Labrador mainly—where he fished and camped all summer, for three whole months, usually with three or four boys our age. The idea of it was agonizingly tantalizing: no parents; living off the land; catching huge trout and salmon on fly rods and camping in tents and making fires and canoeing and buzzing across pristine lakes in rubber Zodiacs. Scott and I instantly lost our minds at the thought of spending our summer like this. I was on the verge of turning ten and Scott was almost eleven and all we wanted was to camp and fish, to enter into the fairytale that most boys long to enter. It would be like building a raft and setting off down the Mississippi. It would be heaven.

That night I told my parents about it and of course they were instantly against it. First of all, five hundred dollars was no small amount, and they would never let me be away from them all summer. Of course the next morning Scott announced his parents thought it was a great idea and he was going. But first, his parents were going to have Mr. Jeske over to talk to other parents with questions, and I persuaded my mother to go. Mr. Jeske showed more films, all of them in those magical colors you see in nature films from the fifties and sixties, with the reds and yellows as bright as those in Jacques Cousteau films. My mother asked why he didn't take girls along, which embarrassed me. "I wouldn't want to get in trouble," he said. So I just kept begging my parents, who kept saying no. Then I heard Mr. Jeske was going camping one weekend on Candlewood Lake, as a kind of trial run for anyone interested in Labrador. That was something my parents could agree to, and the cost was only five dollars, which even my mother thought low, but Mr. Jeske said it covered food and that was all he needed. So Friday afternoon he arrived in our driveway in his beat-up Suburban. My brother John and Joey Nunes were on the floor of the breezeway setting up our green army men, and Mr. Jeske had to step over them to come to the kitchen door, where he spoke to my mother for a few minutes, and suddenly I was riding with him and Scott up to the lake.

We put his small boat in the water at Wildman's Landing and buzzed up the entire lake to Green and Deer Islands, which I had never seen. The idea of camping on an island in a lake particularly thrilled me. We fished till dark and then built a fire and ate and went to sleep, and the next morning we woke at sunup and spent the whole day fishing. I remember at some point we drove the boat back to the truck and went to a pizza place for dinner. In the parking lot Mr. Jeske challenged Scott and me—the fastest kids in our class—to a short race and destroyed us. How could someone his age be that fast? By the end of the weekend I wanted to go more than ever, but my parents wouldn't budge. So Scott went all that summer and the next three summers and I was stuck in Danbury with nothing to do but watch TV and mope.[2]

Actually the best parts of our summers were the weeks we went to Long Island to stay with Tante Eleonore and Uncle Joe, who were always more fun than our parents; and Eleanor and Marion and their other cousins always had

---

[2] In the writing of this book I came to discover that my parents' caution was well-founded. The nonagenarian Jeske is still registered as a sexual predator of minors.

something going on. At worst we would swim in their above-ground pool listening to the Top 40 hits of the mid-seventies. But in Danbury there was nothing to do. My parents both worked and my grandmother couldn't drive and we couldn't ride our bikes far before reaching the interstate, which bisected the universe of our childhood like an electric fence.

But in early August of that summer—it was our third year away from Cutchogue—we decided to rent a small motel room for a week in that area, near the Peconic Bay. It rained every day so we couldn't enjoy the beach, but my brother and father and I got to do a little fishing from the dock there, and we just loved the area. But Watergate had finally wound down and at 9:00 p.m. on Thursday of that week we watched in our motel room as Nixon resigned the presidency, "effective noon tomorrow." My father always loved Nixon, so for us it was sad, and seemed to me a great injustice. The next day he waved from the helicopter and decamped to San Clemente, but the weekend newspapers showed Gerald Ford making toast in the White House kitchen, just like a normal person, and suddenly the country turned a page.

CHAPTER EIGHT

Broadview

I n *Thus Spoke Zarathustra*, Friedrich Nietzsche wrote, "Life is hard to bear." Forty-three years later in *The Future of an Illusion*, Sigmund Freud penned the same sentence. But still more amazing is that neither of them ever attended Broadview Junior High School, which for me and countless others was the bleak nursery of this idea.[1] Long before I set foot in the fluorescent halls of Broadview, I knew it would mark a dramatic and unpleasant transition. I had heard horror stories from other kids, that there were drug addicts lurking in the filthy bathrooms who, if you wandered in at the wrong time would stick you with needles to get you addicted so they could make money selling you "junk" to support their own habits. I realized I must for the next three years never go to the bathroom at school, no matter what. Though these stories proved less than entirely factual, the larger experience was enough of a rude awakening to understand how they got started. After all, in sixth grade, I had been among the older kids in a relatively small school, whose windows were decorated with construction paper pumpkins or turkeys or snowflakes or hearts, while now I was suddenly one of the youngest and smallest kids

---

[1] And to those rare alumni who do not share this sentiment, may I on behalf of the rest of us send along our heartiest best wishes to you in your life of crime?

in a roiling ocean of acne and peer pressure, with nary a hallway lacking magic-markered genitalia. Because Danbury High School was so huge, both junior highs—there was another named Rogers Park, where the rich kids were said to go—went up to ninth grade. And to the eleven-year-old me, most of the ninth graders seemed adult. A few had obviously been left back, and with their facial hair and tattoos looked like they had done time in prison, or must soon be sent thither.

But my new friend John Tomanio would get me through. We shared a study hall period after lunch and sat in the back row of the auditorium in which we were sequestered with our friend Paul Nyland, cracking jokes and mocking the parade of humanity before us. John and I were placed in Algebra in eighth grade and would be in each other's advanced math and science classes throughout high school, but it was here in the skanky petri dish of this proto-*Welcome Back, Kotter* world that our friendship bloomed. Actually these three unpleasant and awkward years made our time in Danbury High School look like Swiss finishing school by comparison. Though we cannot here delve into the monstrous taxonomy of Purple Nurples, Purple Hermans, Dutch rubs, and the other inventive horrors of adolescence, I nonetheless beg leave to dilate for a moment on that which must stand as the *ne plus ultra* of juvenile tomfoolery, and which for me is a signal distillation of the repulsiveness of that disagreeable season.

I must begin by reminding the reader that I was a year younger than the other seventh graders, and being possessed at that time of the physique of a nine-year-old girl, I once in a while during gym class gasped to observe the secondary sexual characteristics of some of the older and more physically mature students. Many were involved in extracurricular sports and even had their own lockers, from which they sometimes would conjure something that seemed to me rather curious. I am referring now to the simple athletic supporter, also called a "cup" or "jockstrap"—or simply "jock." But it is of course not merely to the existence of this now unobjectionable object that I draw your attention, dear reader. How I wish it were so! For it so happened on certain occasions during these gym classes, as we changed our clothes, that one of the more physically mature students would—already having the smirking attention of his evil confederates in this endeavor—proceed with the aforementioned object in hand to sneak up behind a smaller and weaker classmate (and I here thank the ghost of Arnold Horshack that I escaped this fate), and before the hapless victim knew what was transpiring would impiously pull the appalling contrivance over his victim's head and clamp the foul convex center over his nose and mouth until—quite unable to do otherwise— the trapped sufferer finally had no option but to do what anyone must do who wished to continue living during this deeply hateful interlude—*and inhale through the ghastly jock!* Yet even this was only part of the greater humiliation, for as the offending contraption at this juncture appeared very much like an oxygen mask, the horrendous operation was always and ever punctuated with the phrase "Administering joxygen!"—the words invariably delivered with the faux clinical authority and seriousness of sincere medical · professionals. Thus, Broadview.

If school weren't unpleasant enough, my parents around this time got rid of their lilac-colored bedroom carpet and decided my brother and I should use it upstairs in our room. Also my father, newly enchanted with the savings of fluorescent light, installed in our ceiling a garish industrial fixture he had discovered in the trash at Technicon. It boasted four hideous bulbs, and this— in concert with the carpet—transformed what had been a cozy, piney retreat into something like a morgue for the sexually confused. Being around eleven or twelve, though, we were too young to know that the only proper response would have been to reject both of these things outright, and if we had tried we would have failed anyway.

It was during seventh grade too that one bleak midwinter night our cat, Rudy, declined to come home. He was a male tabby who rarely did this, but we finally all went to bed, knowing he would eventually show up. I typically slept deeper than the Marianas Trench, but for some reason that night I tossed and turned extremely unpleasantly, half waking and falling back to sleep and then half waking again in what seemed like hours and hours on the back of a sea serpent. Finally around six I awoke and realized that there was a stench in my bedroom so powerful that it had woken me up over and over all through the night. It was so overwhelming and close that it was as if my nose couldn't get the proper distance from it to make it out, as though a hundred corpses were rotting under my bed. I stumbled downstairs, blinking and gagging, and learned from my mother that dear Rudy had during his nocturnal wanderings tangled with a skunk, who blasted him squarely amidships at close range. The stink-wattage of what the beast had unleashed was so unearthly that it had somehow—*I still cannot fathom it*—penetrated the entirety of our house, despite its being coldest winter, such that every storm door and double-paned window was tightly shut. It was outstandingly horrific, like something you would associate with a demonic presence or with the torrid belches of Beelzebub or a giant's vomit containing gobbets of half-digested peasants and oxen. And poor Rudy, staggering about the house, was constantly blinking and confused, because the funky spunk on his fur was so toxic it obviously hurt his eyes.

We believed the solution to our problem involved tomato juice, which we didn't have, but we had shelves of mason jars containing the tomato sauce my mother made from my father's tomatoes months earlier. So we put Rudy yowling into the slop sink in the laundry room and poured quart after quart of the homemade marinara over his body, trying our best to "wash" him with it. As he understood we were trying to murder him, he fought heroically, and in the end we were happy to give up, towel him off, and let him scamper away. But our efforts had not put so much as a scratch in the adamantine stench, which appeared to be something so advanced and impenetrable that we were tempted to take a page from Erich von Däniken and assume this olfactory evil had been ferried to earth by aliens with a technology eons ahead of our own. Perhaps it was their idea of a prank.

In any event, when it was finally time to go to school, I had never been so glad to do so, to exit the suffocating skunk-mosphere! So I grabbed my books, put on my royal blue down coat, and walked the half mile through the bitter cold to the bus stop. But when I took my seat on the bus Luke leveled his gaze at me and boldly accused me of smelling like skunk! Scott politely agreed. But how? My body had been under several blankets all night and my clothes had been folded in my dresser. Had my coat caught the scent, being downstairs in the front closet? When I got to school I put the coat in my locker and went to homeroom. But within twenty seconds of sitting down, Jimmy McMinn— alphabetically tethered to me for years—picked up Luke's baton: "You smell like skunk!" I was now amazed, and even a little bit hurt. But the kids adjacent soon agreed, as eventually did those less adjacent. Mr. Frankel, my homeroom teacher, finally appreciating the situation at his desk, gave me permission to go up to the office and call my mother to take me home. What else to do?

But the office secretaries rolled their eyes. They had heard every excuse. Within seconds of their scoffing, however, they drank in the skunk molecules for themselves. "Whoa!" they said. "You'd better call your mother." When I came over to their desks to use the phone they backed away. My mother said she would be there in twenty minutes, so I walked all the way down to my homeroom to retrieve my books. But as I approached the room I saw a pile of books on the hallway floor! Evidently they too were contaminated! But how? How could the teensy anal glands of a cute animal unleash such shattering, unrelenting carnage? When my mother pulled up, she said my brother had been sent home too. When we got back home, we took another crack at "washing" Rudy with tomato sauce, but again it had no effect. Somehow the stink clung to him for several weeks. And though we scrubbed and scrubbed with soap and water and ammonia that part of the asphalt driveway that had constituted ground zero in the blast, it reeked for *months*. It all seemed positively supernatural. I hope the aliens are happy.

Of course most of our experiences with animals were more positive. We saw every kind of bird and many snakes, all small and harmless—including a hognosed snake that when we approached it played dead, as they are known to do, and for good measure vomited up a small half-digested frog—and always saw raccoons and possums and wild turkeys and innumerable deer. My mother once even saw a bobcat.

Another time, some Baltimore orioles were building one of their impossible and seemingly miraculous nests in the thin hanging branches of one of our willow trees. We could hardly believe it possible that these creatures with their literal birdbrains could create something so exquisitely complex and fragile, a veritable hanging sack of twigs and grass interwoven so expertly that it clung securely through every kind of weather. Who had thought up this baroque confection? Surely there were a thousand easier ways to build a nest in a tree. But eggs were soon laid and hatched, and we soon watched the mother flying out and back, out and back, feeding her babies. Then one day one of them fell a distance of ten or so feet onto our lawn. There was no hope the mother could retrieve it. So we snatched it up and brought it into our breezeway, making it a little box nest, and removed the screen facing the weeping willow, hoping the mother would see her prodigal and continue to feed it. And she did, feeding her babies in the nest and the one in our breezeway. Finally this little bird and her brothers could fly, but because we had been near her so much she became like a pet to us, until one afternoon she was with us in the backyard, flying around like our friend until she suddenly took off into the distance to live her life, which made us all happy and sad at the same time.

A few years afterward I was deep in the woods that we still called the cow pasture when I came upon a shallow pond and saw that—clinging to the vegetation growing in the water around the edge—there were clear jelly-like globules about the size of a fist, whose insides contained what I suddenly realized were amphibian eggs. There were two kinds of these globules, so I went back to the house and got a bucket and returned to take a few of each kind and put them in a ten-gallon tank in our breezeway, where we watched them develop and then hatch into the water. Half were black frog tadpoles that we watched eventually develop nascent legs to become the tiniest frogs we'd ever seen. The other amphibians were the brown-yellow larvae of tiger salamanders with tiny red gills. It was a daily revelation to watch them and we gave some of each to the Schemmels, but before I got to see ours mature much further my dad sprayed the roses on the trellis outside the breezeway with something that drifted through the screen, killing them all, saddening us, but making us glad we had given some to the Schemmels, who let us come over to continue to watch them develop.

Our hours outside were probably the single most dramatic difference from life in Queens, and of course every winter when it snowed we built snow forts and went sledding in our backyard, whose extraordinarily long sledding hill was the single feature that sold my brother and me on the house. Our backyard hill was the place to be on snow days. The Schemmels and Joey Nunes usually joined us and sometimes my mother and father took a run, and our grand-mother once dared to go down the hill on the uncontrollable saucer. We usually got to the forsythia bush and sometimes to the stand of pine trees beyond it, but if it was icy enough we sometimes made it all the way down along my father's trails to the bottom of the property where Lulu was buried. And when we came in my mother made us all cocoa at the kitchen table and we watched the birds and squirrels eating from the feeder on the dogwood tree. One especially snowy day I sat there alone when a pair of red cardinals and two blue jays visited the feeder together for a few minutes, unwittingly putting on a performance I couldn't help find movingly patriotic.

Russian Orthodox Church

Just after the end of seventh grade something happened that never hap-pened in Greek Orthodox circles, which is to say we moved beyond them. I have no idea how it happened, but one day the local Russian Orthodox priest—who was American and relatively young—invited all of us in the GOYA (Greek Orthodox Youth Association) between the ages of eleven and fourteen to spend part of a day with him for a mini-retreat. And amazingly—though he was of course not Greek—we were allowed to go. His church was very small, but had a distinguishing golden onion dome, and one Saturday morning in late June, a dozen of us were dropped there by our parents, with instructions to pick us up at two.

As we sat in the pews he first talked to us about the basics of our faith, of Jesus's death on the cross and how this was God's love toward us, that he was paying for our sins himself, so that we could return to the perfect relationship with God that Adam and Eve had before the Fall. Amazingly I had never heard anything about this till that morning. I was in church virtually every Sunday of my life and everyone assumed everyone knew all these things, but almost no one did.

But as this priest spoke it all made sense. Then he invited us to perform a standard Eastern Orthodox practice by meditating on the crucifix over the altar and thinking about what Jesus did in suffering and dying for us—for each of us individually, whom he loved personally—and then quietly inviting him to live in our hearts. For a time we all sat there quietly and did just that. It was the only spiritual exercise most of us had ever done.

After a time the priest handed out papers and pencils and said we should write letters to Jesus in our own words, thanking him for what he had done, and expressing our desire to have him live in us forever. When we were finished he said we should go outside—we could go anywhere on the small church grounds or could remain in the church if we preferred, and should spend time talking to Jesus, continuing to thank him for what he had done for us. We should also invite him to speak to us. When our time was up the priest would ring the church bell and we could come back inside.

I wrote my letter and then walked outside and turned left, settling under a tree near the back of the church, praying and talking to Jesus as best I knew how, though I didn't "hear" anything or sense anything particularly. But it all seemed real and true and I found myself in a sweet and wonderful peace. When the bell rang, I arose and went back inside with the others, but the sound of the church bell itself was so sweet and good to hear, like something I had always been longing to hear. Soon we were released to wait outside for our parents, and I spoke to my closest friends there, Dino Kolitasas and Adam Fourkiotis. Dino told me that an amazing thing happened to him while he was praying. He said a man wearing white appeared to him, with white hair and a white beard. He thought it was Jesus, and I instantly knew it must be. To know Dino was to know he would never invent such a thing. I remember the wonder on his face as he related it and then Adam joined us and his eyes grew wide and he said the same thing had happened to him, that Jesus had also appeared to him! We were all staggered, and I knew Adam's reverence for

God would not allow him to concoct such a thing either. It was a wild and wonderful moment, standing there with my friends and hearing them express their astonishment at this miracle.

But there was no follow-up. That day was the end of such discussions or teaching on what it meant to walk with Jesus, and we never saw the priest again. Nonetheless I had been changed somehow and for the next several years—almost every night through my teenage years—I prayed before falling asleep, usually just saying the Lord's Prayer, or praying for my family, but never telling anyone I was doing it. It was as though I had met God and knew he was real, but because no one ever showed us any next steps I had no way of knowing what I could or should be doing or not doing about it, and so in time I simply drifted away from this simple faith.

It was also during this year that the good parishioners at Assumption Greek Orthodox Church in Danbury decided they had had enough of Father Stavropoulos and dismissed him. Dino's father proudly told me he himself had "put the soap under his shoes"—a Greek phrase meaning "greased the skids"—to get rid of him. But things didn't get much better, because we were now sent the small and slightly stooped figure of John Ziotis. He was kind to me, almost courtly, but he spoke English with difficulty and there was an air about him as of one whose days with us were inevitably numbered, as though perhaps he didn't have the knack for making friends. My father claimed the Archdiocese in Manhattan didn't care about us in Danbury. "They send us the lemons," he said.

With Father Stavropoulos gone, it fell to Father Ziotis to attempt to teach us Greek on Tuesday afternoons. But he never got very far. In fact, seeing I had some verbal talent he once privately asked me whether I knew of any colloquialisms I might share with him. He said he had recently learned the phrase "What's going on?" He put a Greek "*Chi*" sound at the beginning of the word "what," and repeated the phrase a few times. "*Wh*-at's going on? *Wh*-at's going on, eh?" So he asked me if I knew of anything like that. I thought for a moment.

"Well, you could say, 'What's up?'" I said. He considered the phrase.

"*Wh*-at's ap?" He brightened as he pronounced it. "*Wh*-at's ap?" I was pleased to see I might have brightened his day slightly, because even though I was twelve, I saw that there was a sadness to him. But it wasn't so long before I saw another side of him too. I had by then become an altar boy, along with Adam and Dino and my brother John, and we quickly learned the ropes from the older kids. But once in a blue moon we might make a small mistake. Once four of us stood in front of the altar holding our candles atop their long wooden poles, two on either side, when suddenly Father Ziotis stopped everything dead and right then in the midst of the liturgy berated us rather loudly and sternly for whatever mistake we had just made, which none of us ever understood. It was a ghastly moment that horrified the whole church. No priest had ever reprimanded altar boys like that, although this was a stifled hiccup when compared with the unpleasant explosion some months later.

Greek Haircuts

I will always think of eighth grade—when I was twelve—as the physical and social nadir of my childhood, being then short and chubby and awkward. And yet even before that memorably unpleasant school year, I got not one but two unforgettably bad haircuts.

I should explain that after Father Stavropoulos left as our priest, my father nonetheless maintained a cordial relationship with him, and one Sunday not long after his official defenestration we were invited to his home for an afternoon meal. My mother strongly protested our acceptance, but in the end we went, and all went smoothly. Until after the meal when I learned that I was intended to receive a haircut from Father Stavropoulos. Could this be happening? But there seemed no escape. I couldn't openly disobey my father, who insisted on this, as though his relationship with Stavropoulos depended on it. But Stavropoulos gaily boasted that he always cut his own kids' hair, although I wanted to protest that his daughters had longish hair and his son had a crewcut! He said he would show my father how easy it was. I knew we were saving the eight or so dollars haircuts cost, and knew we had to make financial sacrifices, so being the dutiful son—and like a sheep silent before its shearers—I endured it. "I will make him look like Levendis!" Stavropoulos declared. To be a "Levendis" meant that you were the very definition of handsome, a ladykiller![2] So he sat me down on an ottoman in his living room and went to work. But alas, by the time he was done I looked less like a *Levendis* than like Shemp Howard. And of course my brother, ever the cannier one, escaped the corrupt cleric's shears by running away into the yard when his turn came.

For me, though, this was but an appetizer of indignity, because my father, now tutored and emboldened, would himself launch a tonsorial career. As he reckoned, cutting our hair would save over a hundred bucks per annum. For context, our last car had cost two hundred, although to put *that* in context, it was a navy Dodge Dart with a hundred thousand miles whose interior reeked so sourly of cigarette smoke that no matter how my mother tried, she couldn't get rid of it, and to put *that* in context, my mother is German, and if she cannot get something clean, it's likely God's way of saying you should throw it out. In any case, we had just opened a checking account and one of the gifts the bank offered for this—among the toasters and irons—was a "professional" hair-cutting kit. So worse than the initial butchering was what I could look forward to facing two months later. Everything was prepared and all that remained was for my hair to grow, which it certainly would. It was as though my own head were my enemy, one from which I could never escape.

In retrospect I still cannot imagine how my mother let either haircut happen. But in her defense, it was the mid-seventies, an era when the notion of men's grooming had effectively sprinted like a streaking lunatic off a cliff. Who can really say what was going on? In any case, the day came and I was summoned and made to sit like a condemned prisoner on a chair in our breezeway, with my father oblivious to my suffering and only too eager to try out the snip-snappy shears and mint-condition neck-shaver from the bank. I wonder now why I didn't do what my brother would have done and simply run away? Is it possible

---

[2] *Levendis* came to mean someone from "the Levant." From Italian *levanti* "Levantine," "people from the East," i.e. the eastern Mediterranean, in particular armed sailors or pirates during the Middle Ages. In Italian the word took on a negative connotation and came to mean "pirate" and hence "undisciplined youth," but in Greek the term has positive connotations of fearlessness and gallantry.

that I too was rooting for my father, naively imagining he might surprise us all and emerge from the breezeway that day as some kind of Rodin of hair? But alas, though my father has many talents, even a generous soul would not put any of them in the category of aesthetics. In retrospect, compared to my father, Stavropoulos was a very Vidal Sassoon. In fact my father's talents tended so dramatically toward the practical—what he always called "engineering"—that his fixes were often visually grotesque. He pronounced "engineering" with a Gallic emphasis—so it is not "engine-EAR-ing," but "engine-YER-ing." It lends the word an elevated dignity, and whenever he used these skills to solve a problem he said the word, as a kind of *sotto voce* "Ta-daaa!" For example, when I was five my brother and I jumped on our parents' bed so wildly that my brother hit his head on the sharp corner of a night table, spurting blood and requiring stitches. Even though we were banned from jumping on the bed, my father nonetheless insisted on affixing ghastly black foam rubber over the corners of the otherwise attractive Swedish modern night tables just in case we ever defied his orders and had precisely this same accident a second time. So the day my father cut my hair he was thinking along strictly practical lines, such that his list of goals consisted of a.) saving money, and b.) removing hair. Making me look like a "*Levendis*" was not on the list. And by the time he was through I looked less like Shemp than like Moe. Even Tante Eleonore visiting the next day instinctively recoiled to see me, insensitively asking, "What happened to you?"

The next summer would mark the greatly anticipated culmination of the Bicentennial mania sweeping the country, and we would go to the parade on Main Street. The only thing I remember was a float with some kid whose hair was cut in the style of the local Mohawks, years before this was fashionable. "Now that kid has guts!" my mother said. "Would you let somebody cut your hair like that?" I might have reminded her that I had indeed let someone cut my hair in a way that was just as unfashionable, though not for any particularly patriotic or historical reasons. But I didn't.

CHAPTER NINE

The Bicentennial

In 1976 the nation was patriotically focused on preparing for the many huge celebrations in July, and there was also a presidential race, in which a young peanut farmer from Georgia was emerging as the man who with his trademark smile might finally carry the country past the dark memories of Vietnam and Watergate. But that March every Greek was focused on our own upcoming anniversary of independence—the 155th—from the despised Turks. Danbury wouldn't have anything like a parade up Fifth Avenue, but we would mount a humble pageant in the church basement, so during Greek school in February Father Ziotis assigned a bunch of us kids poems to recite. Believing me especially capable, he handed me a mimeographed sheet bearing a poem so long that I gasped. It was titled *"O Gero Demos"* ("Old Man Demos") and was three times longer than any of the other poems. Memorizing it would be a protracted agony and when I got home I complained bitterly, begging my father somehow to get me out of it. Of course he wouldn't hear of it. Whatever Father Ziotis said, I must do. I sensed that my father's good standing in the Greek community was on the line. We got into an awful argument over dinner until my pleading turned to caterwauling and tears.

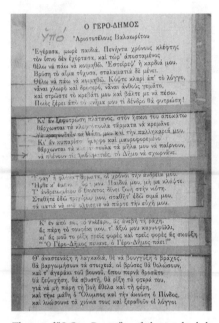

The text of "O Gero Demos" my father used to help me memorize the poem, 1976

Uncle Joe happened to be with us at that time. He often used vacation days from the fire department to do side jobs and had been hired by our friends the Manolakeses to finish their basement, staying with us for two weeks. So after dinner, he took me into the living room. Uncle Joe didn't go to church, but had grown up Catholic in Astoria and didn't have a high view of priests. And not being Greek like my father, I knew he would take my side. But it wasn't quite that simple. "Listen," he said to me, "You want to get back at this priest?" I hadn't thought of that, but when my uncle talked, I listened. He seemed to have understood the assignment as a power trip on the part of this sadistic priest. That wasn't the case, but in my whining over dinner it might have come across that way. "Here's what you do," he said. "You memorize that poem so well—" and here he got passionate, as he could, "—that when you go up there on that stage and you recite that poem, you'll be showing that sonofoabitch priest that he didn't get to you! Because your Uncle Joe knows that his nephew Eric Metaxas has got such a head on his shoulders...that when he puts his mind to it, he can do anything!"

How do you repay someone for something like that? My uncle's love generally, and his taking the trouble to say this to me that day, are gifts one can never repay, except conceivably by doing the same for others when you get the chance. And whenever someone does something like what he did that day, they are of course helping make you the kind of person who will. So each morning I got up a little earlier than usual and sat with my father in the living room and memorized another line or two until the big day came, and all went well. But it is those mornings with my father that now live with me as among the most cherished moments of my life. I remember how sitting together on the couch he would explain the meaning of the lyrical Greek lines before I attempted to memorize them, and often got so choked up that I had to look away in embarrassment. *"O Gero Demos"* was about an old soldier of the Revolution reminiscing about his days of heroism decades earlier, asking that the younger generation listen and then let him depart to "sleep" and live on in their memories. I now know that the author of the poem was Aristotelis Valaoritis, who hailed from the Heptanisa—the Seven Ionian Islands of which our own Cephalonia is the largest, and which were briefly their own nation before—in large part thanks to Valaoritis himself, who became a statesman— they proudly joined the young Greek nation. So Valaoritis in extolling liberty and the "Greek" values of liberty and independence was in his own way a Greek Henry Wadsworth Longfellow, whose "Paul Revere's Ride" I led my own daughter to memorize, just as my father had led me to memorize *"O Gero Demos."* And just as my father had in teaching me that poem, I too got choked up teaching Longfellow's to my own daughter. Both poems celebrate in powerful language what every generation ought to celebrate and teach its children: a love of liberty and sacrifice and honor. I blanch with embarrassment and yet marvel too to think how I despised Father Ziotis for assigning that poem to me, because of course I now regard it as one of the greatest gifts of my life.

Not long after this event I decided I needed spending money. My dad didn't believe in giving kids an "allowance," but he also didn't believe there was a minimum age for getting a job. Our friends Takis and Joanne Biniaris had opened a luncheonette in nearby Bethel, and as minimum wage was two dollars an hour, I brightly offered my twelve-year-old self as a dishwasher for one-fifty, and a deal was struck. I was dropped off every Saturday at nine and picked up at one, and got six bucks; and when I wasn't shuttling back and forth to the kitchen, I'd sit at the counter and eat scrambled eggs or a burger and read the *Daily News* to see if Dave Kingman had hit a homer, about which more in a moment. And whenever my parents were delayed in getting me I'd go to a nearby store and covet the fishing lures.

My brother and I treasured our collection of fishing lures, and whenever we were bored we would open our tackle box and stare at our treasure. There were jars of pork rind and salmon eggs in florescent colors and red-and-white Daredevil spoons and Arbogast Jitterbugs and Hula Poppers and Rebel minnows and Helin flatfish and Mepps spinners and red-and-white bobbers and a plastic dispenser of lead-shot sinkers and boxes of Mustad hooks and monofilament spools, and a tape measure–scale combo marketed as the Zebco De-liar (get it?) and pliers and hemostats for dislodging deep hooks; and at the bottom were all the saltwater tackle we never used, the monster sinkers and flounder spreaders and snelled hooks and an unfinished striper plug Uncle Joe had made. There too sat my little aluminum fly box with dry flies and wet flies and poppers. A few years later we added Ziploc bags of plastic chartreuse worms and grape- and smoke-colored grubs. And after staring at these things for a while we were content, like a king who has counted his gold.

Our boredom those summers was barely alleviated by the Mets, whose games we often watched on the black-and-white TV in Grandma's room, and who were consistently disappointing. Their best "sluggers"—John Milner and Rusty Staub—never hit more than twenty homers per annum. But then in 1975, it happened. The Metropolitans acquired an awkward six-foot-six power hitter who that year whacked thirty-six extremely long balls, obliterating the previous club record. And as the 1976 season began Dave Kingman quickly got on pace to hit as many home runs as Babe Ruth had in 1927—or as Roger Maris had in 1961. For the basement-dwelling Mets, this was on the order of an Old Testament miracle, and every Mets fan lost his mind for joy, and we checked the paper every day to see if "Kong" had hit another one—or two or three—as the total drifted upward toward history.

Then Theo Taki got tickets to a double-header on the first day of August! And even better, it was "Banner Day," when between games fans paraded their homemade banners right onto center field! Of course my brother and I had to make one. Since "Sky King" was one of Dave Kingman's nicknames, I coined the slogan "The Sky's the Limit for Sky King," with an image featuring a baseball flying through a cloud, having been blasted from tiny Shea Stadium thousands of feet below. We drew this with colored markers on an old sheet my mother gave us, and my father helped staple each end to a one-by-two so we could carry it. We were a cinch to win.[1]

Then on July 19, disaster. Kingman had been averaging a homer every twelve at-bats, and already had thirty-two. But in the third inning knuckle-baller Phil Niekro popped a ball into left field and the gangly Kingman fielded it so goofily he managed to severely jam his left thumb into the outfield turf, effectively ending his season. Horrible luck of the normal kind would be letting a pitcher get a double from a routine fly, but the Mets' version of this was on the order of Greek tragedy. The race to touch the hem of Ruth's garment was instantly over, and like innumerable others, my brother and I were crushed back to grim reality.

So when we drove to Queens for Banner Day, Kingman was out of commission. But we hoped he might be back soon—he wasn't—and were sure one of our heroes would pitch one of the games. But neither Tom Seaver nor Jon Matlack nor Jerry Koosman did. Both games featured newly acquired pitchers we had never heard of. Nonetheless we goggled to see the Phillies' Greg "the Bull" Luzinski blast a grand slam that went so high and far it took our breath away, although the idea that a grand slam by the opposing team went in our plus column tells you everything about being a Mets fan during those years. And we had the singular thrill with our cousin John of unfurling our creation behind the fence in center field and then walking onto the field between the games amidst the sea of banners—somehow we didn't win; the winner was "Thumbs Up, Dave." Ha!—to walk on the same grass as our heroes! Incidentally, the Mets lost the first game six to seven in extra innings, a real heartbreaker, but made up for it by losing the second in nine short innings, two zip.

---

[1] One of the stranger things growing up where English is not your parents' first language is asking them the meanings of words you've heard and their having no idea. One day I was watching Leo Gorcey and Huntz Hall in the Bowery Boys when "Slip" Mahoney said, "Why, it's a cinch!" What did he mean? I wouldn't know for many years.

Fire at the Church

One morning in eighth grade I awoke to learn there had been a terrible fire at the church. The newspaper even had a photo on the front page. No one knew what happened, but our community was staggered, and that Sunday we held our liturgy in the basement of St. Peter's, the large Catholic church on Main Street, which offered this venue until our church was restored. But being in the basement of this huge church was awkward for us altar boys, because there was no *iconostasis* to hide behind, so we had to stand in the open during the service, or hide in a small side storage room from which we could make our entrances like actors. Nonetheless everything seemed to go well enough and soon the service was almost over. When Father Ziotis began his sermon we altar boys sat in the storage room, only half listening.

The sermons were usually as short as those in Catholic churches, never being the focus of the service. But that day we got something along the lines of something from one of those crazy Protestant churches, where the priest screamed and carried on. At some point we noticed that the tone of what Father Ziotis was saying—all in Greek—was dramatically different than anything we had heard before, homiletically speaking. He seemed to be angrily berating the congregation, atypically pacing around the "stage" and wielding a heavy golden cross. Eventually we realized he was ranting and raving, but we could only make out some of what he was saying. It was an awful scene. At one shocking point he even feigned hurling the heavy cross at someone in the congregation! But how could boys our age fail to find this at least somewhat entertaining? It was the only time a sermon held our attention. Eventually Adam, who understood Greek better than any of us, began translating. He explained that some people in the congregation had accused Father Ziotis of setting the fire! Adam was always in the know, mainly because his father was a hilarious storyteller and had probably communicated the gossip on this subject. Adam said Father Ziotis was telling the congregation what he thought of them for spreading such rumors, but Adam said some people maintained the fire was started at approximately where Ziotis would have lit it, given his height, which struck even us altar boys as idiotic. But there was Father Ziotis taking it on publicly, now bitterly shouting at his accusers, and we feared the

Catholics upstairs might hear it and wonder what sort of people these Greeks were. Finally some of the people in the pews actually began talking back, arguing with him from their seats, taking things to a new level of madness.

The next day I told John Tomanio what happened. In a way it was hilarious, and yet as I was half milking the story for laughs I also came to see how sad it was. First, there was the case of Father Ziotis. Where would the poor man go now? How many other churches had he left like this? Then there was the question of whether we would ever find a halfway decent priest? It wasn't looking good.

In any event, it was a tragic coda to a somber tale. Of course we never saw Father Ziotis again. In my mind, though, I will always remember him as he was those months earlier, brightly pronouncing the phrase "What's up?", looking forward to trying it out on someone, looking forward to speaking English better and to being accepted by a community of people who loved and understood him.

Some weeks after the debacle in the basement of the Catholic church, Father Germanos's replacement's replacement's replacement arrived. He was Father Nick Petropoulakos, who shocked us by being an American in every way, even boasting a hip pair of muttonchop side whiskers. We couldn't help being excited.

Of course the spiritual instruction remained virtually nil. Talking about God or the Bible or praying just weren't part of the Greek culture, even in church. But to be fair everyone we knew—non-Greeks alike—also avoided talking about faith. If anyone talked about faith too much—except maybe for Billy Graham—we thought it weird and to be avoided, just as the Hare Krishnas were to be avoided. And the plucky "Jehovah's Witnesses" who came to our door were sent away with a "Thanks, but we have our own religion."

Although John Tomanio's father came up with a more creative way of dealing with them when he once opened the door to a hapless pair of such innocents, and being in a funny mood drove them away by taking on the role of a hostile mute, grunting and pointing his finger "away" with louder and louder and angrier grunting.

John and I were in Mr. Barchi's social studies class in eighth grade when Darlene Chelednik, a sweet blonde girl, gave an oral report extolling the experience of being "born again" and accepting Jesus. I knew and liked Darlene, but couldn't help cracking some snide jokes until eventually she said, "You know what, Eric, I'm not mad at you. I feel sorry for you." I didn't mean to be mean. Mocking things was a reflex for me; and what else was there to do with someone going on about something like that? I went to church, but we weren't fanatics about it!

Three years earlier my parents had become friends with the Kakadelis family. Mr. K. was a successful Greek American who personified what I thought I might someday become, and my parents socialized with them regularly. But around 1975 he and his wife had a "born again" experience and couldn't seem to avoid the subject, so my parents began to decline their invitations. This was not any decision to avoid God, but in our world the only people who talked about him were the priests in church, and even that was limited. We believed in keeping faith in church, and only on Sunday mornings and the second floor of the building. Beyond that we just wanted to be "normal," to fit in, as most immigrants do. We certainly didn't want to become weirdos for Jesus. As far as we understood it, being neither atheists nor Jews meant we were Christians. We had been baptized and even attended church regularly!

Of course there was something in the air at that time. Jimmy Carter taught Sunday school and talked about being "born again" during his campaign, and his own sister was an evangelist. When we were driving around town we often saw bumper stickers that said "I've Found It!" We never knew what these drivers had lost, but eventually we came to understand they had found a "personal relationship" with God. We also saw chrome fish on bumpers, but my father, ever zealous about being Greek, explained that the reason people put those fish on the backs of their cars was because the Greek word for fish was

IXTHYS, and the letters of the word made an acronym—IESUS CHRISTOS THEON YIOS SOTIR—which meant "Jesus Christ, the Son of God, our Savior." My father said the Christians in the first centuries had been persecuted, so they used this Greek acronym-inspired fish symbol to represent their faith, although at the time I got the impression he was mostly excited about the Greek aspect of it.

CHAPTER TEN

"Because He's Your Father"

Fall 1976

Ever since I'd had my tonsils out in 1970 I'd been slightly chunky, but during that bicentennial summer I got the idea that raw wheat germ was the key to losing weight, so I ate a lot of it and lost twelve pounds; and at the beginning of ninth grade I thought the new me should try out for the wrestling team. I could squeeze myself into the ninety-two-pound category. My brother—then in seventh grade—joined me. The first days of practice were something out of a Japanese prison camp, consisting of vomit-coaxing hill sprints and squat thrusts, all obviously designed to weed out losers like me. After three afternoons I decided to drop out, not that persistence mattered, since my brother later checked the new list and told me I'd been cut anyway.

In Mr. Toscano's English class we read George Orwell's *1984*, which being eight years away frightened me as distinctly possible, since at thirteen, eight years was forever, and I knew the book was a fictional account of a world that essentially existed. A friend recently had read Aleksandr Solzhenitsyn's *The Gulag Archipelago* and shared parts with us. It seemed too painful for me to read, but I got the gist. The horrors of Communism my parents had told me about were real and had been in full flower in the Soviet Union for decades. But the idea that there was a place where kids told on their parents and people were tortured and killed for—like Solzhenitsyn—cracking a joke about Stalin or believing in God shook me deeply. For my class project I build a diorama, in clay recreating that scene in which the protagonist from *1984*, Winston Smith, has a cage affixed to his head containing rats intended to devour his face.

My father had always made it clear the world was a dangerous place. Still, although I understood his own past evidenced that—and places in the world that moment existed that were horrifically unlike Connecticut—I still thought my father's generally precautionary attitude went too far. For example, to someone who grew up in Greece, baseball was as foreign as curling or ice dancing, so when my brother and I played it—and not with a softball, but an actual hardball—my father made the indisputable point that if the ball hit you in the head or face at top speed, it could kill you. As for wooden bats, he cited the story of "a guy from Technicon"—in many arguments, my father's evidence involved the testimony of "a guy from Technicon," whose stories we could never identify or refute—whose son had been killed during a game by being struck in the back of the neck with a bat. It was a grim story, but didn't most kids play baseball and not die? So our father's warnings were often eventually ignored—never willfully, because we couldn't knowingly disobey him, but because we simply forgot, as he did too—and we over time drifted to playing the game here and there. But once, he spotted one of our baseballs in the backyard, and to underscore his sentiments about these potentially fatal missiles he dispatched it in his Old Country way by—rather impressively, we thought—chopping it clean in two with a hatchet on a railroad tie. My brother discovered the bisected corpse near what we assumed was the murder weapon. We were fascinated by the inside of it: it was tightly wound with endless yards of twine under the white cover, and at the center was a pink rubber ball, and inside that was an oily liquid. Who would have guessed?

Our father's sense of danger always seemed exaggerated, but because he grew up during the war, we understood his perspective was at least well-meaning. Still, if we helped him cut down a tree, he insisted we wear our Mets batting helmets, even though they weren't real batting helmets but were, as the Mets announcer Bob Murphy called them, "handsome facsimiles." Getting a BB gun or minibike was out of the question, even though John Tomanio had both. Go-carts were out, too, though Scott Bennett had one, and a .22. Eventually we were allowed a BB gun, but only after years of focused whining.

Fishing was not entirely safe either, and my father seemed to suggest we should try fishing without hooks. Then he segued to tell us of a kid who suffered a horrific injury while fishing during the war. He threw dynamite into the water and the dead fish floated to the surface. But one day the dynamite went off too soon and the boy lost his hand, but my father said that in order to feed his family he continued the practice nonetheless, now placing the dynamite on his foot, lighting it with his good hand, and then kicking it out into the water. We weren't using dynamite, but there was of course no arguing with stories like this.

The value of money was also driven home to us, almost hourly. My father often told a story from his days as a waiter in the late fifties, when a fellow waiter asked to borrow fifteen cents for bus fare. My father lent it, keeping precisely fifteen cents for himself, since he took the bus home too. But arriving at the bus stop he realized he had two nickels and four pennies, not five. He wasn't sure where the fifth penny was, but rather than try to convince a potentially hostile bus driver that he should be allowed to ride the bus for a penny under full fare, he walked home. As a thirty-year-old man with a strong accent he understood not everyone was friendly and knew the look he might get from a beleagured and potentially xenophobic Ralph Kramden. It would be less embarrassing simply to walk. So after a long shift, he hoofed it all the way from the west Forties to East 75th and four flights up to his bed. That, he said, was when he learned the value of a penny. So my dad's experiences of both penury and difficulty sometimes caused us some embarrassment. But our greatest embarrassment had nothing to do with either.

One day our father took us to McDonald's. My brother and I ordered our quarter-pounders and fries and cokes and stood aside to let him order, but my father rarely ate fast food and without looking at the menu and in his Greek accent, he said, "Ehh … give me one WOO-per!" Our lives flashed before our eyes. Of course saying "WHOP-per" and not "WOO-per" would have been its own whopper of a mistake, since they have never served Whoppers at

McDonald's. So had he pronounced it correctly we still might have fainted from embarrassment. But when the word "*WOO-per*" came out of his mouth we knew our lives were over. We froze instantly, like bananas dipped in liquid nitrogen about to be shattered with a hammer. We were beetles pinned in a display case of shame. If I had a putty knife or screwdriver I might have dropped to the floor and begun prying up the linoleum tiles to crawl under them. But alas, we could only stand there and hiss insistently as mortified children do: "*It's a Whopper, Dad! A Whopper! And they don't have Whoppers here. That's at Burger King!!! They don't have them here!*", praying the teenager who had taken the order would instantly forget what had just happened and never ever tell another soul ever please *please* …

Of course we lived to tell the story, and my poor dad could laugh at it in time too, but as a parent myself I now know the sting of being goose-hissed at by one's own thankless progeny, which sting is compounded in recalling one's own participation in this vicious activity. Thus the thorny progress of our fallen race. Putting this aside, however, it has struck me not a few times that the mistakes my dad made—and by God's grace still makes—were often freakish double-headers of this very sort. So unless you were reasonably fluent in the way my dad spoke and thought, as I was, you probably wouldn't know what he had *meant* to say, and therefore could not register the error, but would simply be baffled to a sheer standstill. I now doubt the teenager at the register had any idea what was transpiring. Any father might say "Whopper" at McDonald's and embarrass his kids, but to drop-kick the confusion into the stratosphere with a straight-faced "WOO-per" was something of another order. Had I known Aeschylus at the time, I histrionically might have pretended to blind myself with two ketchup packets and staggered off like Oedipus. And of course decades later this is precisely what I find charming and endearing about my father.

A similar double-headed boner occurred a few years after the scarring "*woo*-per" incident. I was eighteen and home from college and my father and I were at the kitchen table doing something agonizing, like filling out financial aid forms. An argument ensued, during which—in a fit of late adolescent pique—I idiotically blurted a cliche, hoping to end the painful discussion. "I don't want to talk about it," I said, which I had obviously heard someone say on TV and now repeated, as though that would settle things, as it usually did on TV. But one didn't say such things to my father.

And yet his response to my imperiousness was not anger. Instead, taken aback by my cliched refusal to continue the discussion, he completely uncharacteristically now pulled out a cliche of his own that—had he said it *correctly*—would still not have seemed right coming out of his mouth. Indeed it would have seemed slightly off the point. The eighties-era phrase I realized my father meant to say—that was then sometimes used when someone felt ill-treated—was "What am I, a leper?" It was the contemporary Gentile version of the oft-heard "What am I, chopped liver?" "What am I, a leper?" was in the air around then and I'm sure he had heard it in the lunchroom at Technicon or in the vanpool and now meant to repeat it, just as I had repeated my own dumb cliche. But to hear such a contemporary phrase from my father's mouth would have been undeniably and unintentionally funny. Of course that's *not* what my dad said, though I knew he meant to.

So what did he say at the height of the unbearably increasing tension at our kitchen table? He responded to my forceful statement with another sentence entirely. "Who do you think I am?" he demanded, angrily. *"A leprechaun?!?!"*

My father exclaiming the word "leprechaun" at any time would have been enough to cause me tremendous amusement, because I knew he had no idea what one was, nor cared. But to say it now instead of "leper" at this high emotional pitch, evoking the image of a leprechaun springing into the middle of our heated battle, was just too much. I gagged to hear it and then exploded in laughter. Who could fail to do so? And then I explained to my father what he had just said, completely deflating things between us, as he laughed too. From my point of view, nothing can ever top it: "Who do you think I am, *a leprechaun?*" Would anyone but me have known what my father had meant to say?

Still, it would be decades before I could begin to love him as he deserved, or even to see the deep joy he took in his garden, as though whenever he was there he was a young man again in Mavrata. During the endless adolescent hours I spent there I was inevitably itching to be elsewhere, though I couldn't help learning a few things, such as how to pinch the suckers off tomato plants and how to compost for "organic gardening."[1]

"Because He's Your Father"

So I was during my adolescence a long way from such equanimity toward my father and was sometimes even dismissive and disrespectful, though rarely openly. In the summer of 1977, we were all near Cutchogue, staying at the Sarrantonios' bungalow, which never quite got finished, though it had a roof and the basics, so we sometimes spent a few days there while Uncle Joe continued to work on it while we went to the beach—or went to see how our "Moon Trees" were doing. One afternoon I half-wittingly said something disrespectful about my father and soon after found myself alone with my brother and Uncle Joe, who had heard what I said and then did something he had never done before. He gave us a talking to.

We sat at the kitchen table while he stood, and though he never yelled, he delivered something like a sermon whose unmistakable point was that whatever our father said or did, he was our father, and because of this and because of this alone we must respect him. My uncle did not try to humiliate us or raise his voice and was very measured. Over the course of about forty-five minutes he gave us many examples from his own childhood with his own father— "Pop"—who I am sure made our father seem like Robert Young in *Father Knows Best*. I don't remember the examples he gave, but he repeated a phrase time and again as though he had rehearsed it, and that phrase I will never forget. *Because he's your father.* It was not said very loudly, but he repeated it as a preacher would, over and over to make his point amidst the rest of what he said. *Because he's your father.* It got through to me and seared me, so that

---

[1] I even almost know how to graft a branch, as my father did many times as he experimented with various fruit trees, both wild and domestic. And as the great-grandson of Panagis Vergotis I learned that the word "graft" comes from the Greek word "*graph*," which means to write, and from which we get the word graphite, which we find in pencils. So the verb "to graft" refers to the shape of each of the ends of the branches grafted—because they are each cut diagonally, so you can lay one on the other with the most interior surface area touching—looking something like a pencil.

I can never forget it. *Because he's your father.* My uncle's moral authority with my brother and me was utter, and somehow the innate truth of his refrain was for us clear as a bell, as though every cell in us knew it was true, even though we might not logically be able to explain why, as though its truth were a part of creation and a part of us and was therefore inescapable. So all we could do was listen and agree, because we did agree. We simply knew it was right and were actually glad to be reminded of it, and by the end of what amounted to a grand peroration I felt rightfully embarrassed to have often disrespected the man who had sacrificed more than everything for us and still was doing so. I felt appropriately ashamed. I have by now myself repeated the phrase and sentiment behind it to young men I thought should hear it, as I did then, and tears form in my eyes when I think of it, because these deepest truths are glorious and painful both, are impossibly beautiful, and heartbreakingly so.

CHAPTER ELEVEN

Falling into the Future

Fall 1977

That September I found myself in the middle of a full-blown race riot. Danbury High School began at tenth grade and was a bit overcrowded. Three classes amounted to well over two thousand students, but the school was big enough, and I found myself excited to be there, although simply leaving Broadview was like what I assumed it felt like to be released from a Turkish prison.

John Tomanio and Luke and I knew that to take calculus as seniors meant taking pre-calc as juniors, which meant a *double-period* math class as sophomores to cover trig and analytic geometry in a year, which meant forfeiting our lunch period. It was completely unnecessary, but I believed it would "look good on my college applications," toward which end John and I also started the school's first "Math Team," competing at "Math Meets" with other freaks, nerds, and nebbishes throughout southwestern Connecticut.

We were in the aforementioned double-period class with Mr. Passarella when a voice over the loudspeaker announced that school was dismissed and everyone should go home. The buses were waiting. As we hustled to our lockers to get our things word spread that a race riot was brewing—or already occurring. There had been riots in the years before, the worst being two years earlier, in which a white girl had been killed by a rock intended for black students. I never mixed with the roughneck potheads or macho jocks who were openly racist, so it stunned me this was happening. How could a few troublemakers shut down a school of 2,200? Nonetheless, to a physically small fourteen-year-old, the prospect of walking the long halls toward the buses was frightening.

When I emerged in the front of the school I blanched to see a vast swarm of what appeared to be every black student—something like three hundred—roaming as a tight unit between the school and the buses. I was scared, not realizing they had banded together for their own protection. I also saw that the white provocateurs had taken the high ground near Clapboard Ridge Road and were tossing verbal bombs containing a certain word. I was thrilled to find my bus and was relieved that it left quickly. Nothing happened that day or the next, nor ever again along such awful lines, but I sincerely wondered what world I was living in that something like that could take place.

In the summer of 1976, my brother and I got very excited watching the American Frank Shorter winning the Olympic Marathon, only to be bested at the last moment by what we suspected then—and now know—to be a doped-up East German. But Shorter so inspired us that immediately after the race we put on our sneakers and began running inanely around our yard, imagining that we too might someday take up the sport.

But a year later I did just that, going out for the cross-country team. Greeks never seemed to bother with sports—except perhaps soccer, which was just then beginning in the United States (although I wasn't "Greek" enough to know anything about soccer either)—so it wasn't something I'd ever thought about. But when I heard my old nemesis Luke was trying out for the cross-country team, I had to do it. I'd been faster than him since fifth grade! So I decided I must join, but found that I mostly enjoyed it, even though I ran the entire season in worn-out basketball sneakers, as money was tight and who needed fancy running shoes anyway? When my mother's best friend Brigitte first arrived in Altenburg she shared a pair of shoes with her mother for a year, and only one of them could leave the house at a time. So I could probably manage in my basketball sneakers. But I hated the races, which I found agonizing, and could already feel myself tensing up as I ate my lunch during math.[1]

In a way running cross-country was another of those times I could feel myself trying to fit in—to pass as one of *them*, whoever they were, other than not me—but always sensing I couldn't quite. One Friday afternoon an older teammate in the locker room with whom I had gotten a bit friendly said something about the deadly Lynyrd Skynyrd plane crash the night before. I had heard something about it and said to my teammate that I didn't know his music, but was sorry he had died, at which point he said, "That's the name of the band, you idiot! It's not a guy named Leonard!" Oh.

Our coach Mr. O'Grady was a legend who had coached since the Second World War and wore tweed jackets, Tom Landry hats, and an infectious twinkle so that he looked and talked like a preppy version of Burgess Meredith in *Rocky*. "When you're tired at the end of a race make sure you use your upper body!" he told us. "Punch the air like a boxer! That's it!" The iconic blue-and-yellow Nike Waffle Trainers were just out and as we stretched on the grass of the football field he explained that Nike was the Greek word for "victory," swelling my Hellenic pride. Halfway through our home course, which began behind the high school and looped through a housing development, there was an extremely steep hill. Mr. O'Grady said that as soon as we got to the top we should sprint, to demoralize our opponents. "That'll take the starch out of 'em!" he said with a wink. The memory of those days is so golden that it seems almost as though I had never truly experienced autumn before then, as though during that fall for the first time I felt the essence of fall, the goldenness of it,

---

[1] Seventh period all through high school was always German class, which seemed like a free period, since I knew a decent amount of German from my mother and grandmother, and also because our teacher was an Italian man with a strong Italian accent and an excessively friendly demeanor, neither of which lent themselves to helping us overcome the difficulties of this Teutonic tongue.

and as though that feeling—or the memory of that feeling—pierced through to the deeper meaning of it, so that I could see in the beauty of fall the hope of spring and summer too, but in a slightly different way. I can still remember what I felt as we did our stretches on the green grass under the blue sky of what we didn't know was our youth, that the whole world really was full of hope and future without end.

Our last race—the Fairfield County Interscholastic Athletic Conference (FCIAC) championships in November—featured every runner from every team in our division, and was run on a golf course in Stamford, a long bus ride from Danbury, on the other side of the world, it seemed. I had improved as a runner over the course of the season but didn't have the raw talent to run varsity. In any event, this was the last race and perhaps I would run again next year. But I remember that I was overwhelmed by the limitless crowd of runners and in my anxiety went out too fast, so after the first of two long mile-and-a-half loops I felt so awful and was filled with such despair that I stopped. I had never dropped out of a race before and don't know why I did, but I instantly felt like a coward and a failure in a way I never had before. After the race everyone congratulated everyone else on a great season but I just felt awful and confused. I remember on the bus ride home as it began to get dark listening to Carly Simon's wistful "Nobody Does It Better" playing on someone's cassette player, mostly feeling sorry for myself, feeling sad that the season was over and had ended this way, but also dreamily and wistfully listening to the music as I watched the autumn trees passing and passing as we drove northward. I have thought of that ride with that song playing a hundred times over the years, and have remembered the new feeling I then felt that somehow combined my great expectations for the future with my strange disappointment in myself, as if the beauty of autumn and its intrinsic sadness were somehow combined and were a part of each other in a way I didn't yet understand, but could feel. So it was as though over the course of that short season I saw and felt for the first time both aspects of the thing we call autumn, and which like all things, if we look at them rightly and clearly, open up onto an impossibly deep truth, onto a vista that would lead us all the way to Heaven itself, if only we had the infinite courage required to look.

Fishing

I was fifteen during junior year, but all my friends turned sixteen and could drive, including Scott, whose old blue Ford pickup now took us to our favorite new fishing spot, Byram Reservoir, forty minutes away. We arose at four to drive there, the boat strapped overhead, and as we rode along in the dark we listened to the same eight-track—"Country Hits of the Forties"—over and over, but only to the three songs that were funny: Tennessee Ernie Ford's "Mule Train," Al Dexter's "Pistol Packin' Mama," and Tex Williams's "Smoke! Smoke! Smoke! (That Cigarette)". It might as well have been the forties or fifties as we rode along in that old truck listening to that old music. It's strange now thinking that that music wasn't much more than twenty or so years earlier, but at the time it seemed another eon. But as time has passed since then I have known more and more that time makes as much sense as death does, which is to say none, that both are the self-negating conundrums inside which we live uncomfortably, in all we do twisting and groping to find an exit, which we somehow know or hope must exist, and mustn't it?

Scott and I always pulled up in the dark and carried the camo-green metal rowboat—or long canoe—into the water and then glided out onto the reservoir. We would then work our way along the shore, casting our lines toward what was called "structure": stone walls that slunk into the water like retreating prehistoric serpents, or fallen trees—"deadfalls," they called them—or docks or submerged tree stumps. This was where fish typically congregated, and with our quiet two-horsepower trolling motor we moved slowly along the shore, also casting underneath hanging tree limbs, beneath which fish lay in wait for falling insects. In spring we worked the shallows where we could see the bass as they "sat" over their sandy nests, fanning them with their fins and protecting them from predators.

Though it was illegal to fish reservoirs from boats, we were minors and never kept the fish anyway, so we assumed it was fine, although there was some thrill in it too, and since no one else fished there, the fishing was spectacular. Byram was loaded with smallmouth, a rare and prized creature that although not as large as its fat brother largemouth is a much better fighter, and far prettier. Largemouth are a dull greenish color and often have a sagging abdomen, like an NFL-addicted sluggard; but the smallmouth is bronze-hued and lean and when you hooked him he would often explode through the surface and in his fury sometimes propel himself with his tail across the water for many yards.

If we got half a dozen two- or three-pounders we were thrilled, but sometimes they ran to four pounds or even five, which was unheard of. By this time in my fishing career I was able to "lip land" fish, meaning with my bare hand to firmly grab his lower jaw, at which point the fish gave a shudder, which made novices instantly let go, dropping the fish. But if you didn't let go the fish thereafter hung limply and you could remove the hook. Being purists and sportsmen, we used ultra-light tackle with four-pound test monofilament and single-hooked lures, and as I say, we threw everything back.

Purer yet still was fly-fishing. In junior high we had done nothing else, scrambling around obscure streams, and tying our own flies with supplies from Charlie White, whose small shop behind his home was the destination for any serious fly fisherman needing anything from rooster hackles to impossibly tiny size-twenty hooks. The one time I visited when I was eleven I bought a thirty-cent spool of chartreuse floss, for which meager spending even my mother was embarrassed. That year for a class demonstration, I decided to tie a fly in front of the class, explaining as I went and using a jumbo hook so everyone could see what I was doing. I went to the front of the classroom and took all my supplies out but realized I had forgotten the vise to hold the hook. So I embarrassedly just drew the whole thing on the chalkboard instead.

Scott and I took great pride in fishing "the right way," in not being "sooners."[2] Just as sailors scorn the tacky motor-boater and cross-country skiers scorn the vulgar downhill throngs, we scorned bait fisherman and all who kept their prizes.

---

[2] "Sooner" was the pejorative assigned to those who would fish before the season officially opened and who didn't care about other fishermen or abide by the reasonable rules set down to be of benefit to all.

For us, killing and eating fish was as if the Apollo astronauts had rigged a cable to the moon and hauled it back to Earth for quarrying purposes. Where was the romance? The fish was a wild creature and we were free to borrow him for a bit, to tire him out and look at him and maybe weigh and measure him, but then he had to be released back into the mysterious depths of his society, and perhaps one day in the future, both wiser, we would tangle with him again. Of course this seemed like madness to my father, who grew up when hunger was a real thing, and spent countless days with a slingshot trying to kill the doves that flew near the cliffs in Mavrata, just so they might have something for supper.

I only went ice-fishing a few times. It was dramatically duller than normal fishing, which consisted of expertly casting a lure—*whizz!*—in a long arc toward an intended target—*plop!*—and then intently working that lure back—*click clack click clack click*—while watching it carefully approach, of course standing up in the boat and not sitting, so that you could see better, as you waited for the fish that *just* as it hit made the bright lure disappear, at which moment you paused for a half-second and then—*bang!*—set the hook, and quickly tightened the drag and furiously began to reel in, hoping he might explode through the surface so you could get a look at him, reeling even faster if he did so as to take advantage of his being ever so temporarily out of his natural medium. Ice fishing was something else entirely. If I did it with Scott we did the more sportsman-like thing called "jigging"—sitting atop an overturned plastic bucket and with a tiny pole working a weighted jig near the bottom until you were too cold to continue. But when I went ice fishing with the Tomanios it was more like camping, which like anything I did with the Tomanios, was fun, mainly because Mr. Tomanio was fun.

The summer after ninth grade he took John and me and Paul Nyland camping at the top of what we called Mount Squantz, one of the taller hills overlooking Squantz Pond in New Fairfield, ten miles from where we lived. This was before John and I got serious about backpacking, so we used small school backpacks that didn't hold much, and Mr. Tomanio carried the lion's share of our gear in two heavy canvas-wrapped bundles tied with insulating wires from his garage, one in each hand. Half our journey was off-trail, scrambling through brush and over rocks, because we didn't yet know there were trails to the top, and watching him carry those heavy-looking bundles was impressive. One of them contained a raw eight-pound beef roast. When we set up our tents at the top and built the fire John used his Bowie knife to slice it into chunks that we skewered with sharp sticks, cooking them over the flames. We got grease and soot all over our faces and felt like we were in *Lord of the Flies*, only with a responsible adult alongside. But the joy of Mr. Tomanio was that he gave you the deepest feeling of security while still being so much fun you wanted him around. To wit: the second canvas bundle contained a loaded .357 Magnum. Before dinner and darkness, he took it out and let us blast at things, including the coke cans we had emptied in our insane thirst after making the long sweaty hike to the top, stupidly never thinking water might be a smarter option and therefore suffering an agony of thirst all night long. Other than this, we loved every minute.

So ice fishing with Mr. Tomanio was similar, meaning it was less about catching fish and more about being outside on the center stage of winter itself. We weren't much focused on the fishing, since catching fish through the ice wasn't easy, and you couldn't kill the boredom by casting your lure at a changing shoreline. But being there on the frozen lake amidst the snow and ice under the bright blue sky with John and his younger sister Susan and Mr. Tomanio and my brother was always a joy. They even brought along their German shepherd Sheba, whom they harnessed to pull our sled with all our gear, and which I discovered included two packages of frozen breakfast sausage links. We gathered wood from the shore and built a fire out on the nearly foot-thick ice, warming ourselves as we kept our eyes on our four or five tip-ups. We had set them up at pre-existing holes that had been cut by more serious ice-fishermen with augurs, some of them diesel powered, so we only needed to hack through one inch of recently formed ice. And when one of the tip-ups at some distance popped its red flag we all raced and then slid to it, but as always seemed to happen, by the time we reeled it in the fish and bait were gone. So we re-baited the hook and reset the tip-up, lingering there for a few minutes, since there was no reason to rush back to our fire. We could see all the tip-ups from wherever we stood anyway. But when we finally did return to our campfire we saw that Sheba—evidently indifferent to the temperature of her pork—had snarfed down the frozen sausages. Both packages! I writhed to learn this, feeling those sausages to be the crowning moment toward which the afternoon was building. Of course it was mainly funny, especially when again and again she quietly burped the flavor of what had so maddeningly been lost to us.

CHAPTER TWELVE

"You Have Gell-Friend?"

Spring 1978

I n the spring of 1978, Father Nick Petropoulakis announced he was leaving, stunning all of us, who thought we'd finally found a priest who would stay. We had just missed Germanos and then endured Stavropoulos and Ziotis, and now we had someone we liked and he was leaving. Didn't it figure? So one Sunday yet another priest appeared. His name was Father Alex Karloutsos. He was a striking man of about thirty, who promptly told us he wasn't staying long either. He was only filling in for a couple of months until his younger brother Peter could join us, who would be our new priest. But having blown through four priests in six years, we were understandably skeptical.[1]

The Mount Squantz trip the previous summer had whetted John Tomanio's and my appetite for backpacking, and we wanted to buy some real backpacking equipment, which was expensive. I was still fourteen and couldn't get a real job, but John had just turned sixteen and got a job at Grossman's Lumber. He enjoyed working outside, hauling lumber, and hanging out with the regulars, and particularly revered one of his colleagues—a black man named Colin—who seemed to him like an exotic folk hero, since working-class

---

[1] Last year, Father Peter celebrated his fortieth year in the community, and his son Father Nick has been our priest for the last several years as well. Father Peter's father was also a priest.

Danburians so rarely mingled outside their own race. John related some of the things Colin said. "Yeah, I writes," he said. "I writes a lotta things. I writes poetry. I writes Shakespeare." But I understood that in this John was actually letting me know how much he liked Colin.

My desire for backpacking equipment made me ask my father if he had any job ideas and he quickly volunteered that Father Stavropoulos might be able to use me as a busboy at Hilltop, which he still owned, along with the on-the-nosily renamed "Exit Five Motel." I hadn't seen Stavropoulos since the haircut and had mainly forgotten about the downside to him. My father had continued their friendship, which seems to explain my own genetic predisposition—for good and ill both—to defend the indefensible and retain friends most others have long abandoned. My mother never lost an opportunity to say how ridiculous it was that Stavropoulos was allowed to be a priest in Manhattan—where the archdiocese had almost surreptitiously installed him—while running a diner and a motel, and how hypocritical it was that the waitresses actually called him "Father." Besides, my in-the-know friends Adam and Dino said Stavropoulos was known for pinching these waitresses' polyester behinds and worse. But like my father, I ignorantly ignored such things. In any event, I was soon working under the table as a busboy on Friday and Saturday nights, though Stavropoulos didn't pay a dime. I would get what the waitresses gave me from their pooled tips.

I hated the job, but it was only two nights a week and wouldn't be forever and I needed the cash. The diner's booths were covered with shiny maroon vinyl and each had an individual mini jukebox where Chuck Mangione's "Feels So Good" seemed to play endlessly, with Gary Wright's "Dream Weaver" and lots of Bee Gees and Wings, and as I wiped tables and bussed dishes the music helped substantially.

> There is no end to what we can do, together ...
> The willow turns his back on inclement weather ...

The waitresses were sweet and always said how "cute" I was, but I don't remember Father Stavropoulos showing me any kindness, and as his employee I saw a less friendly side of him now and again. But the diminutive short-order cook was happy to take my mind off Stavropoulos. Fanis was the most vulgar person I had ever encountered in my life and was like a chimera, being half Minotaur and half Satyr. Every time I came through the swinging doors with my filthy plastic gray basin of dishes he would bleat something disgusting to me. I was still fourteen and looked younger, but my innocence obviously encouraged his degrading patter. "Eric," he would ask, leeringly, "You have gell-friend?" And then again: "Eric, you have gell-friend, *eh?*" Evidently he was going somewhere with this, as my non-answers and their implied negative did not stop it. "You have gell-friend, *eh?*" So eventually, to get him off my back, even though I didn't "have gell-friend," I fell for the trap and said I did, and of course this only stoked the fire. "Eric!" he continued, "you gell-friend … she give you somethin', *eh?* She give you something nice, *eh?*" And so it went.

Finally at some point to end the nonsense I said: "You've gotta be kidding! I'm fourteen!" At which point he gave me more than I had bargained for.

"That doesn't matter!" he declared. "Eh, leesten! I was eight years old the first time I have a gell!" Was this possible? He continued: "I was in the barn with the tsee-kens, and my gran-mather see saw me and *BAM!* See give me a black eye!!! But that doesn't mah-reh because I fix her up! I give her a kick with my soccer boot! *PAH!!!*"

Another day, Fanis asked me in a similarly leading tone whether I knew the priest's teenage daughter and commenced to effuse crudely over her when Stavropoulos entered to overhear it. But as Fanis was probably the only cook he could keep, he macaronically told him to shut up and called him a baboon in Greek: *"Ela, sar-RAP, vre Boubouna!"* Every Monday I would fill John Tomanio in on what Fanis had said. It was a never-ending fountain of filth, and as revolted as I was in the moment, by the time I shared it with John it was of course the funniest thing imaginable.

Stavropoulos instructed me that when I bussed a table where customers had eaten king crab—which lived in the hinterlands of the deep freeze and was blasted to "freshness" in the old mic—I was not to throw out the melted "butter" in the little metal cup with the flame underneath it, but rather should pour this used liquid back into a white plastic bucket that sat next to where I dumped the befouled dishes, as he showed me. Of course this yellow substance would be served again, although people had dipped their chewed seafood into it many times, never dreaming it had been used before, or would be used again, and that they were themselves now part of an endless moist-mouthed chain linked through that drawn butter to other diners who might have had TB or STDs or advanced pyorrhea. But when the economy is struggling under Jimmy Carter, small business owners will do what they think necessary.

I had been working three months when I turned fifteen and finally had enough money to buy my backpacking equipment. One night shortly after my birthday my parents had to go to an event and wouldn't be able to pick me up after my shift; so we decided they would drop me off with my blue Schwinn ten-speed, which I could ride home at the end of the night, even though it entailed riding along the highway. But it was just a mile and a quarter and downhill, so I chained my bike outside the diner and went in, past the alcove with the cigarette machine and the game that teases you with the possibility of grabbing a small stuffed animal. But as soon as I stepped into the air-conditioned diner, I saw it was busier than ever, and sensed a palpable tension.

In fact, I wasn't there five minutes before Father Stavropoulos harshly snapped at me to move faster, something he had never done before. I was stunned. But it only got worse. At one point he came over and angrily threw the dishes from a table into my rectangular grey tub, this time angrily cursing at me in Greek, shocking me to my core. I had never been cursed at by an adult, and whatever errant words my father had spoken had never been viciously directed at me. It was unthinkable to hear this from someone I thought of as my father's friend, much less a priest, but it happened several more times that night, with the words *Panagia*—the All-Holy (Mother of God)—and *gamoto* eventually added, this latter being the Greek equivalent of our F-word.[2] I was still just an over-sensitive kid and although I was able to hold it in all night, by the time I got my money from the waitresses and walked out the glass doors

---

[2] When I was twelve I came across the word "gamete" in science class and realized that this word, meaning a sperm cell or egg cell, was the Greek root from which the less refined verb *gamoto* derived. The Greek word for marriage—*gamo*—has a similar derivation.

and into what I now saw was pouring rain, I burst into tears. The rain and darkness—it was now eleven thirty, much later than I had ever worked—camouflaged my tears as I walked down the steps to my wet bike, undid the lock, and began riding home along the slippery black highway. My tears continued to mingle with the falling rain, but I was also now becoming very angry. By the time I pulled into our driveway, I was soaked and furious, despising Father Stavropoulos as I had never despised anyone and I bitterly vowed I would never, ever go back.

The next day I related what happened, but my father insisted I must return. Stavropoulos would know why I had quit and it would be embarrassing to everyone. But I didn't care. I had never disobeyed my father, but I knew I could never go back, which I didn't, and I proudly nursed my bitter hatred of Father Stavropoulos for many years.

I often have thought priests like Stavropoulos drive people away from God, but that wasn't the case with me, perhaps because I never really connected him with God. It seemed clear to me that God—whoever he might be—must be good and loving, like my own dad, so Stavropoulos didn't confuse that for me. Of course a priest is supposed to draw people to God, and I never got any hint that he did that. But after that awful night, I never saw Father Stavropoulos again.[3] But Fanis, the vulgar short-order cook, I would see again, and in some decidedly surprising circumstances.[4]

Summer 1979

Days after finishing junior year I turned sixteen and could work legally, which my parents certainly expected. Our church friend Steve Kaplanis

---

[3] Twenty years after this he went to prison for tax fraud, and just a few years ago I made a point of forgiving him and praying for him, and asked my father if I might see him somehow, hoping that I might tell him I forgave him and share my faith with him, but alas, he passed away before I was able to do that.

[4] In my book *Miracles* I tell the denouement of this story.

worked at the local Holiday Inn, so a few days after my birthday I reported for duty to a Mrs. Wall, whose title was "Housekeeper" and who ran things like a drill sergeant. Actually her stout appearance, short dyed hair, starched uniform, and bleak office gave her the generally fearsome demeanor of the head matron of a women's prison in a *film noir*. She sat at her desk eating popcorn from a bowl and looking me over. Although minimum wage was $2.91, she would start me at $3, which I was to interpret as a generous vote of confidence out of the gate. My job was to keep the maids' carts supplied with sheets and towels and whatever else was needed, so I was constantly running from the laundry room up and down the hotel's four floors until it was finally time to punch out and I could ride my blue Schwinn up the hill and home. It was precisely as far down the hill as the Hilltop diner was up.

But at some point I realized the Marshalls just across Route Six needed cashiers weeknights and Saturdays and I could make even more money. It was there that I met George Duncan, a friendly redhead two years older than me, who attended what was called Danbury's "alternative" high school. I assumed that was where potheads and other troubled souls went, mainly because it was true, but George was neither. He was from a humble family that, though white, lived in Mill Ridge, which most people considered the "black" section of town. But because George was artistic and had something sweet and simple about him, his not fitting into the swarming chaos of the "regular" high school made sense. He was always sketching and painting and invited me to do things with his friends. After the race riot two years earlier, I was amazed these lower-class whites were actually friends with the blacks in their neighborhood, which there were.

As our friendship developed George told me about something called "the Community," a loosely configured group of sixties-style Jesus-people whose leader was a Catholic priest. Father Larry had come of age in the "Charismatic" movement that practiced speaking in tongues and hearing from God personally, and George attended their nightly prayer meetings and sometimes invited me along; though it was all new to me, it felt very natural and unthreatening. This was a part of the tail end of the "Jesus Movement" and consisted mostly of college-age people who gathered every night to pray spontaneously, and as

I sat there I heard this one and that one saying, "Thank you, Jesus. Thank you, Jesus!" And sometimes they prayed softly in what I gathered were "tongues." It was all very gentle and beautiful and although I figured I was covered on the religious front through the Greek church and couldn't join this group, I got to know a few of George's friends and they were all kind, and through them I began to think of myself more as a Christian than previously. By the time I graduated, I knew following Jesus was important and said something to that effect in George's yearbook. I wanted to deepen my faith, though I certainly had no idea how this was supposed to happen.

CHAPTER THIRTEEN

Senior Year

1979

In fall of senior year it was time to apply to colleges, about which I knew nothing, nor were the guidance counselors in our huge public high school much help. By the time I spoke to mine I had already made a number of irrevocable mistakes, like idiotically taking a full load of advanced honors math and science courses, such that my grade point average slipped just below an A. Still, my SAT scores were impressive enough, weren't they? I filled out the applications myself and had no one to help me with my essays, so I wrote them and typed them; but what I wrote I dare not recall. As for where to apply, I thought the shotgun approach best and applied to a raft of schools, including Harvard, Yale, Princeton, Dartmouth, Brown, Williams, Georgetown, and a few others. I assumed I wouldn't get into Harvard or Yale, but assumed I'd get into one of the others.

That year I found a paperback New Testament in my parents' bedroom. I don't know where it came from, but it was titled *Good News for Modern Man*, so the language was as plain as could be. I had never read the Bible, and what it said began to get to me. Somehow I felt I must do something to get my life "right with God," though I had no idea what that meant. So the next day in AP physics I told John Tomanio about it, hoping he might have some ideas.

But his response was decidedly negative. I had given him the impression I was thinking of turning into a saint who would never crack another smile or joke or be sarcastic again and he said that was what made me me, so it would be terrible if I did that. But because I myself hardly knew what I was saying, I let the whole thing go.

That year I finally saw the limits of my academic aptitude. John and I had taken both Mrs. Strouse's AP calculus and Mrs. Rynciewicz's AP physics. Until then I had always gotten straight A's in math, but I suddenly found myself struggling, with no idea how to handle it. I had never struggled in school. Physics was another story. Mrs. Rynciewicz was a cartoon super-genius who stood five feet tall, with thick, filthy glasses, a shock of white hair, dandruff, and halitosis. She was very generous to the smart kids, which was her fatal error, for she assumed that anyone with a high IQ loved physics and learning just as she did. So in our "self-study" AP class she never looked over our shoulders or bothered us with any quizzes or tests. She let John and me do literally nothing but chit-chat and give her the vaguest inkling we were going along in our workbooks, which we certainly weren't. There was a utopianist strain in her approach, as though we were examples of a New Intelligent Humanity who would render the pedagogical crudities of the past obsolete. But in April when we took the AP exam the shameful and ghastly truth was revealed. I got the expected *one*—the lowest score possible—which must have given Mrs. Rynciewicz a heart attack when she saw it, which I didn't realize she would, and the memory of letting her down like that stings still, and is by far the worst aspect of the whole debacle. I am still ashamed to remember it, but simply did not see it coming and blundered blindly along until it was too late.

But in the same year I discovered my left-brain limitations I also discovered a pronounced affinity for words and literature. I never dreamt I would be a writer, nor that such a thing was possible. I knew no one who read much, much less wrote, and of course having parents whose first languages were not English was part of that. But whenever I showed any aptitude for words, my father always and immediately said I had inherited this from his grandfather Panagis Vergotis, whose Plaster-of-Paris bust loomed at us from a high shelf in the living room. In 1977 I opened the large crate in which it arrived, lifting from the excelsior my high-foreheaded forebear—such foreheads in his day being proof of great intellect. Had not Goethe such a forehead? Its bronze original was unveiled on the street where he lived and now bears his name. My father had always sung his praises, whose achievements began with his first book, *O Mikros Politis* (*The Little Citizen*), published in 1872, on the importance of teaching young people virtue and civic-mindedness, and was translated into many languages—and continued with his translation into demotic Greek of the first five cantos of Dante's *Inferno*. A devotee of the liberalizing trends in Europe during his time, he was a vocal advocate of the demotic "language of the people" and for these egalitarian views was hounded out of Argostoli to Lixouri across the bay, then a bastion of artists and political liberals. My father often boasted that his grandfather had also written a two-volume work on the preposition "of"—in Greek, "*Apo.*" So whenever I seemed literarily inclined, my father pointed to him, figuratively and now literally too.

During my junior year I chose to write a paper on John Milton's poem "Lycidas." Milton was a seventeen-year-old Cantabrigian when he wrote it, but this did not impress me overmuch, as I was sure that in the infinity of the next two years I should be able to pen something similar. As would become a pattern with me, it was less what Milton actually said that grasped me than the language itself, as though I were listening to music and loving the words for their sounds and not their meaning. There were phrases from his 1620s teenage quill I remember still: *O fairest flower no sooner blown but blasted… The pansy freaked with jet… Lycidas is dead, dead ere his prime. Who will not mourn for Lycidas?… The perfidous bark, rigged in th' eclipse…* What was it in me that responded to this, though I had never read anything like it, and knew no one who had? I was touched by the elegiac quality of it and then in later decades was moved by the idea that this teenager knew this was his first major poem and that he would never be young again, but would go on to do much more in the years ahead, such that the poem was him self-consciously and ambitiously clearing his throat, as it were.

During senior year my delight with poetry increased and I loved the foreignness of the inscrutable lines excerpted from *Beowulf*: "*Scolde Grendel thonan… Sicean winleas wic, wiste the geornor that his aldres taes ende gegongen, daegora daegrim.*" I memorized them almost as an incantation, as a way to summon the atmosphere of the thousand-years-gone heath, and I drank in the archaic language of Mary Shelley's *Frankenstein* and began annoyingly using phrases from it, talking about "quitting my lodgings" and "slaking my thirst." But I never thought of being a writer.

That spring, I heard from the colleges I had applied to, whose letters typically arrived the same day. I fairly floated out to the white mailbox with the happy metal cutout of the bird feeding her babies, but when I opened it and saw what it contained, my heart sank full-fathom-five beneath the waves. I heard large envelopes contained acceptances and that standard-sized envelopes contained rejections, and one glimpse was enough. The school I applied to as an afterthought—Trinity College in Hartford—was the only one that had accepted me. I was so unprepared for this that I could not take it in. As a tiny sop to my ego, I saw I had been wait-listed at Yale and Dartmouth—but so what? I stood there in the driveway crushed, in a way I had never known. In a way my whole life had been leading up to this moment. I was the smart kid. The one who skipped a grade and always got straight A's. Now what?

April 4, 1980

I did not run cross country again, but as a junior ran the unpleasant 1,000 in indoor track (eleven tight laps!) and in senior year went out for spring track. I was slated to run the quarter, but never broke a minute and since they hardly needed my middling speed the coach asked whether I would try the pole vault, so for the better part of two weeks I discovered how hard it was to do what looked so easy on TV. But one week before our first scrimmage, something happened that scotched forever my dream of pole-vaulting into the record books; and as it happened, it happened on Good Friday, on what was the thirty-sixth anniversary of my grandfather Erich's death.

The Muscular Dystrophy Bike-a-thon was on Saturday, April 5. Angelo Defazio and Pete Moeller convinced John Tomanio and me join to them in riding it; and we all bizarrely thought it advisable to "practice" for the thirty-mile ride by biking the entire route the day before. It was one of those rare Good

Fridays when Orthodox Christians celebrated (and Easter, too, of course) the same day as the rest of Christendom.[1]

When we set out it was a chilly fifty degrees and had just stopped raining, but some miles into the ride we hit our stride and were really cranking along—"booking," as we used to say—without the slightest thought that we might be incredibly sore tomorrow when we would repeat the whole thing. Someplace in Danbury's upscale Aunt Hack neighborhood—in the farthest part of the city from where I lived, so unknown to me—we came to a very long gradual downhill. It continued for almost a mile and I stupidly thought it might be fun to see how fast I could go, this perhaps being the day when my adolescent sense of invincibility peaked.

In a few moments I was soon pedaling hard in tenth and easily pulled away from my friends until I was eventually going fast enough actually to pass a Volkswagen bug sputtering along at nearly forty miles per hour. But not long after that I must have hit a deep pothole. I have no memory of it, but before you could say "Evel Knievel at Caesar's" I went flying over the handlebars and struck the pavement so hard with my helmetless head that I should have died within minutes. The X-rays eventually showed a skull fracture five and a half inches in length and fully one millimeter wide. I doubt a baseball bat could have done worse. Nonetheless some minutes later I floated up to semi-consciousness in the middle of the road feeling cold and dizzy and nauseated, with John and Angelo crouching over me. They carried me to the side of the road and lay me in the cold, wet leaves, where I shivered for something like half an hour, waiting for help. Pete had run to the nearest house to call an ambulance while I lay there shivering and swimming in and out of consciousness. At last the EMTs arrived and helped me stand up and slowly walked me to the ambulance, asking me how I felt. A strange sentence followed: "Both my senses of vision and balance seem to be somewhat impaired." Perhaps I thought it important to be precise. Once I was strapped in, the ambulance rocketed toward the hospital, and whenever the vehicle went around a curve I thought my thousand-pound brain would

---

[1] This is because the Orthodox still follow the Julian calendar, while the rest of Christendom has adopted the Gregorian. Orthodox Easter is normally a week or several weeks later.

exit my head. On the gurney at the hospital I began to throw up and again drifted in and out of consciousness. John called my parents, who soon arrived, and I was checked into the ICU.

Whatever the doctors said was not good, because Father Peter while performing Good Friday liturgy was informed of my condition and immediately excused himself, explaining he must go to the hospital to administer Holy Unction—the Orthodox version of Last Rites—to me. The church was of course packed on Good Friday and for an hour the overflowing congregation waited for Father Peter's return. When he arrived at the hospital and said prayers over me I continued to go in and out of consciousness. He anointed my head with oil and gave me communion, and after he left, I overheard a doctor telling my parents that if my brain began to swell—this was their principal fear, since that could be fatal—they would drill a hole in my skull to relieve the intercranial pressure. This got my attention, and for the first time in my life I prayed earnestly and passionately—albeit silently—asking God please to spare me and my parents this dramatic unpleasantness.

Late in the evening my mother went home, but my father sat all night in the chair by my bed, unable to sleep as he watched the lines on the monitors as though his son's life depended on them, which of course it did. The protocol for patients with severe head injuries was to check them every fifteen minutes, which among other things entailed forcibly opening my eyes and using a flashlight to check my pupils. It was obviously not something one could sleep through and continued all night, with my father by my side. When morning came, there was still no evidence of brain swelling, which was of course what I had prayed for, and a few hours later the doctors reckoned me out of the woods. I slept some and by the afternoon of that Saturday, I felt much better, and several of my high school friends visited. The next day—Easter Sunday—the doctors thought it safe for me to go home, which I did. My father says it was the worst Good Friday but the best Easter Sunday of his life, as though his own son had been resurrected. And hadn't I?

CHAPTER FOURTEEN

Graduation

1980

At the end of junior year I discovered that our school's tradition was that the student who gave the big speech at graduation was not the "valedictorian" with the best grade-point average, but was simply the student who gave what a panel of faculty judges deemed the best speech. I instantly knew I must do this, though I have no idea why, and when a year later my own graduation drew nigh, I struggled to write a speech, though I had never written one before and had no idea what one was supposed to say on such an occasion. Part of it I wrote lying on John Tomanio's bedroom floor as he did homework on his bed; and at some point when he mocked me for what I was doing—as we always did to each other—I told him to knock it off, explaining: "This is serious!" I still can't imagine why I felt it so important, but I did, and somehow the panel chose me, even claiming the choice was unprecedentedly unanimous. I was proud to be chosen and in it somehow had a sense that God was with me. Because I had been hanging out with George Duncan and fitfully reading *Good News for Modern Man*, I quoted the New Testament in the rambly speech; and because I was nervous—never having spoken in front of a crowd, much less one of three thousand—I wrote "Trust Jesus" at the top of the first page.

When the day came I mounted the vast stage set up on the football field and saw that the new mayor was there. He was thirty-four and for me meeting him was meeting a celebrity. When the whole ceremony was over I suddenly felt something like a celebrity myself. My classmates and their parents gushed over what I said—but what had I said?—and the next day my picture and some quotes from the speech were in the paper. It was heady, but after another day the whole thing had faded to almost nothing, and the long boring summer stretched out before me. It didn't look good. I would have to work two jobs that summer: the cashier job from the previous summer, plus a weekend job parking cars at Candlewood Inn on the lake. And in the fall I would be going to the college where I didn't want to go.

But Monday as I lay in bed the phone rang. My parents were at work, but my grandmother picked it up and then shouted up the stairs. "Eric, come *qvick!* It's de may-or!" *What?* I ran downstairs and suddenly found myself talking to the mayor, who was genial and said he would like to get together for dinner. I was flabbergasted and immediately hoped he was impressed with my speech and wanted me as an intern.

His live-in girlfriend Sally joined us and at some point during dinner I asked him whether he thought I might work for him that summer. He laughed that I had brought it up before he did, but he said that yes, he was about to ask me. When I got home I was flushed with excitement, as were my parents. I wouldn't have to work as a cashier now. But I was still expected to keep the weekend parking job.

Though I was thrilled I would be working for the mayor, I was furious I had to work two jobs and stay alone in Danbury with my father while my brother got to go to Greece with my mother. My Uncle Othon had invited them and offered to pay the airfare, since it was "their turn," but the unfairness infuriated me. I had been there in the winter when I was nine, with my father who was not fun, and now my brother would go for a whole month in July as a teenager and spend every day at the beach or on a boat. And I would have all summer to sulk about how I hadn't gotten into Dartmouth or Brown. But suddenly now into this difficult period rode the dashing young mayor in his black Corvette. He also had a deluxe condo and more money than he needed;

and for reasons I didn't question he would choose to spend a fair amount of it on me. Within days of starting my job at City Hall, I was being feted in a way unimaginable to me, and the idea of Cephalonia grew impossibly distant. He and Sally regularly took me to fancy restaurants and engaged me in mature conversations and repartee, all of which flattered me tremendously. My parents and I almost never went out to eat. We certainly didn't have a Corvette.

I remember that one night early in our friendship the subject of New York Mayor Ed Koch came up. My Theo Takis worked for him now, having successfully helped him get the vote of New York's Greek community. But when Tom and Sally asked whether it would make any difference to me whether Koch were gay, I said that I thought it would. I remembered my mother saying how she couldn't stand the way homosexuals talked and acted, shuddering as she did so. And when you love someone as I loved my mother you take their opinions to heart. But I went on to explain that as a Christian—which I then considered myself—I even believed sleeping with my girlfriend at that time would have been wrong, which shocked and troubled them. They couldn't believe I was so uptight and argued forcefully with me, though I stubbornly held my ground until Sally pronounced me "an arrogant little shit," which was the first time I sensed that perhaps she didn't like me quite as much as Tom did.

But working at the mayor's office was a dream. I wore a coat and tie and was treated like a golden boy by everyone, and whatever I did hardly seemed like "work," compared to my previous jobs. The gang at City Hall was a blast to hang out with, especially Joan and Maryanne, the political operatives in the back room. There was also Mark, another intern I enjoyed immensely, whose brother was a state rep. I was suddenly part of what seemed like an in-crowd and it was intoxicating. To use the cliche, I felt I belonged, that I was where I was supposed to be and was "going places." And being young and impressionable, Tom had no small influence on my outlook. Under his tutelage I soon lost my inhibitions regarding cursing and even began to crack some dirty jokes, which proved a huge hit; and with Tom, the sexual innuendo was constant, though it didn't take long to figure out where he got it from. Once when a birthday cake appeared in the office, his eighty-year-old father slyly intoned, "I tell ya I wouldn't mind a piece ..." By that time in the summer, I got the joke.

In August Tom—now "Tommy"—got me to say that we were "best friends" and one night when I had a bit too much to drink at a bar featuring a Beatles tribute band, he said I should stay with him instead of driving home. So I called my parents and in what I didn't realize was a drunken-sounding voice told my mother I was going to do that. But hearing this, she began to cry, which absolutely broke my heart. I would never ever want to hurt her, so I tried to reassure her I was fine, but I was very upset that she was upset. Tom said I could sleep on the couch, and that his good friend Senator Chris Dodd had slept there recently, which impressed me.

That summer the 1980 Democratic Convention was at Madison Square Garden and Tom got tickets and took me along for the final night. On the distant stage I saw Jimmy Carter. Although he was a hundred yards away, I had never seen a president before, someone who stood in that hallowed line of Washington and Lincoln. I was agog at the idea. Earlier that year, sensing Carter's weakness, Ted Kennedy had aggressively challenged him, to which news Carter reportedly said, "I'll whip his ass." Kennedy landed a plum speaking spot at the convention and two days earlier had given a speech evoking the memory of his fallen brothers and ending with the phrase "The dream will never die." The media ate it up. So I saw Carter accept his party's nomination, but the party leaders wanted Kennedy to come out and lift their arms together in a show of unity. Kennedy peevishly refused. But he did emerge eventually. I was struck by the physical disparity between them. Kennedy was a bearish—and later unpleasantly fat—man of six two, while Carter was a slender man of five eight. Seeing them together was striking, because on TV everyone seemed the same size. But when the balloons came down and everyone was singing "Happy Days Are Here Again" it was elating. I knew I belonged in this world and when we left the Garden I saw a tall black man next to me wearing an afro and a blue Super Fly jump suit. I immediately recognized him as Jesse Jackson. He was the first celebrity I had ever seen up close, and eight years later I voted for him to become our first black president.

I knew I had been bitten by the political bug and decided I would be a political science major. It seemed fated, somehow, as though my increasingly close friendship with Tommy was God's way of making up for my not getting into the colleges I wanted. Because of him I saw much of the world in a new way; he had opened many doors for me and made me feel important.

One weekend he and Sally wanted to take me to the city. We would stay at the Plaza. When I told my parents, they didn't say anything. We were working-class people who wouldn't dream of staying overnight in Manhattan—and at the Plaza? That was for millionaires. Toward the end of the summer the mayor invited me to Boston too. I had never been. We stayed at the Parker House, but there was only one king bed, and he and Sally thought that it was big enough for all of us. From my perspective it was innocent enough and I never felt pushed in any uncomfortable direction, though in retrospect, the invitation to yield to the Free Love Vibe of the seventies had certainly been proffered.

One day Tom said, "What if I told you that I was bisexual? Would you love me less?" I knew that there was only one possible answer and could feel myself being manipulated. He seemed to have the keys to my future. But there was no question I didn't feel open to whatever he might be suggesting.

I eventually learned that Tom had a habit of cultivating young men, but it wasn't until that Christmas that he told me he had slept with them. I knew everyone he mentioned, and one who was fourteen when it began, but I had already gotten the idea it wasn't cool to "judge," whatever that meant. But that was part of what everyone in the know seemed to "know" without knowing what it was they actually knew, nor how they knew it. But now I knew it too. When I was in seventh grade Elton John said he was bisexual, but of course that didn't stop me from loving his music. Sally sometimes referred to "the boys club" around Tom in a tone I now see as expressing hurt. I didn't then dream she felt we were competing for his affections. I just thought she was annoyed as any woman would be if the man she lived with made her play second fiddle to his male friends.

There were conversations in which he was clearly pushing me to "love" him, and to persuade me that "love" was something that happened on a continuum.

Didn't I believe that a man could "love" another man? I did. And wouldn't I say we were close enough that I loved him? It seemed rude to say anything but yes. And didn't I believe that love might sometimes express itself physically? I wasn't sure what to think, but nothing ever happened and suddenly the summer was over and I was heading to college.

CHAPTER FIFTEEN

Trinity College

Fall 1980

O ne of several things I disliked about Trinity was getting there, driving a long, bleak, and boring hour up Interstate 84 through Waterbury and then through a genuinely dangerous part of Hartford. But at last we came out on a strange oasis of late-nineteenth-century buildings and green grass and a magnificent chapel tower like something out of Oxford or Cambridge. But as my parents and I unpacked, I palpably felt the foreignness of this environment. Everywhere were characters who had stumbled drunkenly out of *The Official Preppy Handbook* holding martinis and squash rackets and wearing ribbon belts and boat shoes, unloading Volvos and BMWs. For the first time in my life, I felt embarrassed for having working-class parents with accents. And I felt ashamed for feeling embarrassed.

I soon gathered that life here was mostly less about the joy of learning—to which I had so looked forward—than about continuing the prep-school vibe and then getting a job in a bank or on Wall Street. Until I met John O'Brien. He had piercing blue eyes and a mop of hair that went with what I quickly learned was his philosopher/rock guitarist persona, and he loved literature and history. So John generously showed me the ropes of the preppy-verse from the point of view of someone who had suffered in it at nearby Suffield

Academy, and scorned it deeply. He was a brilliant guitarist whose life was music, and at Suffield he formed a band called Nietzsche and a Horse, referring to an episode—drunkenly recounted by Jim Morrison in a Doors bootleg—in which the mad philosopher had remonstrated on behalf of a horse being beaten. The drummer, Gig—Gilbert—Ahrens, and the lead vocalist Ian MacKinnon, whom they always called "Shaman" and sometimes "Satan"— were still seniors at Suffield and visited many weekends to join us in whatever bacchanalian hijinks we engaged. Their collective posture was decidedly anti-prep—they called Trinity "Camp Trin-trin"—and in retrospect I see there was something of Holden Caulfield in their disgust with what they saw as the ethos in which they had been existing for many years, but to which I was only just now being exposed. I had never heard of *The Catcher in the Rye* or half the things they seemed to assume, but I learned quickly and felt privileged to

My parents and grandmother visiting me at Trinity, 1980

be included in their circle, although truth be told I always somehow reckoned my presence probationary, being there mainly because of John's genuine kindness, but as though I hadn't yet fully proved myself with the others on whatever Dionysian scale they used to weigh such things.

As much as I now learned about music, John's principal influence on me came from his love of books and ideas. I was always learning new words, like "albeit" and "ethos" and "debacle" and *"enfant terrible"* and *"cause celebre,"* though we often used them in a self-conscious manner, which made them the more attractive. Who knew the life of the mind could be such fun?

John was the one who persuaded me to join the honors humanities program, called Guided Studies, an introduction to Western Civilization. Whatever we studied provoked endless joking, as did the mannerisms of most of our professors. Our favorite course was with Hugh Ogden, a Donald-Sutherland-in-*Animal-House* hippie with longish hair and sandals.

Under him the first books written and the first we studied—the *Iliad* and *Odyssey*—became utterly mesmerizing. I took one poli-sci course because I assumed poli-sci would be my major and politics my future, but hated it as much as I loved the rest of them. I also took a survey philosophy class where I learned that Thales of Miletus was a pre-Socratic and the professor a womanizer, the difference between them being that Thales was unaware of it at the time.

Though I never mentioned it to anyone, every Friday after dinner I snuck off to attend the Christian group on campus, where I never said boo. It was as though I were fulfilling an obligation, perhaps an unspoken one I had made to George Duncan. God had somehow barely come into my life and this was all I knew to do to about it, but whatever happened during those ninety-minute meetings never bled beyond them.

The smartest person in the Guided Studies class was Ian MacFarland, an outspoken atheist. Like me, he had skipped a grade and was seventeen, but seemed years wiser. He knew he wanted to major in classics and his love of learning encouraged me as much as John's did. John was Catholic and some Saturday nights I went with him to mass to hear the hip young priest, Father John. Ian and I sometimes debated about God, but always in a friendly way, and though his atheism didn't shake my nascent faith, it made an impression.

But one way my faith did affect me was that I didn't have any college girlfriends. I always somehow knew whether I was interested in someone for the long term—which is to say for love and marriage—and since I didn't find anyone I felt that way about, I wouldn't be able to move forward as though I did, which seemed to me a way of lying and using someone. I sometimes wished I could be less self-conscious and have the kind of "fun" others seemed to be able to, but perhaps because I lacked what is called "experience" with women, I simply found I couldn't, which somehow makes something of an argument for deferring such "experience" generally. But even three years later at Yale, when I finally found someone I did feel that way toward, I was physically diffident. One night we found ourselves kissing, at which point she suggested we move to her room, but because I was a virgin and an innocent I felt I couldn't. I had not been sexualized such that kissing would vault me toward doing more, and although we did go to her room, I kept my clothes on and we talked till dawn, which must have mystified her, but I was simply not ready, and of course in retrospect I'm glad I realized that.

Spring Term 1981

It was precisely noon on January 20, as we began the spring term at Trinity, that some of us were walking through the arch beneath the chapel carillon when the carillon bells began pealing wildly over our heads. Someone said President Reagan had just been sworn in, and the Iranian hostages had just been released too. It was a tremendously joyous moment and seemed a particularly auspicious beginning to the year. The long national nightmare of the captured hostages was finally over. That semester in Guided Studies was every bit as wonderful as the first, though at the time I simply assumed this was what all colleges were like, which I would find out was not the case. We studied medieval history and the Rule of Benedict and *The Divine Comedy* and most of Edmund Spenser's *The Faerie Queen*; and John and I took a class that required reading all thirty-three extant Greek tragedies. What had I been thinking in wanting to major in poli sci? It was around this time too that I began to want to be a writer, to attempt somehow to contribute to this majestic centuries-long river of words and beauty and knowledge and wisdom in which I had only just begun to swim.

Part of what impressed me about what we studied was how the ideas we were studying mattered to the people at the time, so that they would fight and die for them. As though life had real meaning, and the people then were truly alive. One day Ian said that an aged stone slab outside the chapel was the very one from which the fifteenth-century martyr Jan Hus had once preached. The idea that Hus, about whom we had read and who had burned at the stake for his ideas, had touched that very stone—and from there had spoken truth with such fearlessness—stunned and captivated me. I began to wonder what it might have been like to live when ideas mattered that much, and lamented that I seemed to live in a world where they no longer did, where every idea was somehow equal to the others, where ideas mattering was either ignored or mocked. But it was true that we were learning that when ideas mattered that much it usually ended in violence. So couldn't we just surf into the future without that heavy ideological baggage? I didn't know. But I missed the sense of meaning that had infused these previous epochs and wondered what had happened. Was living without that sense of meaning really living?

So I understood I was not merely studying books, but was through them trying to touch the ideas in them—truth and goodness and beauty. And eternity too, I supposed. I hadn't put God into the picture, but I knew I was not merely trying to understand what the authors thought about things as much as I was trying to understand the things themselves. What was the nature of reality, and was there a reality beyond nature? When Goethe in *Faust* calls the devil a "negating force," was he right? Was evil a "privation of the good"—to use the term I had learned in a lunchroom conversation with Ian—or was it a thing unto itself? How did Dante's poem of the afterlife correspond to that reality, and could we know? Reading these classics became a tutelage in intellectual history, but every book or play or poem on which I wrote our weekly paper seemed to teach me something profound about my own life. I was not so much doing literary criticism as primary philosophy, trying through these minds to understand the world and my place in it. This was hardly what the professors seemed to intend, but was simply what I found myself doing, and it seemed to flow naturally out of what I read. The world around me seemed devoid of these ideas, but they came to me now through the centuries, through the pages I was reading.

When I read Goethe's *The Sorrows of Young Werther* I had never been so transported. How I ached with the feelings evoked in that early masterpiece, and I wondered if I had read it when it was first published if I might have been among those many youths who took their own lives in imitation of their new Romantic hero. We also read William Blake's *Songs of Innocence and of Experience,* some of which almost undid me with their simple beauty. The ending to "Little Black Boy" choked me up every time I read it and does still.[1] At the end of the semester I wrote about *Death in Venice,* relating it to something I read in Nietzsche, in which he said Apollonian art is like a marble bust, like the Platonic ideal, cerebral and cool, while the Dionysian is earthy and embodied, like African tribal dance, in which the participants become the art itself. In one we objectively observe the art; in the other, we subjectively become the art. I saw that the pomaded protagonist Aschenbach, in his pederastic longing for the beautiful Tadzio, reaches for a kind of Apollonian perfection that ends in his staggering further and further downward into an orgiastic Dionysian swamp, so that what had begun as some kind of pure and disembodied love of an ideal ends in degradation. It was exciting to be making these connections, to see that there seemed to be a deeper order to things, ancient and invisible, but discoverable, like the laws of physics.

So my studies had become personal; and wasn't this the project of education and of art, to help us attain self-knowledge and wisdom? It was what Socrates quoted, written over the entrance to the Delphic Oracle: "Know Thyself." But beyond Trinity College, where in 1981 the noble ideas of attaining self-knowledge and wisdom were still somehow alive and generally treated seriously, these ideas were already disappearing or long gone, as I would soon see. Guided Studies was as perfect an intellectual primer as I could have gotten, though I hardly knew it at the time.

I only remember one curious deviation from the norm, when all Guided Studies students were expected to attend a poetry reading. I had never been to one, and had no idea what to expect, but the poet was a woman whose poems struck such a different tone from what we were reading that I was confused. One poem I remember principally because it seemed so pointedly earnest it almost dared you to giggle. "These hips be big hips!" the poet declared, defiantly, and with a kind of put-on cla-ri-ty that was part of the larger affectation. "And when a man see these hips, they turn his head a-*round* ..." She gave it in a reveling-in-my-earthy-sexuality voice that a year or so later I connected ideologically to William Faulkner's "eternal fecund feminine." But now it seemed merely

---

[1] See Appendix.

trendy. We had studied such unadulteratedly great poetry that we had become harsh critics, and these faddish poems didn't clear the bar. Of course we listened politely, we young men with our longish hair and pin-waled Levi cords and rugby shirts, and the young women in their yoke-necked Fair Isle sweaters and clogs. But how could this hold a candle to Homer and Dante? What were we missing?

This was the first time I had ever felt pushed in how to think, that I felt a not-so-subtle implication that I had some prejudices against this which must be corrected. But I felt that meant I had been reduced to a stereotype myself. I knew I was the son of immigrants struggling in menial jobs while I listened to poetry, and I knew my mother that weekend would be cleaning someone's house so I could sit here. I also knew that my father had experienced the humiliations of being treated like an unworthy foreigner by genuine bigots, so it was confusing that that their child could somehow be identified with—and should even adopt an apologetic posture for—those self-same bigots. Nonetheless, this was the only time I experienced anything like this until I got to Yale.

Because I hadn't been raised in a culturally sophisticated atmosphere, college was for me much more than academics. For example, for the first time in my life I saw certain movies like Martin Scorsese's *Raging Bull* and David Lynch's *The Elephant Man*, both of which I still revere, the latter being almost shockingly Christian in its message. I also saw *A Clockwork Orange*, which I despised for the violence, and *The Exorcist*, which I despised more because it portrayed demonic evil so realistically, although in this it pushed me toward God. I knew evil existed, but actual satanic evil never came into the picture until I saw in that film the unspeakable horror and hopelessness of the real nightmare of a world without God or goodness or love. But precisely because Satan was less an entity of evil than a non-entity of God's goodness, the film showed me in negative form something of the real thing against which Satan raged and rebelled. Through some of what I was reading I began to see that only God can create, and that Satan can only pervert what already exists of God's good creation. In other words, Satan cannot stand on his own hooved feet, and if he presented any twisted reality, that reality was stolen from God. For some reason I cannot remember, my mother had given me a five-by-seven postcard of a Rembrandt, "Head of Christ," which I had posted on my bulletin board, and I was so shaken that night after seeing that film that I looked at it and prayed.

As much as I loved my friends and the courses I was taking—never appreciating how rare such an education was becoming—I badly wanted to transfer to the sort of larger university I had always envisioned. Trinity had fewer students than my three-year high school and the preppy Gestalt was genuinely suffocating. Since I had been wait-listed at Yale and Dartmouth, they seemed the logical choices for possible transfer, but because I was still considering a life in politics—I assumed in Connecticut, since I lived there—I thought I should go to school there, too. So during spring break I applied to Yale.

I needed two recommendations from professors, but the professors that first semester thought so well of me I thought I should ask all four for recommendations. Then I wrote my essay—in it pretentiously using the word "traumata"—which Tom's girlfriend Sally generously typed for me, and I sent it off with my application. And I prayed, believing God had a plan. I wouldn't hear back until summer, and had no idea that if I went to Yale I would enter a world where reading books for themselves and for the eternal truths they contained had already ceased, and where academic trendiness was not the surprising exception, but the fatiguing rule. I only knew that it was my dream.

Summer 1981

That summer, when I returned home, Tom hired me again, but something had changed. I had the sense that he felt rebuffed by me, and the fact that I had never allowed things to go where he seemed to have hoped upset him.

I had no idea whether I would get into Yale, but I remember one day driving down West Street toward City Hall and thinking that if I didn't I would transfer someplace else, to Oxford or Cambridge or West Point. Even if it meant joining the French Foreign Legion, I couldn't survive Trinity for four years. I wanted to strike out into the wide world, whatever that meant, to do something dramatic and important.

And then came my answer. It was late May and I had just come home for the summer. My mother was outside in the driveway when the mailman came, so I ran to the mailbox with the cutout of the birds and saw the large envelope and tore it open. I had never been so happy in my life, so I did something I had never done. I grabbed my forty-six-year-old mother, and swung her around in her sundress, over and over.

That afternoon I called one of my newer friends from Trinity—we had in mere weeks become "best friends"—to tell him, but instead of being happy for me it was obvious he was not, that he was hurt, but couldn't say as much. At the time I had no idea he was in love with me, because I was that naive, and now his plans for us together had suddenly been smashed.

I soon discovered that not everyone would look positively on what I thought such good news. In the mayor's office one day he mentioned to a visiting colleague I was going to Yale and the man quickly and bitterly mentioned his brother, who had gone there and become so full of himself that he couldn't bear associating with his family. He didn't congratulate me, but rebuked me, sternly implying I would likely turn into an elitist jackass, too.

Since my acceptance at Yale was not effective until January, I thought I should do another semester at Trinity to stay on schedule so I could graduate with my class at Yale in 1984, though why that was so important I am not sure. And my last semester at Trinity was decidedly unpleasant. My classes were wonderful as ever, and the last gasp of the kind of education I would never get at Yale; but everything else was a mess. Because I was going to Yale I changed my plans to live near the friend who had so curiously reacted to my good news and instead found a room on the opposite edge of the campus across the hall from John O'Brien and our friend Joe Massaro. But my own roommates were nightmares and seemed to actively aspire to the pejorative cliche of jocks as beef-witted and inclined toward drunken rape. Meanwhile John and Joe across the hall lived with a character of the sort who gave closeted gays a bad name, being a cross between Clifton Webb's Waldo Lydecker and Jonathan Harris's Dr. Smith. While I hung out with John and Joe, he would eavesdrop and then dish across the hall to the jocks, until one day my roomies confronted me with some things I'd said, threatened me physically, and then expressed their fury at my daring to leave their school for Yale. I was happy the semester was almost over.

And then it was. Over Christmas break Tom didn't call. It seemed he really did think me ungrateful in not reciprocating his affections and decided to move on. I really did care for him and enjoy his company, so it was confusing.

Yale

Like an impatient kid on Christmas morning, I wanted to get to Yale as soon as possible so I arrived the first day students were allowed to, finding myself alone in the vast suite to which I had been assigned. But slowly they arrived. They were all juniors and immediately made me feel more welcome than I could have dreamed. Already that weekend they invited me to join them in Puerto Rico for spring break, since two of them were pre-meds who lived there.[2] And the following weekend they threw me a "coming out" party to introduce me to

---

[2] That Sunday I learned Tante Ella had died. The next morning my father and brother picked me up to drive to the funeral in Queens. My father and I got into an argument when I said Tante Ella was in a better place, and we shouldn't be sad, because didn't we believe going into God's presence was the greatest thing imaginable? But no one we knew saw it that way, and my Polyanna glibness contradicted the grim idea most people I knew seemed to believe, that death was the winner and what did God have to do with it? The only thing to do was fret and feel guilty you weren't dead, or at least behave that way out of common decency.

their friends—advertising it with a cartoon poster of me in a debutante's gown, courtesy of my talented new artist friend Tom Fahsbender.

As the semester began two roommates were cast in the musical *1776*, and they suggested I try out, which I did, being cast as John Hancock. I also was thrilled to begin working on the *Yale Record*, the campus humor magazine. It was as if I suddenly felt born to write comedy and only now was realizing it. And I got a part-time job shelving books in the funereal stacks of Sterling Memorial Library.

But none of my classes excited me especially, and whatever foundations were laid at Trinity were not built upon. I drifted from thinking about the deeper meaning of life until something like the opposite began to happen, as though I were being encouraged to think about the meaninglessness of life, though I hardly realized it.

That first semester I still snuck off to the weekly Christian meetings, but never felt comfortable. But in a phone call with John O'Brien that semester I learned that our genius friend Ian was no longer an atheist, but had become a Christian. I could hardly believe it, but I confirmed that it was indeed true, and it bolstered what flicker of faith I still had.[3] But after spring break, I decided to stop attending the Christian group, yielding to my building repulsion toward them as uncool. I had chosen to trade up and hang with a cooler crowd, mostly of the literary and artsy set.

Soon after this decision, however, I heard Billy Graham was coming to campus. I was hugely excited, though it was his celebrity far more than his theology that attracted me, and if Gerald Ford or Dean Martin had come, I would have been just as excited. But on the evening he was to speak I saw something that knocked me for a decidedly unpleasant loop. I was in the Calhoun dining hall—probably recounting lines from *The Little Rascals*—when I glanced toward the door and saw something I couldn't believe. The twenty or so Christians from the group I had quit were filing into the room, past the unpleasant Cerberus-like Sophie who checked our meal tickets as we entered—and who was with them? It was Billy Graham! They all disappeared into the private Fellows Lounge. I was instantly beside myself with jealousy

---

[3] He is today a professor of theology at Cambridge University.

and remorse, knowing that if I hadn't left that group I would be having dinner with Billy Graham! That was the first and only time I felt I had made a mistake in leaving that group, and of course it was only for a selfish and superficial reason. But it certainly stung.[4]

That evening his talk in Battell Chapel was so packed I was forced to find a seat in the balcony. I went by myself and don't remember anything more than agreeing with whatever he said generally, but his familiarly sonorous voice and cadences made it all somehow distant. At the end when he prayed that we receive Jesus into our hearts I prayed along, just as I had many times watching him—or Pat Robertson or Jim Bakker—on TV, but as with all of those times, nothing magical happened, and that was the end of it. I went back to my world and didn't give it another thought.

---

[4] Indeed it really has never stopped stinging, for although over the decades I tried, I never did meet the great man, although I assuage my feelings by remembering that even Moses himself was not allowed to enter the Promised Land.

CHAPTER SIXTEEN

"Summer of Destiny"

When the semester ended and summer began I still hadn't heard from Tom and gathered I wasn't being invited back for a third summer. But I had moved from wanting to be in politics to wanting to be a writer, whatever that meant. But when I got home that summer and one feckless week turned into two, my father put pressure on me to get a job, eagerly offering to contact our friend Gerry, who had a thriving painting business. I perceived this as a threat, and before that terrible fate should befall me I would look hard at the want ads in the Danbury *News-Times*. One day something fairly leapt out at me. It read: "English Major wanted for writing projects of a philosophical nature. No experience necessary." It also said something about typing and flexible hours. It was obviously a sign from God, and I called immediately. The woman I spoke with—not the "author" himself but someone in his employ—sounded vaguely browbeaten and told me that I could show up the next day at two. But before hanging up, she asked me my date of birth, which I gave her, wondering why she had asked.

The summer of 1982 was an odd juncture. I had four semesters of college behind me, one at Yale, but had no sense what my future held. I cared about ideas and about how those ideas were expressed through art, particularly writing. But what did that mean? My faith was more than ever inchoate. I had some sense of God and the Bible, but had floated away from the real thing toward a vague pop-cultural faith and the idea that I could probably figure out the meaning of life on my own, and was surely on my way toward that, toward something that was more "inclusive" than the parochial Christian faith to which I had been exposed. But I still seemed to believe in what the Bible said about the end of the world, and around that time stumbled across *The 700 Club* on TV and heard Pat Robertson say that this summer was "a Summer of Destiny." He spoke about what the Bible said about the "end times" and the Antichrist and explained that the Beast from the Book of Revelation had ten horns, which almost certainly represented the reconstitution of the Roman Empire, and that it would be the ten nations that now formed the European Union, Greece having just joined to become the tenth a year earlier. The stage was set.

Shortly after this, I was on the phone with one my high school friends, Stacey, who suddenly asked me if I watched David Niven, a national talk show host. I didn't, but knew who he was. "Well," she said, half-giggling, "my mother was watching him the other day and he had a guest on who said that the Antichrist was alive—*and that he was living in Danbury, Connecticut!*" I gulped. What?! That was insane. She said that the guest had said there was an ad declaring as much in the *New York Times,* saying not that he was the Antichrist per se, but that he was the "World Teacher" or something. I found this very creepy, and wondered why he would he have chosen Danbury, Connecticut, of all places. Years before I had heard that the Antichrist was a ten-year-old boy living in India, which was vague enough. But the idea that he was in Danbury was on the one hand preposterous, and on the other deeply horrifying. I changed the subject and put it out of my mind.

But the subject was all the rage then. Hal Lindsey had written his megabestseller *The Late, Great Planet Earth,* which John Tomanio's grandmother had a copy of and which he borrowed and let me glance through. I honestly found it chilling. Ever since *The Omen* with Gregory Peck had come out in 1976, the Antichrist and the number "666" had been part of the cultural wallpaper, but we somehow figured it wouldn't be until the year 2000 that the bad stuff began to go down, and that was so far in the future anyway.

The day after speaking with the "philosophical" author's assistant I drove to the address in what I thought a strange part of Danbury, where the houses were worn down and depressing. Being there was like being in a dream. Why had I never seen this neighborhood before? The house itself was bizarrely squat and its roof was made of something like foam rubber, giving the whole thing the appearance of a mushroom house in which gnomes dwelt. I parked my parents' black Ford Granada and went down the side of the house along a chain link fence to what I presumed was the entrance and knocked. A woman let me in and told me to wait in the small hallway, but as I was waiting I was shocked to see a young woman I recognized from Trinity. I'd never spoken with her, but knew her brother. They lived in the neighboring town of Ridgefield. It really was like a dream. Evidently she was already in this man's employ, but seemed curiously unable to talk and was xeroxing something. But a moment before the other woman summoned me to meet the "author," the young woman looked at me earnestly and with the half-twirl of her index finger toward her temple mouthed: "He's crazy."

At last the man appeared. He looked and sounded like Carl Sagan, with similarly longish dark hair and a tan turtleneck and a kind of glum seriousness. I was led down a couple of steps through a narrow, low hallway into a small, circular, low room with a round table at its center. He said he would be right back. There was a large Egyptian bas-relief and bookcases lining the walls, whose titles I quickly scanned. They were all of a curiously mythological bent. I began to wonder what I had stumbled into.

After what seemed a long time the man returned and sat down. He asked again when I was born and was looking at what I guessed were astrological charts. I remember that the ensuing conversation made me uncomfortable.

But this was only the beginning. The trouble began when I politely asked him what exactly he did. I was still eighteen and very unsure of myself, but I at least finally thought I should clear through the fog. But my question seemed too much. He stared off into space and sighed, as though fatigued at having to answer this. Still looking away, he finally said: "Some people say that I am the Messiah ..." *Eh?* If I had been drinking a beverage I would have involuntarily spit it across the room, as is sometimes done for comic emphasis. But there was nothing funny about this. Suddenly my mind was gasping to keep up with what I had just heard. First of all, had I even heard correctly? But I knew I had. And when I took it in I suddenly began to do something I had never done before: I feared for my life. Who was this madman a few feet from me and how had I come to be here with him in his strange house? And then the bombshell. He casually remarked that some of his "friends" had taken out a full-page in the *New York Times* declaring this fact, and instantly I remembered what Stacey had said to me on the phone a week or two earlier. When he said this it was as if a five-thousand-ton vault door had just chunked shut. I don't know what else he said or whether he even said anything else because I was suddenly seriously weighing whether I should find a heavy object and brain this fiend and run for my life. In that moment I very sincerely believed I was probably sitting in the presence of the Antichrist, so there is no way I can do justice to my mental activity at this point. If this man had in fact declared himself to be the Messiah, or perhaps his friends had jumped the gun in taking out the ad but he would himself soon enough do so, then of course he was not the Messiah at all—or to use the Greek word for Messiah, the *Christ*—but was in point of fact the false version of that, which is to say the antithesis of that. Did the fact that I understood this mean that God had brought me here for this purpose? Though suddenly choking with confusion and fear, I tried to appear calm, but my brain was flapping around the room desperately, like a bird trapped in a garage. But surely it wasn't so simple as my being able to help mankind avoid the terrible prophecies in the Book of Revelation by dispatching this queer goose with an ashtray or paperweight, and inasmuch as I had never before felt myself at the center of world history, I had never before imagined myself capable of killing a human being, if human being this was. But as the milliseconds passed slowly, affording me every option of action, I considered it. What if I could bludgeon the Ancient Serpent once and forever, and had been chosen by God to do such a thing? Would I shrink from it? I could not. But had I indeed been chosen by God for this? Wouldn't I have to be more clever than that, more subtle than the arch-Serpent himself was said to be? Wouldn't I somehow have to match wits with th' eternal Foe, to play my part and represent God's interests in this everlasting battle now come to this historical head—and then leave the results in God's hands? Wouldn't I better play dumb and see how this chess game played out over the weeks ahead?

Nonetheless, my vague presentiments of playing a principal role in the cataclysm of the End of Days was at last coming true. I it was who should have to do battle with the forces of evil now concentrated in this devil in the beige turtleneck. It all made sense. Why had my parents settled in this part of the world, and why was I now in this very room? But the "author" then left again and my mind continued whirling about, as though here in this circular book-lined room with the terra cotta plinth of some ancient deity I was myself playing out the Last Battle on the Plains of Megiddo. This man would try to tempt me with the kingdoms of this world, with wealth untold, but I would resist. In any event, the conversation didn't go much beyond this. He returned and said something about how he thought I would work out and we could start soon. So our meeting was over for now. But I knew we would meet again to continue the prophesied drama.

But when at last I was allowed egress from that nightmare house I felt like a prisoner freed, like Injun Joe scampering away from the Cuckoo's Nest, only much, much faster. I could again breathe the air of the Outer World, could drink in the colors of nature! I was Scrooge on Christmas morning. But not quite. I was still scared to death, so I got into my parents' Ford and like a man in a movie escaping from approaching webby creatures I turned the ignition, yanked the shift to "D," and blasted out of there like a madman until finally I was far enough away that I felt I could slow down. But even then I was half out of my mind, so I drove and drove around Danbury's back roads, wondering what I was to do, wondering why God had chosen me for this inestimable honor.

When I got home I of course tried to explain the story to my mother. But she only scoffed: "You must be kidding!" It was just like in those movies, where no one believed you—and then they all ended up being witches too! So then I called up George Duncan, who I knew would be more open to what I was saying, who knew what the Bible said was real. But actually George wasn't sure how to respond. But he said that Larry Carew—who headed up the "Community" and was an intelligent theologian and Catholic priest—would know, and I should talk to him. I could come over in an hour, and Larry should be there. In the meantime I called John Tomanio and told him the story too, but he seemed more amused and humoring me than actually concerned.

When I finally saw George and Father Larry I was hugely relieved and told them and their friend Karen the whole disagreeable story. At some point Larry laughed in a gentle, pastoral way. "Oh, yes," he said. "I know who you're taking about." I was stunned. Larry explained that he had some dealings with the man, who was a troubled and sad soul, but was essentially harmless. He was sure that I shouldn't worry about it. To have a man who knew and believed the Bible as Larry did say these things was tremendously comforting, but it was also a strange letdown to realize I was no longer at the center of history.

Larry advised me to avoid the trouble of working for this man, which I was only too happy to agree to. But what then would I do that summer? It didn't take me long to realize, and I now sheepishly told my father that if Gerry Efthimiatos still needed help, I was available. So I spent the summer of 1982 neither working for the mayor, nor the Antichrist, but perhaps having an even stranger experience than if I had.

CHAPTER SEVENTEEN

National Socialism in Danbury

W hen we first arrived in Danbury, my father became instant friends with a fellow Cephalonian. Gerry Efthimiatos was six feet tall, with a full head of thick black hair and a robust black mustache, strongly suggesting Omar Sharif. It was to Gerry I would report that Monday for work. I was to be at the Olympic Flame diner at seven. Horrors. My mother dropped me off in my white T-shirt and jeans and work boots and I entered self-consciously, looking fifteen years old and strikingly untried in the field of manual labor. Most of the men in the diner were fueling up for a day of carpentry or plumbing and making me feel like a carpetbagger walking into an Old West saloon. In a booth in the back I saw Gerry, who like many tradesmen relegated excessive emotion to the province of women. He was careful not to be too loudly welcoming, and bade me sit across from him and ordered me a coffee. Over the days ahead I learned that he always pushed coffee on his employees, hoping to goose their productivity. I didn't want anything else but that morning Gerry began a habit of ordering himself buttered wheat toast with grape jelly which he never touched but always pushed in front of me, and which I ate. Gerry's three principal employees showed up momentarily, and to describe them must stretch the reader's credulity, though if there is any distortion in what I say it is in my painting them as less eccentric than they actually were.

Ollie entered first, sliding next to me in the booth across from Gerry. Gerry's standard greeting was "Mornee', mornee,'" delivered in a dull-lidded way calculated to be both gruff and yet not entirely unwelcoming, and mostly to communicate that working-class cynicism that this is one more morning like all the others and we cannot pretend it is good, because we know it to be just another in an endless procession of mornings in which we must get up before we would like and show up to do work we would prefer not to but here we are and there you have it. Toward the end of summer he sometimes jokingly literalized the implication, saying, "Money, money."

Gerry's cynicism was not unpleasant, in part owing to his unavoidably good heart. His hardness seemed a necessary balance to his deeper instinct to be overly generous, which he often was. I knew from my father of Gerry's brutal upbringing by his violent and alcoholic father in a coastal section of Cephalonia that was impossible to reach except by donkey. Indeed we understood that his father had beaten his mother to death, but was never prosecuted, and on my trips to Cephalonia I saw this withered old fellow and shuddered. But Gerry now ran a thriving painting business in which he was awarded one large contract after another to paint entire condo complexes, many of which were blooming in the newly booming Reagan economy.

Ollie—along with Alex and Anna, the Hungarian couple about whom more in a moment—formed the generally dependable trio of Gerry's stable of employees. There were others who came and went, but these three were the stalwarts. Ollie was a redneck and racist of the type that exist in profusion in those parts of Connecticut without country clubs. But to me he was a known type, though Ollie—whom Alex always mocked as "Oliver"—also affected a distinct cowboy persona. He looked the part generally, like a rummy in a Western, being slim and small. He was likely in his fifties but had the wizened look of someone two decades older. He was also an inveterate gambler who one day pulled a worn paperback from his back pocket, titled *Gambling to Win*. "People will spend all kinds of money gambling," he said, "but they won't take the trouble to read a book you can get for two bucks." Whenever he got enough money Ollie disappeared to Atlantic City to make merry. His estranged wife and eight kids lived on welfare and I guessed his own family's parallels with many of Danbury's poorest blacks contributed to his racism, and he clung to the idea that, low as he was, he was still somehow better than "them n******s."

Ollie's cowboy hat was so vital to his created persona that he never took it off—save once, which proved the point of not doing it more often. His pate had just a few hairs, and as I beheld him, I suddenly saw him for the sorry old man he was. He never took off his high-heeled cowboy boots, carrying and climbing tall ladders with them, and I was even once horrified to see him walking up a steep tar-shingled roof in them. But his love of the cowboy world went further. I heard him boast about a station wagon he once owned to whose grill he had bolted an actual pair of Texas longhorns. He had also covered the side panels with fake snakeskin contact paper and glued to each of the two front doors a holster with a silver toy pistol. "The cops didn't like that," he said with a grin. Ollie was the sort who, if someone asked whether he was staying out of trouble would proudly answer: "Not if I can help it."

But even Ollie could not begin to compete for eccentricity with the couple who formed the heart of Gerry's batting order. At three and four in this thinner-and-varnish Murderers' Row were Alex and Anna, a Hungarian couple who were industrial-strength workhorses of the rarest kind, and who were generally unimaginable. To begin with, I had never in my life allowed the possibility of a married couple as painting partners, but here they were, to challenge my ossified ideas about many things, as we shall see. Alex was then forty-nine and wore an unfashionable handlebar mustache that seemed a nod to the European soldiers of the First War. His perpetually squinty mien and usually darkly tanned face always made me think of a cat forced to wear a doll's bonnet, wearing a similarly uncomfortably pinched face. Being from Hungary, Alex had an accent that sounded very much like his countryman Bela Lugosi. It was every bit as mysterious and sly, though choppier and more matter-of-fact, without the drawn-out syllables. But we have not yet mentioned the golden key to his deepest identity: Alex was a dedicated National Socialist. A few weeks after I first met him he showed me in his garage a smart-looking and nicely varnished wooden swastika that he had made, displayed next to a handsome framed portrait of *der Führer*. Would my Yale friends believe this?

Alex's wife, Anna, was ten years his senior, and had the look of a pear-shaped twelfth-century peasant from the Russian Steppe, with a face wrinkled beyond her years and horned hands with which, had tools been unavailable, she might have dug a moat. Often she struck me as prehistoric, bearing no small resemblance to a Triceratops. She did not talk as much as scowl bitterly, and though the two of them often worked side by side they were perpetually at each other's throats, with regular threats of physical violence on both sides. Anna was the more foul-mouthed, having picked up her patois on construction sites they frequented, and I often felt sorry for her, until she did or said something especially foul, as when she eschewed walking to a bathroom for the simpler solution of scrounging an old coffee can and using it to do her business just out of sight.

The first time I connected with Alex I was on my knees painting the lower part of the railing of an outdoor balcony of a condo in Bethel, not far from our home. Alex had crept up behind me and silently watched my efforts. I was doing my best to draw my brush along the two-by-six that formed the bottom part of the railing. One must load one's brush with paint and then apply it horizontally steadily and evenly to cover the wide side of the board facing outward without slipping slightly upward and getting paint on the two-inch top. Alex revealed himself of a sudden, saying: "You paint pretty good!" He often stood arms akimbo and did so now. And then, without missing a beat, as though it flowed logically, he said: "Hitler was a painter!" I was still kneeling in that heat, trying to draw the paint along evenly when this registered. *What?* What the hell was I to make of this statement? I didn't yet know Alex was a dedicated Nazi, and said nothing. But Alex continued. "He was a great painter! Maybe the best!" You could never tell entirely when Alex was being serious. I soon learned that everything he said had a provocative and often humorous edge.

Alex gave the impression that he too was a soldier from the Great War, and it took me a while to fathom that his dedication to National Socialism and Hitler were genuine. When he discovered I was only half Greek and that my mother was from Germany, he nearly kissed me. In fact he was so beside himself that he might—like Hitler in that doctored newsreel—have danced a jig for joy. In fact he was so pleased with my Aryan lineage that he thenceforth referred to *der Führer* as "your grandfather," not understanding that this irked me no small amount, as my German grandfather had despised the Nazis and was killed wearing a German uniform against his will. I didn't bother trying to communicate this to Alex, for whom the whole thing seemed simultaneously a deadly earnest belief and a childish game.

For example, he would sometimes use his stain brush to paint swastikas—what he inevitably called "de mark of Zorro!"—in surprising spots. There was also sometimes something menacing about Alex, and remembering his face and mustache I think of Bill the Butcher from Scorsese's *Gangs of New York*. But Alex was also so entertaining that in the painful boredom of that summer I found myself longing to be around him, knowing he would almost certainly say something hilarious. But what choice did I have in what he said or whether I heard it? And the idea that the working classes in Danbury were capable of racist cracks was hardly foreign to me. But when early that summer the local paper reported on the plans for a KKK rally in town I thought it preposterous. And the local paper, hungry for something smacking of actual news, reported on the "developments" with gusto.

My first introduction to Anna was when we exited the diner one morning and Gerry said to me: "Eric, you go to Riverbend!" I walked with Alex and Anna to their station wagon, the back of which was filled with rags and cans and putty knives and screwdrivers and box cutters and anything else one might need in their line of work. It was dirty but orderly. There was an incongruous Cadbury yellow and purple Easter chocolate box in which they stored Brillo pads, and there were the coffee cans with brushes. Anna once croaked to Alex, "Gimme one of dem brushes—and don't give me one of dat Phyllis Dillers!" Evidently that was the name for old paint brushes whose bristles were splayed out, due to their resemblance to the outlandish wigs worn by the comedienne. I had no idea as I stood there that a few months hence I would in the different environs of a Yale College Master's Tea meet Mrs. Diller herself, who was the guest of honor. I was agog to do so and did not have the courage to tell her of her fame in the painting industry, but was surprised to see how diminutive she was and how, apart from the trappings of her stage persona—the wild muumuus, crazy wigs, cigarette holder, silver or golden lame gloves, and matching slippers with elfin curved toes—she was attractive and sweet. Her own blonde hair was that afternoon done tastefully in a small braid that crowned her head in a circle. She said a few things about how the more she traveled the more she admired America, a daring thing to say in the budding PC environment of Yale. "You can't believe how dirty some of these places are!" she said, fueling the fire.

The Master's Teas in Calhoun College at Yale were often worth attending. That year I also got to hear Vincent Price, who said he particularly enjoyed his star cameo as the villainous "Egghead" on the sixties *Batman* series, using words like "Egg-cellent!" and "Egg-zasperating!" He also said while a student at Yale in the thirties he had been on the *Yale Record*, in the heyday of the magazine to which we current-day *Record* folks always looked back longingly. I knew him then only as "Egghead" and as Count Sfoza in one of my favorite episodes of *F Troop*—whom Corporal Agarn thought had turned Captain Parmenter into a chicken—and as the star of a few horror films I had seen on TV, most notably *House on Haunted Hill*, which along with *Horror Hotel* were the only films I had seen on TV that genuinely frightened me.

But I was far from Yale as I drove with Anna and Alex to the bleak condo complex called Riverbend on Route Six. It was painted gray and nestled amidst trees in a vale through which Danbury's Still River ran, with nothing by way of sunlit views. Nor was I even there to paint, but to sand and then stain the hundreds of doors to be used throughout the many units of the complex. Alex went off to do something requiring skill—like actually paint—while Anna and I were relegated to the Stygian darkness of the basement, where the raw doors were stored. Each must be sanded on both sides, which was done with a sanding pole to whose end was affixed a metal "shoe" that held the sandpaper. Up and down and up and down on both sides of the door. This took days, after which we moved to the almost-more-exciting step of staining them on both sides. The mere prospect of something different, like staining, held the same enticement as does, say, reaching one hundred and two hundred and three hundred, while counting to a thousand. The number is really no different than those preceding it, but the merest suggestion of difference in the monotony seems ever so slightly to pull one forward.

I was trusted to do both these things, but when it was time to varnish the doors, it would be Alex who was given the honor. Varnishing was much more difficult, and he was the top man on Gerry's team. I soon noticed that Alex was missing two fingers on his right hand—the one he used to hold the paintbrush— and never asked what gruesome accident had resulted in this maiming, though later that summer Anna told me it happened years ago, when he was working in a factory.

I remember a conversation with Alex, before I understood the depth of his antisemitism, and before I discovered his comedic genius. I had rather out of the blue asked him if he believed in God. The question caught him unawares and I could see him struggling to answer it, not yet having established enough rapport with me to kick it away with a joke. "I dunno, Erriko," he said. "Maybe he's up there hiding, maybe behind de clouds ..." It was a rare moment of vulnerability and sadness from him, one that couldn't help indicate some sliver of otherwise invisible wistfulness, though I never saw its kind again.

Over the weeks I sometimes found Alex brilliantly funny. His vicious bickering with Anna was inevitably entertaining, and he sometimes would punctuate a point by pulling back his hand as if to strike her, with perfect comic timing pretending to catch himself as he did this, and then quickly withdrawing it, lest any had seen, which of course, we all had. "Anna," he would sometimes say, "why you not jest *shad*-dap?"—always putting the emphasis on the first syllable. She would often respond with something so vulgar I won't repeat it. Other times Alex said things that perhaps only I found funny. "Anna," he would say, apropos of nothing, "you look like a woodchuck." He also usually referred to the conjugal act as "making de woodpecker."

As much as he purported to hate Jews, Alex reveled in every and any ethnic stereotype he could find. Playing to the idea that Italians were dirty, he referred to every bathroom we painted as "Ee-ta-lian Keetchen!" Once, when someone remarked on having used a five-gallon plastic bucket as a temporary bathroom, Alex said, "Dat's mee-dget Ee-tah-lian keet-chen!" He then went on a rant about how the tapers—whose job it was to plaster over the gaps between the sheetrock—were the guiltiest of using these buckets as bathrooms, and once they had finished, would cover the bucket and forget about, moving to another construction site. Alex complained about coming upon the calling cards of these men. "Some time you open up one of dem buckets and *pah!* Right inna face!" He now grimaced so persuasively that he might have given Redd Foxx lessons. And then, for punctuation, waved his hand in disgust: "De tapers are de worst!"

In his ability to turn someone into a comic prop, Alex was a *nonpareil*. Once, when an older man happened by, Alex was stirring a large can of latex paint. When the man was not quite out of earshot, Alex gestured to the bucket and shouted, "Hey, Pop! Wanna drink?!" The man didn't know what to make of this—had he heard right?—and simply kept walking. The paint in the can was old—which necessitated its being stirred—and Alex peeled a long ring of congealed latex from the rim. He showed it to me and said, "Here, Eric. Why you not give it to dat old goat to chew on it?" Once we were painting the eaves of the roof at a country club in Wilton, lying on the hot shingles and hanging over to do so. When a pretty girl passed below Alex meowed loudly, so that she likely heard it, but had no idea whence it came. It reminded me of Groucho doing the same in *Duck Soup*, except Alex only did it to convey the degrading word to which men like him reduced women. I was embarrassed and annoyed, but had to suppress a laugh. Once we were talking about what we drank with our meals and I said I usually drank milk. "I not can dreenk milk," Alex said in his Bela Lugosi voice ... and then by way of explanation smiled and said, "If I dreenk too much milk, my legs gettin' curly."

And yet this man who entertained me was a full-on anti-Semite, so much so that whatever he didn't like was by definition somehow "Jewish." If he disliked an Italian he would say "Dat's a Guinea Jew!" As for the few Arabs we came across that summer, instead of liking them because of what he might have projected as a shared antisemitism, he bore them ill will too, insisting by way of explanation that they were "cousins with the Jews!" And Anna backed him up on that. "Dey are cousins!" she croaked.

As horrific as some of the things I heard that summer, I almost felt a sense of relief to be surrounded by run-of-the-mill madmen, rather than being in the palpably dark presence of that frightening being in the beige turtleneck, who fancied himself the soon-to-be-revealed Messiah of the world. I rarely thought of him, but now and again John Tomanio or his sister Susan would joke with me by asking whether I'd seen "the Antichrist" lately. But even their teasing was a hugely welcome respite from the dead seriousness and horror of a few weeks before.

A significant part of this painting world was the arrival and departure now and again of other characters, most of them even less rooted and grounded than Ollie. Among these was one Jimmy Lawlor, an undertaker's assistant who himself looked remarkably like a corpse, or like someone who spent a lot of time in their silent company. When the undertaking business was temporarily in the hole, as the standard joke went, Jimmy would suddenly appear looking for paint work. He was tall and rangy, and his face was long and gray, giving him a Frankensteinian air, and I imagined that he now and again may have quaffed a draught of varnish to prophylactically mummify himself against the inevitable future. His long, pendant arms and large hands completed the menacing, funereal picture.

There were also characters who came and went and never returned, one example of which was a dapper and almost courtly fellow in his fifties named Robert. He bore a sad air of lost nobility and would not go by "Rob" or—God forbid—"Bob." Even his bearing and appearance seemed to insist on "Robert." His van dyke beard was neatly trimmed and he wore canvas boating sneakers he might have picked up in Gay Head or Bar Harbor, and rolled the cuffs of his trousers halfway up his calves, never getting a drop of paint on them, and probably knowing the line from "The Love Song of Alfred J. Prufrock" about rolled trousers. Somehow they even hung nicely, a kind of rebuke to the rough working-class clothes of everyone else. But what was he doing here, this thinner and younger Monty Woolley? He had nothing to say to Alex or Gerry, whom he must have thought beneath his dignity, or perhaps it was they who had pushed him away first by signaling they were not buying his act. Alex mockingly referred to him as "Roberto" and, in some instances, as "Roberto Clemente." But when Robert discovered I attended Yale and was a more reasonable chap than these others, he was willing to parlay with me.

We would each morning pick him up at the Hotel Belvedere, which when it opened in 1909 must have been the bee's knees, but was now a vagrant's hotel. It too had an air of lost dignity, tucked behind Danbury's once-bustling Main Street, and that this decrepitating heap should still be operating shocked me. After a week or so we fell into a conversation in which Robert explained to me that he rose at precisely five each morning, rain or shine, and dressed and made his way down to the venerable bar in the lobby of the hotel. "I have three beers for breakfast," he said, "but that's it." He drew his hand horizontally through the air for emphasis. He seemed to think telling a nineteen-year-old innocent that he drank his breakfast at a bar early each morning and limited himself to three beers would make him a model of moderation—or of *Sophrosyne*, as Plato and before him Heraclitus and Homer would have put it. I was of course thunderstruck at this admission, but did not feel I had permission to sputter a response, so I simply nodded, as though his self-restraint were manifestly admirable. He also volunteered to me that he didn't need to work and didn't need the money, that he had holdings of some kind in Alaska, where his daughter lived. He said he just wanted something to do.

One day he aired with me a grievance against Gerry, who complained that Robert disappeared now and again. Perhaps Gerry suspected him of taking a bolstering nip? But Robert thought I should know the truth. "I generally have a B.M. about mid-morning," he explained to me, "around ten." I was confused.

"A what?" I asked, not sure what he had said.

"A B.M.," he repeated. I had no idea what that was.

"What's that?" I asked, a bit sheepishly.

"A bowel movement," he said, embarrassed to have to pronounce the words. But even these words were not something I had ever heard, though I intuited their meaning. Gerry obviously felt Robert spent too much time "indisposed" and sometimes made mention of it. Of course I defended Robert, as in my naivete I defended almost anyone. But if Gerry thought someone was not pulling his weight, that person would eventually disappear, as Robert soon did.

Then there was Bruno, a squat French-Canadian carpenter whose glasses and eyes made me think of Jean-Paul Sartre. But Alex and Anna immediately explained that Bruno was their sworn enemy, though I was unable to discover why. It seemed to be a feud that stretched back eons, into the primordial swamps. Anna explained, "de carpenters are always fight wit de painters!" It was a fixity in the universe, and to question it was like saying the law of gravity was stupid. So it was an inescapable fact that they hated him and must do so. The wily Alex was therefore always looking for ways to cause Bruno grief, and by way of illustration, told me how he had once "screwed" his foe by driving a nail into one of the lower stairs of a staircase that Bruno was using. It protruded just enough so that Bruno stubbed the toe of his boot on it and flew headlong to the unyielding ground. I grimaced uncomfortably at what to me looked like sadism, but this was for Alex a great victory in their never-ending battle, though from all I could see, he was the only combatant. Alex also boasted of once having come upon a long wooden measuring stick Bruno used in his work, quickly using his stain brush to cover it with swastikas. Alex delighted in now and again putting "de mark of Zorro" where he could, including, he once told me, on the undersides of some picnic tables at the "Singing Oaks" children's camp, one of whose T-shirts he sometimes wore on the job, with an incongruous, happy cartoon image of anthropomorphized oak trees singing.

Despite all else—of which there was plenty—there was a certain bonhomie among these characters, in their playful and not-so-playful rivalries. It was something that a few years hence I would remember while reading of the childlike *paisanos* in John Steinbeck's *Tortilla Flat*. I also saw in them bizarre cognates to the characters from *The Wind in the Willows*. But one day as we sat outside at that condo in Bethel, their back-and-forth manifested itself in a darker way. During a lunch break Alex and Ollie took to a friendly enough conversation in which they each put forth their considered views on "Who's worse, n*****s or Jews?" Each had since time immemorial staked out his ground on this vitally important question, but in their closing arguments, whatever limpest wisp of dignity Ollie still clung to was made plain enough when he declared, as a kind of final trump card they surely must all agree on: "Well, my ancestors owned n*****s—and I'll be darned if I'm ever gonna work for *them!*" Such lineage was likely wishful thinking on Ollie's part, but the implication was of course that under some circumstances he might envision himself having to set his fine principles aside to work for Jews, but to do so for blacks would always be a bridge too far. Therefore, all other considerations being equal, he still considered them worse. But before they parted, Alex felt it necessary to dissent sharply. "No way!" he said, forcefully and somewhat angrily. "Jews are de worst!" And there it was, a kind of detente, so that even in their ongoing disagreement, they bore one another enough respect that they could leave things here for now and part with some measure of decorum. I was stunned, as though I had been a silent witness at Appomattox. And again I wondered whether I could share these dyspeptic scenes with my friends at Yale.

Much of that summer I was alone, doing jobs of agonizing drudgery. Sometimes Gerry would hand me a jar of spackle and send me to some units in a condo complex, which seemed the equivalent of the warden putting you in the "hole" for a few days. I would be—for what seemed an unending and seamless brake of minutes blurring to hours—mostly on my unpadded knees, where with my fingers I put a tiny toothpaste amount of spackle into every single nail hole in all of the woodwork in the unit, so that once it was painted you wouldn't see those indentations. Every baseboard along every wall—closets included—must be thus spackled. And every window, meaning the holes in the molding surrounding the window and then every nail hole in the window itself and every door jamb, meaning the molding around *both* sides of the door and then every nail hole in the jambed interior. The closets were the worst of it and every one—but especially the large walk-in closets—took the wind out of my sails as the horse latitudes did for nineteenth-century sailors. I would be on my knees moving along the baseboard at a fair enough clip, just enough to give myself the feeling of some progress—with which of course came the barest modicum of hope that my ignoble estate was not eternal. But then the hitherto hidden interior of a closet bloomed before me, like the open mouth of a sperm whale upon the limitless sea. I was so focused on the horizontal baseboard I had forgotten there were other dimensions, that the possibility of such things as closets existed. And my dull progress around the room was interrupted such that I now had to disappear into the closet's as yet unlighted interior, spackling the baseboard inside the closet, along with the other considerable woodwork therein, such as the wooden brackets for shelves and clothing rods. By the time I emerged from the closet I felt a week older and realized I hadn't finished the room—which I'd seemed well on my way to finishing before I had disappeared into the closet—and whatever momentum I had before being swallowed by the hungry closet had vanished. I was suddenly Jonah, vomited onto dry land among a people he had always hoped to avoid; and now I must face the sinful Ninevites after all.

The drudgery of this job was its worst aspect, and a few times that summer Gerry would remind me I should make sure I studied hard when I went back "to the college, eh?" The implication being that I would otherwise forever be trapped in this circle of Gehenna like these other lost souls. He seemed to know better than I did that this was an anomaly for me, that I was a fish only temporarily out of water and would be returning to my happy liquid home soon enough.

One of the last weeks of the summer Gerry decided to send me to do another kind of job. There was an old three-story house in Danbury that Gerry and some others had bought, wanting to turn it into condo units. But in the summer of 1982, before it could be reconstructed, the interior needed demolishing and gutting. Gerry thought he might dispatch me here for a few days, and at four dollars an hour it was a good deal from his side, as I soon discovered demolition was the most physically difficult of anything I had ever done. The sharp and rusted metalwork and old wiring and broken glass made it dangerous too.

But it was the physical exertion that got me. No one knows the unyielding permanence of things until he is directed to break them apart and then shovel them into five-gallon cans. But with sledgehammers and miners' picks and shovels a gang of us, none of whom I knew outside that week, threw ourselves wholly into this project of demolishing anything there was to demolish, including bathrooms of infinitely heavy old tubs and porcelain tiles, an entire house's worth of plastered lath, and even one massive brick chimney. The childlike joy I initially experienced in being invited to break this chimney apart with a sledgehammer instantly exploded away from me into the surrounding atmosphere when my best youthful crack at this petrified ochre dinosaur's turd produced no movement of bricks at all, but rather the contra-distinctive rebuke of a painful sting through the lithe timber of the sledgehammer to my untried hands and arms. Only a few more of such youthfully hopeful but humblingly useless swings led to the near-instant development upon my writer's hands of blisters.

But once something was sufficiently fractured, we shoveled it into buckets and then carried the nearly permanently arm-lengtheningly heavy buckets two at a time toward the dumpster positioned outside one of the demolished windows, although not near enough that one could avoid walking across a makeshift bridge of twin two-by-tens that bowed politely and frighteningly under the weight of us and our barely bearably heavy cargo. I cannot remember ever counting the hours and days as I counted them that week. And in case it was lost on me, I remembered that I was a half-mile from City Hall where, an eternal year earlier I had been wearing a blue blazer and a rep tie in the air-conditioned offices of the mayor, who had tasked me with creating a scrapbook of his triumphs from piles of saved newspapers, and at twice what I was now making too.

And yet there was something about this summer that I couldn't help preferring to the effete and coddled universe of the previous two. Having looked up to such men as my father and my Uncle Joe and Mr. Tomanio, who had not been above the hardest of hard work, it felt somehow honorable and good to be filthy with sawdust and brick dust and perspiration and the honesty of a hard day's work. I did not wish to choose it forever, but the dignity of it was a consolation.

But one Monday morning, as I sat down at our booth at the Olympic Flame, I got a genuine surprise. "Did you go yesterday?" Alex asked Ollie.

"Yeah," Ollie said, sheepishly. "I went."

"Did they frisk you?"

"Yep." I soon gathered that my colleagues had both the day before attended the KKK "gathering," which had finally occurred and which by the end of summer had been downgraded to what sounded like a picnic of losers on someone's private property. Still, I was hornswoggled. Again, would my friends at Yale believe this?

The last few weeks that summer I went to different sites than Alex and I missed his company, which made the miserable work go much faster. I also realized that despite the horror of his offensive views, I had developed an affection for him, naively thinking him mostly and merely misguided, only needing to see the illogic of some of his positions. So while I was away from him, I daydreamed about helping him see the errors in his thinking. My corrections fell along the following lines. First, all of Alex's posturing against the Jews seemed to assume an insurmountable divide between Jews and Christians, not that he considered himself a devoted Christian, but perhaps he sloppily thought of himself as a cultural Christian, and I could work with that if he did. And my plan was to tell him that the leader of the Christian religion—Jesus—was himself a devout Jew. And all of his followers were Jews. Even his mother—whom the Greeks half-pretended was Greek and their own personal deity, whom they called the *Theotokos*, and whom the Italians half-pretended was Italian, as "La Madonna"—was clearly and indisputably Jewish. So the idea that the "Jews" could be the enemy meant that one misunderstood everything. But in my daydream conversation with Alex I would then pull out my second and more important point, and the very trump card that would itself be revealed at the last trump—that the God of the Christians was a God of love, to the extreme point of having commanded us to "love our enemies." So if it was true that the Jews were somehow anyone's enemies, as Alex seemed to think they were, Jesus had commanded us not to hate them but to love them. What would Alex have to say about that? How could he argue with it?

Not many days later I would find out. He must have known I would soon be rejoining the ranks of Yale students, because there was a sudden urgency in his approach toward me and the issues central to his thinking. If he were to complete his plans for the summer, he must convert me soon. I had never been aware of any such plans, and of course I had been hoping I might convert him. But mightn't I? In any case, there was something different about him now. He was not as friendly and devil-may-care as before and when I eventually brought up how we Christians worshipped a Jew—and then said we were commanded to love our enemies—he did not warm to my theme. I was somewhat surprised and sad to see that the indisputable logic of my points meant nothing to him. In fact, he lightly mocked my Christian faith, which obviously made him uncomfortable, and at some point later in the day as I approached him, he greeted me with "Here comes Preacher Bob!" It was as if suddenly we two who had been friends over the summer were no longer friends and I, being young and sensitive, was slightly hurt. I was fond of this maniac and foolishly hoped he might be open to a real conversation.

But the next day I was in for a richer surprise. He appeared at the construction site with something he thought I would be interested in. It was a "privately published" book bearing the title *World Conquerors*. On its crude black-and-white cover was the ill-drawn image of a globe being choked by a large serpent representing "World Jewry." He pressed it into my hands, singing its praises. Of course I would not take it home, much less read it. But he was sure it was just what the doctor had ordered. "Believe me, Erriko," he said, serious and joking at the same time, "You read dat book, and you gonna kill three, four Jews a day!" I don't remember anything after that.

I don't even recall how I gave the book back to him and broke it to him that I wouldn't read it. And we never said goodbye. I could not help seeing it as a sad ending. I have often been naively hopeful about people, but I knew that there was something lovable in this human being because in my own way I had loved him a little bit, had seen the sliver of him that still might be open to truth and to the love of God, and I wished I might have had the time to speak to that part of him eventually, and perhaps see it grow. But of course, I didn't.

CHAPTER EIGHTEEN

The Meaning of Meaning

Fall 1982

My Yale friends fell roughly into three groups. First there were my roommates, such as Tom Fahsbender and Ken Hewes-Manapol and his girlfriend, Elizabeth Renker, who became one of my dearest friends, and David Lee, whose brother Spike was at NYU film school. Loosely in this circle too was Adam Liptak, though he connected me to yet another group of literarily inclined folks, and then there were of course my friends from the *Yale Record*.[1]

---

[1] The *Yale Record*, founded in 1872, is the nation's oldest college humor magazine, although by the time I became involved with it, it had lost whatever cache it once had, recently even having been defunct before it was discovered and then resurrected by a small group of friends in my residential college, including Chris Hanes, to whom I eventually became closest, and who was a blond economics major from Atlanta. As part of my initiation to the *Record*, he and his roommates Richard and Todd often told me stories of what had transpired in previous semesters, to catch me up, so to speak. My favorite concerned what Chris called "The Blinky Light."

In most stories he tells, Chris usually casts himself in the role of a character from an Evelyn Waugh or P.G. Wodehouse novel, and this story is no exception. As the story went, Chris and Richard and Todd, who became the nucleus of the *Yale Record*, were assigned as freshmen to a suite on the Old Campus, and the day they moved and met each other they also met the fourth suitemate, Jonathan, who without asking if there was any objection immediately affixed to the living room wall a huge timeline poster illustrating the bloodline of the Messiah—Jesus—extending all the way back to King David and then back to Abraham. This would have been a bad move under any circumstances, but Richard and Todd were Jewish. But Jonathan was famously insensitive to such nuances and was the sort of lampoon-ripe evangelical of whom Ned Flanders was but a type and shadow. He had a clipped and imperious way of expressing himself and cut his own hair, whose wavy strands puffed out in an unattractive sandy wedge that, though his hair was not thinning, nonetheless gave the unfortunate appearance of a comb-over. He and a number of other students in Calhoun formed what Chris and others derisively called the "God Squad," though even in this "uncool" group Jonathan stood out as the oddnik at whom even the others in the group rolled their eyes, and of course was their most outspoken and visible member, but as they were genuine Christians they did all they could to show him grace and patience. Chris Hanes, however, did not feel himself under the same obligation. Chris hailed from Atlanta and went to a Christian school called Westminster Academy, where he'd had his fill of evangelical eccentricity, and finding Jonathan assigned to his suite made it seem almost as though the petty God Chris didn't believe in had burst into being just long enough to get Chris's goat by monkeying with the freshman room assignments. One night near midnight, Chris returned from the library to find a priest in vestments administering communion on their coffee table. He found it hostile and creepy, but what to do? Perhaps the universe would suggest something.

We come in this footnote to the story of what Chris called "The Blinky Light." By that he meant those round orange-yellow lights made of nearly indestructible plastic that are affixed to sawhorses at construction sites, one of which Chris saw lying in the gutter near his dorm. It was attached to a broken sawhorse, and as students often dragged exotic trash back to their dorm rooms, it seemed a miracle for Chris to spot this gem—which was even still blinking—before anyone else. It even seemed like a sign that it was meant to be his. So of course he immediately stooped down, detached the piece of wood to which the Blinky Light was wedded, and carried the whole contraption back to his room. Since these lights were attached to these sawhorses in a way that would make stealing them very difficult, prying the cheerful plastic lozenge from the wood proved extremely difficult. But after some hours with screwdrivers and pliers, Chris succeeded, and then even took such pains as necessary to discover how one could turn the light on and off, which involved prying open the stubborn white plastic base. He then generously shared his windfall with his suitemates by displaying it in the living room window, where it could blink for the whole campus. And now, as though having hung the sun and moon both, Chris saw that it was good; and after his labors, he rested. This was the first day.

But only hours later, Chris observed that the Blinky Light was not where he had left it. He asked around until Jonathan informed him that he knew the light was stolen, so he had simply done his duty and taken it to the Yale Lost and Found Department, where it belonged. Of course Chris was irate—as he put it, "cheesed off"—and explained to Jonathan that the light was rightly his, that it was trash in the street that he had found and that it consequently had *not* been stolen—unless one wished to count Jonathan's taking it without asking for Chris's side of the story. Jonathan seemed perplexed by Chris's response, perhaps suddenly wondering whether he might have acted hastily, but saying nothing. In any case, the Blinky Light was no more. What to do? Chris might think of something. In fact, he soon got a capital idea. He reasoned that the only way to persuade Jonathan that his actions were wrong was to convince Jonathan that God himself thought so. And if Jonathan could somehow hear from God directly on the subject, all the better. Chris had an idea that even this might be arranged. It was really only a matter of acoustics.

So, after preparing the script of what he—er, what God—would have to say about the iniquity, Chris and Richard and Todd wandered down to the basement squash courts in Calhoun, where using his best stentorian voice—complete with dramatic background music played on another tape recorder—Chris thundered the blistering jeremiad into the space of the echoey court. The divine plan was to hide the cassette player in Jonathan's bedroom and get it to squawk to life after Jonathan had fallen asleep. Through some trespassing and trial and error, Chris determined that when the recorder was under Jonathan's bed the sound seemed to come from everywhere at once, so it was placed there, with an extension cord snaking surreptitiously from Jonathan's room to a hidden spot in the living room. Of course the recorder's PLAY button had been depressed in advance. All that remained was to wake during the dead of night to plug it in from the living room and then wait for the fireworks.

It was between two and three in the morning that Chris and Todd and Richard awoke. As planned, they crept into the living room, plugged in the extension cord, and ... Lo! Precisely as planned, the machine under Jonathan's bed blasted to life. They cringed and thrilled to hear the loud music, designed to awaken their victim, and then, once the stage was set, the alarmingly authoritative voice began: "Jonathan! THIS ... IS ... THE ... LORD!" From there "the Lord" went on to make his case that Jonathan "had been weighed in the balance and found wanting" and must now "repent of his evil actions." As a result of his Westminster education, Chris knew enough of the Bible that he could make his case remarkably well, using numerous apt scripture passages, and laying on the religious guilt rather effectively, nor was he himself unconvinced of the case he was making. In any case, the three of them remained crouched in the living room listening, sure that at some point Jonathan would understand who was behind this and would come storming out of his room to confront them all. But oddly enough, this didn't happen. They saw that he had turned his light on soon after the tape began to play, so they knew he heard all that they heard. But he never came out of the room. Now what?

Eventually Chris's conscience got the better of him, so he knocked on the door and asked if Jonathan was all right. Jonathan opened the door. "Did you hear something?" he asked them, with an odd look on his face. Chris said that he had not. But it was a miracle of sorts that Jonathan had not yet spotted the extension cord, which now like a serpent accused Chris of what he had done. He felt he must come clean, especially since Jonathan would see the cord eventually. So he told Jonathan the whole story, that he had planted the recorder and had recorded the voice. But Jonathan wasn't angry. He seemed to have been convinced by the biblical reasoning of the "divine" voice, and seeing that it was merely a prank, he simply went back to bed. Jonathan could be strange in many ways. Who was like unto him?

But probably the "coolest" of these groups called ourselves "the Schroed-rats" because we hung out in what was called the Schroeder (pronounced SHROE-durr) Lounge, a wood-paneled room on the first floor of Calhoun that looked out on the courtyard, with couches and a big table where I did most of my work.

These friends were politically liberal, though we rarely talked politics, although the uniform of torn denim jackets, ripped khakis, and ratty red high-top sneakers said enough. There was the general feeling among these friends that pursuing art and literature was good and banking and the corporate world were evil, as were most people with money, except for our friends whose parents were loaded but who thought the way we thought they should, so it was cool. Practically speaking, for example, when the Yale-Harvard Game was played, some of us chose not only to avoid the game but pointedly to go to the art studio to paint or sculpt, as a way of protesting the red-blooded rite a mile away by

---

But in a few days, Chris returned to his room to see that perhaps Jonathan was not quite the Pharisee he had thought. For Lo! There like a dove returned to the ark holding an olive branch of peace stood the Blinky Light! It was in the bay window, just as before, and was even blinking happily. So it seemed that Jonathan had indeed seen the error of his ways and had earnestly repented of his actions and had gone the extra mile in returning to the "Lost and Found" department to reclaim the light and bring it back. So what was found by Chris—and had been lost in the Lost and Found—was found again! And very great was the rejoicing on that day in that suite. World without end. Amen.

Chris took the second semester of sophomore year off and part of junior year too, at which point I was able to become editor-in-chief of the *Record*. But even when not physically at Yale Chris submitted a brilliant parody of T.S. Eliot's "Prufrock" poem, which we decided to put in our next issue of the magazine. He cast the protagonist of the poem as a Yale student being rebuffed at a party. Brilliant as it certainly was, there was one couplet that didn't seem up to the standard of the rest of the poem, so I composed a couplet I thought might be better and suggested it to Richard and Todd, but they disagreed and outvoted me. My line was:

In the room the women come and go,
One of them looks like Barry Manilow.

But I felt so strongly about the superiority of this to what it would replace that I had it secretly typeset anyway, and when we laid out the magazine before delivering it to the printer's, I at the last minute slipped the renegade lines in. And as my guilt about this has over the decades risen to the level of Saint Augustine's over the theft of those famous pears, I thought I would here confess it.

doing something honest and real and true. And whatever art was made must be done for its own sake, not to make money, because that might mean you had sold out. Even writing something that didn't communicate terribly effectively was OK, because logic and objective reality were already becoming suspect as tools of an oppressive patriarchy. I didn't know what I thought of all of this and was trying to figure it out as I went along. One day in talking to a feminist friend I said the Bible said men and women were equal in God's eyes, so wasn't that the whole idea behind feminism? She asked me if I would write this for the campus feminist paper and I said I would and meant to, but never did.

Another tendency in our group was to idolize people we thought "authentic," like the seventy-year-old peroxide-blonde waitress who says, "What'll ya have, hon?" with her charming three-pack-a-day rasp. These people were always called "great," and anyone from a working-class background might qualify. Some of this was our desire to show solidarity with the common man, since being Yale undergrads we were self-conscious of our privileged existence. Folks whom we thought "great" had permission to make mistakes we wouldn't be caught dead making. We missed the condescension in this, or that we might ape their mannerisms and clothing styles now, knowing we could leave them behind when it no longer suited us. Sophie, the grumpy, unpleasant woman who stamped our tickets as we entered the dining hall, was "great" along these lines. But I wondered what these people thought of our treating them like that. Some likely liked it; it made them feel like celebrities. But I'm sure others saw us as privileged kids slumming in their world. On the other hand, there was sometimes a genuine kindness in seeing these people that way and I knew that. It was somehow grounding to be with them. They reminded us there was a world of people for whom things like "Exeter" meant nothing, and who had never heard of Jacques Derrida, much less met him, as I had. Or if they had met him it had been as the weird foreign guy in the dining hall line who didn't know what Jell-O was. But perhaps because I grew up with working-class people, I sometimes found it all slightly off-putting, though I knew my friends meant well.

Maybe because I hadn't grown up with friends like this I gave them a pass, wanting to learn to think the way they did, and the simple working-class world of my parents—of good and evil, of Communism and freedom, of God and the devil—began to seem passe. Obviously the people who ran things knew something we didn't know. For example, they knew that the word "Oriental" was wrong, that the correct word was "Asian." I had never heard that, but someone had decided it and now one must use "Asian." Similarly to say "colored person"—which was a term of respect when I was growing up—was wrong. Although one could say "person of color," which seemed confusing. This was the general cast of things, so it's not as if there were some overt indoctrination going on. And I rarely saw it in the classroom. Although there were moments.

I took a class on the Victorian novel, thinking it would be fun to read *Middlemarch*, for example. But when I wrote what I thought a particularly fine paper I got a flat B—which at Yale was more like a C—with comments suggesting I had insufficiently appreciated the book's feminist message. In another class I read Vladimir Nabokov's *Lolita* and found it brilliantly hilarious, but knew I was expected not to "judge" a middle-aged man for kidnapping and raping a twelve-year-old, though thirty years later there can be no doubt we are expected to do so. In one scene Nabokov's Humbert gropes his "nymphet" with a graphically ecstatic denouement obviously meant to be funny. But everyone I grew up with would have thought the book's entire premise sickening. Yet to have said so in class would have been thought prudish. When the book came out in the fifties it was controversial with the masses, but just as the intelligentsia believed there was really only one "right" side to the *Lady Chatterley's Lover* and *Ulysses* controversies, there could only be one to this too. My professor John Hollander had then blurb-ily declared it "one of the funniest books I remember ever having read." In other words it was the art that mattered—until thirty-five years later the #MeToo Movement exploded, at which point not to be against such books was beyond the pale. But how had we gotten to the point where truth was so malleable?

The Death of Meaning

At the heart of Yale is the Sterling Memorial Library, built in the late twenties for seventeen million dollars—an astonishing amount at the time.

As anyone can see, it was intentionally designed by James Gamble Rogers to look like a great cathedral. Immediately upon entering through what look like cathedral doors, one finds oneself walking a long narrow aisle leading to what looks like an altar, above which Rogers placed what he called the "altar mural." Its main figure looks strikingly like the Virgin Mary, but reveals itself to be a personification of "alma mater"—"our mother"—but of course the mother is Yale herself. The whole affair, while not necessarily mocking religious art and architecture, comes asymptotically close. Indeed, the long, narrow passageway leading to the "altar" is called the "nave," just as in a cathedral, and the part that looks like a chancel is called "the chancel."

It all begins to make sense when we learn that in 1926, Yale abandoned mandatory chapel services, scuttling plans for a new chapel across the quadrangle from the library. Rogers brightly thought he could take advantage of this by incorporating the larger ecclesiastical theme into the library, and of course did, using stained glass and other details to make the building look unmistakably like a cathedral. Except it was the first building ever to do so that was not actually a cathedral. So it was a daring statement in its day. Many found it sacrilegious and deeply offensive, as what it did was overtly secularize what was once strictly ecclesiastical, while cheekily imparting the elements of religious faith to the secular.

I remember walking along the "nave" toward the circulation desk—the running joke is that one need not "genuflect" there—and then turning right and coming to a beautiful cloistered walk with medieval-style carvings, each of which mocked student life. One depicted a student drinking a mug of beer beneath a curvaceous pin-up, another a student snoozing over his books; and another a student listening to the radio, the student distraction of that day. If this building was a secular temple to learning and knowledge, it seemed a curious thing to come upon these literally lapidary homages to adolescent snickering at the idea. But it was the fourth sculpture that took the joke a step further. It struck me personally, when I first saw it, and is the only one that depicts a student reading a book. But what the book says is extraordinarily cynical, if not positively dark. The carved book's left page has the letters U, R, and A carved into it. The right-hand page bears four letters, two on the top and two below:

J O

K E

Of course on one level it's simply a joke itself. But it also seems to be saying that if you are the sort of earnest fellow who—unlike the other three—actually goes to the trouble of studying, you will find that at the end of all knowledge is something surprising and perhaps quite troubling. And that is the idea that you are yourself a joke. And not merely because you are fool enough to bother with studying when ogling, snoozing, and entertainment are available, but because after all your struggles you will discover that at the end of everything is the idea that your very existence is itself absurd. In other words, we have at last found that at the end of the search for truth and meaning is the idea that

Carving at Yale

there is no truth and no meaning. So the joke is on you. And furthermore, if you understand the implications of that, you are *yourself* a joke. In other words, we finally "know" that the universe has randomly and accidentally produced you, who are concerned with searching for the meaning to your existence and life, only to discover in the end that there is no such thing. Isn't that funny? So not only are all the hoary truisms you've heard nonsense, but more vitally the

end of our search for meaning is that there is no such thing. The joke is on us—and we are the joke.

When these carvings were done in the twenties, this notion was generally accepted in the elite precincts of academia. After all, Charles Darwin had shown we arose from nothing by blind chance, and there was no "God" behind our creation. And Einstein had helped us see that everything is relative, such that nothing is subjective, and objective "truth" is a mirage. And Freud helped us see that at the heart of all we do is not something noble and transcendent, but merely the desire to perpetuate the species, as expressed in the sexual impulse.

But once we knew that we were mere accidents, bubbled up by chance through the eons, what to do? The decision—as evidenced by these carvings—seems to have been not to take it too seriously. We might as well all have a good laugh. Just because we now know life has no meaning, we don't really want to commit suicide, do we? There was at least some fun and pleasure to be wrung from our meaningless existences, so let's grab that while we still might. What's more, we can do it with no guilt, knowing that all those old moral codes were so much pious foofaraw. Now at last we knew what was what, so everything could essentially be seen as a joke, and could be held—as if by hermeneutical tweezers—in quotation marks of perpetual irony. I later assumed such ideas came to Yale and the cultural elites in the tumultuous sixties—until I read William F. Buckley's *God and Man at Yale,* published in 1951, about the Yale of the forties; and we may now see these notions were already in stone in the twenties.

Of course I had never encountered such ideas in my working-class immigrant world and had come to Yale really wanting to discover the meaning of life and the secrets at the heart of the universe. Yale's motto is *"Lux et Veritas"*—Light and Truth—and I was innocent enough to take that seriously, to hope to be enlightened by my education, as I had been to some extent at Trinity. But as the weeks and months at Yale passed I realized I was many decades out of step, and that the real thing I was to learn was that these things were ancient fictions whose usefulness had passed, at least for those willing to face it.

And yet who really could? It was so bleak that it was best to avoid. Other than the aforementioned carving, it was usually a bit too taboo to take straight. It was, after all, a seriously dark joke. The only time I remember it being joked about at all in a way that was funny was in one of my favorite movies, Mel Brooks's *Young Frankenstein,* in which the eponymous monster, played by Peter Boyle, being monstrously endowed in ye *"Schwanzstücke"* department, embraces Madeline Kahn's character to consummate their wedding, at which point she bursts into song: "Ohhh, sweet Mystery of Life—I've found you!!!" That was the great Mr. Brooks's way of joking about what most of us some-times wonder: *What is the meaning of life?* Woody Allen's movies take the subject on more straightforwardly, and in his interviews he is explicit about believing life is meaningless, but is also clear that he is unhappy about it. It is deeply unsatisfying and not really something that can be funny. He regards his grim conclusion as unacceptable, but more acceptable than agreeing with those idiots who claim life actually does have meaning, and wrestles particularly honestly with the question in *Crimes and Misdemeanors*.

But Woody's cinematic hero Ingmar Bergman struggled with it best of all. If *The Seventh Seal* isn't a film about this Question of Questions, what film or piece of art is? Woody's films pay many homages to Bergman—sometimes openly parodying him—but about this he doesn't joke, for he knows that if he is right—that this is all there is and there is no God and after we die we cease to exist utterly—he has every reason to be unhappy. The logic is unavoidable.

So it was at Yale that I first encountered the idea that life has no undergirding meaning, and no objective goodness and truth and beauty to carry us through the hard times we endure. I had not bumped into these ideas at Trinity, and even when John O'Brien and his friends talked about Charles Baudelaire and Nietzsche, I mostly took it as fun. But now it seemed serious.

So what to do? It seemed all the "best" people had adopted a winking, post-modern attitude, in which the notion of Truth had been replaced by the idea that there are many "truths" or none at all, and that anyone who talks too much about truth must be regarded with deep suspicion. The old idea of Truth was an inevitably repressive idea that needed to be abandoned, and replaced with something else, with a more open-minded view of things, with something more feminine, something semiotically more like the welcoming and nurturing and open "O" of the female genitalia and womb than the weapon-like and self-important "I" of a phallus.

But the idea that truth and right and wrong were antiquated notions was perhaps even more unsatisfying to me than to Woody Allen, perhaps because I wasn't entirely convinced. And yet I now felt a bit foolish for having expected to find truth and meaning, like the goober who runs toward the oasis that is a mirage. Most others around me seemed untroubled to see nothing where—as children, at least—we thought there was something? Why did it bother me?

"Celery Green Day"

Those I hung out with in the Schroeder Lounge became such good friends that I tended to accept their views, and through them began to see another way of looking at these things. One of them had even brilliantly invented a holiday that summed up their notions. He called it Celery Green Day.

The idea behind this was that every spring as you looked out over the landscape of trees in your neck of the woods, wherever you were—and especially in New England, where we were—the wash of colors slowly changed from sepulchral gray to green. The dull wintry granite of the bare tree branches stayed unchanged for months, as though the trees really had died and turned to stone. But finally, at some point tiny red buds appeared and the trees from a distance took on the slightest reddish hue amidst the gray. Then, some days or weeks later the faintest suggestion of spring arrived in a hint of yellow green, usually in April. That implicit hint of budding color would become more explicit each day until one day, looking out over the hills or trees, you saw a luminescent optic yellow-tinged green that was the approximate color of a celery stalk. This was Celery Green Day.

That color would deepen, so the celery green color only persisted for the shortest window and only the first day on which it appeared was Celery Green Day. Part of the charm of it was its radical subjectivity. It could fall on any day, so no one could know when it would arrive. It arrived unannounced, so planning a Celery Green Day celebration was nearly impossible. But the subjectivity didn't stop there. I might say the day was Tuesday, but you might say the trees hadn't been quite green enough. You believed it wasn't till Thursday. We all had our own "truths"—our own private Idahos—and Celery Green Day was an homage to that idea.

You could take the subjectivity further still. Even to the same person, Celery Green Day in Danbury where I grew up would probably fall on a different day than in New Haven. You could throw your worldly possessions into a VW bus and like a Deadhead, follow Celery Green Day north from place to place for weeks on end. I thought of it then as a wonderful idea, and still do. But it could also easily fall into a larger narrative that is less wonderful.

"Dance of the Macabre Mice"

If Celery Green Day was an illustration of the new truth that didn't take itself so seriously, the old idea of Truth was illustrated by a Wallace Stevens poem I read called "Dance of the Macabre Mice." I loved Stevens, but for his gorgeous words, not for his abstruse ideas. For example I loved the lines:

> *Tum-ti-tum,*
> *Ti-tum-tum-tum!*
> *The turkey-cock's tail*
> *Spreads to the sun.*
> *The white cock's tail*
> *Streams to the moon.*
> *Water in the fields.*
> *The wind pours down.*

I wasn't sure what in the world he meant, but who cared? I just loved the words. I felt the same way about:

> *In Oklahoma*
> *Bonnie and Josie dressed in calico*
> *danced around a stump.*
> *They cried Oho-ya-hoo! O-hee!*
> *Celebrating the marriage of flesh and air.*

I adored "The Emperor of Ice-Cream," which ended with, "Let be be finale of seem. The only emperor is the emperor of ice-cream." In fact I did what I did whenever I loved something: I tried to imitate it. The poem I wrote "after" his "Emperor of Ice-Cream" ended with the line: "With Luna swim to join the Sun in warm eclipseless skies." But even in my own poem, it was less about the ideas than the words.

But there was one poem I encountered in which Stevens's meaning seemed clearer than usual. In "Dance of the Macabre Mice" he writes about the equestrian statue of a military hero holding an outstretched sword. Just as Celery Green Day was like a verb—whimsical and light and unpredictable and somehow feminine—the equestrian statue was a dead noun, heavy and hostile and threatening, and of course, somehow full of itself, and repressively masculine.

So for Stevens the statue is not heroic and glorious, but aggressively militaristic. He lets us know what he thinks of it by having mice crawl all over the statue and then "dance it out to the tip of Monsieur's sword." They do not walk or march, but dance, because they are free and light-footed and alive and therefore victorious over the dead equestrian hero. "What a beautiful tableau," the poem declares with archness and irony. "The arm of bronze outstretched against all evil!" Stevens is not just scorning military heroism, but is chucking the idea of "good and evil" on the chin, too, as though that medieval binary conceit is precisely what gives us marauding colonials on horses.

Such notions were bruited about ad infinitum by artists early in the century and found increasing purchase in academia. Even the idea that humans were created in the image of God became less an apologetic against racism than one for wicked things, like being able to treat animals cruelly, even with "God's" blessing. Evoking humanity's special place in the cosmos suddenly smacked of the arrogance of "Manifest Destiny." The bumper sticker slogan "Question Authority" brought this idea to the popular level, not only suggesting we should question authority to determine whether it is legitimate, but implying all authority is by definition suspect—and hence, all assertions about the truth.

These ideas flew in the face of the line from Solzhenitsyn's magnificent Nobel Prize acceptance speech in 1970, of which I was then ignorant: "One word of truth outweighs the world." For him truth was the thing that makes evil dictators tremble; the thing that cannot lose and cannot long be suppressed, that according to Shakespeare "will out." Eventually it must arise and be victorious. But to us at Yale this seemed dated and overly serious, a little like Solzhenitsyn himself, who after his 1978 address at Harvard was principally regarded as a kind of disappointment and bummer, talking about God and truth like some Old Testament prophet.

And what did I make of these things? I didn't know. The zeitgeist—somehow concentrated at Yale—was blowing me forward with such force that it wasn't possible to get my bearings and think these things through. You really couldn't, unless you already believed in the idea of "standing athwart history" and shouting "Stop!" as some rare conservatives on campus did, though it would cost them every last farthing of social standing, and who wanted to be a social outcast? My friends were too valuable to me for me to debate with them about the possible downsides of their ideas. So I drifted along until such time as I would have the leisure and incentive—which usually meant suffering—to consider such things more critically.

Clockwise from top left: My father's grandfather, the celebrated Panagis Vergotis—"no one will ever reach him"—with his wife, Eleni Vergotis (née Tsitselis), who lived to be one hundred, along with my father's Aunt Kikí and his mother, Regina. Circa 1902.

Clockwise from top left: My grandmother Regina, my father, his brother Takis (Panagis), his Aunt Kikí, and his brother Othon. Circa 1931.

My father in 1938, after his father's death.

My father and his mother, Renee, in Athens. Circa 1950.

My grandfather Yiannikostas's grave in Mavrata after the 1953 earthquake.

My mother with her grandmother,
Minna Grosse, 1934.

My mother, aged eleven.

My grandfather Erich with his
daughters, 1943.

Annerose and Eleonore. Circa 1940.

My parents dating, August 1958.

On their wedding day in New York City, August 22, 1959.

With my father, 1963.

The author, age two.

From left: Tante Ella, Eleanor, Marion, Tante Eleonore, my brother John, Grandma, me, and my mother. Grandma's living room in Sunnyside, Queens, 1965.

The four cousins in Cutchogue, 1968.

Without question, one of the happiest days of my life. My brother John and I had never been sledding before, but Uncle Joe and Tante Eleonore called and said they were all going to Astoria Park, so we jumped in our Valiant and drove there from Jackson Heights. I might have burst for joy, being with the people I loved most. Winter 1969.

With my brother in front of our 1960 Valiant. Cutchogue, 1968.

The Trip to Germany, Summer 1971

Clockwise from top left: With my mother and brother at Tante Toni's birthday celebration. It was on that day I spoke my first German sentence: *"Bitte gib mir ein Glas Milch!"*; my mother, grandmother, and Tante Eleonore on that day; the four cousins in front of the church in Großstöbnitz; the cousins and Tante Eleonore in Hamburg.

The Trip to Greece, Winter 1972–1973

Clockwise from top left: At the Acropolis; with my Uncle Othon on Christmas Day in Lassi, Cephalonia; lifting a kid on our family property in Mavrata; at my grandfather Yiannikostas' grave, Agios Yiannis churchyard, Mavrata.

Above: With my father and brother in our backyard, 1972.
Right: Our house in Danbury, after a big snow.

Right: Doing the Epistle Reading at Assumption Greek Orthodox Church, with Father Peter Karloutsos, 1978. *Below*: Speaking at Danbury High School graduation, 1980.

Yale Graduation, 1984

Above: With Chris Hanes, giving "The Class History" at graduation in front of thousands on Old Campus. The yellow and green ribbons were my concessions to the cultural peer pressure of the day.

Right: After my nightmare speech was over, I got to listen to my future friend, the legendary Dick Cavett, give his own speech. His witty japery managed to raise the ire of some nascently politically correct members of our class, who quickly wrote disapproving articles.

The best part of this day was sharing it with the people I loved so dearly. *From left*: my Dad, my friends George Duncan and John Tomanio, the graduate, my mother, my cousin Marion, my brother, my grandmother, my Uncle Joe, and my Tante Eleonore.

With the people who made my dreams possible.

Summer 1984: "The Grand Tour"

With Chris Hanes in the Cotwolds. "And then you *literally* make a left…"

The author ruminating at sea, Cephalonia:
*"I have seen them riding seaward on the waves
Combing the white hair of the waves blown back
When the wind blows the water white and black."*

I took this photo of my grandmother in June 1984, at the garden cottage of our cousin Rudolf, in Neuenburg, Germany. When I first saw the photo I knew that years in the future, after she had left us, it would become—at least for me—her official portrait.

With my mother at my cousin John's wedding on June 19, 1988, a week before my Uncle Takis's death. Some days after his funeral I had my fateful dream.

There's no place like home

CHAPTER NINETEEN

The Last Bladderball

Junior Year 1982

M y decision to stop attending the Christian group Friday nights enabled me to drift ideologically without being reminded that I was drifting, although I had no particular ambitions to do anything dramatic, like smoke clove cigarettes or sleep with Andy Warhol. But I did hang out more with the literary and artsy crowd, although this too was still part of some vague quest to find the meaning of life. I wasn't rejecting God, only the evangelical Christian version that seemed narrow and "uncool." I assumed—as everyone "in the know" seemed to—that the true path to truth must combine things from all religions. It never occurred to me that just because God loved everyone equally didn't mean he loved every idea equally, or that all religions were essentially saying the same thing. But to parse truth from falsehood would not have been in keeping with the general timbre of things then, where a lightly considered "tolerance" became a tautological telos, and where tolerance of course really meant tolerance to anything, except to those creepy religious nuts who self-servingly held to the view that some things ought not to be tolerated because they said so.

Since I no longer attended the Christian group on Fridays I assiduously avoided anyone who did. But there was a Jewish student—Andy—who had "found Jesus" and sometimes buttonholed me toward lunch in his college, and I didn't know how to say no. In one of our conversations I mentioned that in my Harold Bloom/John Hollander seminar one of them averred definitively that Moses hadn't written the first five books of the Bible. Andy was troubled when I repeated this, eventually giving me a huge book arguing the opposite, which I certainly didn't plan to read. So I now worked harder to avoid him and hung out with friends who avoided uncool questions like who authored the Pentateuch.

But I wasn't doing most of this very consciously. In truth, I was principally drifting along as best I could and having such fun as seemed normal. I hadn't exactly decided to kick out any traces of Christianity. I still thought sleeping with someone outside marriage would be to use them selfishly, and therefore didn't; but neither did I talk about this subject with my friends. Nearly all the time I spent with my eight suitemates was like that—meaning simply fun, within the accepted bounds of college behavior. That year all nine of us—whom my friend Chuck Forrest dubbed "The Big Suite of Great Guys"—continued rooming together and having parties so popular and loud that the new dean once arrived at midnight in his bathrobe to upbraid us. The old dean was Eustace Theodore, a Greek who had so fled his Old-World ethnicity that he smoked a pipe and seemed only to wear wide-waled cords and green turtlenecks. Did anyone but I know his real name was Eustasios Theodoros? His self-invention as a hyper-preppie academic paralleled that of Yale's president, Angelo Giamatti, who had kicked his ethnic first name clean to Calabria and styled himself A. Bartlett Giamatti—and less officially as "Bart," which for those of us who understood German seemed a nice way to underscore his goatee, trimmed with Teutonic neatness. The only concession to his ethnicity—besides his vowelly surname—was a fondness for Dante, who existed in an Italy safely centuries before the introduction of tomatoes from the New World. But this semester a third figure of repressed ethnicity had entered in the shape of this new dean, who had an Italian surname but who, in his blond hair and Main Line lockjaw had so successfully given the slip to any traces of the Old Country that his surname came as something of a shock, perhaps even to him. When he came up that evening he was cordial, as were we, immediately saying we were sorry and killing the volume on David Lee's monster speakers. I relied on these roommates more than any other friends to show me the general ropes at Yale, and it was they who would initiate me that fall semester in something hardly to be believed.

"Bladderball" began in the fifties, when drunken madness among young men was generally considered "a healthy outlet." The "Bladderball" itself was six feet high, made of impenetrable canvas, and inflated like a bladder; and was first "played" across the entire campus. Each of the ten residential colleges would battle for possession of the ball and stampede hell-for-leather around the Elm City chasing the vast spheroid till somehow someone got it into the courtyard of his residential college—or died trying. Cars would be tipped over and children and pets hidden until the mob had at last spent itself.

By the early eighties the game had been "civilized" down to a more modest version that, if you hadn't heard of the earlier versions, sounded every bit as insane and reckless. If I wasn't convinced of its dangerousness, there was a Yale–New Haven ambulance perched nearby, like a vulture. There are four main gates on the Old Campus—a grassy quadrangle the size of four football fields—and this was the playing field, inconveniently studded with mammoth trees and statuary. There were now just four teams, each consisting of anyone who wished to participate from three of the now twelve residential colleges. Each had a color: red, blue, yellow, or green, and the several hundred students on each team gathered in one of the four gates, wearing their official Bladderball T-shirts, ours being designed by my pal Tom Fahsbender, in blue with white writing. I don't remember which other two colleges were on our team, but they wore these shirts too.

So we in blue gathered in the Dwight Arch, anticipating the appearance of the ball. Where did it live the rest of the year? We were restless, and many had been drinking by way of preparation, though it was only noon. But then the monster sphere, doubtless resurrected from some tomb beneath the campus, made its appearance, like a bull trotting out to the middle of the ring. I had certainly never seen a ball as large. The Brobdingnagian plaything was rolled to the center of the green quad as we tensed for the gunshot. *Bang!* What followed, of course, would never happen again. And with some good reason.

Though of course we had no idea at the time. For all we knew, this tradition would continue for centuries.

In any case, there now exploded from each of the four "gates" a torrent of foaming color, each particle amidst this flood hellbent on being the first to get to the insensate canvas zero at the epicenter of the universe. If that day you had been standing like the devil in the New Testament—or an angel in a Wim Wenders film—on the pinnacle of Harkness Tower observing the spectacle below, you would have seen something like a modernist painting composing itself on the rectangular canvas of the quad, with its thick, ornate burnished brown frame of faux-Gothic buildings and would have seen the four colors pouring toward the center and then slowly mixing with each other; and mixing and mixing until blue and red and yellow and green were equally and quite idiotically distributed around the dull, putty-colored ball in the center.

My point of view that day was less satisfying. There was screaming and whooping and then everyone sprinting at once, until hundreds of squirming and writhing bodies tried to move an object made immovable by the hundreds of others trying in the opposite direction. It was a kind of tug of war in reverse and cubed, everything pushing inward from every direction. After a few minutes most simply backed away from the lunacy to watch, but eventually something like a permanent palisade of bodies, ten or twelve deep, formed around the circle, which was ground zero and above which the massy ball bounced, now batted back and forth by those on the shoulders of those in the front line. The pressure on those brave souls at the verge of this bloody maw was tremendous, and many crumpled into the blank hole beneath the ball. But once you fell down into the circle of mashed grass beneath the ball you were in the eye of the storm as it were, the inert sphere above you blocking the sunlight and air. I watched the spectacle from some distance, scratching my head. (To me the ball looked something like a "malignant mushroom" and I pretentiously said so, causing Tom to say "You're such a *writer*.") I had nothing approaching the courage or foolhardiness to push toward that agonic donut of humanity, with its bouncing canvas hole. But the drunken and dim-witted were less hesitant.

Then suddenly, Ward Wheeler—belonging to neither group—appeared, sweating and excited, as he often could be. He had been scrambling around the periphery of the lunacy and now like Caleb and Joshua returned from scouting the Promised Land and breathlessly declared: "I'm goin' in!" Tom and I stared at him. Really? Then he said the words that changed my life: "Metaxas! You're coming with me!" What? I certainly didn't want to and wouldn't. But how to resist the glowing vector that was Ward Wheeler? He inspired confidence and madness both, and was now on a goggle-eyed mission. What was there to do but clamber onto his broad shoulders and pray for survival? In a moment he was screaming and bellowing and bumping and shoving his way toward the center of the churning horde, and all with such unholy vigor he might have sprouted horns. I was exhilarated and horrified at his steady progress, as though riding a rhino in the midst of a cattle stampede, or approaching the crater of a live volcano on the back of a wildebeest, or riding the Minotaur to the center of his maze. Still, from what I saw, getting into that front line was impossible, the humanity thick as stacked lumber. Of course whoever did somehow get there might touch the Bladderball. Theoretically. But that would be as mad as descending into the Underworld and touching the hem of Elvis's bellbottom, like poking one's fingers into the puffy yellow underbelly of the zeitgeist itself! We got closer and closer, Ward carrying me onward until somehow—how?—we were there, unimaginably, in the very front line of the crushing circle, whence with vertigo I now beheld what I had only imagined earlier. The grass in the center was mashed down like a crop circle and the wild, circular mob was inanely and insensately beating the ball back and forth, so that it continued and continued to go absolutely nowhere: Sisyphus at play. It was like a skill-free, multi-dimensional pitcher's duel, and now on the verge of it all, on the trembling lip of the maw, I reeled for fear of falling down below the ball into the blind heart of darkness. I had become Pentheus staggering into the midst of a bloody Bacchanal, and the Dionysian thrumming was pulling me into itself. And so I sat upon Ward's shoulders like a cilium on the upturned flowery edge of a protozoan, existing only to make contact with the floating food particle upon which I with all the intensity of a tropism was focused. The stupid, deaf, and dumb Bladderball was the core of the cosmos, and big enough to eclipse all else as it *ka-bounced* in slow motion just above the circular wilderness of souls.

I remained there upon my friend's shoulders, watching and watching, hypnotized. And then as if I had willed it, it happened. The swollen planet bounced my way and I with my own fingers touched it—and pushed it back to the other side of the crater. Really? Yes! I had touched it! I could sing the *"Nunc Dimittis"* and depart! I couldn't believe it. It was as though I had bamboozled the Swiss Guard at the Vatican and managed to pinch the papal arse! Or had slipped past Kremlin security, smashed the coffin's glass, and audibly slapped the cold waxy pate of Lenin *himself!* Canst thou take in the import of what I am telling you, dear reader? Can anyone? Could I? I had touched the Bladderball! Time as I understood it had stopped, so what was the point of going forward when one had arrived? In this oasis of eternity I simply existed now, like some Aristotelian deity: *thought thinking thought.* But then, as though the timeless island to which I had swum were expanding across the sea, I touched it again! And again! And again! I was at the dead center of the world now, just above the fissure at Delphi and breathing the oracle's sulfurous fumes—γνῶθι σεαυτόν—and it was heady and horrible, and yet at any moment the great maw at the infinitesimal center of the cosmos might swallow me like a great *vagina dentata*[1] and I—unlucky pilgrim—might be smashed to bits beneath the senseless Ivy League juggernaut.

At some point in this reverie, as though slowly waking from a dream within a dream, I remembered that I existed, and where I was, and I suddenly sensed that Ward had begun our retreat, moving slowly backward through the less and less serried ranks until we at last escaped the dark gravity and collapsed on the cool grass beyond the giddy fray. We were exhausted. But by the beard of Zeus we had done it, had immanentized ye eschaton and literalized all metaphors! And were returned to the world of time and space! But for

---

[1] In our class John Hollander once referred to "the myth of *vagina dentata*" and a famously openly gay writer among us blurted: "It's not a myth!" He simply meant to say that that idea could not literarily be properly categorized as a "myth," but of course the room exploded with good-natured laughter, and he blushed to realize the undeniable humor of saying what he had just said.

our transgression we had the Golden Bough of the memory, the mnemonic apples of the Hesperides. *Felix Culpa. Fu Li's Gulpa.* Whatever. Αμήν και αμήν.

Soon after we caught our breath and found our friends we heard a young woman had broken a bone and was being rushed to the hospital in the ambulance. Of course we never learned who won the Bladderball contest, as if anyone could, for the drunken orgy of humanity had eclipsed all such cares. But after that day in 1982 the administration tallied up the situation and decreed Bladderball would never be played again. It was over. Finis. But thanks to my doughty friend Ward I had not only touched the Bladderball, but had touched the final Bladderball—that Omega of omegas—the very last one that ever was or indeed ever shall be! And as the immortal Tony Baretta oft quipped: "And dat's de name of dat tune."

CHAPTER TWENTY

The Game

November of that fall marked the ninety-ninth playing of "The Game"—as the annual Yale-Harvard football contest was called—so some of us went to Cambridge, though of course not so much for the football, which was a good thing, since Yale was crushed into the Cantabrigian sod 45–7. As a remedy against the cold weather—and because Adam Liptak did it, making it the thing to do—I purchased a half-pint of Johnnie Walker, which on an empty stomach at noon soon catapulted me leagues above the stadium. At some point in my haze I witnessed what had to be a hallucination. I saw a gigantic weather balloon self-inflating out of the turf at the fifty-yard line. And then I saw three black letters on it, crudely made with what seemed black electrical tape. An "M," followed by an "I," followed by a "T." Aha. So it wasn't the whiskey. Bravo, nerds. You had to hand it to them; they had a history of cleverly inserting themselves into these exclusivist activities, and in this case had managed to bury the balloon and a gas canister in the center of the field such that no one had noticed it. I never learned how they activated it, but for eggheads of a certain caliber, it couldn't have been very hard. Surely they would be designing Mars rovers soon enough. So everyone was properly transfixed as the balloon grew and grew—and then burst. The gracious thing would have been to applaud, but as that did not happen, these humble sentences must suffice.

When the game was over, sore Elis stormed the field and tore down Harvard's goalpost. Evidently after four quarters of humiliation the only path toward recovering some dignity lay in undignified vandalism. But it took tremendous effort for enough drunken students to climb aboard the metal structure and rock it under their combined weight until at last it snapped off—without maiming anyone. We watched this play itself out as we moved in our boozy indifference toward the exits and eventually found ourselves outside the stadium. But as we drifted in the crowd in our intended direction—lo!—I did espy something passing strange. There in yon gutter lay the very goalpost so indecorously removed not ten minutes before. Evidently some of the vandals had hauled it here and abandoned it. But who in such state as I could let such treasure lie? I shouted that we must carry the booty away and loudly mustered some volunteers, who joined me in lifting it and carrying it along with the crowds. After hauling our monstrous souvenir for about a half mile we began to feel like the dog who catches the car, not knowing what to do with it. So as we came to a bridge crossing the Charles, it suddenly seemed foreordained that we must bid our trophy adieu! I trumpeted this to my men and—*One! Two!! Threeeee!!!*—we together heaved the behemoth ho o'er the railing and watched it plummet and *ker-splash* into the river, where it now swam out of our ken, like a new planet or Rocky Balboa something something something on a peak in Darien. And how many times, dear reader, in the decades since that chilly day past have I winced at the dark thought that there might just then too have swum a motor boat or sculler 'neath that bridge from which we blindly and blithely tossed what might have been a murder weapon upon their unhappy heads? But enough.

Soon after this Adam's friends led us into the fabled and comically thin *Harvard Lampoon* building and we wandered, goggling at the Delft tiles and other curiosities. Of course all I could think was how far our *Yale Record* had fallen—from once having something comparable to this to now having a bathroom-sized basement room with foil-covered heating ducts overhead. The university had seen fit to give our glorious building to the theater arts department, though the stone iconography on its facade made it clear to anyone that the leg-warmer-wearing thespians within were mere eminent-domain scabs and squatters.

But being at the *Lampoon* gave me an idea; and so the next year, following the 100th Game in New Haven, we at the *Yale Record* finagled the use of our old building to throw a party! We invited anyone from the *Lampoon* who was in town, and at some point a very tall, pasty-faced Irish redhead showed up with what was obviously his posse of jesters. This was the head of the *Lampoon.* As the editor of the *Record,* I graciously welcomed him, pretending not to notice his goiter, hump, and horribly oversized club foot. He said his name was Conan. I agreed that it was, and in this history has proved me correct many times. There we stood, the two living titans of college humor. And how funnily we stood! But now it was time to match wits. "How's it going?" I inquired wittily, and then waited for what must surely be a particularly apposite riposte, perhaps even one he and his "gang" had scripted beforehand, anticipating my question. "Can't complain," he replied. And there it was. I have always believed our meeting that day and our now famous exchange constituted something of a Humor Summit—and as a result of our willingness to put aside our differences for those few precious moments, the world after our meeting was left an ever so slightly funnier place.

My burgeoning literary ambitions that first semester led me to a fiction-writing seminar whose professor's surname was Faulkner[1] but whom I liked nonetheless. We read a contemporary story by Mark Helprin[2] titled "The Schreuderspitze," and the first line was so good I have been reciting it for four decades now, including recently to the author himself. It went: "In Munich are many men who look like weasels." Brilliantly omitting the word

---

[1] There was a rumor that he was an unclaimed son of the modernist bore and had taken the name deliberately.

[2] Thirty-six years later I interviewed Mark Helprin at a *Socrates in the City* event which may be viewed at www.socratesinthecity.com.

"there" before the verb "are" made it sound the way a German would talk, or like a German translation. I knew then that the author was a genius and the story revealed such talent as underscored what I suspected, that writing could not really be taught any more than could being funny. His writing was by turns brilliantly funny, deeply moving, and powerfully poetic, and it had a moral clarity that was downright countercultural, though I failed to see this at the time.

That spring I took a poetry seminar, where we read a sampling of the curdled *entres nous* poetry being published in the *New Yorker,* and the idea that anyone could aspire to join this sour company struck me even then as mystifying. But we wrote some poetry too. I only wrote one poem I liked, titled "At the Last Wedding," which I was thrilled to see published in the *Yale Quarterly,*[3] giving me some bona fides in campus literary circles, although their inexcusable typo of "alter" for "altar" made me wax murderous. The poem was my way of talking about God's spirit in veiled terms, since my fading Christianity was something I now thought must be best expressed surreptitiously.

"Veal Fuselage"

My best friend around then was Chris Noël—whom I knew principally thorough the Schroed-rat circle—and he shared my sense of humor and wordplay to such an extent that we often annoyed our friends to the point of actual anger. But there was an earnestness and innocence to it, rather than a desire to display our wit in a show-offy way. It was childlike, but sometimes devolved to a childishness too. We worked together in the Calhoun kitchen dish room and while clearing our classmates' dishes of half-eaten food into the trough once began inventing comic verses about a rat named Reuben (the Dishrat), who lived in the industrial-sized dishwasher we manned during these shifts. The first of the handful of times I tried pot—which I loathed—was

---

[3] The corrected version of the poem is printed in the Appendix and was published in *First Things* in 1999.

with Chris, and at some point, just to crack him up, I pretended to be obsessed with it, crying out in German: *"Ich muss das Geist essen!"* which suggested a compulsion to "eat the spirit" of the smoke, and which may give the reader an idea of how annoying we could be.

But surely the clearest example of our verbal incontinence involved a trip to Peking Duck in Manhattan. Once in a blue moon, the Schroed-rats drove there, and on the last of these journeys our friend Shay drove. Afterward we piled in the car for the two-hour ride back, during which Chris and I began to entertain ourselves by trying to produce pairs of words so unrelated that the dissonance between them was jarring. The goal was to find words that defied the mind's ability to link them.[4]

The inanity began because I spoke the phrase "Veal Fuselage," probably as a semi-intentional mistake, and when it came out, we marveled at it. It defied meaning.[5] But finding two words like this again proved extremely difficult. For example, if one of us triumphantly blurted "Wooden Casserole!" it might get a laugh, but then we could quickly enough imagine a casserole in a wooden dish, or perhaps the casserole tasted so awful someone would say it tasted wooden, or we might imagine a casserole carved of wood, perhaps for a stage prop. It didn't sufficiently defy the mind's poetic ability to make something of it. Chris and I began this game as we got into the car and did not let up for ten seconds. We would always think we had one—as in "Alabaster … foot!"—but the moment it came out we pictured the white carved foot of a Victorian statue. Or "lemon neck!" Not bad, but then you would picture a neck with a lemon tattoo or a spit of land named after the family that first settled there, when old man Lemon made his fortune. Chris came up with

---

[4] Our inclination to connect things is the very taproot of our language abilities. It is that symbolic and metaphorical instinct that makes us human, and that I'm sure is a manifestation of our desire to bridge the gaping abyss between the parts of our split and broken selves, and between us and the God from whom we are separated.

[5] I maintain that nothing has yet topped it. On a similar note, when my wife and I once visited her sister in Bellingham, Washington, we noticed dozens of coffee shops with clever names and invented our own. As with "Veal Fuselage," I spit one out that I believe ended the contest, meaning that the level of cleverness might conceivably be equaled, but not topped. It came in two parts, The first: "Bean Me Up." And then: "Biscotty!"

"Muffin Ion," which was probably the best of all, although for me the double "enn" sound diminished the elegance I thought any winning phrase along these lines required. Or perhaps "ion" was just too vague? In any event, on and on we went! "Criminal Leg!" and "Orange Legacy!" and "Sumptuous Lava!" and "Shiny Swamp!" and "Spiffy Herd" and "Barbecued Cloak" and "Simmering Nose" and "Plaster Sunrise" and "Walnut Ghost!" and "Nasal Hoe-down!" We could not stop ourselves, mile after mile, despite our friends' imploring us to do so. Eventually there were angry imprecations, making us laugh and continue all the more, until finally, unable to endure the hammering agony further, Shay angrily pulled the car over—on the shoulder of the very heavily trafficked I-95—turned around, and talking to us as though we were red-headed twins locked in a never-ending "I got you last!" contest, threatened not to continue driving until we stopped. We were simply that annoying.

Skull and Bones

In the spring of my junior year I wondered whether I would be tapped for one of Yale's secret societies, the eight-hundred-pound gorilla of which was "Skull and Bones," to which Chris Noël belonged, but of which he was unable to speak. It was founded in 1832 and has a storied reputation, with an indisputably ominous building that looked perfectly like a mausoleum, and was, in fact, called "the tomb." Within it were said to be coffins and skulls and bones and other macabre tokens of what was only thinly veiled in its satanic pretensions. One heard that the initiation involved performing an onanistic rite in a coffin surrounded by one's fellows. Chris himself said that at some point in their ceremony they thrice repeated the word "Iscariot," surname of the Judas who betrayed Jesus. One day in the Calhoun dining hall Chris sat nearby while another "Bonesman" stopped by and chatted me up. I cannot recall a syllable of the conversation but remember being unsure whether he was favorably impressed. Had I passed the test?

In any case, weeks later I found a postcard slipped under my door with a curious notation on it. It was a Dewey decimal number. The cat-and-mouse game had begun. I guessed it was my assignment to go to the "stacks" within

Sterling and find this book, which I did. Inside was another card, indicating where and when to appear next. So this was it: I was being tapped to join Skull and Bones. Everyone said that whoever got in would be "set for life," whatever that meant. But the vice president at that time was a Bonesman, as was William F. Buckley, and many leading lights of the Eastern establishment. The organization reportedly wrote its inductees a check for fifteen thousand dollars upon acceptance—an impossibly staggering sum to me—and were annually feted at an island in Newfoundland, which they owned and where they annually mixed with other members of this elitist of elitist groups, unlocking every door to success one could imagine. I began to wonder whether allowing myself to be drawn into this society was right, inasmuch it really did seem to have a diabolical aspect. Would God forgive my trafficking in potentially dark things to achieve what I thought of as "success"? I wasn't sure what to think, but until the time came for my "interview"—or "induction" or whatever it was—I twisted in the wind, and now and again spat out such fragments of prayers as one does who has little idea to whom he addresses them, nor any confidence that they might heard. When the day finally came I was terrified and before I left to go to the place appointed I grabbed the five-by-seven postcard print of Rembrandt's Jesus my mother had given to me three years before, putting it inside whatever book I carried, and when I sat alone in the anteroom, waiting to be ushered into whatever sanctum lay beyond, I stared at it, looking for comfort and protection. At last the doors opened and I was ushered into a room so dark that I could not see those sitting opposite me and questioning me. I don't remember anything, only that one of the voices was a woman's, and one thing I knew about Skull and Bones was that they did not accept women. So I was utterly confused, so much so I could hardly think. At some point after my fevered responses to whatever they were asking they asked whether I had any questions. I said I was wondering why there was a woman present because I knew they didn't accept women. They became flustered and almost offended and said they did, confusing me the more. When I got out of there I didn't know my own name. I felt almost as confused and frantic as when I had emerged a year earlier from the strange man's home on that odd street in Danbury. And then somehow—and I don't remember how—I realized that the society that had tapped me was not Skull and Bones nor any of the three "main" societies, none of which accepted women, but another society that had obviously been very recently formed. I was crushed.

And now I had to figure out whether I should join. I might at least take the next step and see who they were. So one night I was summoned to a spot on Old Campus where some white-masked figures eerily beckoned us "chosen ones" around the campus to come to what amounted to a casual "get together" where all the masks were taken off, at which point I got cold feet, and decided to decline. It was Groucho Marx who said it first and Woody Allen who repeated it in *Annie Hall*, but I can't help wondering whether it is true of me, that I wouldn't want to belong to any club that would have me as a member. And I wonder too whether this helps explain why I so often in life found myself feeling like a fish out of water. Was it I—after all—who was the problem, who was suicidally rejecting the water?

CHAPTER TWENTY-ONE

Bohemian Threnody

Summer 1983

I t was about this time I thought I should find a summer job commensurate with my literary ambitions, and believed it should be in the fabled city of Max Perkins and John Cheever. I would need something "significant" on my resume when I began looking for a "real" job after graduation, and might need to know my way around the center of the publishing universe, not that I knew I wanted a job in publishing or much else about what I wanted, but this was as far as I had gotten in thinking about it. Even though I was born there, I had since 1972 become thoroughly rusticated, without any better concept of New York than your average hillbilly sucking the stem of a corncob pipe and a-taking a pull from the old jug. So one day I skipped off to Sterling, found some literary magazines with offices in Manhattan, and sent them letters with my "resume." I only got one response that was not a form letter of rejection. It was from Megan Ratner, then managing editor of *Antaeus*, which was something like a younger brother of the *Paris Review*, not least since both were funded by the ketchup heiress Drue Heinz.

And since George Plimpton founded the *Paris Review* in Paris with the conceivably gay Ernest Hemingway, Dan Halpern had upped the exotic ante and founded *Antaeus* in Tangier with the exceedingly gay Paul Bowles.

Antaeus was connected to Ecco Press, a small literary house that published Cormac McCarthy before anyone heard of him, and Czesław Miłosz before he won the Nobel. *Antaeus* also published newer names I was coming to love, like the fabulist Steven Millhauser, whom Chris Noël and I parodied in the *Record* the following year. So one day, as smartly attired as I knew how, I walked the bleak graffiti-covered blocks to the New Haven train station and was whisked into the heart of Manhattan.

During our interview, Ms. Ratner said the job didn't pay, at which point I tried and failed to seem unsurprised. But who needed money? Other than me and everyone I had ever known besides a handful of my rich Yale friends. Still, any job so hard to get must be worth doing for free. I realized I was competing with trust-fund kids who didn't need to make money, but before then I had never heard of an unpaid internship. Still, my ignorance of such things and my surprise paled to starkest albino when compared with my parents' near-shrieking reaction. *A job where they didn't pay you? How was that a job?* I might as well have told them I would be making invisible sculptures. Or having an affair with John Cage. They weren't shy in expressing their deep horror. Had my great learning finally made me mad? The question was reasonable, but I had no answer and said I would get a second job to make money, but insisted I still needed the internship for my resume. They knew even less than I did about how to pursue a writing career—and I knew nothing—so what could my poor parents do but take their son's word for it?

So now all I needed was a paying job that didn't interfere with the unpaid internship. And a free place to stay in Manhattan for the summer. But how hard could finding such a place be? After all, most of my sophisticated Yale friends had managed it. Of course what I didn't know was that many of them had relatives and family friends who summered in places like Martha's Vineyard or Bar Harbor and were only too delighted to let Parker or Lelia or Grant or Amanda stay at their air-conditioned penthouses for the summer, and alas, of such magical connections had I none. But that didn't mean I had no connections at all.

My beloved godmother—my *Nouna*—Effie Drogaris, had heard from my parents, who probably called to vent about their unraveling son, that I needed someplace to stay in Manhattan and said she would check with her old friend Andreas Vlastos. "He is Bohemian type!" she declared. In speaking to my parents I gathered that this Vlastos was an eccentric but wealthy old Greek man who lived alone, though they didn't know where. But my mother laughed at the mere mention of his name. "Vlastos!" she said. "I remember him from when we were first married! We all went to the beach. The heat was *awful* and he wore a wool turtleneck! And he never took it off. In that heat! He was a strange bird, let me tell you! I can only imagine what he's like now!"

My father said Vlastos and his brother had published a successful Greek-language newspaper called *Atlantis,* but at some point it had "gone under." When I finally spoke to my godmother—after she reported that Vlastos was happy to have my company—she repeated what she told my parents: "He is Bohemian type!" She pronounced this with a short-voweled first syllable and the hissing Greek "chi" sounds in the second. "Boh-*CHEE*-mee-an!" (There are no schwas[1] in Greek-accented speech.) But this didn't frighten me. "Bohemian" was just what I had in mind! After all, I wanted to be a poet and write fiction! Vlastos probably lived in a fabulously appointed flat in the Village and could regale me with stories of hobnobbing with luminaries along the lines of Bob Dylan or Dylan Thomas or Thomas Wolfe or Tom Wolfe or Wolfman Jack or Jack Kerouac! He probably had an apartment on a picturesque mews with dramatically overstuffed floor-to-ceiling bookcases filled with *mementi* and oriental carpets from trips to Marrakesh in the forties and Astrakhan throws on the velvet sofa and perhaps there was an Empire *recamier* upholstered in a bold yellow Bombazine upon which now lolled Madame Blavatsky, the cat that once clawed Susan Sontag! There would be *objets d'art* and framed *belles-lettres* and maybe the gruesome plaster-of-paris death mask of someone who had previously taken the flat—yes, it must be a "flat," not an "apartment" and must be "taken," not "rented," as when one fashionably "takes" a lover!— and whoever had taken it must be someone like Lou Reed or perhaps even Andy himself! And perhaps there would be a graffito on the wall where Allen

---

[1] The "schwa" is that extremely common vowel sound in American English that sounds like "uh" and is the "o" in "mother," the "u" in "bunny," and so on.

Ginsberg had carved the word "owl," the missing aitch bitten off by a drunkenly raging Norman Mailer!

So when the semester came to an end I moved back to Danbury for a few days and then packed our large avocado cardboard suitcase without wheels and hopped a Greyhound bus to the city. I hadn't really spent any time there since I was eight, so debarking at the notorious Port Authority bus station on 41st Street and Eighth was the proverbial rude awakening. Nothing captured the horrors of pre-Rudy Giuliani New York better, and if the word *skank* could be distilled, the Port Authority of the eighties was the test tube in which it was contained. Drug dealers and pimps owned the place, and I'm almost disappointed that when I arrived a man in a fur cape did not offer to buy me a hamburger and a milkshake. But even once you exited the scuzzy labyrinth you saw that the execrable miasma extended for blocks, this being the gritty core of the Big Apple of that time.

Carrying my suitcase along the avenue I beheld all manner of sights, including a six-five black transvestite prostitute in heels, and schlepped my avocado bindle past the peep shows and porno emporia until at last, fifteen blocks south and two long avenues east I arrived at the address given by Vlastos, with whom I had finally spoken. It was on 24th between Fifth and Sixth, a long mile north of what I had envisioned. This area—one dared not think of it as a neighborhood—was a grim no-man's land, and his block was an unrelieved eighth of a mile of warehouses and loading docks. It was inconceivable anyone could live there. Indeed, there was no apartment, only something that might—but mustn't—be described as a loft.

But first I must leave my suitcase with the Hispanic deli owner next door. I would return at noon to meet Vlastos, who now had another engagement. I then walked six blocks north to the *Antaeus* in another part of the city so unappealing and confusing it can barely be described. It was a repulsive hodgepodge of low-rent businesses including foreign import/export establishments and places where tourists might buy a cheap suitcase. When at last I walked up the stairs to the *Antaeus* offices I felt a little better. It was of course a converted "loft," complete with a baffling bathroom whose bucket and plunger and boxes of cleaning materials let you know no one was concerned with impressing visitors. But the office was lined with book-shelves carrying the entire Ecco Press inventory, including copies of the fifty "numbers" of *Antaeus* then extant, plus four desks and a broad window overlooking the ugly street. Two desks were for Dan Halpern and his wife, who were never there; one for the managing editor, Megan, who always was; and one for the intern, who was suddenly me. And what would we be doing today? It had something to do with contacting lapsed subscribers and involved addresses and index cards.

Antaeus was named for the Greek god famous for wrestling—until he wrestled Hercules and lost—and was one of the big "little" magazines, like the *Paris Review*, that one of the big *big* magazines had dubbed part of "the glit-terati." As we have said, both were funded by Drue Heinz, of the eponymous catsup dynasty, but there were a hundred lesser others, most testifying from coffee tables to their subscribers' good taste, and containing poems and stories that seemed calculated to sound like the other poems and stories in these magazines, where one found words like *gloaming* and *limned* and *moue*. And then *gloaming* again. The poems seemed to spend most of their energy in striking the right pose and were therefore often about the crippled tern on the deck of the beach house that reminded you of your dying mother's cough and the ashtray she used in her last winter, the one with the chip in its side that reminded you of the clever hermaphrodite in Venice.

At some point I realized it was time for lunch and I had to make my way back to the Hispanic deli to meet Mr. Vlastos, who would take me upstairs to his "lodgings." The deli owner called him and in a few minutes he was down-stairs. Vlastos was a small, thin, and seventy-ish Greek man who eyed me rather suspiciously through a pair of old-fashioned and particularly filthy eyeglasses. His eyes, when I would at last get a better look at them *sans* glasses, were fierce and piercing, like those of a hawk, or almost like those of a Moray eel peering from a subterranean crevice. But when he wore his glasses they seemed muted and safe.

"Meta-*XAS!*" he said, with the Greek accent on the last syllable. "I am Vlas-TOS!" He nodded to me curtly instead of shaking my hand. It was almost as though he had clicked his heels. There was a formality to him, even a courtliness almost, which the otherwise grimy appearance belied. "OK!" he said, positively. We entered the building and cranky elevator. On the third floor he approached a strange and oversized gray metal door and opened the locks somewhat surreptitiously, suggesting he had been previously mugged here.

And then we entered. But entered what? It was no Romantic poet's or painter's flat or garret, not by twenty thousand leagues or any stretch of the most creative imagination. Indeed, it seemed for all the world like an auto body shop. Or perhaps a machinist's storage room. Or like a small defunct manufacturing plant. It was so filthy and confusing I had no category for it and my head hurt trying to take it in. It was certainly not any kind of apartment—"Bohemian" or otherwise—and even to call it a loft was to forget that lofts are usually "converted," meaning that they are remodeled into places where people can live and contain things like sofas or futons and TV sets and coffee tables and carpets. This seemed to be a loft *before* conversion. The floor was unpainted cement. As we entered, I passed an old chrome coat rack upon which hung a yellowed white shirt that had seemingly been worn often but never laundered. There was also a maroon polyester sport coat and two pre-knotted ties. In time I came to believe that these things, and what he now wore were his entire wardrobe.

On the right, next to a wall of unfinished sheetrock was the daybed that comprised my "quarters," and straight ahead the main "room," filled with industrial equipment. Everything was gray or industrial green and along two walls stood begrimed and cluttered workbenches groaning with tools and boxes and piles of newspapers and magazines. I remember a drill press. Where I had entered, immediately to the right of the coat rack, was Vlastos's "room."

I deposited my suitcase by the bed and bade my new landlord *adieu* to return to the office. I walked there in a daze, as though I'd just visited a prison. Mr. Vlastos had been nice enough, even sweet almost, but where he lived had overwhelmed everything, putting me in mind of the places mobsters took people to murder and dismember them. Suffice it to say I had questions. But on returning to the office I had to focus on the task at hand, sending out poetry rejections. Around this time a former intern stopped by named Brad, who was tall, gay, and from the South, and whom I liked immediately. He was twenty-four but seemed a full decade older than me and was a friendly breath of fresh air: Oscar Levant with a sunny nature. Brad asked me what my new digs were like and of course I was too confused to give any real answer. There was something specific about it that didn't make sense, something my brain hadn't processed—until then. I now realized what my brain had been struggling with: the place had no windows. While there I hadn't explicitly noticed it, but obviously some part of me had inferred it. But how could any place have no windows? I would be back soon enough and would look into the mystery. In the meantime I must destroy would-be poets' illusions, returning what they had typed and letting them know that although we were grateful they had "thought of us," and "let us see it" that it was nonetheless "not for us at this time."

When I returned to Vlastos's after "work" it seemed even worse than I remembered. His own "room" was almost exactly like the filthy "office" of a roadside gas station. It contained a metal desk with a blotter twice my age and an old hotpot and a bed with a metal frame in which my landlord slept—or so I assumed. Its "sheets" were gray for lack of washing and put me in mind of Victorian winding sheets,[2] being possessed of a canvas-like stiffness I attributed to their accretion of filth. Just beyond this bed was the bathroom, and the idea that I was obliged to creep past his occupied bed when I needed to use it during the night gave me gooseflesh.

At some point I got up the courage to ask Mr. Vlastos why there were no windows and he told me quite brusquely: "I have boarded them up!" I saw that there were things *like* windows, but that indeed they had been covered with what looked like plywood and cardboard. "Because of the thieves!" he said. "One black came in here two years ago when I was sleeping and I called the police!"

When I passed his bed to go to the "bathroom" I saw that his room had a kind of window onto a filthy airshaft and its chicken-wired glass was nearly opaque with the soot of decades. There was no kitchen. The bathroom was a wretched utilitarian affair. There was a drain in the speckled cement floor and Vlastos had jury-rigged a kind of shower. There was no proper hot water, but

---

[2] In which they wrapped the dead in days gone by.

my resourceful landlord—a veritable demiurge in his demesne—had created the possibility of it. He proudly showed me a primitive bolt switch he had affixed to the wall. This, he explained, when thrown—*"So!"*—would activate the diminutive water heater—which for all I knew he had found in a dumpster and had resurrected through some lost art. And thus—*voila!*—a small measure of water boiled and steamed, sputtered, and then trickled from the pitted nozzle above. "It is my invention!" he exclaimed!

But the next morning, when I used the homemade "water-heating" gizmo, I was peevishly less enamored of my inventive host. I had arisen at seven and left the gray gloom of the macabre workshop in which I slept to mince carefully past his sleeping form—if he was indeed asleep. He seemed to me in the gloom like a papyrus-wrapped mummy. I eventually saw that there were old newspapers under the sheets which he read indiscriminately, as though there in his bed he had seized time by the shirttails and bade it stop and linger with him in his gray eternal forever. I slunk as silently as possible past his increasingly sinister form, expecting any moment as I passed with the inexplicable slowness of a nightmare that he might suddenly snap upward like a rigged ghoul in a spook house and fix me in his fiery gaze. *Dost trespass upon mine slumber, knave?* Or perhaps more horribly he would only howl and gibber, like a corpse who has forgotten language. When I had finally slipped past him I went into the bathroom and pulled the door to and breathed a sigh. Of course he was inches from me on the other side of the thin, unlocked door. But I must turn my thoughts to the task before me and see if I could work the dials and switches necessary to take a "shower."

I did what I remembered from his instructions. I turned the water on first—this was somehow very important—and once I was sure it was running, and only then did I throw the bolt—*"So!"*—to commence activation of the heating unit. The water pressure was so close to zero that the way in which it extremely slowly leaked out of the nozzle can and will never be believed by anyone. It was the tiniest of trickles, as if the trickle itself smirked at the word "shower." Nor did this volume or water pressure increase. But what could I do? Shivering, I stepped under this anti-Niagara and waited. But waited for what? The "flow" of water was so pitiful that I had to stand under it until such time as a sufficient amount had soaked into the entire mass of my longish early eighties–style hair before it would actually begin running down my neck and shoulders and—by degrees—actually wet the rest of me, this of course being the well-known principle behind "showering." It was an agonizing experience and the misery of it made me forget all about the inert fellow lying in his moldering sheets beyond the door. The water flowed so restrictedly that I learned to use as little shampoo as possible, lest I spend the rest of the summer rinsing it out.

Of course this was a daily experience, and the state of this "shower" hinted at how often it was used. And every morning after holding my breath past my unconscious host, and going through this humbling ascetic routine, I must once again hold my breath past him in the other direction. But sometimes on the return journey I would find him sitting up and reading a newspaper. If he was up, he would greet me with a bracing "Ah! Good morning, boy!" For the entirety of our relationship he called me "Boy" and I assumed he had forgotten my name or decided that inasmuch as there was no one else in our quaint society, he might as well call me what I was to him, for I was not yet twenty and have always looked young for my age and he was at that time a septuagenarian going on five thousand. So there was something elemental and fitting about the word.

After my shower I went back to my "bedroom" to dress while Vlastos roused himself and performed such ablutions as he did, though I guessed they didn't involve anything more elaborate than putting on his robe and slippers and coughing. At some point he called me back into his room—which was where he ate, too, at the metal desk—to join him in a rudimentary breakfast. He would sit in a swiveling office chair at the metal desk and turn on the hotpot to his left. I had no particular expectations or ideas about breakfast and was even somehow honored to be included in it, for our arrangements had never mentioned anything besides a bed.

His routine was fixed. He always and only made hot Ovaltine for each of us, spooning the powder into two old mugs and then filling them with the boiled water. He always put a shot of whiskey in his own, though I had no indication he ever touched alcohol beyond this. While the water was heating, he invariably produced a ripe banana and peeled it and set it upon a plate, which I gathered—apart from the two mugs—was the only crockery in the establishment. He then sliced the banana into approximately ten pieces using a metal knife he seemed to have filched from a local diner—and next took out a slice of some special bread, a loaf of which he always purchased along with his bananas, and put the slice in the toaster next to him, all without ever leaving the swiveling desk chair. When it was toasted he methodically tore it into bite-sized pieces and put it on the plate. Then he administered the honey from a wide-mouthed jar. Rather than let the spoon sink all the way into the honey, which of course would be messy—and rather than taking the spoon out and being forced to wait as the excess honey dripped from it back into the jar before he set it down someplace—Vlastos did something unexpected. He had at some point considered this quotidian puzzle at length and had come up with a novel solution. Whether it was one year ago or fifty I didn't know, but he had bent a simple metal wire in such a way that he could hang it on the inside of the jar, from the jar's lip. The loop of wire descended about an inch into the jar and he put the honey-laden spoon upon it such that the excess honey dripped back into the jar. He saw that I noticed. "It is my invention!" he declared.

The next step in what became our morning routine consisted of his choosing from among the eight or ten dirty old toothpicks stuck underneath the edges of the old desk blotter. With one of these like a picador he stuck one of the banana pieces and popped it into his mouth, doing the same with the toasted bits of bread and honey. Being offered nothing else but the toothpicks, I elected to use my finger. This was breakfast.

There was one thing about Vlastos I had not known when I came to live with him; and when I discovered it I was staggered. As we have established, he was a rather curious figure who seemed distinctly to pride himself on his small inventions. There was something about him that suggested Drosselmeyer in *The Nutcracker*, and something about him, too, that suggested the old Enricht figure from Nabokov's *King, Queen, Knave*. In the way he moved he was sometimes a bit like an automaton, walking in almost jerky steps, like a wooden figure come to life, and yet he seemed a bit like Geppetto too, although nothing he made quite ever came to life. Except, in a way, for one.

In any event, of the several inventions he would show me, none had made their way past his threshold and into the wider world except the one that I had seen many times in my life, and when I realized this I was dumbstruck.

Ever since I was eleven or twelve, I went with my father to the annual Holy Saturday midnight services, arriving after eleven and counting the minutes to midnight and the dawning of the light that came into the world at Easter. Each person held a candle and to prevent the hot wax from dripping onto one's hands, cups of white or red plastic are pushed down over the tapered end of the candle—there is an X cut in their bottoms to accommodate this—making it possible to hold the candle and focus on the liturgy without screaming. Just before midnight the entire church is made dark, with every candle and light extinguished. Then, with great drama, at the stroke of midnight, the priest declares *"Thefte lavete Fos!"* and he takes from beneath the altar the flame there hidden, lighting with it his own beribboned triple-candles and with these lighting the candles of the altar boys around him, who then leave the altar to fan out into the crowd, lighting the candles of those in the first pews, who turn around to light the candles of those in the pews behind them, who turn around to continue this process until the entire church swells with the golden light of the candles, and with the Light of Christ which comes into the world, and eclipses the Darkness—and "the darkness comprehended it not." The ancient drama of this affected me when I was young and over the years that feeling deepened, so that now I am almost in awe of it. But what I did not know about this great tradition until this twenty-first summer of my life was that the plastic cups that shielded the hands of millions of Orthodox faithful around the world were the brainchild of this wizened gnome in whose presence I now sat. So when I came to realize that that which I took for granted was his invention, I almost couldn't believe it. I was suddenly in the presence of a very Tesla—or a Steinmetz!

Vlastos explained that for years he had watched people struggling, sometimes cutting a hole in the bottom of a paper cup and using that, but never quite succeeding. Then he realized he might solve the problem. He said he initially experimented with different colors, but only the red and white sold well. He said they were manufactured each summer and stored in the very room in which I slept till the following spring, when he sent them out. The room would be stacked from floor to ceiling with the boxes. He also showed me where he printed the labels for the churches to which he sent them. Evidently he did all this himself. It was as though I were in a Paschal outpost of Santa's workshop. (The East Pole?) It seemed to me he ought to be famous and celebrated. He had invented something that was a fixture of my childhood and life, and of the childhoods and lives of millions. Who knew that those cups—he dubbed them "Safe-T-Cups for Candles"—hibernated for nine months in this very room! At some point he said it: "They are my invention!" I knew then I was in the presence of something more like a modern Prometheus, or at least a Greek Thomas Edison, who had not quite brought light to the world, but who had brought containment and safety to the light, without which the light was merely a dangerous flame. And thus, too, was his own bright celebrity contained, known only to a precious few.

But there was one place where he really was something like a celebrity. On Bleecker Street near Seventh there was a McDonald's, and with some regularity he would repair thither. When I went with him, he said as much: "Here I am a celebrity!" I didn't understand. "Here," he continued, "they are calling me Mr. Three-Oh-Five!" I still didn't understand, but as we entered—shuffling and herky-jerky at once—he made his way to the counter. The black teenage girls behind it tittered and seemed to know him. He squinted upward at the menu and then suddenly blurted his order in staccato succession, as though overseeing a bank robbery. "Feelay oh Fees'!" Followed by "French fries!" Followed by "Strawberry S'ake!" Then it was over. They scurried to fill the order and the girl at the cash register punched it in—*Ka-ching! Ka-ching!* The girl smiled shyly. "That'll be three-oh-five," she said.

He one day showed me another invention. Surprisingly it was a shoe, a hideous brown affair that was positively orthopedic-looking, with an implausibly thick rubber sole. But looking more closely one saw that the thickness of the sole had a vital purpose, for all along its length were square holes, perhaps twenty or so on each side and each a bit larger than an eighth-of-an-inch square, like square portholes. Vlastos turned the shoe over and showed me the inside and behold! The bottom of the shoe—that part upon which one rested one's foot—was made of a black mesh fabric. I now understood. The sole of one's foot would literally rest "on air." "It is my invention!" he declared triumphantly. "I call them 'Bree-zee Sooz!'" Breezy Shoes? I am sure my face betrayed confusion. "I will show you!" he said. And now, like some confidence man he produced from among the clutter on the workbench a page of ancient newsprint and—*hey, presto!*—crumpled it and then twisted it into a tight length, like a horn. He quickly lit a match and ignited the end of the paper, waiting for it to burn a bit. I watched in silence. When he was satisfied, he blew it out and, having grasped the ugly shoe with his free hand he turned it over so that it was upside down and then thrust the smoking paper into it. "You see!" he said, and then, as if on command, perfectly square smoke emerged from each of the series of holes along the length of the sole. *Square smoke!* I had never seen square smoke before and was vastly more taken in by this extraordinary phenomenon than anything else. Who has ever seen square smoke? But there it was, being extruded from the square holes in the outlandish shoe in that dreary loft.

But after this, Vlastos's face fell a bit. He explained that the product had failed, had for some reason never caught on with the public. From the rubble he produced a yellowed newspaper clipping and handed it to me. It seemed very old and featured an advertisement for the shoes. "Bree-Zee Shoes," it announced. I wondered when he had gotten this idea; when he had manufactured this prototype; when he had tried to market them, and when had he given up? Perhaps because I saw it was something of a tender subject, I did not ask these questions. The advertisement was in such an old typeface it must have been printed in the fifties or sixties. And yet here in front of me was the single prototypical shoe itself, never worn, never used, taking its eternal ease upon the forgotten workbench, the first and last of its line, a stillborn monarch of airy footwear, never to find its grotesque twin and never to walk about the city that had given birth to it!

In mid-July he said a relative was coming to visit, but he was determined that both of us stay and proposed creating a floating wall of corrugated cartons, saying he would hang them from the ceiling and fashion an alcove for me. But I was disinclined to accept. It seemed like a lot of trouble. "Anyway," he said, "I will think about ..." assuming and therefore omitting the object of the preposition, as Greeks often do. "No, no," I said, "that's OK." I sensed that it was time to move on. A friend in Soho knew of a room I could rent cheaply. But I would miss Vlastos. And for many reasons, one of which happened on my twentieth birthday.

Owing to my typical lack of forethought and my parents' strange forgetfulness that year, the day passed without celebration or note or phone call from anyone. It was depressing. I staggered to the office to send out rejection slips and cannot remember how I passed the evening, doubtless with a friend I drummed up at the last minute. But what I can never ever forget from that otherwise dull and lonely day was its beginning. Upon arising I carelessly mentioned to Vlastos that it was my birthday. When I did, he sprang to life. "It's your birthday!" he declared with more glee than I believed him capable. Within a moment he whisked us both from breakfast and walked me out to the filthy room in which I slept where, hitherto unbeknownst to me, there also slumbered some variety of an early electronic organ. Vlastos uncovered it and plugged it in. It glowed and wheezed to life and then, in halting chords and with a surprisingly fine voice the old man played and sang "Happy Birthday" to me. The whole thing. I was profoundly moved and am even more so in remembering it.

A few weeks after I moved out I met him for dinner again, and as we walked down the street he declared something. "Recently," he said, "I have been promoted!" I looked at him, waiting. "Now," he declared, "I am Mr. Three-Twelve!"

CHAPTER TWENTY-TWO

"I ang Leo..."

Because *Antaeus* paid literally nothing for my literary internship it fell to me to find a non-literary job that literally paid something. One day I stumbled into an upscale Mexican restaurant on West Broadway in Soho called Cinco de Mayo and when I inquired whether they needed a busboy, they did, and in no time I was serving coffee to trendy lesbians like Liz Smith and Fran Lebowitz; I even got to spill Paloma Picasso's coffee! There were two principal waiters, both in their early forties. Tomas was kind and professional. Then there was Felix.

Felix was a Castilian—forgive me, Cath-*TEE*-lee-ang—who had great disdain for many things and people and seemed eternally embroiled in battles with someone or other, not least those customers who didn't spend enough money. If a table didn't order drinks and appetizers out of the gate they would struggle for his attention all evening. "They are berry cheep e-people!" he would say. "Berry low-class e-people!" Felix would pronounce all "ens" as "engs," so "one" was "wang" and "am" was "ang." He would go up to the bar and curtly say to the deth-*peek*-able bartender: *"Wang Doth-Equis! Wang e-peet-cha* mah-*gar-ree-tath!* Two *e-peetchas* thang-*gree-a!"* I was never clear why Felix disliked the bartender, but he dismissed him with the same disgust and sneering facial expressions Kenneth Mars's character deployed against Ryan O'Neal and Barbra Streisand in Peter Bogdanovich's *What's Up, Doc?* His hair was just long enough to cover his ears and he parted it down the middle, as was the fashion. I supposed he was gay, but at the time honestly didn't have any real idea what a gay Spaniard might be like.

When Felix arrived he always went downstairs to a little closet to change and once I saw that he used a "Tummy Trimmer," a rubbery contraption advertised on TV that one put around one's protruding abdomen until *zip!* and *voila!*—a perfectly trim tummy. Over this he wore his requisite white shirt and black vest, in which costume he emerged to spend his shift serving the *cheep eh-people!* I couldn't help feeling sorry for him, even as he annoyed me. He seemed to like me well enough, perhaps because I was just young enough to be respectful of him, although in the pecking order he was effectively my boss.

Once he asked me what kind of music I liked and boasted that in his apartment he had thousands of records: "Brazee-lian, e-Spanish, Ee-tah-lian! All kind of e-music. And I cang cook berry well Cath-tee-lian reh-the-peeth! Song ti-ang I will invite you!" I mumbled something non-committal, now suspecting there might be more to the invitation than paellas and international music.

But one day I was sitting with him in this downstairs area before our shift when out of the blue he asked what my horoscope was. I said I was born in late June, and was therefore a Cancer. "Oh!" he said, clearly taken aback. "Cang-ser people berry berry moo-thee e-people! Berry up, down! Up, down!" He sneered a bit. I wondered if perhaps there was some particular "Cang-ser" person in his past. Then he went further: "Cang-ser people berry berry unlucky in love!" He stated it as though it were accepted science. But really? I was doomed to be "unlucky in love" because of my birthday? But I didn't feel like getting in an argument. He obviously had fixed views; and wanting to shift the conversation I brightly asked him what horoscope he was, hoping to bring things to a less dramatic level.

But now he looked at me deeply, as though about to confide something untoward. Everything in the room seemed to stop as his gaze fairly smoldered. In fact it was almost as though smoke were emerging from somewhere behind him in order to properly frame the declaration he would now make. And then he said it, his eyes widening and his nostrils flaring, with a hint of threat in his voice. *"I ang Leee-o!"* he said. There was an unmistakable "hear me roar" subtext.

"Oh," I said, trying not to respond to the new drama obviously unfolding. We were supposed to move some chairs, so I stood up to deal with that, but as I thought about what Felix had said and how he said it, I couldn't help finding it funny. What was the great drama behind it? Why did he say it in such a way as to imply there was much more there? I realized he had hoped to say more, probably about how he was regal and ferocious, and he said it dramatically to bait me into doing so, but I hadn't. I suppose I could sense that asking him to go on would have meant wading into a swampy psychodrama involving his own "love" story—and how being a Leo was at the growling heart of darkness of it all.

But rather than understanding what was happening and simply ignoring it, I let my immature desire for laughter get the better of me, and did what in retrospect was a terrible thing. The moment I could I ran to the bartender, who was one of the very few relatively normal people on the premises, and related the conversation, culminating in the declaration: *"I ang Leee-o!"* Why I did that I don't know, but in a few moments I would regret my action mucho. Because when Felix next went to the bar to place an order, the bartender couldn't resist. "You know, Felix," he said, "I was wondering what horoscope you were ..." I overheard this and cringed in horror. But it was too late. "I dunno," he continued, "but for some reason to me you look like a Leo." And there it was. It took a moment for the comment to register with Felix, at which point he looked taken aback—and did one of those takes the actor Franklin Pangborn was famous for. But as he realized I had obviously related our private conversation to the bartender, he gave me a look. I was some distance away, but it was a look that haunts me these years later and I hope continues to haunt me for the rest of my life, because of course I deserve it. What makes it worse is that I am sure Felix was used to others treating him this way. His behavior pushed you to it. But that didn't excuse it on my part, and I bear the sin for my part in contributing to his hurt and inability to trust people. But isn't it possible to feel genuinely guilty and repentant and still find something funny?

CHAPTER TWENTY-THREE

Senior Year

1983–1984

Going into my senior year, some of the Schroeder Lounge gang decided it was time to live off-campus. This was what all the cool and artsy people did. My friends Bill and Marc and I found an apartment on the top floor of a ramshackle three-story house on Howe Street, which seemed to form the very border between wealthy Yale and crime-addled New Haven and might aptly be thought of as a literal, paved hyphen separating the words "Town" and "Gown."

My friend Marc's sister had the semester before studied "economics" in Moscow, when the Cold War was still in full fan, making the idea of studying there all the more fashionable among those opposed to Reagan, who had called it an "evil empire." The Soviet elites knew naive Americans studying in Moscow provided a nice way to smuggle their ideas to the West. So when my friend's sister departed they loaded her with "gifts" in the form of a trove of Soviet propaganda posters. Some of them had a wonderfully Stalinist-era look that would appeal to her friends, who posted them in their dorm rooms and apartments as a winking nod to their anti-Reagan views. In fact, she had been given so many that she gave her brother a bunch to give his friends. When Marc generously said I could have my pick, I was thrilled. A free retro poster!

And one that would burnish my credentials as a "right-thinking" member of those in solidarity with the worker. I finally chose a shot of Lenin standing heroically and holding a book, posting it on the sliding door of my closet and never gave it another thought. Until my parents visited.

My mother and father and my friends had gathered and chatted in the living room for a while and before my parents left they came with me into my bedroom, where we talked for a while. At some point my father noticed the poster and asked me where I had gotten it and I told him. Before they left to go home, he asked if he could talk to me for a moment and joined me in the living room where he slightly sternly asked me, "as a personal favor" to him, to please remove "that poster." Suddenly getting the picture, I was stunned. I almost couldn't believe that I had evidently forgotten everything the man who so loved me had taught me, that the atmosphere of Yale had so affected me that I hadn't given him the slightest thought when I chose the poster and put it up. I was shocked at the sudden revelation of the distance I had drifted from him and his values—and from his love for me in this thoughtlessness. Knowing how hard this man was working and had worked so that I could study here, who had himself seen the evils of Communism, I was deeply ashamed.

"Yes," I said, humbly. "I will."

Intimations

It was in that bedroom one night that I had what, for me, was as close as anything I had ever experienced to a vision. I was on the verge of sleep when very distinctly, in my mind's eye, I saw a kind of circular hole in the floor of a ship or something, I wasn't sure where the hole was exactly, but water was kind of sloshing up through it, and at the time I knew that it had some significance. As I thought about it I figured that this was the hole leading from the conscious to the unconscious, and it was the goal of human beings to keep this portal open, allowing passage between the two realms. I had read enough Freud and Jung by then to have an idea of their theories, so this made sense.

In another year or two I thought a better way of expressing this idea was as a hole in the ice of a frozen lake. In life, we were on the conscious side of things—the frozen surface—hacking away to get to the water. Once we had chopped through and found the water—which is the unconscious sea beneath—we would have to skim the ice away periodically to keep it from refreezing. This, in the Freudian sense, would constitute "psychic" health. This model of the human soul seemed right, and for a year or two I thought that the goal of life—and what for many constituted "religion"—must be this, to drill through the ice to the water beneath, to whatever it was on the "other" side. And if that was the real point and project of this life, then that's what people really meant when they talked about being "born again." That was just the contemporary Christian term for what all religions were trying to do, to reach the Godhead, to transcend this world and reach the next, to build a ziggurat that poked through to the heavens. And once we had drilled through to the other side and had struck water and found the collective unconscious, which Jung said was "God," then we would have achieved a new state of being, the one for which we had been born. I had no idea what this meant practically, and had no idea how one would do the drilling, and certainly no idea what would happen when one got through and hit water. I didn't even know how one would know when one had reached the water. Would there be some epiphany or splash? At this point it was all pure theory, with no practical meaning in my life, and no expectations on my behavior. So what was it, exactly? Could a theory that is pure theory really be a theory?

Political Correctness

During senior year there bloomed on campus an effort having to do with South Africa, then still under apartheid. Everyone knew apartheid was unconscionable, so it was proposed that our senior class funds be divested from any companies doing business with this rogue nation. I neither then nor since have fully understood whether divesting was a good idea, practically, but at the time no one who thought it might not be a good idea was willing to voice their objection against the winds of moral rectitude sweeping the campus. In many ways this was the beginning of what we today call political correctness, and to say anything against divestiture was like suggesting Hitler had done some positive things. Anyone daring to dissent would quickly be hissed into silence and shame. So except for those few outspoken conservatives on campus who were already hated, no one said a word.

But my friend Chris Hanes, an economics major and a liberal Democrat, nonetheless told me over dinner that he thought divesting our class funds from South Africa was counterproductive. I did not trouble myself about his argument, remaining in lockstep with all my other classmates, because I too assumed there could be only side to the issue, and Chris must simply be indulging the racism he had brought north from Atlanta. When our class had a referendum on the subject, I duly voted YES. There was a cardboard box outside the Calhoun Dining Hall and one simply wrote one's YES or one's NO on a piece of paper and folded it and put it in the box. The next day I asked my close friend Sam how the vote had gone. He was involved in calling for the vote and had manned the Calhoun polling box. He said it went well. Everyone had voted YES—"except for your buddy, Chris Hanes." It took me a moment to process what Sam said, but I quickly gathered what was obvious enough, that he had seen Chris scrawl NO on his piece of paper. It was at this point that something deep inside me caught, like the tooth of a gigantically large gear. The idea that someone had looked at someone else's vote outraged me, but more than that, I was bothered that there was a "right way" to vote, and that those administering the "vote" should have this kind of vested interest in the outcome—that they dared to observe whether everyone voted "the right way." It seemed perfectly Communist. Years earlier I asked my mother how there could be elections in the U.S.S.R., and she explained that it was all a show, with a predetermined outcome. Everyone voted for the party candidate, and you made sure you did. It helped me understand how totalitarian systems worked. But to hear that those concerned with the fate of South Africa would behave like this shocked me. It was then that the campus zeitgeist along with which I had been drifting first concerned me. I didn't do anything about it, of course, but kept drifting along, but it was a marker for me in a larger journey. I didn't know anything then of Lillian Hellman's Stalinism, or of Leonard Bernstein's fashionable limousine liberalism, but I was nonetheless fellow-traveling with their ideo-logical children. What would become of me?

John Hersey

And so we approached the sheer cliff that was graduation, though I certainly didn't see it coming as such. In my last semester I thought I would try to get into a writing seminar regarded as the ultimate level of cool in certain circles. It was taught by the legendary John Hersey himself. Only ten seniors made it into this course, offered each spring, and this year the competition would be tougher yet, because it was his last year, and it was open to talented juniors too. Mr. Hersey was a Yale institution, though I knew nothing of him at the time. He had won the Pulitzer Prize for *A Bell for Adano*, the fictionalized account of an Italian village in World War II, but was most famous for *Hiroshima*, a classic work of journalism that detailed the experiences of six people living in Hiroshima when the terrible bomb exploded there. In a decision that made publishing history, *New Yorker* editor Harold Ross published the thirty-one-thousand-word article not in four installments, as originally planned, but in a single issue. It was prob-ably the earliest example of what came to be called the New Journalism, incor-porating the devices of fiction in reportage.

Albert Einstein ordered a thousand copies and that issue of the magazine became a collector's item. When I tried to impress my parents by telling them I'd gotten into this course and referenced *Hiroshima*, they said they thought they had heard of that book, but confused it with *Hiroshima, Mon Amour,* an avant-garde French film from 1959, though as they were hardly aficionados of the avant-garde, this was not unimpressive. Recalling this and similar episodes sometimes reminds me of a Carol Burnett sketch in which Eunice (played by Burnett) and her husband Ed (played by Harvey Korman), along with "Mama" (played by Vickie Lawrence) visit the home of Eunice's brother, a celebrated Hollywood screenwriter played by Roddy McDowell. We soon see why he doesn't visit them much. Ed tells him he "orta" put more of that stuff like "them Three Stooges" do in his screenplays. My wonderful family were hardly like the characters in that sketch, but there was something in Roddy McDowell's pained expressions at their failure to understand him and his world that now and again resonates with me. It is hard to want to share something with people we love and be unable to do so.

The class itself was held Wednesday afternoons for two hours. We sat in an open square of desks. In one class Mr. Hersey wanted to teach us about the follies of fame, though he was too respectful of us to say so. Instead, to underscore the point, he read us some of the fan letters he had received, one of which was a letter from someone claiming to have a "Glasses Hall of Fame," asking whether Mr. Hersey might be willing to donate an old pair for the collection. But this hardly succeeded in dissuading any of us. How happy we would have been to get such a letter!

One of the things he taught us I never will forget, not least because I have come to see it as true but crucially important. In talking of the power of words, he said that the breakdown of communication leads to violence. We weren't sure what he meant, but he wanted us to understand that there was something sacred about writing, that it came with grave responsibilities. Writing was not merely an aesthetic exercise, but was a moral act of truth-telling, so the writer has an important place in society, one he must not take lightly as a mere path to fame or self-aggrandizement. Hersey seemed to embody the older and truly liberal idea that there is a right way to do things and a wrong way, that chest-beating histrionics are vulgar and in being vulgar are in fact morally wrong. He never mentioned Norman Mailer, but he didn't need to. Hersey would not have said it for fear of sounding self-important, but seemed to think the writer—and in saying "the writer" he confirmed this thinking—was to be something of a prophet, and was to "speak truth to power."

More important than these classes were the weekly private sessions in his office, where we discussed our work. Hersey was a forbidding figure, certainly to me, who had no previous dealings with diffident patricians. His office was in Davenport, where he had been Master during the tumultuous sixties, when he had written a little book titled *Letter to the Alumni*, attempting to persuade more staid Old Blues that they ought not worry about what was happening at Yale with the anti-war activists.

My sessions with Mr. Hersey didn't do much for me, probably because I was less interested in learning how to write than in being confirmed as the genius I believed I already was—though to be fair to my past self, it is probably also because whether writing can be taught remains an open question. The idea that one can learn to write has not been exploited until rather recently—the most venerable of such places, the Iowa Writers' Workshop, opened in 1936—but what are such places really but opportunities to write and hone one's already established talents? No one believes Flannery O'Connor learned to write in Iowa. It was a gift she had long before she went there. For genetic evidence of where my gift came from I only need glance at a small notebook of my great-grandfather's from the 1870s which my father keeps in the back of his clothes closet, in which Panagis Vergotis wrote in a tiny hand the etymologies of various Greek words. That I should have myself inherited whatever genes propel one toward an affinity for etymology is incontrovertible, and what is etymology but a fascination with the stem cells of words, and with the very nature of language? But that he and I—born 120 years apart—should share this says something about the nature-versus-nurture aspect of this question.

But when something comes into fashion, a way to make money from it is likely to follow, and toward the end of the twentieth century a universe of MFA programs in short fiction and poetry sprang up in which students learned more than anything how to teach fiction and poetry to younger versions of themselves. There also emerged from this the aforementioned world of "little" magazines, which few read, but which afforded writers an opportunity to see themselves "in print" and collect necessary credentials.

Part of what made my time in my sessions with Mr. Hersey difficult too was my then being hopelessly in love with John Cheever, so much so that—as has happened to me with other writers—I only wanted to mimic what he was writing, probably in some effort to vault into the world of his art, or to build for myself via my own sentences a bridge into it. Whenever I have found something so tremendously appealing I have often tried to create more of it myself. So when reading Cheever I wanted to write more Cheever, and probably wanted to become John Cheever. This is related to the parodic instinct some people possess and which I certainly do. When I've seen a particularly powerful movie I find that I want to be inside the world of that movie so badly that I cannot stop imitating lines from it until everyone around me runs away. It also happened to me a few years later with the written humor of Woody Allen. But when I read Cheever during this period, it was particularly pronounced, as though his writing began a bridge to another world I hoped my own writing might complete, and I could enter that world forever.

During spring break I wandered into a thrift shop in Danbury and spotted a paperback of his first novel, *The Wapshot Chronicle*. Reading it was like a religious experience. Such experiences are the inviolable mysteries of our race. In fact, the phrase "the inviolable mysteries of our race" is precisely what Cheever might have written and which I find myself writing when thinking of him as I am now. I had an internship at the *Hartford Courant* that week and was daily taking the bus to Hartford and back while reading the book, and I fell into it so hopelessly that even the woodcuts in the book—which Cheever may not even have approved—transported me, as though they were clues to the world inside the book. Part of the parodic instinct is an ear for rhythms, and most writers have rhythms in their writing that are almost like fingerprints. So after reading that book I found that all I could do in my writing was ape the recently deceased Cheever's prose, as though the greatest literary achievement would be to write a short story no one could tell from a Cheever story. Of course this got me nowhere with Mr. Hersey, although it would in a year's time get me involved in my first and only serious relationship outside of my marriage.

Reading my Cheever-mooning prose was probably what led Mr. Hersey to tell me he and Cheever were close friends for many years. When he said this I believe my breathing changed and the blood drained from my face. He might as well have told me he had once purchased a frog from Sam Clemens, or had carved scrimshaw with Hank Melville while Nate Hawthorne whittled a bust of Hester Prynne, or that he'd ridden to Canterbury with a company of pilgrims that included a man yclept Geoff Chaucer. I couldn't get over it. Mr. Hersey suggested I read an interview he had done with Cheever that some years before was published in the *Paris Review*. He even said a tape recording of it had been made. My eyes started from their sockets, not because I cared a fig for Cheever's thoughts on fiction, but because I might actually hear his speaking voice. Hearing him read the first three hundred names in the Boston phonebook would have been divine.

Adam Liptak lent me his Cheever's *Collected Stories* paperback and I saw—gulp—that it was signed! How I stared at that signature! My obsession with Cheever didn't much abate over the next few years and I read his stories often, as though a healthful draught of his sentences could assuage whatever ailed me.[1]

"Cheever was a very religious man," Mr. Hersey once said. I hardly knew what to make of this, but began to notice moments in his writing where his faith revealed itself. The most dramatic was "The Death of Justina," about a hapless advertising copywriter getting increasingly frustrated with the garbage he had to write. Cheever ends the story with the haggard man typing the Twenty-Third Psalm, which Cheever includes in full. And then, the last sentence: "I gave this to Ralphie and went home."

There were many places where Cheever's theological predilections are in evidence, and he believed people should disport themselves with what he called a certain "fitness." Propriety and character mattered. The last page of *The Wapshot Chronicle* quotes the end of the diary of the hero's beloved father, Leander. It is advice for his sons, and the last words are: "Cherish the love of an honest

---

[1] This kind of literary puppy love had befallen me before, though. It happened a year earlier with Thomas Pynchon. In an American Lit class we were assigned Pynchon's *The Crying of Lot 49* and I instantly became obsessed, although part of that probably had something to do with his Salinger-like reclusivity, too. I soon read his first novel *V.* and then—God help me—tried to read the busted goober that is *Gravity's Rainbow*. But I cared nothing for what Pynchon was saying, only for the rhythms of his writing and, to a small extent, for his odd humor. It reached an apogee in the spring of 1983 when I wrote a short story published in a Yale magazine called *Zirkus*. It was as close to writing an actual Pynchon story as I would ever come. Writing it felt very much the way one feels who can so well imitate someone that they are able to improvise in that other person's voice—so much so that what they say, even if it never was said by the person they are imitating, might well *have been* something he said or could have said or would eventually have said. In fact, I was so deadly in sync with the rhythms and voice of Pynchon that at one point in the story I wrote two short sentences: "Was it x or y? He wondered." And then a few weeks later while reading *V.* for the first time I came upon virtually the same sentences. I had so utterly internalized his voice and rhythms that I really could write what he would write—and now I had proof, because he really had written it, and there it was. But my ardor for Pynchon cooled to freezing when I fell for Cheever, though even Cheever wouldn't be my last goo-goo fest, because at some point I would look up and lo! there would be Nabokov swinging his pens Cyrillically in the on-deck circle.

woman. Trust in the Lord." Such sentiments were rarely far from Cheever, and over the next years they would call to me now and again, as from a distance.

At Yale, the magical realism of Gabriel García Márquez—and to some the writing of Jorge Luis Borges, too—influenced me. I felt that perhaps I ought to write stories or a novel about Cephalonia that was something like Márquez's approach to the fictional world of Macondo in *One Hundred Years of Solitude*. Márquez's winning the Nobel Prize the year before, plus his close friendship with Fidel Castro—especially at that time of fashionable opposition to Reagan's Nicaraguan policies—made his writing better known in the circles in which I ran. During my senior year *Vanity Fair* was resurrected after a half century, debuting with a formidably thick issue that like the *New Yorker* edition of Hersey's *Hiroshima*, published the entirety—in Gregory Rabassa's English translation—of Márquez's most recent novella, *Chronicle of a Death Foretold*.

I read it in the spring of 1984, and it combined somehow with the background Cheever radiation in my mind to help me write a short story titled "The Wild Ride of Miss Impala George," for which I won a major literary prize at graduation, and which eventually became my first published work. In that story I seem to have transmuted what I loved about Cheever and his work into something of my own, in which I explore what I now see is a theme for me, of boundaries and their transcendence. It begins with a fictional stand-in for me in a small aluminum outboard on Lake Candlewood, wondering about the world beneath the water. As I have said earlier, Lake Candlewood is man-made, and covers much of what was once farmland. The story purports to be the account of a woman displaced by the lake, and who, as soon as she popped out of my mind and into the world via the story, I loved. I still love her and see in all women I admire and love something of her. The narrator of the story says that sometimes while mapping the underwater contours of the lake he has an urge to slip overboard. In retrospect I find this very telling, as though the shape of my psyche had in this story revealed itself, much as a tree stump or some such "structure" would actually poke up and show itself above the surface of the water during a drought.

CHAPTER TWENTY-FOUR

Graduation from Yale

1984

We produced two issues of the *Yale Record* senior year, the second being a parody of the *Yale Daily News*, which took itself so seriously it desperately needed mocking. Our headline revealed the existence of a race of "chicken-men" living in the stacks of Sterling Library.

As we approached graduation, Chris Hanes and I thought we should try to give the Class History at graduation. This was a satirical speech that is a Yale tradition. Chris wrote most of it, to be sure, and the judges chose us from the many entrants, reportedly unanimously. So we would deliver it in front of thousands on Class Day. But first there was a battle to be fought. Someone demanded we remove certain lines, and it fell to our class secretary, Larry Lawrence, to communicate this to us.

The theme of the speech—if theme it had, being a concatenation of silly jokes—was that Yale had in our four years become more uptight and politically correct, though as that term did not yet exist, we used the term "tight-ass." For evidence we cited the banning of Bladderball and other things. Of course at twenty—which I then was—one frowns on restrictions, even those designed to prevent dismemberment and death. And editing was censorship! We reluctantly changed a line here and there but secretly vowed that at the podium we would surreptitiously revert to our original text. If we must take a bullet for artistic expression and free speech, we were prepared. Also, the battle betwixt us and our—we now saw—power-mad class secretary had been unpleasant enough that we considered adding a line or two to even the score.

At last the great day came. The setting was glorious. Everyone was in full regalia, with their long Revolutionary-era clay pipes that were our tradition, gathered on the vast quadrangle that was Old Campus, the very ground where Nathan Hale's dorm still stands and where the faux-Gothic buildings enclose the four hallowed acres. And there we sat overlooking it all, in the umbra of Harkness Tower's patriarchally oppressive phallus, just beyond which were the doors of Skull and Bones in whose crypt-like basement sat the skull of Geronimo, stolen by U.S. Vice President George H.W. Bush (Yale '48). To our left on the stage sat the conversationalist nonpareil Dick Cavett (Yale '58) and President Giamatti (Yale '60), and finally our class president, suddenly no longer sporting the younger twin of Bart's goatee, which he mock-sadly explained had gone on "to that Great Chin in the Sky."

Everyone that day—except perhaps for courageous Chris Hanes—wore ribbons on their caps and gowns, one gold and one green. One expressed our disapproval of South African apartheid; the other our solidarity with Yale's Union workers. Chris and I walked onto the gigantic makeshift stage and out in the sea of ten thousand were my beloved parents and grandmother and brother and my cousins Eleanor and Marion and Tante Eleonore and Uncle Joe and John Tomanio and George Duncan. Everything was a blur until we came to a tremendously solemn part in the ceremony. It was a short memorial service for our classmate Roosevelt Thompson.

Two months earlier I had gotten a phone call from my friend Kirk Hughes, saying Rosie had just been killed. Rosie was a legend even before his horribly premature death. He was a black preacher's kid from rural Arkansas who was soft-spoken, brilliant, and humble, and who had a work ethic that made bees blush. Though no taller than I, he was on the Yale football team, and back in Arkansas was a protege of the young governor, Bill Clinton, in whose footsteps he was already following by having just won a Rhodes Scholarship. But driving back to Yale near the end of spring break a semi jumped the divider, killing

Rosie instantly. His death was a rebuke to anyone with easy answers about the meaning of life, or about how everything happens for a purpose.

Many of my friends—Tom Edman and Bill and Kirk and Sam—had roomed with Rosie as freshmen and flew to Arkansas for the funeral. Kirk said Rosie's preacher father in the eulogy said he and his family loved Rosie with all their hearts, but they loved God more. The idea staggered me. That kind of faith was far beyond anything I had conceived. How to make sense of it? To tell the world you loved the God who allowed this to happen more than you loved your son was a more powerful statement of faith than anything I imagined. Saying such a thing in the Orthodox world I knew would have been shocking and distasteful, as though one didn't sufficiently love one's son. So it struck me powerfully when Kirk said it, and suggested God might be real.

Chris and I took in this short reprise of the Arkansas ceremony and before it was over, thousands were weeping. But I was not. Because in the midst of this I had glanced at the sumptuously printed program to see something that, if true, was a door leading to a nightmare. I saw that somehow—impossibly, inexplicably, insanely—following this unbearably sad moment was "The Class History," with Chris's name and mine next to it. Evidently momentarily, following the Noahide flood of tears over this magnificent young man's death, Chris and I must step to the podium and crack puerile jokes. I was instantly out of my mind with bowel-shifting fear. This couldn't be happening. The day was too beautiful and the company upon the stage too august.

Had a bird-like demon now leapt from a Hieronymus Bosch painting to impale me with its devil's beak as it carried me wriggling and shrieking toward eternal perdition, I don't think I could have been more horrified. Indeed, in my current state, I could neither shriek nor wriggle to protest. I was on a great stage with dignitaries in black gowns—with Dick Cavett! But I understood that Chris and I, a pair of callow clowns and insensitive buffoons, must nonetheless now arise and dare try to extract guffaws from this sobbing sea of humanity. What could be more blasphemous and hateful? My mind reeled and staggered like a drunken sailor with two peg legs on the deck of a pitching ship. Then I gagged to realize that the one who likely had orchestrated this was none other than our class speaker, he of the former goatee! Now I understood everything and had I a broadsword to hand I might have risen to unseam him from nave to chops, for even a cloven fellow upon this stage and my subsequent imprisonment could not be worse than what was about to happen—than what silent second by silent second drew nearer and nearer, as like synchronized worms we two inched forward to our Fatal Doom.

Surely Larry would quietly smirk for joy as we were feted with the modern-day equivalent of a thousand hurled rotten cabbages and tomatoes. Larry! He it was and none other who had created this order of events, who had placed this unfathomably sad moment just before our sophomoric japery! And there was no escape. Neither Chris—suddenly beginning to understand my blank stare and dumb pointing to the program—nor I were clever enough to come up with a plan in the next sixty seconds that ticked and tocked away. Larry had, of course, done this because of how we had mocked him for insisting we clean up our act. But now the clean-shaven nerdnik would taste sweetest revenge—would hoist the slick funnymen on their own petard to basest ignominy and would for decades over cigars and brandy regale his banker friends with this triumph!

In seconds there would be the briefest pause as things transitioned from this memorial, during which people would continue to cry and honk. And then we would be introduced. I already imagined that as we dared to begin our idiotic speech someone in the crowd would boo loudly, quickly followed by a righteous chorus of boos and jeers, until a tidal wave of the same would wash us off the stage and down, down, into a Davy Jones's Locker of humiliation such that two years hence, having historically fluffed Mookie Wilson's grounder in Game Six, Bill Buckner would beam with the happy notion that at least he had not suffered the worse fate of Hanes and Metaxas!

Part of the agony of these moments was that, though there was no way out, my mind nonetheless desperately scrambled for one. Yet over and over none was found, and the seconds continued to count down. And then at last—almost as a mercy—the hangman rose and walked to the podium. And out of his newly shaven jaws there came the words that with every muon and neutrino and quark we dreaded. "Ladies and gentlemen!" he said, the electronically amplified words ringing out across the illimitable expanse of tear-streaked faces. "We will now hear the 1984 Class History—by Eric Metaxas and Chris Hanes!" The impropriety alone of this brief, cheery introduction was an oppressive foreshadowing of what was to come. But to us the words seemed to echo forever. Had he really said them? I wanted to shrug haplessly and semi-comically, like Giuletta Masina in *La Strada*. But we did not have time to process anything anymore. The noose was waiting. Chris and I looked at each other dumbly, and then like waxworks automatons rose lifelessly from our seats to face our deaths. I imagine Cavett was now inwardly leaping for joy that it was not his turn, as even the great Groucho would have been daunted by this unrelievedly grim and still mostly blubbering audience. Although Groucho being Groucho, he might have been able to get away with saying: "For the love of Christmas, get a hold of yourselves. It's not like somebody died or something!" He could have gotten away with that. And probably only he. And we were not he.

Chris and I took our time settling at the podium, he on the left, I on the right. Why rush? Perhaps a bus-sized meteor might strike nearby, or Connecticut's historically quiet tectonic plates would suddenly shudder, throwing us all to the ground and saving us the looming horror. Had I an M-80 or smoke bomb I certainly would have used it and bought some time. Anything. Except what we now must do. Because it was up to us to begin our own hanging, it was the more agonizing. Had there been someone to pull the lever and spring the trap door it would have been far better. But no. We must ourselves now leap in unison from the lonely crag.

But the first words on the page in front of us were a surprising sop against the grimness. I forgot that we planned to begin by together exclaiming "Greetings!"—as a way of making fun of our class secretary. He was infamous for saying this word, always delivered in an orotund basso so forceful and direct that it sounded threatening. Opening with this was not in our "official" scripts, for who would be dumb enough to telegraph such a thing? But as we looked down now I saw it and remembered. I had previously thought it a hair much, but now, knowing him to be the one handing us our tumblers of hemlock, we would not shrink from delivering it, and with gusto. We looked at each other to synchronize the word properly, as it was the only one we would speak together, and quietly mouthed *one, two, three* to each other and then after a pause, looking out over the hostile desert of humanity, we spoke. In a solid imitation of the fiend who had put us there we loudly said: *"GREET-INGS!!!"* Our doubled voices exploded through the hopped-up sound system and bounced and echoed off the pseudo-ancient walls of ivy and brown stone all around. And *incredibly*—like a BB hitting a mosquito—our missile found its mark. Impossibly, miraculously, our classmates laughed. And howled. They screamed. The pressure of sadness and solemnity built up during the memorial service was now—*gloria in excelsis Deo!*—released. We could not continue for the laughter. And behind us, slunk down in his chair and fuming like a silent screen villain, was the object of everyone's fun, for whom I suddenly now, as the howling continued, actually felt a bit sorry.

Ten thousand mouths open in laughter. It was one of those unutterably glorious moments in life, because it came from something we had written and had now said. It was that feeling stand-up comics live to repeat, that home run off the sweet spot in the bat that makes every batter labor to do it again and again, until two decades later his bones creak and the fans look away in embarrassment. *GREETINGS!!!* To be awash in that much laughter, and all of it contained to greater effect by the halcyon walls of Old Campus, like some Olympic cocktail of love and *schadenfreude* combined!

After that heavenly opening salvo, the speech was a cinch to succeed, and by God's grace it did. As planned, we reinstated each of the forbidden phrases, unable to see our class secretary scowling behind us, and we sailed on, from glory to glory. When at last we turned around to retake our seats amidst further thunderous applause, Larry—half-jokingly?—gave us a "hoo boy, you're gonna get it!" look.

I was far too joggled by what had just happened to be very attentive to what my future friend Dick Cavett now said. My head was swimming in several atmospheres of ether and laughing gas. At the end of the ceremony we stood and pulled out the white handkerchiefs we'd been given to sing "For God, for Country, and for Yale" and the sheer feeling of being up there with Chris, waving our handkerchiefs with the thousands across Old Campus, and with the myriad thousands waving them here across the decades,

I got a lump in my throat. It was as if we were waving goodbye to all of this, and it was the more poignant because this was the first time many of us—I for sure—saw it for what it really was, the beginning of the end of our youth. Somehow in that moment it all came to me, that this was the end of something movingly beautiful, something green and young and innocent and golden, and there I was as one awake in his own dream, walking through that present as though I had stepped back into it from the future and could appreciate it as such, in the eternal now that is the state to which all of our broken world aspires and to which one day it will again be redeemed and restored. On this side of that veil we get these glimpses so rarely, and even then see but through a glass darkly, but even these rarest glances are so powerful and affecting that they haunt us forever, and draw us forward toward their final and full realization. They are sign posts of eternity and transcendence all around us, and yet not yet fully accessible. They are not teases but are blazes on the trail, so we must look for them, must be open to them in our hearts. For if we are not, we miss these moments and only stagger on in the dark.

Even now I wonder how that golden moment in the past can be past and those happy young faces be gone forever. I see them smiling back at me now so vividly and it is this minute as real as it was then, and perhaps more so—not just more real but more present too, in this future time that is as much then as that past moment then was. Is that what memory is, a kind of explosion inward unto eternity and transcendence? Is this the glory of our human minds, made in the image of God, through which, though fallen, nonetheless preserves some dim echo of eternity and Eden in its unfathomably deep fibers, and thus is able, Godlike, to shuttle between past and present and future with the infinite speed of thought? The most glorious animals cannot do it, but we can. Nothing can hold us, because our minds were created to yearn toward the borders of our world, to yearn to return to that place where they were created, outside of time and space. And in them we retain something of that freedom we had in our first state, and our memorializing minds remind us of what we once were and of what by the grace of God we can once again be, flying forever beyond the ramparts of time.

The actual graduation the next day was heartbreakingly dull because it rained and the ceremony was in a church that had no resonance for any of us. Graduations were supposed to take place in the more intimate settings of our residential colleges; ours should have been on the emerald sward of Calhoun's courtyard, where stood the elm that had miraculously survived Dutch elm disease and outlived its doomed generation and from whose swing I had often swung and on whose grass I had sat and talked and where the future had beckoned me. There too I had shepherded the visiting Jacques Derrida across a temporary whiffle-ball outfield in the light rain, holding an umbrella over his swollen head.[1]

But at least we were all together, my Calhoun classmates and our families. The highlight for me was receiving two senior prizes for my fiction, one for my "Impala George" story and one for an account of my mother's escape from East Germany in 1951. My friends applauded and howled and jeered. And then it was over. I was a Yale graduate. I packed my things into my parents' trunk and said my hurried goodbyes to Chris and Bill and Kirk and Tom and Sam and Chaz and to everyone else I loved—and to so many others too, with whom I suddenly realized I had shared so much—and then I got in the car with my still young parents and drove with them out of the Elm City toward Danbury, making our way through the rain along the road to my future.

---

[1] This poem can be found at this link on my website: http://ericmetaxas.com/writing/poems/derrida-and-umbrella/.

CHAPTER TWENTY-FIVE

Grand Tour, Einzer Schtück

If ever there were a season when the disparate parts of my identity—usually separated in my life, and allowed to ignore their other selves—were compelled to mingle, as at an unforgettably uncomfortable cocktail party, surely the summer after my graduation was that season. Understand that I had envisioned myself traveling first to London, where gazing in the British Museum at the black basalt of the Sennacherib Stele I would have glimpsed in its ancient and dusky mirror the reflection—now floating, now swimming—of that pale beauty who should become my wife; but before I could persuade her Baronet papa that I was worthy of her ivory hand I must skip across the Aegean and the Dardanelles to take in Heinrich Schliemann's butchery of the mound at Hissarlik and then traverse the Levant to observe the ancient crocodilians half-sleeping in the Nile, until at some point I found myself having coffee served to me by fez-capped nonagenarians who had themselves warned Howard Carter not to disturb Tutankhamen's pyramid as I myself adjusted the perspective on my sketch of the Sphinx whilst thinking of the strawberries and cream I would be eating with Gwendolyn on the terrace behind her family seat, watching the sheep just beyond the clever ha-ha designed by Inigo Jones himself.

But before I could begin this journey, I must sojourn first among my own people on Long Island. For as it happened, my Uncle Joe had informed me at graduation that he was overseeing a construction job in Brooklyn, and what, perchance, did I think of earning three hundred and fifty dollars for a week's work? I realized I needed money for the trip to Europe, and so I leapt at the chance, this of course being yet May, and my scheduled departure across the Atlantic weeks away.

By the time it was time to leave my parents in Danbury for my week in Long Island I had had more than enough time to adjust from the dizzying heights of my graduation, and I was only too glad to get away from my parents to the relative freedom and fun of the Sarrantonios. On my first morning there, Tante Eleonore got me up at five, since we would start at seven and it was a long drive into Brooklyn from Bellmore. I groggily pulled on my jeans and a T-shirt and hooded sweatshirt and work boots and staggered out to the kitchen for coffee and a buttered roll, and then climbed into the passenger seat of my uncle's van. As when I had worked with Gerry two summers before I felt real pride in my working-class status, however temporary. I was suddenly like one of those characters at the Anchor Bar whom my Schroed-rat friends had deemed "great" for what we supposed was the "authenticity" that came with a lack of education and means. Of course we wanted to be as they were just as Marie Antoinette wanted to be a shepherdess: on our own terms. We never dreamt of what it would feel like to be trapped there. My mind wandered as we drove and drove.

At the site I was surrounded by people my Yale friends would either have deemed "great" in their charming unselfconscious authenticity, or fascist a-holes, depending on how long you let them talk. My first task was helping a sullen muscle head named Kevin carry plywood and sheetrock from a delivery truck to a prep room. We didn't have anything to say to each other beyond "You got it?" and "I got it." Throughout the day I crossed paths with my uncle, who'd stop his colleagues to introduce me as his nephew "who just graduated from Yale!" at which juncture I would semi-proudly and semi-embarrassedly endure their looking me up and down and obviously thinking, "If your nephew is so freaking smart what the hell's he doing here carrying sheetrock with Kevin?" Of course these fellows would have been unfamiliar with the Grand Tour upon which I must soon embark, for which one required such green stuff as Eurail passes[1] are made of, Horatio. Usually the colleague would politely say "Congratulations!" but then they might quickly shift to address a subject closer to their hearts, like the tools that were missing: "I mean, we got these black kids running around here and they're all frigging thieves! I got a lot invested in these frigging tools. I think tomorrow I'm gonna bring down my gang box and lock all this shit up." Now it was I who did the polite nodding.

One afternoon my uncle offered a colleague a ride home, so I was relegated to an uncomfortable seat atop one of the five-gallon buckets in the back of the windowless van. Whatever morning glamour attended the trip had evaporated. But there, in the sweltering van, I found something to do. It began when I noticed my uncle and his voluble colleague employing the eff-word—or one of its unofficially recognized permutations—remarkably, and really almost impressively, often. Perhaps it was that time of day when fatigue seems to centrifugally scatter more nuanced words to the unreachable edges of one's consciousness, and perhaps Uncle Joe, never famous for this sort of language, felt it might be somehow rude to depart from the vocabulary rut that his colleague was laying down ahead of him in their conversation, so that not to talk that way might be perceived as a kind of pointed rebuke. In any case, by the time I became aware of this phenomenon—as when one suddenly in the fifth inning realizes the pitcher is throwing a no-hitter—I suddenly began counting. I had no idea how many had already passed me by, but I would at least know how many times the word or a variant thereof was spoken between now and when we got home. I caught every one with a kind of secret glee, like a wild-eyed Forty-Niner finding gold nuggets. By the time they hit a hundred

---

[1] Eurail passes were available to all students and at a very low price, enabling one to travel throughout Europe by train.

I began wondering how far it could climb, and as at last we pulled into the driveway in Bellmore, I had counted 172! If only I had started earlier they would easily have exceeded two hundred. I knew my Yale friends would have thought this exceedingly "great," until perhaps they heard my uncle and his colleague's views on homeless people and interracial marriage. But after a week of this I hugged my dear aunt and uncle goodbye, for I loved them with all my heart, and went back to Danbury to prepare for my trip to Europe.

Germany

The plan was to meet Chris Hanes in Germany, but a week before I would meet my mother and Tante Eleonore and grandmother in Munich. We would rent a car and drive hither and yon for a week, ending up in Neuenburg, where my mother's cousin Rudolf lived. It's rare that a twenty-year-old would want to spend time with his mother and aunt and grandmother, but I knew how much fun it would be. And my mother always spoke of Rudolf's legendary hilariousness. So the prospect of the fun and of immersing myself in my real Germanness before taking off with Chris seemed a good idea, not least because Chris aggressively styled himself as the ugly American tourist, saying things like "we kicked your asses" (Germany and Italy) or "we saved your asses" (Britain and France) in the war. While it was my desire to blend in Zelig-like, often to a fault, perhaps fancying myself a kind of Byronic figure, Chris's was to do the opposite, Lord Elgin being more his model in these environs. So if I tried to dress like a native—for Byron this would have meant a turban and some curved shoes, while for me it meant striking what I thought a European insouciance, perhaps involving a French-striped boatneck sweater—Chris wore plaid shirts and Bermuda shorts and carried in front of him as he duck-footed forward an open map. There can be no question he was also somehow affecting the persona of a nineteenth-century English gentleman sizing up the classical sculptures he would soon haul back to the Ashmolean Museum. For him the natives were simply background local color. Of course being in my literal bones Greek and German, this annoyed me. But for this one week at least I would enjoy Germany with my German family—as a German, which I was—and after Chris and I finished our Grand Tour I would go to Greece, to enjoy Greece with my Greek family as a Greek, which I also was. That the people in those countries might have other ideas as to identity—that I was an American—was not yet something I had considered.

I found a cheap flight to Frankfurt and since all train travel was free with a Eurail pass, I thought I could fly to Frankfurt and take a five-hour train ride to Munich. Besides, the idea of a train ride alone through Germany seemed *Romantische*! Who knew whom I might meet? Maybe the Princess of Thurn and Taxis would be traveling incognito. And if not, I could read Friedrich Schiller alone, taking in the countryside flecked in the green-yellow garb of flowering rapeseed.

When on the plane to Frankfurt the stewardess asked me what I would like to drink, I unflinchingly requested a vodka on the rocks. I looked seventeen and she clearly wasn't sure what to make of my request. But neither was I. I never drank alcohol alone, and certainly not vodka. But I was at that time reading Cheever and in my reverie wanted to remain inside the book as much as possible, and since his characters might have ordered this while traveling to Europe, I would too, though of course I would have preferred it in a stateroom aboard the Queen Mary instead of wedged in coach on Lufthansa, but one made do. The flight attendant brought it to me, trying and failing to reserve judgment, and in a few moments I was too blasted to continue reading.

In Frankfurt I boarded my train and found a compartment all to myself. As the journey began I stared out the window, drinking in the marvelous Europeanness of it all! But soon we stopped and into my compartment burst a rude American who put one leg up on the seat, stared out his window cheerlessly, and then told me he was returning from a two-day leave from his base near Munich to avail himself of the highly regarded prostitution services in Frankfurt. He volunteered the prices for me with rhyming Anglo-Saxon bluntness, while I tried not to look shocked, as I now knew to regard things sexual with a blasé attitude, connoting sophistication. I also hoped to communicate my social solidarity with the unenlightened jughead addressing me.

After all, what had I seen of the world from my ivory tower? But the oafish fellow staring out the window soon began making disparaging references to "Konrad"—which I took to be his word for the Germans, Konrad being the first name of their first prime minister, Herr Adenauer. For some reason he was bursting with contempt for the national population, so I felt not a little conflicted, as I would soon be meeting my "Konrad" mother and aunt and grandmother at the end of this very train ride, which was turning out less and less as I had hoped because of the saturnine jackass holding court across from me. Every time we stopped he regarded them milling about and said: "Look at 'em! Stupid-ass Konrads!"

When I got to the Munich airport I met my mother and Tante Eleonore— and Grandma! As ever she was full of energy and humor, and soon we were in our rented car driving south toward Switzerland. The plan was simply to drive and enjoy ourselves as we wended our way toward Rudolf in Neuenburg. My mother told me innumerable stories of growing up with him during the war. He was Tante Walli's youngest son and his appetite for kidding around was insatiable. One would not expect one's humorous affinities to come from one's Teutonic genes, but as we have said, the Saxon world is the world of that comic maniac known to the world as Martin Luther. To know his story as I now do is to know that not all Germans are dour.[2] Indeed my own relatives were more like peasants who had fallen out of a Pieter Brueghel painting, as much at home in their sexuality as the animals around them, and that Luther himself consummated his marriage with a close friend bearing witness offers us a dramatically more humble and frank view of our physical selves than anything one might see in either the puritanical or hedonistic poles of American life.

As I have said, my grandmother was always joking. Even some years after college when I brought Chris Noël home to Danbury, she hid behind a screened window in the kitchen and as we passed just under it, made a growling sound I can still hear, hoping to scare us. Whose eighty-something grandmother does such things? I grew up in a world of non-stop joking, and processing the world in any other way is nearly impossible to me still.

---

[2] I wrote a biography of Martin Luther (Viking, 2017).

My grandmother was even sharp and funny until her death at ninety. But I recall once when she was in her seventies that I suddenly wondered whether she might be slipping. I was watching *Green Acres* in the den with my brother when she came in and said she was going to make us French toast. We were thrilled. Until five minutes later she returned, looking slightly confused. "Eric," she said, "can you remember what you need to make French toast?" I was amazed at the question. She'd made us French toast many times.

"Sure," I said. "Egg. And milk. And cinnamon. And a little vanilla extract." She was tracking along with every ingredient. And just to complete things in my own mind I said, "And you just soak the bread in it ..." My grandmother's eyes widened in surprise.

"*Ach!*" she said, hitting her head in amazement. "I forgot the bread!!!" I looked at her, not believing this could be true, but then realizing she was not kidding. "Can you imagine?" she said. "The bread! I must be going nuts!!!" She howled with laughter, and then I did too. And as she turned to go back toward the kitchen, she spoke one of the favorite sentences of my life. "I vas vondering," she said, "why dat vasn't coming out square!"

The four of us stopped in Salzburg, Mozart's hometown, and afterward found ourselves near Berchtesgaden, taking a boat ride on the breathtaking, beautiful blue-green waters of the Königsee. I saw why the beauty of this area typified for Hitler that aesthetic Alpine ideal to which he and his confederates aspired, but we declined to visit his famous Eagle's Nest on the mountain. My companions didn't have much of an appetite for such things, linking that period—*Der Hitlerzeit*, my grandmother always called it—to the great pain of losing my grandfather and so many other horrors.

From there we drove westward through the beauty until in a tiny hamlet called Ebbs we saw a sign for a bed and breakfast and stopped. It was just below the Alpine pastures where the local cowherds grazed their flocks for months at a time and was so idyllic I felt I had entered a picture postcard from the 1930s, as though everything existed in a hand-tinted, color-saturated realm.

In the morning we arose to the smell of hay and had a typical breakfast of strong coffee, served with those small hard rolls I've only seen in that part of the world, with butter and cheese and cold cuts. I half expected to find a fresh-faced milkmaid and marry her and make a life amidst the cowbells and lederhosen. As we have said, this odd desire to fit in, to somehow ingratiate myself and then fully enter another world, is a constant in my life, but what is it? Is it simply insecurity, or merely an aspect of my sympathy for others combined with my gift for mimicry?

We thereafter wended our way through the medieval village of Oberammergau, where every ten years since 1634 the town's inhabitants perform their famous Passion Play. The facades of the medieval buildings are colorfully painted with *Lüftlmalerei*, frescoes bearing extraordinarily evocative images and scenes from German fairy tales and religious subjects, along with some *trompe-l'oeil*. From there we continued westward, toward the Black Forest.

At some point we stopped at what is called a *sesselbahn*, which is really just a ski lift that in the summer months is used to carry tourists up into the glorious snow-white heart of the mountains. Each seat held just one person, and to non-skiers, which we all were, it looked intimidating. I had never been on a ski lift. Though my mother and grandmother declined, my aunt and I decided to try it—and up we went. Every foot of the ascent was glorious. I had never seen such beauty or experienced such stillness, and as one ascended, the air seemed to grow cooler and cleaner and clearer. There was a halfway point at which one debarked and chose to return or continue upward, toward the snowy peaks. The second leg looked steep, so my aunt declined, but encouraged me to continue. She would return and tell everyone I would be along soon.

As I rose further, the air continued to grow clearer and brighter. Ten years later when I encountered C.S. Lewis's fantastic book *The Voyage of the Dawn Treader* I read about something like what I was experiencing now. In Lewis's story, the ship is moving through the sea at the end of the world. There are white lilies everywhere and as they proceed the light becomes brighter and clearer, so much so that they cannot look at it. But when they drink of the sweet water all around them, their capacity to take in the light grows. So thinking now of my ascent up that mountain I can't help but wonder how clear and how bright it might conceivably get? The snowy brightness and clarity as I ascended were intoxicating and seemed irresistibly to draw me into themselves, as if everything in me wanted them more than anything, as though I were moving toward Truth and the resolution of every Question in the universe. But at what point would the brightness and the clarity become unbearable? Would they burn me and undo me? And was there a real remedy, a draught of something that I might drink to make me able to handle more of what I so craved? These, as it happens, were profound theological questions, but none I was yet asking.

When at last I was delivered to the end of the line and got off, I was half crazy with joy. I simply stood there transfixed, and beheld the eternally white brightness of the snowy peaks as one who has arrived in some antechamber of Heaven. I was dumbstruck by their beauty, and by their sheer Otherness, as though I were beholding a golden goddess shimmering in a sunlit clearing in the woods. For the first time in my life I was experiencing what can only be called awe. It was bright and clear and terrible and wonderful and somehow paralyzing too. I didn't want to leave, only to stare and stare and drink in whatever gloriousness there was to be drunk. I knew this somehow touched upon what people called God, but I hardly knew how. When at last I tore myself away and got back on the lift and descended I was almost in a trance, simultaneously giddy and utterly peaceful. Was this what Moses felt as he descended from Mount Sinai, his face literally glowing from his encounter with Deity? When I finally returned to my waiting mother and aunt and grandmother, I didn't know how to describe what I had seen and experienced, but as we drove off toward the west, I remember that they listened patiently as I tried.

The next day we would arrive in Neuenburg and I would finally meet that renowned jackanapes Rudolf, whose inspired lunacy I had heard about my whole life—who as a teenager had donned a potato sack and beat a bees'

nest with a stick, only to have the bees ascend through the open bottom, with predictably ill effects. But before meeting this legend, we would first travel through the fabled and still convincingly primeval Black Forest. What we sought in those haunted woods as we drove was some version of what I had found in the bright whiteness of the mountains. We were looking for a portal to that something beyond us, to the fairy tale past of talking animals and witches and ogres and heroes. We almost expected to find a witch selling apples at a crossroads, or to stumble across a cottage of gingerbread and candy—or to find an impossibly ancient tree with a small door in its trunk. The joy of being with my aunt and grandmother and mother was that none of them had ever "matured" beyond these things and with me seemed to hold out some possibility and hope—was this faith?—that at last, here, in this ancient place, we might find what we always and in every search in our lives had been seeking: the boundary of this world, beyond which the truth of fairytales still existed. Hadn't my aunt and mother just twelve summers before earnestly believed they had stumbled across a prehistoric turtle crossing the road?

And so we followed our noses toward whatever seemed to look most like the primordial Black Forest in our minds. As the light began to fade through the thick brake of trees all around us, and knowing we had to stop soon, we came upon what looked like the ideal candidate for our fantasies. It was an old restaurant and inn, nestled in the very center of that haunted world in which we had been searching for our otherworldly treasures, for our passageway to the world of faerie or elfland, as some have called it. It would make me happy to say that when we crossed the inn's threshold we beheld an old woman—older than Methuselah—spinning at a wheel in front of a fire, and that she bade us come closer that she might touch our hands and faces, for you see she had been blind since the time her eldest son was killed in the Napoleonic Wars; and that she had then regaled us with the selfsame stories with which she had regaled the Brothers Grimm when they visited here 180 years earlier. But—alas and alack!—that was not what happened.

We went to the desk, got our room keys, unpacked, and hustled down to dinner where the innkeeper, an unkempt middle-aged gent with the potbelly and long hair of an aging hippie, came over to our table as we concluded our meal. When he understood we were from America he harangued us on the evils of our home country as we sat trapped in our *gemütlich* wooden booth. We thought it would be bad form to argue with him—but not nearly as bad form as this churl insulting his guests with his inanities against their beloved homeland, and after they had

My mother and her cousin Rudolf, 1935

spent a goodly amount of money in his establishment, too—so we heard the rude fellow out on why our president and country were evil, and then went to bed.

The next day we at last arrived in Neuenburg, where I instantly saw that Rudolf was everything my mother had described. He spoke in the *Schtiemzer* dialect, and my mother, aunt, and grandmother's German immediately bent further to their roots, such that merely listening to them talk was an entertainment. Rudolf was a housepainter and divorced recovering alcoholic now living with his girlfriend of five years. My mother had hailed him as the gold standard of funny and although I only understood half of what he was joking about, it made no difference, because he cracked jokes incessantly and then laughed at them so hysterically himself—going into paroxysms and slapping things—that you couldn't help joining in.

In his backyard Rudolf had a circular grill that swung from chains attached overhead. He built a crackling wood fire under it and began grilling platters of meat and sausages. We did this three nights running, and as we ate and joked I felt more German and more connected to this part of my family and my German family than I ever had before. Much of it was him reminiscing with my grandmother, remembering old jokes or sayings, such as *"Er hat gefortzt wie 'ne Waller!"*[3] They had all been carrying on with Rudolf like this since the early forties, and my grandmother had been carrying on with his

---

[3] "He broke wind like a brewery horse!"

parents since the First War, so as we were joking it was as if all that time fell away and we were back in that past, being the same people and doing and saying the same things we had done then, except of course I hadn't been born yet, so for me the time travel was the more dramatic. But I felt returned to the womb of the German past for which I longed. It was so intoxicating that on our third night I actually found myself thinking in German and then even dreaming in German, as though I had at last entered the gill-breathing liquid world for which I was created. So for me the trip was more a pilgrimage than a tourist adventure. But when Chris arrived, things would change.

I met him at the train station in town, and as we walked to Rudolf's house he gleefully said, "We sure bombed the hell out of this place!" neither realizing nor caring that it was my relatives who had been bombed. This was the kind of thing we would argue about for the next six weeks, with Chris reveling in playing the ugly American and me trying to pretend I was really European— and wasn't I, somehow? But when we got to Rudolf's and the wild japery resumed, Chris felt right at home. His family in Atlanta were dramatically like mine. His father and grandmother, whom I'd met, were hilarious too. After seeing *Dances with Wolves* his grandmother complained that there was only one wolf in it—"and he didn't dance!" Chris knew just enough German to love Rudolf's jokes, and our mutual favorite concerned a man once lost in the desert. The man tells his friend how awful the experience was, saying he was even chased by a lion! When his friend asks what he did, the man says he immediately climbed a tree! Of course his friend is confused. Everyone knows there are no trees in the desert! "*Ja,*" replies the man, "*aber in dieses moment was es mir Ganz egal!*"—which translates to "Yes! But at the time it made absolutely no difference!" Of course it's funnier in the original, and Chris and I have repeated the German ever since.

CHAPTER TWENTY-SIX

The Grand Tour, Zweiter Schtück

The next day I bade my family adieu to begin the Grand Tour part of my trip. Chris and I hopped a train back into the Black Forest, from which we would then continue toward Munich, to meet Robbie, Chris's friend from Atlanta. After we met I knew it was the right decision having him along. He was redheaded, with the genetic penchant for mischief that is the boon and bane of his kind, but his wildness proved to be a necessary balance to Chris's positively Hammurabic need for order. We would meet him the next day, but now Chris and I were on the train together and eventually thought we had gone far enough. There was a large youth hostel up ahead, and we decided to stay there. It was clean and rather modern and very cheap, and we were shown to a simple dorm-style room with four normal beds and one bunkbed. There were backpacks on the four beds, but the bunkbed was unclaimed, so I threw my gear on the top bunk and Chris threw his on the lower and we wandered out to see about food. It wasn't much of a social scene, and we soon decided after eating our German meal that the only thing worth doing was going back to the room to get a good night's sleep. When we returned, we observed that three of the four beds were already occupied by young men already sleeping. The only bed still unoccupied was the single bed nearest our bunk bed, but there was a backpack on it, so we realized it had been claimed. In any event, we undressed and climbed into our bunks, shutting our eyes to prepare for sleep.

But it was a bit earlier than we normally would have gone to sleep, so we lay awake for a bit, and before either of us drifted off to slumberland the door opened and a stout older gentleman entered. He was perhaps sixty—sporting lederhosen and hiking boots, as was the custom among older hikers. In short order he undressed and clambered into his bed near us, and with impressive alacrity quickly fell into a state of deep unconsciousness, which we only knew because of the shattering and utterly terrifyingly airhorn-loud sounds suddenly emerging from his head in the darkness. We understood it to be a kind of snoring, but what sort of snoring was this? The volume made no rational sense. No human being could be large enough to make these bone-shuddering noises, and we had seen that he was not a giant, but simply a slightly portly older gent on his holiday. Had someone slipped a drug into my sauerkraut?

When it first commenced, I shuddered in my bunk, fearing the End of All Things was upon me. And now what to do? The three others who had arrived before us may have been asleep, but it is likely that their pleasant dreams were soon transmuted into chaotic ones, in which they were eyewitnesses to the Battle of Midway. I cannot say whether Chris had fallen asleep yet, nor whether the dead in surrounding cemeteries were at this moment already fleeing their tombs, grave clothes aflutter. All I knew was that I was reeling from the regularly timed blasts ten feet from my soon-to-be bleeding ears. Each time the man inhaled another soporific draught of healthful mountain air it was to me as though the circus had come to town with trumpeting elephants and clowns honking horns and ringing bells. Actually each snore was something more like an entire amusement park that suddenly flew screaming and flashing through my skull. Again and again a dizzying salad of rollercoasters, merry-go-rounds, and shrieking spook houses exploded out of this man's nose and mouth several times per minute and then, at the height of it all and with only the barest Doppler effect very suddenly retreated to the safety of his sinuses, wherefrom it would soon enough seconds later explode with every clanging bell and screaming siren and whooping spook voice intact.

It was not possible even to imagine falling asleep under these circumstances, much less actually sleeping. I am sure no healthy human could have done so. And yet it was all just a single reasonably sized man snoring. But the sound was so outrageously and monstrously outsized that anyone would have sworn it was no mere human lying in that bed. To produce such a sound it had to be some sort of armored, prehistoric beast, several times more massive than any human. Or if historic, it had at the very least to be a wounded rhino in agony or some other kind of oversized ungulate rasping its last and raging with all of its might against the dying of the light. And yet, behold! it was merely yon sturdy retired businessman from Stuttgart or Mannheim making a hiking tour of the Schwarzwald! He had only an hour ago with his heightened appetite partaken of a traditional German repast—at the center of which was an ample serving of

wurst and potatoes, and had of course then washed the lot down with several excellent steins of beer—and now he lay sleeping irenically, like a very cherub on a cloud, as his stomach struggled to digest these ancient roiling rivals of pork fat and pilsner.

In any event, it was not long after he had begun his recital that I realized I was not the only person awake. For sometimes, amidst the riotous clangor of this one-man band, I heard deep moans of desperation from the distant bunks. And there is no other way to put it: this went on for hours, without respite, though here and there he cruelly teased us with heavenly oases of one or two minutes of perfect silence before again choking into a full-blown and unremitting Six Flags wall of sound.

The three young men in the other beds by now revealed themselves to be German, for it was in this language that they cursed the *Snarcher* (German for "Snorer"), who slept so blissfully nearby. At one point one of them clapped loudly, hoping to startle the raucous perpetrator into silence. Then the same man beat his own wooden bedstead loudly with his hands. Each time this method worked, but only for some seconds. And then again there came the bitter imprecations and foul oaths directed at the human foghorn happily abed beneath his covers. After an eternal hell of this, the Germans actually took to beating the cinderblock wall with their sturdy hiking shoes. This too, worked, but again, only temporarily. It was all maddening and exhausting and unendurable. Some hours after this had begun, in the middle of the night, and quite inexplicably, I—and I presume the others—fell asleep. But what sleep we got could not have been long, nor anything better than shallow. It was the sort of sleep one might have snatched in a trench during the Great War as the shells exploded. But at some point the young body can take no more and passes out, as it were, from the pain.

When at last we arose in the morning the businessman was already putting on his lederhosen and stretching happily. He was gloriously rested and ready to start the day. He pulled on his rucksack, smiled at us all—the young lads!—bade us good day and then trundled off like a hedgehog, out of our lives and into legend. As soon as he left the room one of the Germans, blotchy and bloodshot with fatigue, exclaimed *"Mensch! Das elende Schnarchen!!!"* ("Man! That damnable snoring!!!") In any language, he spoke for us all.

The next day we staggered toward Munich and met Robbie, and the next I turned twenty-one. Chris and Robbie knew it was my birthday, but never mentioned it, and as the day wore on and we wandered about the city, hitting every church and building that Chris insisted we hit, it began to get on my nerves and eventually put me in a foul mood. I knew Chris would have thought it somehow feminine—"gay," he would have said—to make any fuss of a male friend's birthday. Real men ignored each other's birthdays. That was the masculine thing to do. Finally we ended up at the famous Hofbräuhaus, the biggest and most touristy beer hall in a city full of them, and we sat there and each drank three liter-sized steins of beer, quietly launching ourselves into outer space, though not realizing it till we stood up. Before our third round, however, Chris grudgingly tipped his hat to my special day by offering that he and Robbie should pay for my third stein, which gesture I appreciated.

We made a day trip to Neuschwanstein to see Mad Ludwig's famous castle. Boarding a bus for the trip back to Munich I stepped in the way of a local man of about sixty and heard him with a bigoted sneer say: *"Genau wie ein Auslander!"* ("Just like a foreigner!") Of course I understood and was infuriated. Wasn't I German? My family had grown up here and most were still here and my grandfather and many great-uncles had been killed wearing German uniforms. I might have murdered him I was so angry, but this was always the difficulty of my hyphenated identity, and of course mine was doubly so. Wherever one found oneself, one never fully belonged. But I reasoned that if it bothered me when Chris said things like "we bombed the crap out of this place" because my people were *from this place* I should somehow be able to escape being regarded as *ein Auslander, nein?*

We next went to Salzburg, where I had just been, and the only thing I remember about our time there was that as we were walking home from dinner along the Salzach river it was getting dark when I heard someone say, "Eric Metaxas?" I stepped toward the voice and out of the gloom stepped three young men, about our age. "We're in the Class of '84!" they said. "You spoke at graduation, didn't you?" I suddenly felt like an international celebrity and beamed. Until I remembered that Chris, standing next to me, had also spoken, and had written most of the speech, and realized he was now seething in my peripheral vision.

"Uh, yeah," I said. "And this is Chris Hanes. We did it together." They nodded, but somehow still didn't seem to remember him. I knew this bothered him greatly, and I have teased him about it through the decades.

From Salzburg we took the train to Vienna, where it rained all three days we were there. Chris was sick and stayed in bed much of the time—at the *Hotel Zum Goldenen Bären*, a seedy hotel run by a curiously ursine man. One night

Robbie somehow hooked us up with four random young people with whom we had nothing in common except Robbie's enthusiasm that we should all connect. Two of them were the French son and daughter of a diplomat, one was Austrian, and the last was Belgian. Trying to have a conversation with them was sheer agony, and Chris and I hated Robbie for putting us through this. Another night we took a taxi to the Prater, site of the world's oldest amusement park, which we visited principally to ride the gigantic Ferris wheel, built in 1897 and featured in *The Third Man*, which I had not yet seen, but to which my father had sometimes referred and which Dick Cavett in the future would call "at least perfect." In 1984 it was still the tallest in the world, but before the taxi dropped us at the entrance we passed along what was a gorgeous avenue of chestnut trees, although that summer the nineteenth-century ambience was destroyed by the many parked and cruising cars and prostitutes stretched all along the avenue, separated only by such distance as professional courtesy demanded.

We took a tour of a Viennese cathedral and the tour guide seemed to know no English whatever, but had evidently phonetically memorized an English translation of his speech, such that everything he said came out mispronounced and awkwardly stretched, as though by a machine on Quaaludes. Our minds grappled for a handhold, but rarely found one. When we got to the place in the crypt where after the Black Death hundreds of bones and skulls had been stacked, the man pointed to them and said: "We zee in he-arr de boh-one room ... and in he-ar it isss werry dark and SPOH-kee!"

A similarly crippled English clouted us in Paris as we stood in the long, hot line for the Louvre. A short man, with bristly upturned moustachios, held up a long stick festooned with various postcards and glossy pamphlets as he patrolled the perimeter of the line; and in every imaginable European language he spat out a revolving carousel of come-hither phrases. "Sights and sounds of ze big city!" he said. Our favorite English phrase was: "Let's commit some business, Colonel!" Was this the straightforward sort of come-on he seemed to think would produce results with no-nonsense American types? And where in the world had he picked it up?

From Vienna we went to Venice, where we dutifully gawked at St. Mark's and the pigeons and the bridge where Dante had met Beatrice seven hundred years earlier. We observed that wherever we went in Venice, we seemed to be shortchanged. When I finally realized it, I determined to take greater pains with the details of my next transaction. Sure enough, soon after, while I was boarding a *vaporetto*, I handed the man my fare and didn't get back the change I had coming. So in my incipient but sufficient Italian I rather boldly said something to him about it. It was only now that I saw he was a menacing-looking fellow, old and large and missing one of his eyes. With the concentrated force of his remaining eye he regarded me rather threateningly, as though he might with an effortless swipe from the knife in his belt gut me like a fish, toss me overboard, and having not missed a beat, collect the next tourist's fare. It was then that I realized this unwillingness to subtract was a local epidemic, a long-accepted part of their culture to pocket whatever extra the tourists gave them as a well-deserved and customary tip. But I didn't have to like it, did I? It was immoral, and part of the immemorial Italianate swamp that spawned the Borgia popes and La Cosa Nostra. The next morning, immediately upon waking, I spoke the aphorism that my unconscious had been formulating all night. "All Italians are thieves," I declared. "Even a good Italian is only a good thief!" Of course I didn't believe it, but still.[1]

When we came to Florence I called one of the numbers in my book—*Europe on $10/Day*—and was told they had rooms and we should come over. But when I hung up it occurred to me that in the conversation, which seemed to cover all the necessary bases, I had been speaking with what sounded like young girl. Surely no adult could have faked a child's voice so effectively. And at the top of a flight of dreary steps the door upon which we knocked was answered by two girls of approximately nine and five. The elder showed us our room and bathroom and shower, asked us how many nights we would stay, and gave us our key. Chris thought this suspicious and going downstairs

---

[1] On our last day in Venice, Chris benevolently reckoned Rob and I had earned an afternoon off from visiting churches, so we all went to the Lido, where the men's dramatically abbreviated bathing suits elicited the terms "banana hammock" and "grape smuggler."

called out, "Hello!" until he satisfied himself in discovering in a dimly lit room a corpulent woman who spoke no English, but seemed to be the girls' mother.

In Florence I beheld the only work of art that ever gave me a feeling of overwhelming transcendence and awe. When I turned a corner in the Galleria Accademia and took in Michelangelo's *David* I was staggered. The majestic seventeen-and-a-half-foot height and beauty of it were unlike anything I had seen, and I could only stare and stare, much as I had stared at the snowy peaks at the end of my *sesselbahn* ascent weeks earlier. It was literally breathtaking. Afterward I foolishly repeated to Chris and Robbie what I had heard from friends at Yale, that the statue's proportions—its large hands, for example—were Michelangelo's way of rendering it somehow homoerotic. Much at Yale was framed in these terms, and Chris and Robbie thought it hilarious, thereafter describing everything we encountered similarly. "This pasta seems homoerotic," Robbie would say. And Chris would reply: "It's the proportions."

When at last we arrived in the Eternal City, we found a *pensione* with a room on the sixth floor, though it sounded like the cars and motorbikes on the street below were in our room. The sound rose without losing a single decibel and dove straight in. The stairs to our floor were interminably long, with each step the width of two or three average steps, so you couldn't run up them, as they didn't seem to gibe with any human gait. Perhaps they had been constructed for horses, or the workmen had misread the architect's plans, or had misread them intentionally to spite the architect, who owed them money.

Happily there was an "elevator"—actually a motorized cage, in which three well-acquainted persons might squeeze, though it was surely intended for fewer, much like the elevator Gene Wilder and Zero Mostel enter with Andreas Voutsinas's character in *The Producers*. More to the point, this quirky anachronism was operated with ten lire coins that, when the venerable apparatus had been installed, had some small value, but by now had less value than some fraction of an American penny. And yet these coins were still necessary to engage the thing. But why did such a device ever require coins? This was the sort of puzzle one encountered throughout Italy. We got the idea that the population had become resigned to a thousand similar things, such that nine-tenths of the national demeanor consisted of a weary shrug, as if to say, "What do you want from me? I'm-a just-a pass by." But the *pensione's* landlord gave us all the coins necessary, and we hauled them about in our pockets, lest upon returning we be forced to negotiate the equine stairs.

We visited everything Chris required, goggling at Trajan's Column and the Pantheon and the Spanish Steps and the Trevi Fountain. And who could miss the ubiquitous louche *uomini* on their Vespas? I was overwhelmed to take in the sheer size of St. Peter's as we approached it, and marveled at the undulating marble columns of Gian Lorenzo Bernini's altarpiece, but what struck me most in the Vatican museum was the fabled Laocöon, which Chris Noël and I had referenced in a piece for the *Yale Record* titled "*Universität Meat*," about a sculptor who worked with flesh and whose postmodernist triumph was a replica of this masterpiece made from raccoon, predictably called the "Raccoon Laocöon." But staring at the two-thousand-year-old masterpiece now provoked such awe as made me suddenly feel guilty for our pretentious undergraduate joke.

Laocöon and His Sons by Gian Lorenzo Bernini, circa 1506, Vatican Museum

On our last evening in Rome we fell into dinner and conversation with two American girls from the South, one of whom was cute in a way I knew appealed to Chris but not to me; so when she began bibulously indicating interest in me, I could smell the invisible smoke curling from Chris's ears and knew the evening might not end well. Generally when Chris drank wine he needed less confirmation that the world was a dark and unpleasant place ruled by an indifferent—or even capricious—deity, one who—if he existed—favored idiots like me, and probably for no reason other than to get Chris's goat. We all had more wine than we realized, sitting and eating and talking for some time, but what did anything matter? We were young and in Rome—and the night too was young! But behold, the relative youth of the night was only an illusion brought on by the wine, for the cranky innkeeper at the *pensione* enforced a strict midnight curfew, which none of us had remembered—until suddenly at ten to twelve we did, and leapt up. Suddenly, everything swirled into motion. We must leave immediately!

The only good news was that we didn't need further excuses to extract ourselves from these sweet girls, and with all the dignity of madmen chased by white-coated fellows with butterfly nets, we sprinted away into the night. We knew if we had jogged we might not make it back before the doors were locked, and the *pensione* was a significant distance, but when we finally arrived the door was still unshuttered, thank goodness, but between the endless pasta and wine, followed by our quarter-mile sprint, we stumbled into the lobby on the verge of forfeiting the chance to digest anything. So we stood there for a moment, catching our breaths and allowing our roiling innards to find equilibrium, then staggered forward to the inane lift that would haul us the six flights to our room.

But while we were cramped aboard the ancient lift, one of us must have joggled the door slightly, because the steel cage suddenly ceased its ascent, *thunking* to a dead halt. Of course this lift was nothing more than a cage without benefit of a surrounding shaft, so we could see down in every direction, and despite every effort could not get it to move again. Worst of all, we were between floors, stuck in our dangling cage like lobsters in a trap. So eventually we began gingerly crying out, hoping the unpleasant landlord would come to our rescue. What else could we do? In time the old fellow emerged, but savvily intuited that we had been drinking, so before he released us from our cage, he let us know he was on to us and angrily—and somehow triumphantly too—put his thumb to his mouth in the international symbol for immoderate drinking and croaked, "Aha! You drink, eh? You drink!" But were we not legally allowed to do so? Nonetheless he behaved as though he had caught us with his wife, and immobilized in our cage, we had no choice but to weather his rant. Finally, he relented and opened the door so we might crawl out onto the floor above, because even in his great sobriety and with decades of experience he did not seem to know how to get cranky old Concetta to budge from where she had decided to end her day.

Switzerland

By the time we stumbled through Switzerland, something like Euro-fatigue had set in and we were constantly sniping at each other. So when we spotted a theater playing a movie called *First Blood*, starring Sylvester Stallone, we figured it might be a nice cultural palate cleanser. When it had come out in the U.S. two years earlier, we had missed it, preferring at Yale to see more sophisticated films, like *The Rocky Horror Picture Show* and *Eraserhead*. We did not know at the time that this movie would spawn the *Rambo* franchise and that in its full-throated Reagan-era pro-American tone would effectively sum up everything the European cognoscenti and my Schroed-rat confreres hated about America. So in its way it was just the ticket for us. We also noticed that in Switzerland the people were even stricter than the Germans. Crossing streets against the light in Germany evoked stares and wonder, but when we did this in Lucerne an old woman shouted her disapproval in a very firm and insistent voice: *"Nein! Nein! Nein! Nein!"*

At some point soon after this, Robbie had enough of Chris's and my bickering-old-couple routine and decided to split for a few days to Amsterdam, where pot and prostitution were legal. Chris never tired of the running joke that Robbie had visited the Low Countries to pursue his "low pleasures."

The Arctic Circle

I found the idea of the Eurail pass fascinating, principally because it afforded us literally endless travel throughout most of Europe. But there is a utilitarian and greedy side of me that inevitably tries to maximize such benefits, and one day I noticed on the Eurail map that one could travel clean into the Arctic Circle! This was the very sort of thing I had envisioned doing on this trip, something spontaneous and open-ended. We could get on the next train headed to Northern Sweden and be there in thirty-six hours! The Arctic Circle! But Chris was unenthusiastic. Deviating from his predetermined plans was like asking the mailman to come in for a half hour and help you put up some wallpaper. "What would be the purpose?" he asked.

"Just to go there!" I replied, "And say we did it!" We could throw a few snowballs and send a few postcards and eat a walrus fritter and be on our way! The idea thrilled me. We had no real schedule anyway, and the whole loopy lark wouldn't cost a sous! But Chris wasn't buying. In the heat of what became a real argument he maintained that Robbie and I were just "pig ignorant"— which epithet he used for the rest of the trip. As I have said, Chris had fixed nineteenth-century ideas about traveling on the Continent and knew the young Gladstone or Macauley wouldn't have been caught dead going to northern icy wastes where there were no ruins to sketch. So of course sneering Moe Howard prevailed over the chuckleheads again, though to this day I regret failing to fly northward to that fabled circle atop our planet—and by Kris Kringle's icy beard, I may go yet!

Paris

When we got to Paris we found an odd hostel where at check-in we were presented with a xeroxed copy of rules in French, German, Spanish, and English. Chris copied the English in his journal: "Regarding sexes, mixity in the rooms is not allowed ... radio and record play is not strictly permitted between the hours of 24:00 and 8:00 unless sanctioned by the authorities and also loose living."

We were there four days, but what do I remember? I recall shuffling like cows past the *Mona Lisa*, her Sphinxy smile safe behind bulletproof glass, and recall climbing the Eiffel Tower and visiting tacky Versailles and eating in cafés and riding a bus past the aggressively hideous Centre Georges Pompidou. But my only vivid memory is of phoning John Tomanio's parents from a phone booth, pumping in my franc coins, and giddily getting Mr. Tomanio on the line to tell him with more pride than I can explain that I was "in Paris, France!", saying it that way to him because in my mind I could hear him saying it that way to me—"Paris, France!"

London

Chris planned everything in London too. He purchased and unfolded and pored over the maps, determining where we would next go. What would

I do without him? But alas, when I departed his company two weeks thence, we would see. Chris explained that we would that night see a play, implying the phrase "you numbskulls!" as he did. But when I heard more, I was impressed. It starred Rex Harrison, then seventy-six, and Claudette Colbert, eighty. They were paired in a revival of *Aren't We All?*, a 1923 comedy! That these legends were yet among us and sentient staggered me. But in truth Miss Colbert on the stage seemed a veritable fossil, a fragile bit of peanut brittle in a size-zero dress whose most recent previous appearance on the London stage had been in 1928, the year Thomas Hardy died.

Our seats for the play cost two pounds—about three dollars—a price so low it seemed impossible. Until we saw where they were. I had no idea anyone could be seated so high, because we climbed increasingly narrow stairs for what seemed forty minutes. Eventually we passed pipes, valves, gauges, and workmen's ladders. Was it legal to sell tickets up here? I would have sworn we were above the dome of St. Paul's, and we were sweating like ditch-diggers in our jackets and ties—which Chris insisted we wear. It seemed impossible we could have climbed so high and still be under the theater's roof. But there was the roof itself, so close we could touch it; and had the Nazis dropped one of their incendiary bombs on it, we would have heard the hissing, and since Chris never ceased discussing the War, the idea occurred to me. When we groped our way into our tight velveteen seats and I finally looked down to what I supposed must be the stage I started with fear, instantly dizzy. We might as well have been watching from a dirigible. The stage was the size of a penny postage stamp between my feet, almost vertically down below us, and when they appeared, Rex and Claudette were so small it was like watching a flea circus. It was impossible to hear much of what they said, old as they were and no longer able to project as they had done in their prime, when Britannia ruled the waves. Nor would they have thought to project their voices vertically upward, likely unaware the Haymarket sold seats where one might be brained by a passing satellite.

Throughout the play we strained to pick out the bon mots, and since heat rises, the concentrated body warmth of every patron below us rose to our concentrated garret and became trapped, gagging us into a semi-asphyxiated stupor. Halfway through the miserable affair a boy staggered toward us selling cups of ice cream with wooden spoons, and in our overheated haste to get them we almost tackled him—but one daren't move too swiftly up there, lest one lose one's footing and fall and fall, like the Jack-chasing giant in the fairytale, all the way down upon the frail heads of Rex and Claudette a hundred leagues below, still speaking their clever dialogue like insects.

Of course we visited Westminster Abbey and St. Paul's, but my favorite visit was to the well-preserved home of Dr. Samuel Johnson, where the large and stout-looking wooden chair that had supported the great man's broad fundament two centuries earlier became for us a hallowed memory. How we longed to sit in it and feel his literary breadth. But the velvet cordon made it plain this was not to be.

In London Robbie departed for home and we were joined by our friend Louise, with whom for a week we drove through the Cotswolds. As with everything else, it was Chris's plan; I was no planner, rather affixing myself like a lamprey to those who were. First we had to rent a car. Both men who ran the rental company were named Miles, so the company was cleverly called "Miles & Miles, Ltd." I had never used a stick shift before, nor driven a car in which the steering wheel is on the right, nor driven on the left side of the road, so I was amazed and am now retroactively frightened to think these men rented us the car—and we survived. We visited Oxford and Stonehenge, too, but found the latter tremendously disappointing. "That's it?!" I said, obviously expecting something four times larger. It was like traveling to Easter Island to find stone heads the size of pumpkins. I also remember one tall, middle-aged woman giving us directions, saying, "And then you *literally* make a left."

We returned to London for one day before I was to depart for Greece. On the street someone our age provocatively asked me, "How's Ronnie, eh? You like Ronnie Reagan?" To prove my good liberal bona fides and to show I wasn't like all those other Ugly Americans, I said, "No, I don't. Not all Americans love Ronald Reagan, you know!"

Before I left for the Continent I needed a haircut, and when the pretty young woman who cut it learned I was from America, she asked, "Do you see a lot of stars?" She was under the impression, fed I presumed by the tabloids of her social station, that America was Hollywood and that movie stars graced every acre, and I realized with some sadness that we ugly Americans hadn't cornered the market on parochialism.

Finally it was time to say goodbye to Chris and Louise. I would now make the long journey by myself across Europe to Cephalonia.

CHAPTER TWENTY-SEVEN

Alone!

I said goodbye and took the ferry across the Channel, boarding a train that rocketed me through France and all the way to the south of Germany where I visited Rudolf again and dined again with the Neuenburg Mertzes, and the next morning took a train that carried me through the Alps, where I shared a compartment with some Swiss who shared their wine and bread and cheese with me and made me feel I ought to do more of this traveling alone! Was this not what I had always envisioned without the encumbrance of hide-bound Chris? For his part, of course, Chris had always been immovable in maintaining that I (and Robbie, too) was an idiot who should be grateful for him, that without him I should certainly become irrevocably lost and worse. So if in reading what follows, dear reader, it happens that you find yourself taking not my part in this disagreement, rest assured you may do so with a clear conscience, for mayn't I myself too have decades ago come to that conclusion?

For example, when my train pulled into Naples, things changed dramatically. I arrived mid-afternoon and realized I had five hours in the stultifying heat in which to do nothing in the empty, down-at-the-mouth, Jadeite-green-colored train station. It was the middle of the summer in the middle of Italy in the middle of the day. I was a bit exhausted and found a sad corner with some tables and ordered a baked good and sat and read. It was unspeakably depressing, not least because I was reading Faulkner's *The Sound and the Fury*. To Chris's point, what could possibly be more idiotic? That I did not hang myself that afternoon must itself alone stand as evidence of the hand of Providence on my behalf. Something like an hour before my train departed I thought it not indecent to make my move, hauling my backpack of literary gravitas and glumly proceeding to the sun-baked track.

Finding my train sitting idly and as hot as Hades, I saw that I had my pick of the capacious brown compartments, which themselves were a far cry—really a haunting yodel—from the smart, clean, state-of-the-*kunst* compartments of the Germans and Swiss! But my compartment was empty! Might I be rewarded for my idle hours in the Naples train station with a compartment to myself? The seats were not individual seats but benches—something like those on the school buses I took for years: springs covered with cracked putty-colored vinyl. So I took my seat and stared out the window at the rest of the sleepy trainyard. In less than an hour the train would thrum to life and depart for Brindisi, where I would board a ferry to Greece! The train would whisk me through the night, and though it was now about five o'clock, eventually I would sleep. I could even stretch out on this long bench seat!

But then a deeply tanned, well-groomed young Italian fellow poked his head into the compartment and asked in broken English whether it was free. What could I say? He was in his mid-twenties and as he took his seat across from me my heart sank that I was obliged to share my compartment. But I kept my eyes in my Faulkner to avoid conversation and eventually the train shuddered awake and soon pulled away from the station. In twelve short hours I would be in Brindisi!

My ruse of being captivated by my Southern gothic sludge did not work for long, though. As my companion lacked for literature of his own he soon made aggressive efforts to engage me in conversation, asking some vaguely prying questions that, being an innocent, I did not parry as I might have. When I said I liked to read, hinting that I wished to return to my book, he missed the hint and suddenly glowed with excitement: "Have you read Oriana Fallaci?" I hadn't. At Yale we had covered Julio Cortázar and Borges and

Márquez and Zora Neale Hurston, but this was about as *outre* as we had gotten. In our exotic reading we meant to show our political solidarity with the
Sandinistas and the African-American women of the Jazz Age, but we hadn't
taken the trouble to wade across the Atlantic. After all, hadn't Europe been
done? And who cared what modern Italians thought? We had of course
acquainted ourselves with *The Bicycle Thief* and some Federico Fellini. Anita
Ekberg in the fountain had been on the test, but beyond that I was blank. So
I admitted I hadn't read Oriana Fallaci, but not that I hadn't heard of her,
which I thought might have been rude.

But my interlocutor was not prepared for this. He seemed unable to take
it in, as though I had declared I was a conjoined twin, or oviparous. *"Che se
dice?"* He almost gasped. He seemed to recoil, really, as though a cudgel had
been raised by my ugly words. "Ah!" he said. "This is a great, great pity!" It
was as though I had said all pasta tasted the same! "Oriana Fallaci is very well
known!" he said, in what I now took as an open-handed clout for this inexcusable ellipsis in my learning. But there was little he could say further, although
as I returned to my Faulkner, he paused to reload.

"You have of course familiar with Oscar Wilde!?" he said. I looked up.
Yes, sort of. I had read *The Importance of Being Earnest* in a freshman survey
course, and may even have remembered who Lady Augusta Bracknell was,
and the hilarious line about how losing one parent was a "misfortune," but
losing *both* parents looked like "carelessness"; but beyond this simplest of
Wildean staples I had not ventured, and said so. Even Wilde's masterpiece *The
Selfish Giant* was still years in my future. I knew my traveling companion
would take it hard, and I almost heard him say *"Ai!!!"* As this exchange was
transpiring I half-recalled that Wilde was a large, sexually adventurous man
in velvet suits that, if not themselves flouncy, nonetheless tacitly suggested the
motion, and that he had been sent to Reading Gaol for some reason.

There followed a brief *caesura* in our conversation, but we would reenter
the lists soon enough, and my clever opponent would wield a new lance too.
He was tentative in all he said, preceding everything with an "eh" and then a
pause, as though to find his balance before he said what he was going to say.
"Eh," he said, pausing, and then: "You have a girlfriend?" Where had I heard

that before? I didn't have a girlfriend, but if I said as much, might I send the wrong signal? So I did what I thought best and said yes, I did. Now we knew where we stood: I was a typical man of the world, a hearty fellow traveler of the standard masculine type. I had now made it clear enough, if there had been any question.

Perhaps to be polite I then asked him whether he did. And he said yes, but then quickly added that he missed her very much. I was encouraged. *He only appears as he does because he is a modern Italian man*—un uomo!—*wearing fashionably pointy shoes and tight pants and cologne.* Such details are there the height of masculinity, just as high-heeled shoes and monstrous perukes had been in the seventeenth-century French court! I mustn't let my American parochialism confuse the situation. We wore sneakers and baggy khakis and loose-fitting shirts—and had somewhat shaggy hair, but what of it?

But this *uomo* was not yet through communicating what suddenly seemed a dramatically vital piece of information. "I miss my girlfriend very very much!" he said, as though this was something I really mustn't miss. I didn't respond. After all, what was I supposed to say? *Absence makes the heart fonder, old chum! You know women! Can't live with 'em, can't live without 'em!* But as it happened, this fellow was merely hauling in the mainsail to try another tack. With some pain and force and almost some umbrage, he now said: "It is not right for a man to be away from his girlfriend for so long!" What was he getting at? But before I had a chance to consider it further, he asked me another question: "Are you also miss your girlfriend?" I was now finally beginning to get annoyed. I didn't have a girlfriend and his pushing this issue now forced me to extend my lie rather uncomfortably, which I resented. "Um, sure," I said. Of course I had no girlfriend to miss, but wanting the conversation to end, I mumbled the most anodyne thing possible. I wanted to move on. But I was thinking, *Wow. You need to get a grip, dude!*

So I continued to pretend to read, but who can really read Faulkner, even under less confusing circumstances? I wondered what I was dealing with. In any case, I was sure the only way forward was to dive deep into my modernist mush, never looking up. If I did anything else, I would be continuing this inane conversation all the way to Brindisi. But my eyes were trudging across the bleak plains of Faulkner's prose, and it took great effort to continue. Nonetheless, my companion seemed to have gotten the clue that my somewhat curt response to his question, coupled with my show of ardent devotion to the literature in my lap signaled the end of the conversation for me.

But he was not about to be put off so easily and now, monkey-like, swung down the evolutionary ladder to non-verbal methods of attack. And what were they? There was only one. He sighed. It is not a sound one hears often, and certainly not when one is alone in a train compartment with a stranger. But it was clear that he had sighed, and for my benefit. And then he sighed again. He needn't any longer use words to communicate that he missed his girlfriend, but it was evidently important to him that I know. But I had had enough and coldly refused to take the shiny bait of these exhaled lamentations. So I did not look up and would not. I refused to tear my eyes from the page! *Sigh on, ye hurricanoes! Blow as ye will!* I was resolute and reread the same handful of sentences four and five times over as my mind reeled for a way through this increasingly curious thicket. But the pomaded inamorato before me was not finished. If his plaintive sighs could not raise my eyes from the depressing postage-stamp-sized patch of Yoknapatawpha County in front of me, he had more. Was I ready?

To get a running start he first repeated his sentence, "I miss my girlfriend very very much," and then came the punchline, which was rather clever. He said: "Do you miss your girlfriend *so much?*" I heard what he said, of course, but what in the world did it mean? *"So much?"* It was undeniable genius on his part to throw that in, because no sane person could resist wondering to what particular muchness it was that he now referred. It was a maddening perfume; and of course it was now that I made the fatal mistake of glancing up, ever so briefly. But that was all it took; for my eyes now fell like Satan from Heaven upon the terrible muchness to which he had been referring. Indeed, I goggled to behold the very muchness itself, and none other, albeit mercifully sheathed in the worryingly thin cotton of his right pant leg. My glance was itself glancing, lasting perhaps a quarter second. And yet that was all that was necessary. I quickly pretended to plunge back into the Faulkner, but I could not choke down another word. They were now less decipherable than ever, because my eyes could not unsee what I had just seen. And yet what had I seen? It had been a blur, like unto an otter ascending from the murky depths, on the verge of splashing to the surface. I glimpsed enough to understand that my companion had wished me to see it, to see that it was a muchness with which to be reckoned! I might have blanched when I quickly looked away. But what exactly was the meaning of this grim revelation? Really, what was I to make of it? I didn't know, nor was I interested in knowing. But what is most remarkable to me now is that it was only then that I wondered whether the girlfriend he missed so palpably was as fictitious as the one I myself said I missed. But I pushed all of this away. I was not interested in thinking about these things. In any case, what was I supposed to do now, stagger to my feet and applaud? I had been disgusted and was now even a little bit angry.

As my Faulkner was still idling at the curb, I simply stepped in, put it in gear, and drove off again, down the dusty road, a fur piece … riding and riding along with that rhythm older than the planet, riding and riding along the tired dusty ribbon of road, a fur piece. But dad-blast it if I didn't still hear this idjit sighing like the low wind soughing through the outhouse where Benji done them things he known was wrong, what knowing knows is wrong and foreknowledge remembers …

I realized this might not simply go away. The renewed sighing was obviously for my benefit, but what did this buffoon expect me to say? He missed his girlfriend very very much. I got it. Everything was now quite clear, every obscene millimeter of her absence. I was now seriously annoyed. All I could think of was that this Italian stallion needed to snap out of his sappy reverie. And while he was at it he could send yon grandaddy hog skedaddling back to whatever rustic pen it had escaped. But my interlocutor had other ideas. For having understood that his sighing was drawing me back into the conversation, he now began that phase of things in which he struggled to give a certain bare notion the clothing of English words. But it was not easy.

"Do you mind, em …" he said—and then retreated. And then again: "Do you, em … do you mind … ?" And then retreated again. But then at last, finally girding his loins as it were and muscling all the way through the nasty thicket, all the way through to the bitter verb, he pronounced such sentence as I will never forget, no never. "Do you mind ..." he said, "em, do ... I, em ... *eh* ... *Como se dice?* ... do you mind if I ... em ... eh ... em ... eh ... *masturbate?*" And there it was. One now had all one's cards on the table. And Grandma, what big cards they were!

I must pause here to dilate upon the situation before me, since such situations were unprecedented in the world I had traversed till then. I was in an Italian train compartment alone with a man who seemed to think it reasonable to inquire of a stranger whether in that stranger's company he might bring to fruition something which by all rights ought never to have been planted in the first place. One must therefore wonder: Had this fellow had some success with this art form amongst other strangers in similar circumstances? Did he perhaps even routinely ride the rails performing this parlor trick, such that I was one of many who had been made the great gift of this opportunity—or was it I and I alone who had blundered into this heady bonanza of concupiscence? I cannot imagine that I gave much thought in the moment to these questions, although in retrospect one cannot help wonder about them. And to wonder too—egad—what further turns this sport might have taken had the innings been played out. But was one meant to pretend to ignore the proposed activity? Or was his question merely a ruse to upgrade the solipsistic verb he had used?

But if there can be a last straw in something this absurd, this verb was that. This fellow had now pushed even me too far. *Did I mind?!?* It just so happened that I did! The fellow's behavior had at last discovered the limit of my patience.

"Yes!" I said, rather forcefully, becoming another man than I had been till then. "I *do* mind. Yes, I *do* mind!" And then for emphasis and unmistakable clarity I added: "Do not do that!" In truth, I was so offended I might have done anything, might at least have beslapped him about with my Southern Gothic paperback. But I didn't do anything. I simply let that sentence, spoken forcefully, describe the dimensions of my indignity. And that, dear reader, was that.

In retrospect I have many times thought that I should indeed have threatened him with physical violence and forced him to leave the compartment. But my Yale training prevented this most natural of reactions. I mustn't be so vile as to express any real shock over something of a sexual nature. That would be blue-nosed and unpleasant. After all, I didn't believe in *censorship*, did I? Nonetheless I had been clear enough and went back to my reading, as if I could ever read another page of that awful book. I don't believe I read one dopey paragraph further, but I forced my eyes to stay put on the page nonetheless, *going over and over the dusty ribbon of wheel-rutted words over and over and over.* But the sighing had stopped. Beautiful Narcissus just sat there now, quite stumped and stymied—and surely feeling almost as stupid as I then thought him. He had been soundly rebuked and now, for the next hour, newly bereft of his swollen hopes, he sat opposite me as we each counted the uncomfortable seconds that passed like minutes and hours and days. But truth be told I was angry enough to now ignore him with something approaching elan.

But I would soon have my revenge. For at some point now the train pulled into an unknown station someplace south of Naples. It was at this backwater berg that an infusion of such heterosexuality entered our scene as would make the angels blush. It arrived in the form of three cartoon yokels who now like gibbons jabbering entered our compartment. It was a knuckle-dragging company of rural swains who at some point claimed to have hailed from Palermo, although how they had scrambled overland and where they were now going was an open question, perhaps even to them. One of them appeared to have cut his hair with a dull scythe; and if I had learned that it was not pig-manure upon their buckled shoon I would have been bowled over. If this trio did not all wear overalls without shirts it was only because I have forgotten that they actually did, or because they had a woman to impress, and any shirt under Heaven would have done the trick with the ultra-accommodating damsel who had poured herself into the compartment with them. For in truth she was no damsel, looking more mature than these gap-toothed fellows—if not in actual years, then in bumpy local mileage—and her pixie-ish dress was so evanescent as almost to necessitate turning one's head from side to side to make it out. To complete the presumed effect of countrified insouciance, her shoes were non-existent. Where, pray, had they been lost, the poor things? But who has need of such sophisticated *accoutrement* in the happy haylofts of Sicily?

The next minutes were filled with such raw energy as one would expect from hopped-up farm boys in a train compartment. And what had become of my nattily attired Neopolitan lothario? It was as if with the advent of these simian theatrics he had retreated into the crevasse between the seat and the window.

But dear reader, do you hope that the arrival of these satyrs and their nymph marks the end of our story? Alas not, for Maestro Fellini was not yet through with the set piece he had been constructing. The train soon stopped again and now into the compartment—filling it fully—stepped a middle-aged woman and a sixty-something nun. At last the eight spots in the compartment were filled. Before we proceed, may we review the seating chart? You will remember that I was in the first position by the window, across from the now chastened man, let us call him *Signore Onanissimo*. To my left were Swains #1 and #2, and then the middle-aged woman. Across from us, to the right of my former interlocutor were the aforementioned milkmaid, followed by Swain #3—and then the Nun. I delineate this because what followed would not have been possible without this arrangement.

It now shortly followed that Swain #3, sitting between the young woman and the nun, produced from some interior pocket a certain folded magazine, flashes of which interior he cleverly flashed to his compatriots opposite, not because they were especially interested in the pictures, which on the well-worn pages were no longer shocking to them, but because they found it the height of hilarity that he did this unbeknownst to the sister in holy orders inches away from him. The *hyuk-hyuk* hilarity of it grew and grew with each successive pictorial flash, the nun's proximity and ignorance of their shenanigans being the necessary and fixed object against which they could perform their con-stricted *opera buffa!* But their increasingly poorly hidden snickering and apish grinning was inevitably too much for the middle-aged woman, silent until now, but as privy as I to their asininity and the goofy *bob-bob-bobbing* of their yokels' Adam's apples. Without a hiccup of warning, she suddenly exploded at them like a jar of spoiled marinara whose expanding toxic gases had sud-denly overtasked the glass containing them. Her precise words were of course lost on me, but their effect was pyrotechnically spectacular. She went on and on in such magnificently blistering tones of umbrage that I was inwardly cheering and hooting. It was as though a cold shower of propriety and maturity had suddenly besoaked them to their cores. I suppose she was to them an analogue of what they had all been to my original companion.

Now, as the sun settled over the blasted landscape a silence came over the compartment as the rebuked jug-heads sulked. But still one more small scene must play itself out before our troupe of actors leap away into the wings and out of our story. For now—though my eyes were yet fixed on the pages in front of me—I began nonetheless to pick up another series of muted signals from across the aisle. Somehow, though I knew not precisely how, I came to intuit that the shoeless woman across from me, forced to look elsewhere than to her companions for diversion, was now expressing to them some interest in the young man reading the paperback across from her. There were occasional glances in my direction and some quiet words, and then eventually my instincts were proved correct as she made so bold as to assay a word or two in my own language, albeit not yet for my ears. She seemed to be asking her companions what the English was for some simple phrase, which phrase must first be correctly shaped before being directed toward its intended object. *"Como se dice ..."* she said to them. *"Eh ...* I like ... I like ... *Si?* I like ... I like ... Me? I like *me ...* ? I like me. *No?"* As I refused to acknowledge the attention being paid me by my now antique ruse of being engrossed in the book before me, so now too I declined to pipe up to aid this tottering communication to me-ward by proffering what was quite obviously the second person objective pronoun. In truth, hearing them struggle to find it powerfully tempted my naturally helpful instincts ... but in the end, like Melville's Bartleby, I simply preferred not to. The magic word must remain my own secret and I would hide it in my bosom forever. To her credit, she gamely tried to discover it for some time—rummaging around the monosyllables of my language with no help from her pre-literate companions—so much so that I could not help but be flattered. At one point my muscles tensed when the word "you" broke the barrier of her lips once or twice—the jig was up!—but somehow that word never struck her as quite right, so she rejected it. I couldn't believe my fortune. Had she really discovered it only to set it aside? It seemed she had and would be unable to declare herself to me after all. Now what? It seemed the drama was at last coming to an end.

In any event, I now had another trick up my sleeve. The light was going, so I closed my book and closed my eyes. I would simply feign sleep, death's second self, until at some point if I feigned it long enough it would mercifully no longer be feigned. I would have to fall asleep eventually, wouldn't I? I would have to leave my contact lenses in, but what was eye pain compared with finding an escape from this unpleasant dream? In seven hours the train would pull into Brindisi, would it not? Sitting up in this uncomfortable seat surrounded by this gang of Chaucerian characters would not under normal circumstances have been conducive to falling asleep, but now that I saw it my only option, I would not relent from seeking it. So I kept my eyes shut until finally, I fell thither at last, headlong into a better world.

Brindisi!

When I was jostled awake at dawn, I saw that we had stopped someplace. The man who missed his girlfriend now got off, and only literally. I was informed we would be in Brindisi soon and twenty minutes later, we were. Brindisi! I pulled my book-heavy backpack from the luggage rack, scrambled off, and began walking. I had forgotten that there was a world outside that train compartment and was excited to be rediscovering it. I was on my way to Greece! So I just kept walking down to the gigantic ferries, wherever they were. Some signage with the graphic of a boat led me along, but I never saw what I was looking for. Where was the dock? These crazy Italians! Who knew how far it might be, eh? So I simply kept walking. However tired I was, I was so glad to be out of that train compartment that nothing else mattered.

I'm not sure where I was headed during this trek, but in time I began to get the sense that I was not on the best route to the ferries. Nonetheless, I kept on. One had to find one's way eventually, and I knew that I would. But at some point, even for such as I, one comes to that point in one's forward wanderings when one wonders whether turning back is the better option. But of course the farther one has gone in a certain direction, the less one wants to admit one might be wrong—and have to walk all the way back in the direction from which one has come. When I came to a cemetery, I paused. It was still so early in the morning that I had not passed anyone all this time, but suddenly now I saw a woman dressed in the manner of women in Italian villages. I asked her in a few words of broken Italian which way I might go if I wanted to get to the ferry. *Traghetto.* That was the word: *Traghetto.* When she understood my meaning her eyes widened dramatically and she repeated the word to confirm—*Traghetto!?* The good woman could hardly contain her dismay. She spoke some dramatic words, which I clearly understood to be her inexpressible horror at my miserable predicament. Finally she made a hand gesture that was a cross between a chopping tomahawk and the pan-European hand gesture for "Boy, are you gonna get it!"—to communicate that it was very, *very* far. Unbelievably far! My God, you cannot imagine how far!

I wasn't sure how to respond. But then, taking some pity on me, the woman told me to walk with her. She seemed to be headed in the general direction of the ferry, and I could go with her for part of the journey. And so I did, sweating and unshaven and blinking painfully because of my calcified lenses. Of course I had little to say to this woman at this early hour as we walked and walked along these empty roads. I tried and failed to make some small talk, but she was old enough to be my mother and looked twice as old. Also, to be frank, I was embarrassed, because each step was an admission of my foolishness. And of course neither of us spoke the other's language.

Finally the quiet awkwardness was relieved when my Virgil bumped into a woman she knew. But then in Italian—I understood enough of what was being said to be freshly humiliated—she raved and raved about the ridiculous—the impossible!—situation of this wandering American foreigner! *It was unbelievable!* My God! Here it was six o'clock in the morning and he wanted to go to the ferry! *Il traghetto!* And listen to me now … are you listening? He was by the graveyard! *Il cimitero! My God—do you understand? Il cimitero!!!* The other woman looked at me, aghast, and then repeated the phrase. *Il cimitero!!!* At this she recoiled physically, as though defending herself against a vicious blow! It was beyond anyone's life experience to comprehend! I stood there patiently with my backpack as they loudly grieved and grieved over my unprecedented stupidity from just a few feet away. What could I do? Finally she thought it was time to continue our journey—*What else could she do? She had exhausted her powers of description!*—so she bade her neighbor goodbye. The neighbor said goodbye and looked at me and shook her head again. *Foreigners!*

After some considerable time my host sent me on my way as she went on hers in another direction. She was still shaking her head at me as we said goodbye. But finally she stopped, and eventually, I found the port and the ferries. Next stop, Greece.

CHAPTER TWENTY-EIGHT

Home, Eric

In the line for the Brindisi ferry I found myself next to an Australian chap, tall and thin with tousled sandy hair and a few years older than me. It was a wild joy suddenly to be speaking unbroken English with someone—and someone, let us be frank, who did not have designs on me. We traded life stories and remarked upon what a perfect hellhole Brindisi was. It seemed since Roman times to be a way station on the way to somewhere else. There was no here here. We were standing next to a gigantic greasy coil of the thickest rope I'd ever seen in a line of other Eurail students headed to Greece. The ferry ride to Patras was a slow twenty-plus-hour journey. When we finally boarded, my new friend and I hustled to the uppermost deck, whose vastness was covered with dirty indoor-outdoor carpeting, and found a spot near a riveted tower. We purchased some toasted ham-and-cheese sandwiches and I continued inanely wrestling with my opaque modernist fiction.[1]

---

[1] I later learned that the morose, alcoholic Faulkner preferred the characters in his writing to real people, declaring: "I can invent much more interesting people than God can." Also, that when his only daughter was twelve and piteously remonstrated against her father's drinking, he bitterly growled: "No one remembers Shakespeare's child." *Touché!*

The next morning—after an unmolested sleep on the unyielding deck—we passed the Ionian Islands and Cephalonia, my eventual destination. But of course I had to steam past them to the mainland and then find the ferry to take me back to Cephalonia. When our huge ship neared the Patras dock I spied the *Agios Gerasimos*, named for the hermit monk whose mummified body I had venerated a decade earlier. If I missed it I would likely spend many hours at the bleak Patras docks, so the moment I could I bade my Aussie friend adieu, ran down the gangplank with my groaning backpack, and hustled across several parking lots to catch the ferry.

I know now and I knew then that I was looking for the meaning of life, and not really anything quite that dramatic, but more the meaning of my own life. I had done everything expected of me, had graduated Yale with honors and now must find myself somehow—but how? I felt that returning here, to the Homeric home of Odysseus and to my own ancestral home, must be part of the answer—such that the word Homeric made me stoop pun-ward to "Home, Eric." My lineage had been here forever, so to land here now had for me something mystical about it. What would I find? Was my destiny here, among these people who were my people? Would I finally fit in here in a way that I had never fit in anywhere else? Would I find myself?

Three hours later I beheld the ancient contours of the mythic island and fir-covered Aenos, rising a mile out of the sea. I felt I was coming home. The *Agios Gerasimos* docked in Sami, from which I had an hour-long bus ride on the precipitously high, narrow roads wending their way down to the island's capital city, Argostoli.

I knew that my father was already there and that of course my Theo Othon lived there, but my Theo Takis was there too, and the three brothers hadn't been together on the island since the 1940s. Seeing them together there would be a once-in-a-lifetime experience. But first I must get to Argostoli. So I followed the crowds off the ferry and toward some parked buses. I saw an English girl wearing a straw hat with a blue ribbon and followed her toward the bus. Who was she? Would I marry her? The future lay before me pure and unadulterated, like hope itself.

Taking a seat near the front of the bus I saw that the bus driver—one of those crazy Cephalonians the other Greeks talked about—had with white twine hung a jerry-rigged black-and-white TV above his head, like a sword of Damocles. It was August 4 and I remembered that the Olympics were taking place in Los Angeles. How strange to be here where the Olympics were invented twenty-seven centuries earlier, and for them not to be here but of all place in Los Angeles! But there they were, on the TV above the driver's head! Although the picture was impossibly snowy I could make out hurdlers hurdling and remember the absurdity of riding in this bus along dangerous mountainous roads watching the tiny figures leaping over the hurdles in black-and-white California, two continents and an ocean away.

When the bus arrived in Argostoli, I had enough memory from 1972 to think I could find my uncle's home, but I was wrong and wandered aimlessly again. But nothing mattered more than that I was here. I was like Odysseus when he landed on Ithaka, and like my first forefather, I had arrived unannounced and incognito. No one knew I was there and I wandered the streets, awed simply to be there.

At one point I passed a group of young people talking to each other and perceived that one of them—an almond-eyed beauty—looked something like my father's goddaughter, Xenia, whom I had last seen twelve years earlier. I wasn't sure it was she, but stopped and asked her directions to the library; and as we spoke I thought, *It is as though I am disguised as Odysseus was disguised, transformed by Athena after he had been deposited on the shore by the Phaekians, so that he could*

Odysseus sits by the fire as Eumaeus discovers Telemachus at the entrance

wander his own homeland without being recognized, and talk to people he knew
but who did not know him ... I remembered how he talked to Eumaeus the
Swineherd and to his son Telemachus and to his father Laertes and even to his
wife Penelope and yet they had not known him—and here I was now talking
to Xenia, but she did not know me. I was now just another American tourist
wandering the island. When would I ever see her again like this, with this
cloak of anonymity? I was an invisible man, freed from all constraints, a
stranger wandering my own homeland.

I made my way up the hill of the town and saw the library, with its imposing steps. I knew I was not far from the house. Then I was amazed to see at
the top of those steps none other than Theo Takis, surveying the view with
the authoritarian air he often had about him: chest out, arms akimbo. To have
traveled for months and finally to be here and to see my own uncle was a
strange and thrilling moment, and I hustled up the steps to surprise him. For
some reason, though, his response was muted, as though he had seen me ten
minutes before. When I asked what direction I ought to go to find where my
Uncle Othon and Aunt Katy lived, and where my father must be, he pointed
toward the church. So I said I would see him later and made my way there.

I felt that in my days-long journey to this house and to my father I was
somehow reprising a journey he often related, of being in Mavrata during the
war and of not having heard from Kikí for days. She had gone to Argostoli,
but ought to have been back and he and his grandmother worried until eventually very early one morning he set out to walk the sixteen miles to Argostoli
to find her. But when he arrived at the house he found no one, just an open
book in the garden, as though someone had been reading it and suddenly
abandoned it. A neighbor said she had gone across the bay to Lixouri to visit
some Vergotis relatives, so my father eventually found someone with a boat
willing to take him across, and on the way passed the bloated corpses of soldiers, and because the fish had eaten away the flesh on their heads, saw the
bright white of their skulls. When he arrived in Lixouri he made his way to a
distant village on that part of the island, and to the door of their relative, and
when the door was answered he frantically asked, "Is Kikí here?" And the
woman said, of course, she's inside, at which he fainted. The next thing he

remembered was waking up in a bed and sweet Kikí rubbing his forehead with a washcloth.

These memories mingled with the craziness of my own journey from London, and now at long last I approached the house I had through all of Europe and all these years been thinking of, the physical locus of what I thought my truest self, the place where Panagis Vergotis had written his great books and where my father had grown up too, and so much else in our history had transpired.

And as happened to me now and again, I found that being with my father now was like entering another world, as if the past were not past anymore. As in 1972 we drove with Uncle Othon to Mavrata, stopping at a bakery to get some fresh bread, when my uncle related a joke whose punch line involved Georges Clémenceau and I realized they were referring to the French prime minister during the First War, as though it had happened yesterday. My father spoke of a bronze ashtray his father had brought from France before he was born and which in 1938 after his father's death he had shown his French teacher. It featured a little boy peeing upon an image of the Kaiser, and read *Apres L'Yser, Mon Dernier Salut!*, which the teacher translated as: "After the [German defeat at the Battle on the River] Yser, [Here is] my Final Salute!" The events of the past really were commingled with the present now, through my father seeming so recent. How many times had he told me the horrific story of how the Germans had murdered five thousand of the Italian Acqui Division in cold blood in October 1943, how he had himself heard the bursts of machine-gun fire, and now we passed the very spot where it took place.

Most of my time was spent with my cousin Yangos and his English girl-friend Martine, whom I hoped he would marry. The three of us took a several days' motor-boat excursion to Lefkada. But traveling there my mind often flew backward to the more ancient history of this island, too, to Homer and to "Odysseus and his Cephallenians," as the *Iliad* said. I was fortunate that my cousin had enough time to take me out on the boat and the most remarkable thing for me was that everything we saw was essentially unchanged from Mycenaean times, when Odysseus and his men lived there.

As we sped across the water I sat on the prow bouncing with the waves and recalled the mermaids in Eliot's "Prufrock":

I have seen them riding seaward on the waves
Combing the white hair of the waves blown back
When the wind blows the water white and black.

I saw Eliot's genius of giving this image back to us transmuted to what it always ought to have been in the first place, redeemed from our broken and fractured vision, and isn't that what poetry does, what all art is meant to do, to help us see things as they truly are in the deeper reality beneath the quotidian, so that we might see all the way through them to the beauty and the truth beneath, without losing sight of the things themselves? I mumbled to myself the haunting lines at the poem's end.

We have lingered in the chambers of the sea
By sea-girls wreathed with seaweed red and brown
Till human voices wake us, and we drown.

I hardly understood them, but what did it matter? Even to have a glimpse of whatever lay beneath seemed enough. Wasn't it the haunting quality I was after, anyway? But what exactly appealed to me? What dark truth was there that seemed to bear light upon the true nature of things? Why did anything strike me as it did? What was in me that I should like this and dislike that, that I should mark this and ignore that?

Why did Poe's "Annabel Lee" strike me as it did and does? *And neither the angels in Heaven above/ Nor the demons down under the sea/ Can ever dissever my soul from the soul/ Of the beautiful Annabel Lee ...*

It made me so sad, but it was a weirdly satisfying sadness, as though that sadness were somehow getting me closer to the real happiness and truth of the universe. *"And so, all the night-tide, I lie down by the side/ Of my darling— my darling—my life and my bride,/ In her sepulchre there by the sea—/ In her tomb by the sounding sea."* In reciting those lines I wanted to scratch beneath the surface of the world to find the gold and ivory and lapis beneath, to know the meaning of the universe and to give myself to it, whatever it was, if only there were such a thing. But who knew whether we longed for something that really was there or whether that for which we longed was a vestigial phantom limb left over from the meaningless progression of evolution, something that made as much sense as my appendix or my wisdom teeth? I only knew I ached at times in certain ethereal directions and I believed that in this direction there might lie the object toward which I ached, the Real Thing that would satisfy the homeward aching and make me feel at long last as I long had longed and longed to feel.

And so I went off on such reveries, but every now and again my father—like Mrs. Rynciewicz inquiring about our AP Physics progress—would ask when I planned to return to the United States. I had for three months been making my Grand Tour without a word on what I would do after—and what *was* I going to do? I wasn't sure, but my father saw clearly that whatever I did, I must get home and get a job and pay back my college loans. I cringed to hear this because in my mind there was something small-minded about this. I was an artist and a writer trying to find myself and the meaning of the universe. Why rush that? Did the twenty-one-year-old Goethe have to pay back college loans? Had Byron written *Childe Harold's Pilgrimage* under fluorescent lights? When my father was preparing to leave Cephalonia he expected I would go with him, but I wondered if staying there might be the better way deeper into myself, toward the home port for which I thought to be sailing. I had no real commitments. Why should I rocket back to nothing and for no real reason? If I was trying to find myself, why return to where I had always been and hadn't?

My cousin Yangos hoped I would stay. He is brilliant and charismatic and can be very persuasive. "You are a somebody here," he said. And it was true, in its way. I daily passed the bust of my great-grandfather Vergotis on the street that had been named for him, and there was a marble bust of my great-grandmother Eleni's brother in front of the archaeological museum. Yangos said that in the village, in Mavrata, "some of the old time villagers will actually address me using the word for Lord or Master." Living here would be something like returning to the place where we had been something, would be like returning to the great manor house from which I had been exiled years ago, like Tarzan discovering he was Lord Greystoke. But where was the manor house and where was the wealth? Alas, it had all been squandered in the nineteenth century or lost in the Second War or, most recently, in the 1953 earthquake. Both glorious villas had been reduced to rubble and most of the heirlooms destroyed.[2] Even before the war, my great-grandmother sold the volumes in her late husband's library until in the end, none remained.[3] In the late thirties there were still five or six armoires in the library on the second floor, and anyone who wished could go upstairs and purchase what he liked. Eleni put the books in a sack and sent my father to the library to ask deaf Kyrios Moschopoulos their value, and would then ask that price. Moschopoulos—the venerable head of the library—had in the previous century been a pupil of Vergotis's and sang his hero's praises to the man's eleven-year-old grandson, saying *"Kaneis then than ton ftasi!"*[4]

But Yangos was only thirty-four, with the ambition to be a gentleman farmer on our family land, which since at least the 1680s had been as it is now. He would grow grape vines and reconstitute the winery our family had since time immemorial. Now he owned a car dealership, where he said I could work, and a photographic shop, and a gorgeous house on the cliff in Lassi. I could stay there with him and find my future and my past. I might one day alone stumble upon a fissure in the rock and clamber inward to the dead center of

---

[2] An invaluable set of China brought from the Orient by Yiannikostas—so exquisite that when Greece's king in the twenties visited the island it had been borrowed for the occasion—had been stolen.

[3] We have only one volume from all those books, appropriately enough a bookworm-eaten 1541 edition—in Homeric Greek—of the *Iliad and Odyssey* combined into one volume, and set in the smallest type imaginable, and bound in desiccating calfskin.

[4] "No one will ever equal his intellect!"

the universe where time had stopped, to some vaulted grotto that opened onto that interior ocean upon whose sunless shore lay the bleached bones of Odysseus himself, next to the planted oar of Aenos fir he had carried thither and whose last drink had been just here at the world's end from that stream from which I too would now drink, here where he had talked with the bloodthirsty shades whom he had then at last joined at his journey's end, and whom I might join too, to mingle forever among their company, far from the false light of the superficial surface world.

So after my father left, the world was open to me. But what did I do? Nothing. I remember late one afternoon tagging along with Yangos and Martine to meet up with two friends of theirs at the harbor. We arrived and boarded an impressive sailboat docked along the quay. It belonged to an Athens-based lawyer, Makis, who was visiting the island with this brother, named Mikios, also a lawyer. The similarity of their names instantly lent a comic edge to their introduction. Makis and Mikios? They wore crisp polo shirts and expensive swimming trunks and the requisite boat shoes; and both spoke British English, giving them a refined air. Makis seemed serious, but Mikios seemed mostly to pretend to be serious so that his deadpan comments were the more funny or ironic. For some time we simply sat, mostly in silence, on the deck of the beautiful boat and took in the pleasant harbor scene. Finally I broke the silence.

"It's so peaceful," I said.

"Yes," rejoined Mikios. "Highly peaceful." Had he really said "highly peaceful?" The term struck me as hilarious, the idea that peacefulness could be raised to the level of "highly"—or that he should think to describe it that way. If peace rose to any kind of extreme level, wouldn't it contradict itself and vanish? Was Mikios being serious when he said this? Was his English not quite sophisticated enough for him to realize how funny this might sound to someone like me? Or was he so sophisticated that he knew precisely how ridiculous it sounded, and so had said it to amuse himself and anyone else sophisticated enough to find it funny? But no one laughed.

I soon realized there was a dry comic edge to much that he said, though I still can't say if he meant "highly peaceful" to be intentionally funny. But if one said something innocent, like "I'm starving" or "I'm exhausted" he would usually pause—and then in a very serious tone, as though he really wanted to know, would ask: "Do you mean *sexually*?"

After some time on the boat we found a café by the quay and decided to order what the Greeks call *mezedakia*: a few hors d'oeuvres like feta and olives and grilled octopus. And a beverage: perhaps some orange Fantas. *Portoka-ladia*. Or some shots of ouzo.

But I wasn't sure what I wanted and as I dithered Mikios offered: "Perhaps you can have *hybo-brichio*?" (pronounced *ee-poh-vree-chee-o*).

"What," I asked him, "is an *hypo-brichio*?" He looked confused and almost put-out, as though it was impossible anyone could be unaware of this, as though I had asked what a cat was, or a shoe.

"A submarine," he said, somehow embarrassed to have to translate it, in a shrugging tone that itself said, "What else could it be?" But I was still baffled. In my world a submarine, or "sub"—which in some places was called a hoagie or a wedge or a grinder or a hero—was simply a sandwich in a long, oblong white roll, reprising the shape of the vessel. But what did it mean here? Mikios seemed amused that I had no idea what I would be getting and so he said, dryly, "Order it. You will see." Was I being set up? But I did order it, and I waited.

But as we waited I grew annoyed. What was I in for? Now that I had taken the bait and ordered it, perhaps someone could tell me. Would it be some ghastly exotic horror, like the entrails of a fish in a greasy puff pastry? Had they allowed me to order it to amuse themselves at my expense? And so I asked them again. At last Mikios relented and said in his plummy English: "It is a *vanilla*." As though that would clear things up. What the hell was "a vanilla"? I still didn't get it. And said so.

"Ah," he said, and then again, "you will see," tilting his head and moving his eyes in a way that I didn't like, that portended trouble. At last the waitress appeared holding a tray with five glasses, four containing normal beverages, two Pepsis and two pale orange *portokalades*; and one containing—or perhaps it was—the *hypo-brichio*. The streaky water glass set in front of me was filled with what looked like plain tap water, but vertically in the water there was plunged a long metal spoon upon whose end, submerged in the glass and resting upon its bottom, was a gooey chunk of what I supposed must be vanilla taffy. Thus was it served, and thus explained its enticing appellation.

Still, I was stymied. What the heck was I supposed to do with this bizarre oddity? Even now that it was here, the thing itself didn't seem to offer any clues. Was I to drink the water without disturbing the spoon, and would the water be faintly vanilla-flavored as a result? Or was I now to wait for the white clump to dissolve, or perhaps to stir it to hasten its dissolution? So I again bothered Mikios and now Yangos and Martine, too, who were sipping their sodas and staring out at the harbor, indifferent to my struggles. "What am I supposed to do with this?" I asked. And now Yangos, looking at me as though I were an idiot, said "Eh! You take out the spoon and you eat it! What the hell do you think you can do with it? My God, cousin! Where you were born? *In a fah-keeng cave?*"

Ah. Now I understood. Or did I? In any case, I took out the spoon, stared at the moist taffy, nibbled at it indifferently, and then replaced it in the water. It was overly sweet and I was never any big taffy fan, so had I known I was ordering taffy I would not have. They couldn't have told me? Furthermore, I still didn't get it. If one were a taffy fan, what exactly was the advantage—or affectation—of keeping the taffy wet? Or would serving this taffy-laden spoon on a plate simply look less festive? Or perhaps this presentation was meant to keep the taffy moist and reasonably cool? Or perhaps it was an age-old prophylactic against aggressive insects? Was that it, that the water protected it from the ubiquitous flies and hornets that were already arriving to climb into Yangos's Pepsi bottle? So I could nibble at the taffy I didn't want at my leisure, without having to shoo anything away? But then I wondered if perhaps there was something to this presentation that had once held some other meaning, decades before, perhaps during the war when German submarines were a hot topic? I never learned the answer. And how it still tortures me these decades later. *Why was the taffy submerged?* Who had invented this, and when? Where on earth had this infernal idea originated? Was it in the bazaars of

Constantinople, a thousand years earlier? What did it all mean? Somewhere in the distance, a Greek dog barked: *γαυ γαυ.*

So what then would I now do and what was I looking for? I had no idea what the shape of my future would be, but perhaps I would live there forever and marry a Greek woman and raise my children there—and the years that my father and family had spent in America would seem a mere blip of three decades in the numberless centuries of Metaxas Greekness. And thus would the wound be healed, the breach atoned for. But that would make my mother the breach and the wound. And wouldn't it mean that I was half valid? And yet surely this is how many of the Greeks I grew up with felt. For some being Greek itself was their principal object of worship, the place from which all meaning was derived. And others simply were proud to be Greek. My aunt's brilliant and otherwise kind and wonderful artist sister once in a fit of pique expressed her horror at my insufficient Greekness. I must have stared dully at some clever snippet of conversation to set her off. "Why have you not learned to speak Greek?" she asked, upset. "Your father ought to have teached you this wonderful language! It is a tragedy! We have ancient poetry, history, dramatics! It is a tragedy. How it can be this?" And I sat there and listened to this, the dutiful son, as they implicitly devalued my dear mother, as though she had been some grasping harpy who had flappingly tried to wrest from the arms of noble Pallas one of Athena's choicest ephebes, had entered the Parthenon under cover of dark and stolen me from the goddess's ivory arms. Of course, it would not be charitable or Christian to say it, but it was inevitable that, under certain circumstances one might at least momentarily mentally bid these voices *adieu* something to themselves. But I had heard such things many times over the years. Was my wanting to stay in Greece my acceding to this kind of thinking? Was Cephalonia really the atmosphere in which I was born to swim?

As the summer turned to autumn, I wondered. And then one day in the mail there was a package from Adam Liptak containing a long letter—I can see his handwriting now—and two copies of the *Harvard Lampoon*. There was a world I'd forgotten all about, a city called New York where I had friends and where everyone spoke English as I did, and got the same cultural references, and where perhaps I belonged more than I had realized. Where no one knew what an *hypo-brichio* was. I knew I must go back.

CHAPTER TWENTY-NINE

Onion Skin and Nothingness

"Never mind, sir—things will shape themselves."

"Shape themselves, eh?"

"Just so, sir."

—*Anna Karenina*

O
f course no sooner had I arrived than I wondered why I had done so: to what exactly had I returned? I had no job and was again under my parents' thumb. So I fell instantly into the queer post-adolescent adolescence of the over-educated gadabout, those grim horse latitudes between college and "life" in which one floats and drifts aimlessly and imperceptibly. To do that in gorgeous Cephalonia may be regarded as unfortunate, but to do it in one's parents' home must be regarded as carelessness. For just what were my plans now? But wasn't the very idea of planning itself a bourgeois conceit I must avoid? In any event, I hadn't been raised in a home where going to college was normative, so the world after college was never something I had thought about clearly. I was now on that part of the map where dragons be and knew the comforting academic grid of latitude and longitude was sunk forever, Atlantis-like, beneath the blue waves.

So suddenly now I would feel the lack of a plan as a man overboard feels the lack of a boat underneath him. But somehow—and yet how I knew not—I earnestly believed things would "shape themselves" of their own accord. I had a destiny, hadn't I? I seemed to think that I did, although I don't know why I did, or why I should. Perhaps part of this feeling came from a genuine sense

of destiny, but I hardly knew. And if I really did have any destiny, how was I
to proceed toward it? Or was I? Would it not find me? I suppose that it was
now, in my increasing misery that I began to look for something like "the
meaning of life," the thing that might help me know what it was all about and
how I might fit in to it. But I also suspected that perhaps there really was no
meaning to life, or to anything at all, and this could be a problem.

And yet I still somehow had some inane sense of some kind of guaranteed
predetermined happy future. But couldn't this be not a faith in something real
but a false faith, a bouquet of stupid ideas, an excrescence upon my hull of
barnacles I'd picked up as I floated along aimlessly? What did I believe in,
really? I suppose I could say I believed in *myself*, to use the celebrated cliche.
But did I? Or perhaps I believed that everyone possessed a secret and wonderful destiny and fate, as though the universe owed me something exquisite and
fulfilling. But what? And why would we believe this when so many people's
lives are full of agony and tragedy? Why in the world *should* such a thing be
true? But like all false ideas and all lies, there is enough truth in it to fool us,
if we are willing. Somewhere in the culture there was still the idea that we are
each created in God's image and have a purpose for being here, so perhaps
even if we don't believe this exactly there is nonetheless enough of that image
within us—albeit broken—to which we might affix our dreams, which are
likely themselves to be broken at some point, though we would never believe
it if anyone tried to tell us. But I simply didn't know, nor knew that I didn't
know, nor whether one could know or hope to know, and the days passed.

But as they did my parents questioned me persistently about less ethereal
matters. What was I planning to do with myself? And so I soon came to see
that—at present, anyway—things were not "shaping themselves" at all. I was
living with my parents with no job prospects. And because my parents had
come to this country with nothing but hope and the wisdom born of their
sufferings, and because they had worked extremely hard since their arrival,
giving my brother and me opportunities they never had, they were hardly
content to watch me blithely treading water. I was almost an affront to their
own dreams. I had gone to Yale and graduated with accolades and prizes; why
shouldn't I have the world by the tail? Of course I had some vague plans of

getting a job "in publishing," but I think my real plans at the time revolved around being "discovered," which was the antithesis of having a plan. But if all went as I was idiotically sure it must I would be publishing stories in the *New Yorker* very soon and would be the toast of the literary circuit. And then, of course—when I was ready—I would write the novel. And yes I must use the definite article because my goodness how it would be talked about! It would be my *Buddenbrooks*, my *The Naked and the Dead*, my *V.*, only so much more! The critics would scarcely know what to say, would sputter and stutter on the page and practically spit in their stupefaction at the book's unprecedented order of genius. Its appearance would be compared to that of a tornado dropping down out of the sky and altering forever the literary landscape! It would mark the debut of an astonishing genius "in our midst." A moment ago no one had heard of him, but now we can hardly imagine "our fiction" without him. They would use phrases like "to be reckoned with" and "in our time." And finally Pynchon—and then Salinger too—would come out of hiding to blow bubbles and kisses of praise in the pages of the *New York Review of Books* to the one to whom their work had all along been pointing, in whom they had at last been fulfilled! People would recall Bernstein's debut at age twenty-five, but that could hardly compare to what they were seeing. And of course my little book would sell like crazy too, would become required reading in all the right high schools and colleges, and before I was thirty there would be CliffsNotes to help the dumbfounded kiddies make sense of its baroque symbology and byzantine allusions! I would stand alone as atop a butte in the midst of the vast flat culture—I alone—saying to a thankful and admiring world: "Thus and thus and thus have I willed it!"

Except that didn't happen. Instead I skulked about the house like a guilty dog, dodging my poor parents' questions, until one day my friend Bill said he and Tom Edman were subletting an apartment on 54th Street and First Avenue. Might I join them? It was a one-bedroom, but at twenty-one the idea of three guys living in such quarters is perfectly acceptable and in no time I arrived with my suitcase and IBM Selectric. Suddenly my future was "shaping itself" after all.

But how did that "shaping" express itself?

I wondered what was at the bottom of everything. If you peeled away the onion layers, and peeled away and peeled away, what would you find? Was there something at the bottom upon which the universe stood and depended? And if there did exist a foundation upon which the edifice of Reality stood, what was it? Was that what some called God? And what if there were no such thing, that we stood upon an abyss, and to scratch beneath the surface was to see the howling emptiness below? I remembered having a recurring image of myself on an infinitely large blue carpet stretching to the horizon. You could sprint and sprint and get no nearer to anything; you were upon an unending nightmare of gridlessness, with no escape. You were modern man, unmoored from anything but himself, with no reference outside of himself.

There was a short-lived men's magazine that I tried and failed to write for, but through my *Antaeus* friend Brad I got an introduction to "Chip" McGrath at the *New Yorker* and one day breached the famous rabbit warren of offices. I had sent him humor pieces, and his short rejection letters had been personalized and genuinely encouraging. Through my friend at *Vanity Fair* I got another appointment with an editor at *House & Garden*, and somehow persuaded myself I should work there, although they were not so persuaded.

In the meantime I got invited to some parties and openings, usually with Adam's Harvard friends. One night we went to the opening of a new nightclub called the Limelight on Sixth Avenue and 20th. I hadn't realized until I got there, but it was a former Episcopal church that was sold to someone who had turned it into a nightclub. The official "desacralization" of it—so it could be sold—was of course a knowing, winking con, because the cache of the place as a nightclub was clearly the perceived "trangressiveness" of its having been a church. Even as I got out of the cab I knew there was something wrong about the whole thing. I wasn't sure I believed in such things, but the word *demonic* entered my mind. While the music was throbbing around us and people were dancing and staggering drunkenly, a movie was shown on a screen above our heads featuring a pornographic opening scene, though it was worse than merely pornographic. It was a darkly vicious smearing of faith being played on endless TV screens in this building that had recently been a church where babies were baptized and couples married; where people wept prayers for their sick and said goodbye to their beloved departed.

Though I had walked away from any expression of faith, I was nonetheless struck by a palpable darkness there and I think for the first time in my life I sensed where the cavalier, cynical, knowing attitude I and so many had adopted could eventually lead, and it frightened me. But the next day I woke up and didn't think about it again for years.

Falling in Space

One weekend John Tomanio—still at Wesleyan, having taken a year off—told me that Annie Dillard had read my "Impala George" story and loved it. I didn't know who she was but soon gathered she was a famous writer, and that I should be very flattered. I eventually even got to speak with her on the phone. She generously listened to me and then recommended some books I might read, but when I got off the phone I realized I was still as lost as ever. What had I been looking for from her? A promise to try to place the story in an important magazine?

Around Thanksgiving I drove to Wesleyan to see John and he and I went with some friends to O'Rourke's Diner, a fixture on Middletown's Main Street. But after we paid our bill and walked out, something unutterably odd happened.

I should first point out that this street is literally the widest Main Street in America, as John had often told me. In any case, as we were walking toward my car, gabbling about something inane, like whether the Monkees' Mike Nesmith's mother had invented Wite-Out or Liquid Paper, it happened. What I mean to say is that the bottom dropped out from under me. The sensation was a piercing distillation of confusion and horror. For what seemed like several seconds, but what certainly must have been the tiniest fraction of a second, I was suddenly falling, plummeting, as though I had stepped off a cliff.

And then, after that long instant's disorientation and terror, my accelerating downward flight instantly and awkwardly and harshly was arrested as my armpits—happily swathed in a vintage thrift-store overcoat—caught the edges of the open manhole into which I had suddenly, perfectly, stepped.

But how had this happened? One moment I was deep in meaningless conversation and the next I was up to my armpits in sidewalk. How was it possible to be talking one moment with the certainty of pavement under foot, and the next to be dangling over a bottomless hole as you gasped to make sense of the universe? Was this some grand cosmic joke? My friends suddenly looked down at me, aghast, nearly as baffled as I. There was a construction site nearby with a hose running into the open manhole, but none of us had seen it; we had simply been walking along in our careless reverie until I was sucked away toward the center of the earth. I had been striding along happily, unselfconsciously, and suddenly I was sixteen inches tall, a sawed-off buffoon addressing my friends from ankle height. It would have been perfectly fitting if my voice just then sounded as though I'd inhaled helium.

So I clambered out, dusted myself off, and realized that if I had fallen ever so slightly differently I would almost certainly have cracked my head on the sharp metal lip of the hole and been knocked unconscious, would have fallen to the mucky bottom, a long ten feet down. It was seriously frightening. But what to do? I tried to shrug it off and drove home. My overcoat was torn, a war wound with which to impress my friends. Of course my mother had another view. How could someone have left a manhole open in the middle of a sidewalk? She insisted we sue them—for the cost of the coat, and whatever else. The cost of the coat? Still, she was right. It was outrageous. If an older person had fallen it might have been fatal. There hadn't even been an orange cone. So my mother made me call a lawyer friend from the Greek church, who did his best to help me. But my heart wasn't in it. Why couldn't we just forget it? The lawyer friend wasn't terribly encouraging about my "case," but my mother wouldn't hear of letting it go.

I went back to Manhattan to pursue my "writing career," but now every time I spoke to my mother she hounded me about this. Had I filled out the small claims court form she sent me? But what I did do in the next weeks, alone in the apartment while Tom and Bill were off at real jobs, was sit in front of my humming Selectric and think about the larger meaning of it all. But I didn't write anything. I was not self-motivated in that way and I didn't know how to be. So I stared at the ingenious silver ball inside the typewriter and now and again made it jump here and there, forming sentences and ideas, but no more.

But I was thinking, trying for the life of me to figure out the meaning of life, the way out of my dilemma. I knew that writers mostly had to chart their own courses, while doctors and businessmen—even the driven ones—had grooves into which they could pour their energies, had assignments and offices and titles and deadlines and concrete expectations. The writer had none of these. He was a kind of fish out of water, existing within society, but strangely separated from it. While the world hustled and bustled in its well-worn rhythms, while commuters swarmed in droves—bringing to my mind *Koyaanisqatsi* with the Philip Glass score—I, the artist, lived outside those rhythms, observing them. What to do?

I kept returning to the vomit of the manhole. Did it *mean* anything—and if so, what? Did anything mean anything? Perhaps I could write an essay about it and sell it and make some money. That would mean something! And it would stop my mother from bugging me about it. So I tried to write something, but it never went anywhere. Whenever I tried writing on the subject, it was as though I were going through the motions of making the carcass of an uncooked chicken "walk" across the table. It would never come to life and walk of its own accord, much less fly. Still, I continued to brood upon the whole thing. Was the larger message that there was no foundation in the world, that even the sidewalk was a phantasm, that there was no bottom to things, no Ground of All Being. Were we really adrift in infinity with no bearings except the ones we invented? This idea floated in and out of my mind, but I was too dumb to grasp the full horror of its implications.

I was also in fits and starts—how else?—fiddling with a novel about Cephalonia and my family. But to call the paragraphs with no semblance of a plot or structure part of a novel was to kid oneself. Nonetheless I thought about Cephalonia and about the seismic event that in 1953 had propelled my father across the ocean, and thought about how it had made beaches and whole villages disappear forever, how it had uncovered ancient statuary and opened graves, how roads had vanished and cliffs had fallen into the sea. All of this made me wonder whether I really was on to a larger idea with my manhole thesis, that perhaps everything was transient and reality itself was protean and therefore "unreal." I thought of the image of an onion, which one peeled and peeled to get to the center, but there was no center, just onion skin and more onion skin and then nothingness, eternal nothingness at the heart of the universe, nothingness without beginning or end.

I even thought of the manhole semiotically and hermeneutically, and then even typographically, the manhole somehow being a period on life's page into which I had fallen, the idea being that one couldn't even take the letters and words on the page for granted. They gave the illusion of certainty—of meaning and order—but were phantoms. You could walk upon them and feel sure of your footing and then slip between the sentences, knocking letters as you went. You might even fall through a period as I had, into the endless blank abyss of the thinness of the page itself, into the infinite whiteness beyond the ink, the fathomless mystery of the White Whale of nothingness and everythingness, because even that blankness that seemed like nothingness and whiteness was neither nothing nor white. John Hollander once said that etymologically *black* and *blank* and the French *blanc* and therefore *white* were all mixed. It was where the abyss of unformed chaos uncreated everything back into itself. It was not a pure nothing of black or white but an erasure of *something* … a meaningful something smudged into meaningless nothingness. So we were on a rickety catwalk above that abyss and I, in falling through the manhole, had only immanentized that inevitable and bleak eschaton because we were each Ralph Waldo Emerson's all-seeing eye, alienated in our prisons of total subjectivity. God help us! Oh yes, and then more bad news: God didn't exist.

But who had time to worry about such grand bad news when there was bad news on a much smaller scale: Bill said our wonderful sublet was over. We'd have to move out after January, and suddenly I had to think where to go next. John O'Brien kept trying to convince me to join him in Boston with the other members of Nietzsche and a Horse. We would all live together and be artists. They would finally give the band a serious go and I would write. We were the Beatles in Hamburg, soon to be discovered as the geniuses we were. Ian was there and Gig would be there soon too and the idea was appealing. But I had my vague idea of making it in New York.

But suddenly I had nowhere to live. Then, a possibility leapt up. I had been proofreading at law firms during the midnight-to-eight "graveyard"—or "lobster"—shift, as it was known, and once or twice had as my proofing partner an affable dude named Charlie, who was so laid-back that seeing him here was like seeing someone in surfer attire on a commuter train. He had a classic seventies shag and a beat-up jean jacket with a sheep's wool collar and seemed to be a vintage pothead right out of my high school, down to the thin-waled Levi cords and shit-kickers. I felt I had many times watched him slump and shuffle to wood shop or to his rusty El Camino in the parking lot. But here he was proofreading three-hundred-page legal documents for Cadwallader! One day he said his roommate was moving out and I could move in. It was a sublet from a Frenchwoman on East Tenth Street in the Village—a to-die-for location—and my share of the rent would only be four hundred a month. Really? I visited the apartment and couldn't believe it. I could move in the following Monday. The Village would make much more sense for the writerly lifestyle I planned for myself anyway, *non?* And I'd finally begin working on my novel in earnest!

But before I moved in, I would finally that weekend make the trip to see John in Boston. I drove up and stayed with Bill Taylor, who was at the Boston Opera Company. But that Monday I was back at the law firm with my suitcase, since I'd be moving in with Charlie after our shift. But where *was* Charlie? Charlie's friend said something bad had happened. I was confused. "What are you talking about?" I said. "I need to know. I'm supposed to be moving in with him. Like tonight. There's my suitcase."

"You'd better let Charlie tell you himself," his friend said, infuriating me. But we couldn't get Charlie on the phone. So at last his friend spilled the beans. Charlie's roommate had died of a drug overdose over the weekend. The Frenchwoman subletting the apartment was understandably infuriated to have her place swarming with cops and coroners, and she demanded Charlie move out. But why should this affect me? Actually the woman was generously willing to interview me to see if I might work out, and the next day we had a pleasant conversation at a café, but in the end she decided in favor of a young woman, and can you blame her? And so it was because of a drug overdose that I moved to Boston.

But before that I went to a party at Tom Edman's new digs and slept over. Tom was way downtown in the financial district and his new roommate was a high school buddy of his to whom I took an instant liking. The morning after the party the two of us talked for a long time. Bruce was driven and disciplined, and I longed desperately for his focus and organization. Where did it come from? He shared with me his plans for the year and then for the years and decades. He opened a loose-leaf notebook in which he had inscribed his goals. It was all there in black and white, on graph paper, of course. He showed me how by thirty his net worth would be X and by thirty-five it would be 2X. It was all meticulously planned and to me was mind-boggling. He was the sort of fellow who would do a hundred push-ups before breakfast and a hundred after lunch, who would excel in business because he arose at four thirty for that purpose, who would cut his hair militarily short and who would inspire thousands to follow his lead. If I could have done so that morning I would have signed up as his first recruit.

But who was I kidding? Or whom? I had always been easily inspired, subject to fits of inspiration that soon waned. I was looking for a quick fix, and knew nothing of actual self-discipline, nor how to get it. I had never really had to apply myself. On the strengths of my genetic intelligence I had been praised since earliest childhood and had skipped a grade and gotten straight A's for little real effort. Even when I had studied it was less that I needed to than that there was little else that held my attention. Everything had come to me easily, even at Yale, where I had edited the humor magazine and had gotten awards for my writing. Why shouldn't I expect this to continue? But I had begun to realize it might not, that I was for the first time adrift in the great uncharted waters of the wide world. I had been an able sailor on the large, well-run ship of academia, where I was told what to do and I did it. But suddenly I was on my own in a dinghy, drifting and wondering where to go. I wanted Truth and the Meaning of Life and worldly success too, but wasn't sure the first two existed and had no idea how to get the third, but sensed if I didn't understand who I was and what life was about I might not have anything to write about. And like Faust I wanted it all now, and didn't know that to get it now was to pay a monstrous price, one so large it would negate everything.

Nonetheless that morning I thought it was in my sights as I listened, under the spell of the militaristic achiever with the graph charts. Self-discipline was the key. Naturally. It was the thing that would undergird you. You must pull yourself up by your bootstraps! But what the hell did that mean, practically speaking? Obviously the very idea of pulling oneself up by one's bootstraps assumed there was no Ground of All Being, or God or Truth. One must assume we were ourselves all we had, and needed to make the best of it and somehow— arbitrarily it seemed to me—impose order upon ourselves. We would be our own gods and create our own reality and future. But how? What resources where there upon which to draw? I didn't seem to have anything like that within me, though I might be willing to look for it if I thought it was in there someplace— but I was sure that people like Tom's roommate, who thought they had that whatever it was within them, were actually mistaken, that they had thoughtlessly internalized some form of order from someplace else, that they had never deeply thought about it, but had simply adopted some form of self-discipline and order because it appealed to them, or because it was already in their natures, just as it was not in mine. In other words, they were kidding themselves. Not that I wouldn't have liked to kid myself along the same lines, if I had been able to, but for whatever reason I didn't seem able. I suppose I saw through it all, for some reason, whether I wanted to or didn't, and so I just couldn't make myself play along. Which left me where, precisely? Who knew? Anyway, what did it matter. I was going to Boston.

CHAPTER THIRTY

Boston

Spring 1985

The house John O'Brien was living in was far from downtown Boston. A large dog owned by one of the other housemates roamed freely within it to do his business. Who lived like this? But John promised he and the rest of the band would find another place soon, and of course I would join them. In the meantime I would stay with Bill, whose living room's wooden floor was unoccupied. I would sleep in my blue sleeping bag, the one I had purchased with the money I made at Hilltop Diner. But neither the bag's thin synthetic fill nor the varnish on the wood floor provided the cushioning for which one hoped. But as it was only for two weeks or so, I would hold out. Tom Edman's cousin Lisi lived upstairs and worked at the Boston Opera, and had opened the door for Bill there. So while living with Bill I got to know Lisi, and some of Bill's other friends.

As the weeks passed I realized I needed some money, so I got another proofreading job, but it was at a filthy and smelly printing plant in the industrial section of Southey, near the water. It was almost unbearable and I lasted eight horrible weeks. In the meantime, John was no closer to finding another place to live, and sleeping on Bill's floor had begun to lose its charm. Two weeks became three months. Then Ian told me Harvard Business School rented its dorms every summer. Did I want to room with him? In addition to being lead singer for Nietzsche and a Horse, Ian was also a poet and a dedicated anti-Reaganite political activist who created giant papier-mâché heads and wore them around Boston Common to support the Sandinistas. Though I was politically unaffiliated, you still couldn't have found an odder couple. Nonetheless we moved in together and flew what freak flags we could. At my printing job I had made a bunch of eleven-by-seventeen black-and-white prints of Nabokov's author photo, and we covered a wall with them. And Ian had a cassette-tape boombox on which we played the same Smiths album—*Meat Is Murder*—over and over.

I was then obsessed with Nabokov and with John Updike too, reading almost everything by him, but drawing the line at reading his novel about an African dictatorship, nor could I bother with his *Bech* books. I spent that summer walking to Harvard Square, daily passing the Agassiz Museum and realizing the multivalent Nabokov had walked this same street in the forties, when he was the chief lepidopterist there, just before writing *Lolita*. I often sat for hours at the red outdoor tables outside a chain coffee shop, and one week labored over a long paragraph describing a kidney-shaped pilsner stain on a piece of sheet music. I was obviously reading too much Updike.

One day that summer I was lying on my mattress in the dorm room when I heard the opening strains of that black symphony I have heard often enough since. I didn't know it was depression, but remember from my window glimpsing one of Harvard's beautiful Georgian brick towers with a white steeple and wondering how any human being could ever have the will and the energy to build something like that? What was the point? Even having to shower and dress during this period was too much to be borne. Eventually I went to a doctor, who told me nothing was wrong with me, that I should take a tablespoon of castor oil every morning and exercise. He should have told me to get a job, too. But of course I did neither. What was the point? In recent years Dick Cavett has described depression as something that puts you in a state such that if someone were to say there across the room lay a genuine magic wand that—when you waved it—would unfailingly and instantly cure your depression, you simply couldn't bother.

Chris Hanes was just beginning to get his doctorate in economics at Harvard and invited me to a party, where I met someone who had a room for rent in a house on the outskirts of Cambridge. So when the dorm gig with Ian ended, I moved there. It was an odd group of people, none of whom I knew. I recall a beautiful young dancer there, who at one point in a conversation admitted she had "never read any Jungian." It reminded me of the famous exchange: "Do you like Kipling?" "I don't know. I've never kippled."

One weekend I learned my old friend Jim Shapiro from Yale would be in Boston for a few days, so we made plans to hang out on the steps of Widener Library, whose Corinthian columns make it the kind of ennobling public architecture that recalls Yale professor Vincent Scully's remark, "One strode into the Old Penn Station like a God. One scuttles into the 'new' Penn Station like a rat." As though following an inner divining rod we mounted the steps and sat near the top, with an inspiring view of Harvard Yard. I wanted us to collaborate on a humor book of some kind and tried to talk Jim into it. We finally hit on doing a parody of the *Ripley's Believe It or Not* books whose paperbacks we had both devoured in grade school.

Jim and I immediately sprang to remembering our favorite entries, all of which were insane, but just believable enough that you couldn't discount them, which was the genius of the genre. There was the Chinese emperor whose eye sockets each contained two irises! We both remembered it instantly and guffawed. And then there was the medieval duke who had a false hand made of pewter, in which he kept phials—"phials"!—of poison with which he dispatched his enemies. And there were less baroque entries, like "Charles Darwin kept a Mynah bird as a pet for thirty years, saying it improved his powers of concentration." Or "Smokey, a cat with thirty claws." Jim and I realized parodying these books might indeed be just the thing for our sick imaginations. But was it possible to parody what was already on the brink of incredibility and lunacy? Yet there was more to parodying this form than screwy facts. These books had odd and archaic phrasings that somehow made the whole thing work, that made it funny to us. Could we duplicate that? We must try, and with the afternoon yawning ahead of us in the way afternoons yawned at that point in life, we set to work.

So I would start one and he would try to finish it and then he would start one and I would try to finish it. It wasn't easy. Finally, from our noodlings, Jim thought he had the beginning of a winner. "OK, I think I got it," he said. "No, no, seriously. OK, this is *amazing*." I listened. "No, no," he reiterated. "This is *amazing*." I told him I believed him and for the love of Pete, please continue! "OK," he said, pausing dramatically and then daring to begin. "In World War One," he said, and struggled to continue, over-pronouncing every word as though chiseling them in stone for all time "... chefs ... in a mountainous region of Switzerland ..." and then he choked on a laugh, unable to disgorge the enormous verb and final clause ... but then he did "... buttered an entire mountainside!" But wait, I said ... what about *"chefs under siege"*? OK, again ... "In World War One, chefs under siege in a mountainous region of Switzerland *buttered an entire mountainside* ..." Then, suddenly, I leapt onto the genius of Jim's shoulders and blurted: *"—and slid to safety!!!"* And there it was. We both collapsed in laughter. But we had done it. We had at least once in our lives parodied *Ripley's Believe It or Not!* to both our satisfactions, a feat in its way as impressive as much of what one reads in the actual books.

But once we had recovered from laughing and congratulating ourselves, the question arose: Could we do another? So we soldiered on, stopping and starting. Jim said, "OK, wait! What about the entries that are just so totally insane that they dare you to throw the book away?" What if we tried to parody that subgenre? And then, haltingly, he came up with: "Dachshunds are born ... wearing bright green fur." OK, that was a beginning. But he continued. "It is only as they mature ... that they take on their characteristic nut brown hue." Even when he pronounced the word "hue," Jim did it dramatically, as though to say: "Can you even believe the total insanity of the word 'hue'?" The way he pronounced it and much else in this session and other similar conversations was itself a provocation to laughter, as though he were himself gagging on the tickly words in our throats, always on the verge of exploding with laughter. This went on for hours. "OK, what about ... The Ursine Abbess?" This was Jim's idea, and he seemed to know where he wanted to go with it: "Trained to ring the bells as a cub at the Montreax nunnery, a common brown bear eventually rose in the ranks of the order ... to become Mother Superior of the Convent." I then added "—before being killed *by poachers* in 1549!" Who wouldn't want to buy a book full of these?

That summer I often rode the T across the Charles and into Boston, watching the white sailboats and reading my Nabokov and wondering about my future. One day I bumped into Tim Howard, the redheaded guy who had led the Yale Christian Fellowship. "Hey, Eric!" he said, excited to see me. "How are you doing? What are you up to?" I half cringed to see him, sensing he wanted to pull me back into the born-again Christian world, and I certainly wasn't interested. "A bunch of us are living here this summer, just off Harvard Square," he said. "We've got a great house. You should stop by. We're having a barbecue tomorrow night." I smiled uncomfortably and tried to say something noncommittal. I said I was just trying to write. I didn't tell him I was struggling and adrift because I hadn't struggled or drifted far enough to know that I was struggling and adrift. I still had plenty of hope in the tank. I wasn't sure why I didn't want what he had, but I had moved on and wanted to stay moved on. I didn't think about it logically and didn't want to. I just wanted my space. I wasn't asking the big questions. I was avoiding them. I was fine. But as C.S. Lewis said, there comes a time when if we don't say to God, "Thy will be done," He says to us, in effect, "Okay, *thy* will be done. Have it your way." He turns us over to our desires, whatever they are, which is about what happened, though I certainly didn't see it at the time.

And of course I wasn't doing fine, although there were enough breadcrumbs to keep me interested in continuing along my path into the forest. One day from a pay phone I called Bill who said I got a letter accepting my short story, "The Wild Ride of Miss Impala George" for publication—and they offered four hundred dollars! I had sent it to the *New Yorker*, but of course they were then interested mostly in fashionably fatiguing suicide bait from such as Raymond Carver, Bobbie Ann Mason, and Ann Beattie. *The Atlantic* passed, too, but somehow I thought the story might fit in at this magazine called *Country Journal*, which had never published fiction before, and I was right. They even surrounded it with two pointillist illustrations. After it came out I heard from the *Ziegler Magazine for the Blind*, which wanted to print the story in Braille. They sent me a copy, which was fascinatingly thick, with pages of something like brown grocery-bag paper.

Then Ian and I got another apartment together, a fourth-floor walk-up on the unfashionable side of Beacon Hill. In my first weeks there I read an ad someone had placed, offering to sell seven hundred back copies of the *New Yorker*. I had no money, but for some reason had to have them, and purchased the lot for eighty bucks! Who knew what was in them? I hauled the many heavy boxes up to our apartment and later learned the seller had culled out all the issues with Updike or Cheever stories. *Caveat emptor.* Still, the covers were nice, some from the thirties and forties. I saw that what the magazine had become—and was still becoming—was a far cry from what it had been during the glory days of editor Harold Ross. It now took itself so horribly *seriously.* But so much of elite culture had gone that way. PBS once aired Monty Python. Poetry once included light verse. What had happened to make everyone so dour?

It was toward the end of that summer that my friendship with Bill's friend Clarissa bloomed into something else. She seemed to me like a character out of one of Cheever's books. Even her name and where she lived. So it seemed fated to me that we should be together. This was the first relationship in which I allowed myself to move forward without thinking, as I had once been unable to do. Somehow that inhibition vanished and suddenly we were spending as many nights together as possible, and not thinking much about the future. But in early 1986 something happened that would force me to do so.

I was visiting Chris Noël in Vermont, and when I returned Clarissa said she needed to talk, and the next day came over and said she was pregnant. I was so ridiculously naive that I had somehow never considered this. I had so internalized the cultural idea that sex existed apart from procreation that it just didn't cross my mind. I knew she was on the pill. Before I had room to be upset or process it, she removed the need of my thinking by quickly saying she was going to "take care of it," getting an odd sideways look on her face, unable to look me in the eyes. But then I immediately thought, yes of course, that's what people do, right? I hadn't even thought of this avenue, but when she said it I immediately accepted it as what she must do and did.

I somehow knew I was expected to "be there" for her and recalled some scene from a TV show reminding me that "the guy" probably should offer to pay toward the "procedure," and/or to accompany her whenever she was scheduled. But she demurred on both counts. Maybe she felt that involving me at all would only underscore the unpleasant thought that I was the father of what was inside her, giving that "what" too much of an identity. I had similar unspoken thoughts. The procedure was scheduled for a few weeks hence and that was that. But I remember somehow being proud she was pregnant, proud to know I was capable of producing progeny, though it literally never occurred to me that what we had agreed to dramatically contradicted whatever odd pride I felt. I couldn't have been more muddled about it. I assumed we were talking about a "mass of cells," but the way she preemptively made her decision took any pressure off me to think more deeply about it. We didn't refer to it again in the weeks before the procedure and some hours after it she called me and said it felt like having a vacuum inside you, and half-laughed, trying to make light of what I began to guess was not as light as either of us had thought.

Our relationship was problematic from the beginning, but it soon got worse, and there now sprouted in my mind the idea that Clarissa had violated herself and knew it, though she never said anything. Over the months and years afterward, there were times she seemed not herself and I wondered if she had a sense that something deep inside her had been broken, something that neither she nor I had the power to fix. The closest we came to speaking of it was eight or ten months later when one day, out of the blue, she said, "I think maybe it's not right to be in a relationship that's physical outside of marriage." I reacted as though she had thrown boiling water at me. "Are you kidding? That's ridiculous!" I said with conviction, though with no actual thought behind my emotion. It was what everyone did and because I didn't know anyone who didn't, the idea was patently crazy and the conversation ended. Little did I then think many women were having such thoughts and being shot down as I had then shut Clarissa down, who was unwilling to risk the relationship, unsure of what was the best path and then, as I, simply going along the one of least resistance.

After my year with Ian was up, I lived with Clarissa for a few months in the Back Bay. One Sunday she suggested we go to church. I found this surprising, but didn't see any reason to argue, so we dressed appropriately and walked over to Trinity Church in Copley Square. It was culturally very different from the Greek church, but I understood it was somehow important to her to go. But I had no theological thoughts during the service. It was as though I were now sleepwalking through the important parts of life. I had somehow forgotten whatever Christian faith I once had or thought I had, had drifted away from it by degrees, never noticing how far.

CHAPTER THIRTY-ONE

The Opera House

Clarissa was no longer working at the Boston Opera House. In fact she was doing nothing. But Bill was still there and said they needed someone in the ticket booth. It paid minimum wage and I took it. The building itself was Dickensian, being one part Miss Haversham's dining room and another Fagin's hideout. The theater itself bordered Boston's Red Light District and was run and run-down by the infamous Sarah Caldwell, a musical genius of Orson Wellesian proportions—egotistically and otherwise—who hobbled about the stain-carpeted hallways plotting a way to keep the doors open for another week. Like Welles, she was the prototypical enfante terrible who had so much early success and acclaim that it had ruined her for the long run, and now in her sixties she couldn't manage to keep costs down— because who could put a price on Art?—and like so many others who put Art first, she put people third, meaning she only pretended to put Art first, because what would Art be with such conduits as herself? And as ever with such outsized personalities there gathered about her dark sun various dys-functional planetoids and asteroids, simultaneously drawn to her—and desperately avoiding her too—as they described their eccentric orbits. The late great Beverly Sills once gave her the following fatally mitigated

encomium: "Sarah did present challenges—it was a challenge to be her friend, to be her colleague, her employee, but in the end it was worth it...."
Yes, yes! Throw your hat in the air and shout "Huzzah!"

The building itself was so fragile it seemed perpetually one bribe away from being condemned and razed. One got the impression that as with four-thousand-year-old linen in a lightless tomb it might evaporate if exposed to enough light and air. The paint peeled more than it stuck and there was hardly a seat in the house that didn't squeak or whose velvet wasn't more threadbare than thread, but the whole gaudy, decaying hulk seemed to have been held together against all odds by one Astley, a prancing French-African queen, who worked miracles with a broom and dustpan—and who like an ebon fairy flitted about the old building and did everything but sweet talk the huge rats into taking other quarters. At the other end of the octave, sitting at the moldering switchboard like some displaced pirate, sat Roger, a gay man of the old style, who wore leather vests and a handlebar mustache. The world to which his appearance paid homage was already fading fast, but not before it had the opportunity to give him the mysterious night sweats and weight loss that would soon decimate that community, and lead him and so many dear souls into an early grave. I had the night shift at the desk he manned during the day, and often seeing his handwriting on messages I came to admire his old-fashioned nines, with a curved tale. It was from these foetus-like digits that I learned to make my own, and have done ever since, sometimes remembering Roger when I do.

Further behind the crumbling scenes was a larger cast of crazies who backbit and backstabbed each other like characters from some badly overdone Italian opera, scheming and smirking and pouting like a bunch of children wearing costumes. But always at the center of this vast dilapidated death star was Sarah, a superannuated and malevolent potentate whose sole delight and *raison d'être* somehow lay in the dark drama unspooling around her and put on for her benefit: the chaos was the thing. It fed her genius artist's ego, as if that were the larger and more important drama, and sometimes in my daydreams I cast her in my own opera, which is set at the bottom of a black hole, from which light cannot escape, so no one will ever see it.

In fact, during my time there, there were very few productions, one or two. The financial situation was so horrendous that when Sarah fell gravely ill everyone who had subscribed—meaning "pre-paid"—for the season of operas got a letter asking whether the opera might keep their money as a donation anyway. Although the word *chutzpah* could be used to describe such behavior, I did not hear anything so anodyne from the subscribers who called the ticket office to vent about this.

Desperate for income, the theater was rented to bands and various traveling acts. I saw Chuck Berry, and Morris Day and the Time, but most enjoyed Garrison Keillor, who, through Bill's radio, had become someone I loved. What touched me more than anything was when, at the end of the evening, he had the audience sing with him. The final song we sang, a cappella, was "Amazing Grace." It is one of the extremely few songs whose lyrics are known by most people, so we all sang it together, with harmonies too, and a holy hush came over the room. I knew that I was touching something ineffable and numinous—the same something I had touched at the top of my *sesselbahn* ride in the Alps a year or so before. It was extraordinary. I would have floated home, and was on the verge of doing so, but just after the concert Bill and I hung around for a bit to talk to our friends in the ticket booth, and while we were doing that we saw Mr. Keillor had come out to sign copies of his new book *Lake Wobegone Days*. People began to line up and Keillor, a very tall man, stood there in jeans and an untucked white shirt.

The thought at that time of purchasing a fifteen-dollar hardcover was as remote as eating at a five-star restaurant. I made three dollars and change per hour and was so broke that even brand-new paperbacks were far beyond my reach. I made something on the order of six thousand dollars that year, so I had a library of remaindered and secondhand books. But even though Bill and I couldn't afford to buy a book, we were so enamored of the author that we hoped to meet him, and Bill suggested we simply wait in line with the others to shake his hand. Bill was unfailingly polite and knew his way around etiquette, so I joined him in the long line. Just before our turn a blind woman came up to Mr. Keillor and he dealt with her very graciously. When it was our turn, I hung back and let Bill do the talking. "Hello, Mr. Keillor," he said. "My friend Eric and I don't have books, but we are big fans and we just wanted to shake your hand." Keillor seemed taken aback by this, because he didn't say one word but gave each of us what can only be described as a dramatically perfunctory handshake, and then pointedly turned away to the next person in line. It was a ghastly moment. Had we been snubbed by our hero? But it was late and he was obviously tired and needed to sell books, so we wandered away and tried to forget it.

Mostly we did, because whenever I told people about being there all I could say was that it had ended up being "a religious experience." Like standing there looking at the snowy heart of the mountains after that *sesselbahn* ride and staring agog at the *David* in Florence. The transcendence I felt as we sang "Amazing Grace" was undeniable. We had touched Beauty itself, and Goodness itself, and Truth itself. But what did that mean? I couldn't say anymore. I could only feel these three things meeting in that moment. But what it was exactly and why it touched me I simply didn't know.

During this otherwise bleak period I continued reading everything I could by Nabokov. I read *Ada, or Ardor* and *Pale Fire* and every other one of his novels, underlining everything funny. I especially liked his early novel, *King, Queen, Knave,* of which he wrote: "Of all my novels, this bright brute is the gayest." Some of the words he used I found hilarious. He described the teats of a lolling dog as "bubs," which I found funny, and which immediately put me in mind of Thomas Mann's use of the dramatically unfunny phrase "dugs of finger length," which he uses in describing the grotesque hags who devoured a child in the horrific *Walpurgisnacht* scene in his *Zauberberg.*

Nabokov made me want to write, but I didn't. But I reveled in how he reveled in words, in his strange descriptions of things, physical objects. I realized that in this he was very much like John Updike—or rather, that Updike was like Nabokov. They would describe a rectangle of sunlight on the floor of a room or a weird stain in the wallpaper with as much attention as they would describe the most important thing in the world. But what, in the end, did either have to say? I loved Nabokov because he was unbelievably funny, and in its way that was enough. If he had only written *Pale Fire* as Ralph Ellison had only written *Invisible Man*, it would have been sufficient to put him in whatever pantheon existed in my mind. But Updike was another story. He took himself very seriously, and while Nabokov would focus his genius for language on something extremely quotidian to brilliantly disgusting comic effect, as when describing the extrusion from a popped whitehead as a "waxy eel," Updike used his similar genius in another direction, almost piously dwelling on the most graphic descriptions of sexual intercourse, and even stooping to describe with poetic interest the stools in a toilet, as he did in at least one short story and later, a poem, as though his words would lend these things their proper dignity in the world. He cast himself as the progressive and revolutionary Renaissance Master who dared to dignify the mundane with the same attention formerly accorded only the world of royalty. Yet somehow Rembrandt never felt the necessity of using his great gifts to immortalize the contents of chamber pots.

I felt similarly about what Updike was trying to do in focusing on human sexuality. I felt it merely trendiness, and I found it interesting that Cheever had a dramatically different view, which he detailed in his story "A Miscellany of Characters That Will Not Appear." "Out," he writes, "with all explicit descriptions of sexual commerce, for how can we describe the most exalted experience of our physical lives as if—jack, wrench, hubcap, and nuts—we were describing the changing of a flat tire?" Cheever was a romantic and a Christian who believed that what was transcendent could not and ought not be reduced, but Updike thought that in reducing these things he somehow lent them a nobility previously denied them, giving them the place they had long been denied "in our fiction," the highfalutin' phrase always used when people praised him for this. But when I read his passage describing feces in a way intended to be some kind of brave artistic breakthrough I knew it was time to move on.

Updike generally seemed to be saying that the world is fallen and there is little we can do about it beyond be aware of it and describe it, to say that people are not terribly nice and the possibility of rising above this is slim. But at the beginning of his career he was far more hopeful. In fact, he had been a full-on Christian, as anyone familiar with his early work would intuit, not least by reading his extraordinary poem "Seven Stanzas at Easter," which is as theologically straight as St. Paul. But this was before the sixties bent the cultural plumb line of our flawed but optimistic culture, and when Updike's *Couples* came out, helping to normalize adultery among the sophisticated reading classes, the die was cast. Updike claimed merely to be documenting the changing culture, but had to know he was also using his magnificent talents to change culture.

Visiting Hersey

During the awful summer of 1986, I wrote John Hersey, hardly sure why. His response was on cleverly diminutive stationary that gave the appearance of a full letter while only requiring the writer to peck out two or three sentences. But my colleague in the ticket booth was so impressed that Mr. Hersey had responded that she insisted I must visit him. Perhaps she was right. So I wrote again, asking whether I might do so. I hoped he might offer some guidance that years hence in a memoir would stand out as what set me on the brilliant career for which I would at that point already be internationally celebrated.

Mr. Hersey's reply was terse but positive, saying which boat I should take on what day. So on the appointed day I took the two-hour bus to Woods Hole and the ferry to the island where in the parking lot stood the great John Hersey. I now feel awful for having imposed on him and deeply grateful he allowed me to take up his afternoon, but at the time I was probably hoping he'd ask me to stay over, that some literary world would be magically opened to me. Perhaps that night we would be trading bon mots with his island friends Lillian Hellman and Ralph Ellison![1] I knew he valued my writing and had put me up for the literary prizes I won, but what to do with me, now that I had

---

[1] The year before my friend Bernardine Connelly Clark had actually worked for the Herseys for the summer and served Lillian Hellman what would end up being her last meal.

visited? He first drove me around the island and gave me the highlights. As we drove past where we might have gone fishing he pointed out, probably with some relief, that the winds were a bit too strong that day. He showed me the Methodist campground in Oak Bluffs and spoke of its history. I hardly understood it then, but his parents had been missionaries in China. In his novel *The Call*, published that year, he gives a semi-autobiographical account of those missionaries to China of which his parents were principal figures, and of the battle between what was then called the Fundamentalists and the Social Gospel proponents. There always seemed to be a sadness about Mr. Hersey, and I now cannot help wondering whether he ever questioned the worth of his own writings as compared to the work of those missionaries. Even if that generation had failed somehow, what had his generation offered? It was easy to see where our forebears had gone wrong, but would we do better? In any case, our children would certainly judge us as harshly.

In the end we circled back to his house and sat in his kitchen, where he offered me a cup of tea and some fig newtons, and then got to the point of the visit, my writing. He remembered my award-winning story "The Wild Ride of Miss Impala George" and said that in it there had been a dream-like quality, and that perhaps there was something in that I ought to pursue. In retrospect that seems right, but it didn't mean much to me at the time. But what was I expecting from this dear man? I'm sure I wanted him to ask me to move into his guest cottage and be his chauffeur and help him edit his memoirs just as he had been asked these things by Nobel Prize–winning novelist Sinclair Lewis when Hersey himself graduated from Yale. But such was not to be—and the genial Mr. Hersey was soon driving not Sinclair Lewis but yours truly back to the ferry that took me to Woods Hole to get the bus back to Boston.

John O'Brien and Gig and Ian had found a house in Brookline and I decided to move in with them. Probably the best part was that Kenny Doroshow would be there too. He was another friend with whom I laughed almost incessantly. I continued not to write fiction, but did try my hand at the sort of humor Woody Allen published in the *New Yorker* and collected into *Getting Even, Without Feathers,* and *Side Effects,* much of which is the best humor writing in history. One piece I wrote titled "That Post-Modernism!" purported to be a publisher's catalog of Post-Modern books, all the rage at that time. The final one bore the title *Veal Fuselage.* I sent it out and soon heard that *The Atlantic* wanted to publish it, which literally made me leap for joy. As far as I was concerned, I had arrived. Encouraged by this success I wrote another, which they also accepted, titled "They Were Ahead of Their Time," and on the strength of these acceptances was invited to their Christmas party, where I met John Kenneth Galbraith, the famous Harvard economist who had served in the FDR, Truman, JFK, and LBJ administrations, and who, in his patrician uniform and floppy hair looked—at six feet nine inches—like a cartoon parody of what I thought a Harvard professor should look like. I now began work on another piece, about a bitter feud between Gertrude Stein and James Joyce. I spent weeks writing it, which was at least ten times as much effort as Gertrude Stein put into *Tender Buttons,* which will only seem a cheap shot to those unfamiliar with her work.

Around this time I decided I should apply to get into Yaddo, the writer's colony where John Cheever spent time. That could at least give me six or eight weeks of free rent and food and "time to write." Amazingly, I was accepted. Not long after I got into the MacDowell Colony, too. Curtis Harnack and his wife Hortense Calisher said the board who made the decision said that I wrote "like an angel!" But while there I wrote nothing. I was less looking for an opportunity to write—write what?—than for something more like direction and yes, meaning. For some reason I took along a King James Bible and lamely struggled to read bits of it, not at all knowing what I was doing but in a way following in the steps of Cheever, whose few biblical allusions seemed to lend me his approval to do this. Of course I might as well have been reading Nostradamus. Dear reader, I was lost.

At the MacDowell Colony some months later it was the same. I watched television; I played racquetball with a composer friend and every night watched *Late Night with David Letterman* with him and my new friend Monica Yates, who was the daughter of the novelist Richard Yates, who laughed at my dumb jokes and kept saying "You have to meet Dad!" And "You've got to meet my friend Larry!" This was Larry David, who she kept saying was brilliant and whom I would love, but who hadn't had much success, being too dark and brainy.

CHAPTER THIRTY-TWO

Backward to Greece

Summer 1987

After the MacDowell Colony, I knew my two and a half years in Boston were at an end. Where to go? I thought I might to go back to Cephalonia. Perhaps there I would find the environment I needed to write the novel I kept talking about. Perhaps I might even live there for good. Perhaps there I would have the distance I needed to get some perspective, or perhaps would find myself, if there was any self to be found. Of course even that was something I doubted. The idea that we can find ourselves is itself fraught with problems, though it's the sort of thing we talk about as though we all understand what it means, but do we? Who are we exactly that we need to be found by ourselves? And which self is finding which other self? Does it make any real sense, or is it simply an empty figure of speech with the barest purchase in reality? Is it really any more meaningful than "um"?

I came back at some point to the idea I had first formed in that strange vision I had during the first weeks of my senior year at Yale, but it had evolved slightly to the literary image of a frozen lake through whose surface we dig and dig until at last we strike water. That is this larger project, I thought, of our lives. It is the journey of our souls, and is the journey beyond our conscious mind to the collective unconscious deep within each of us, to that thing that connects us all, one to another, and that some people call "God" and others "Divinity" and others "Godhead" and others other things. Was I making progress thereto? How would one know? And how did I know there was anything to any of this? Could it be that this idea was really only my pretentiously sophisticated way of saying "um"?

But I did go back to Greece. I was obviously desperate and was looking for a *Deus ex Machina* to save me from my straits. I knew that I wanted to touch transcendence—if there were such a thing, and I felt there was—but I was also wondering whether what might save me was the cataclysm predicted in which the world would end. I had read in *TIME* magazine that there was to be that summer a harmonic convergence, that all the planets would align and that New Agers around the globe were awaiting some leap into another dimension. It would be like raising the Pentagon with our minds, except this time it would work. Would this at last be the "Summer of Destiny" that Pat Robertson had predicted a few years before, the End of the World, and the crashing through into our reality of some other ultimate reality, someone falling through the sky from Heaven into our world like a figure coming through a skylight in an action thriller? We all long for justice, for a final reckoning, don't we? Would it happen now? It never occurred to me then that that was effectively the Christian myth of God's breaking through from Heaven down to Earth to save us, but why should we be surprised if our race comes up with markedly similar images and myths over and over? Wasn't that precisely what Jung had been getting at? And wasn't that my problem, that if everyone said the same thing, maybe everyone was saying nothing?

When I was in Cephalonia the one thing that seemed transcendent, that meant something profound to me, was my connection to my ancestors. There was something sacred there, but what? I certainly didn't know. One day I borrowed the moped and rode by myself down into Argostoli and across the old Trapano bridge to the other side of Argostoli Harbor to the churchyard where my great-grandfather Panagis Vergotis is buried. It was as though I were expecting him to give me some guidance on what to do. So I parked the moped and wandered among the ancient-looking graves. I had an idea where his grave was, having been there before. Some of the larger monuments had been broken in the 1953 earthquake and never repaired. Obelisks several times the size of a man had shifted on their pediments, but no one had ever moved them back, probably because the families of whoever was buried had vanished. I saw cherubs that had lost wings too, and realized that that seismic disaster had sent my father across the ocean to meet my mother and bring me into the world. So why was I back here, and looking for what? When I found the grave I remembered my father had told me of a sign that had been there with the Greek words: "If I speak in the tongues of men and angels, but have not love, I am like a sounding gong or a clanging cymbal ..." My father had not known those were the words from Paul's letter to the Corinthians, but he remembered going there with his grandmother Eleni, who took the sign to a painter to restore the weather-worn inscription.

I stared at the grave. What did I want? I knew I was lost, but I didn't believe the universe really could be meaningless. I just didn't know how or where to find that meaning. So I did the only thing I knew that might have some meaning. I knelt down, far from anyone's sight, and kissed the stone. I paid my respects. One thing that was true to me in the world—without any doubt—was my father's love for me, and my love for him. And in paying my respects to this man who was his beloved and revered grandfather, I was paying my respects to my father too, and to the goodness and truth and love I had seen in him. In a way it was my father's love for me that somehow pointed me to the idea that there could never be a world where that love meant nothing, that there had to be something behind that, somewhere. But where?

My brother arrived in Cephalonia too, shortly after I had, and a week after that Clarissa arrived. I sensed she had come for fear of losing me; and who knew what was in my mind at that time, if anything? One minute I thought we should end our relationship and the next minute I thought perhaps it was time we married. Perhaps we could live in Cephalonia and make a life there. It would be so romantic and wonderful, and take me out of the pressure of living in New York or wherever I thought I would end up, where all you could aim for was selling a minimalist "story" to the *New Yorker*, or writing a similarly sulky novel.

But again here in glorious Cephalonia there were those odd signals of mistrust and miscommunication that made our relationship mostly an unpleasantness and even an agony. But I knew breaking up with her would only confirm her view of the situation, so I didn't. At the end of a few weeks, though, I knew I couldn't stay in Cephalonia any longer. I had been kidding myself again? So I went home again. But again to what? And this time I wasn't going to Boston, since I couldn't afford to live there anyway. I had really come to the end of things. So I would effectively admit defeat, and would now do the one and only thing that feckless college graduates can do after a season of drifting and floating. As surely as the swallows return to Capistrano, I would go home to the only home I ever really had: my parents' home in Danbury.

Fall 1987

I have often said that if someone flounders and drifts after college just long enough, he will inevitably and unavoidably end up moving back in with his parents; that it is a fundamental law of the physical universe, a constant, like Avogadro's number or π. So after my wanderings in the wide world I now came back to the house with the white mailbox with the cutout of the robin feeding her babies. It was embarrassing. Parents of my Yale friends all knew I wanted to be a writer and thought my aimless wanderings would all be grist for some proverbial mill. In time I would of course "find myself," so why worry? But my parents—having survived the war and having worked very difficult jobs to raise me, and then put me through Yale—had a less whimsical view. They were less interested in my finding myself than in my finding myself a job.

And so this time was for me the beginning of troubles. It was a painful time. And what job could I get? My Yale English degree helped me crack witty jokes and indulge in such repartee as almost guaranteed someone seeing my genius and hiring me on the spot for something—but what? I was like some hobo in training, and like Robert the painter who drank three beers for breakfast, I would always have some dignity, even as I slid further and further from anything particularly laudable. And I would aspire to say something witty on my deathbed, or at least to be remembered for having said something witty even if I didn't, just as Oscar Wilde is remembered for having said, "Either the wallpaper goes, or I do." Though he didn't. But what did it matter? In fact, if there was nothing by way of larger meaning in the universe—and all there was was matter—what did anything matter?

The only thing I might do to earn something now—while hoping to write— was proofreading. But where? As it happened, there was a soulless international chemical conglomerate nestled like a stadium-sized extraterrestrial insect in the woods at Danbury's southernmost end—that happened to need a proofreader. And if I wasn't eager to apply for the job, my father was available to hound me to do so.

CHAPTER THIRTY-THREE

Lost at Home

And did you trade a walk-on part in the war
for a lead role in a cage?

—Pink Floyd

During my last year of high school Union Carbide had broken ground on the outskirts of our city to build its otherworldly world headquarters, a building as much like something out of a James Bond movie as exists this side of the movie screen. It pretentiously and quite preposterously aspired to redefine what a monstrously large corporate space could be. The vast structure was situated on a series of "pods," and nowhere rose higher than the trees, so that for all its inhuman hugeness it is never more than four stories high. It was obviously intended to blend in sensitively with the surrounding wilderness, but one could never see it in its entirety, unless from an airplane or helicopter, and therefore one could not get any perspective on it as one can with an ordinary skyscraper or other building, and this had the unintended effect of making it simultaneously maddening and creepy. I could just imagine the winning architect's pitch to the corporate bigwigs in the late seventies, when the future of the endlessly acquisitive conglomerate still seemed as rosy as Homer's dawn.

In order to enter the building one drove into it as into a parking garage and along roads within its quirkily laid-out interior. So one was never "outside" the building even as one was driving to get there, as though it was something of an architectural Möbius strip, or a cement wasp's nest. The trees outside every window were surely intended to give those inside the happy idea that they were not drones laboring in an international industrial conglomerate, but were in fact doing something homey and charming, like playing checkers in a cabin with an old-timer everyone called "Gramps."

But the sense of being down among the surrounding trees more often than not gave those privileged to have window offices an uncomfortable sense of suffocation, such that you longed for a glimpse of the blue sky, or of something—anything—in the distance. And if the sense of suffocation became too acute you couldn't open a window, because there was a strict policy against this, and they were locked. This was evidently necessary to maintain a uniform temperature and humidity throughout all sectors and quadrants and pods, lending employees the unhappy feeling of being a bug in a plastic terrarium.

By way of background, two and a half years before I arrived, something almost unbelievably awful happened. In Bhopal, India, where one of their worldwide chemical plants was located, there was a huge and terrible explosion that released vast clouds of poisonous gas, killing more than a thousand people living along the plant's perimeter in squatters' shacks and blinding many more. It was a disaster among disasters, and the public relations nightmare for which no one can or even should be prepared. The company's stock plummeted and its worldwide image suffered so dramatically that by the time I arrived the building was something like a half-sunk *Titanic*, a sad gigantic shell, entire quadrants of which remained empty, such that walking in those depopulated hallways for me inevitably recalled *The Shining*, and I always half-expected to see a pair of doleful Diane Arbus–inspired twins or a decomposing, cackling hag.

So when I arrived in the early fall of 1987, Union Carbide was a cowed giant, and over the weeks as I proofread chemical manuals and other mind-numbing arcana I grew sadder and sadder and often actually wanted to die. I continued to try to write and finally finished my humor piece about Gertrude Stein and James Joyce, but *The Atlantic* rejected it. If all this weren't enough I decided to rent my body out for medical experiments, needing the money. My brother pointed out an ad in the local penny-saver offering a thousand dollars to anyone taking part in a six-day experiment, requiring one day per weekend over six weeks, so one Saturday I drove the hour south to a building in Westchester.

The doctor was an Indian national named Dr. Mehta, with slightly bulgy eyes and an unintentionally comic demeanor. While I filled out the necessary forms it was clear he suspected anyone participating in these experiments to be a suspicious character. The first day the doctor's assistant attached sixteen wires to my scalp with a kind of white paste that hardened quickly into little white mounds beneath my hair. The sixteen wires were color coded and bound together into a bunch at the back of my head, giving me the appearance of a Rastafarian android. It didn't take long for these conductive dreadlocks to become annoying, and I would have to wear them for twelve hours, during which I would periodically get an EEG. The medicine being tested was a Valium substitute, so I got that, or actual Valium, or a placebo. They also constantly tested my vitals and stuck a butterfly valve into my arm to draw blood easily. Otherwise I could just hang out and read or watch a video. One day when they gave me what I am sure was valium I enjoyed *The Pope of Greenwich Village*, with Eric Roberts chewing the carpet as no one before. The assistant's seven-year-old daughter watched too, occasionally releasing an audible flatus, so that at some point in my haze the thousand dollars began to seem like the chump change it was. The assistant was a young Turkish woman whose name was Demet, accented on the first syllable. But in the mouth of Dr. Mehta it sounded like a curse. At one point he angrily exploded: "Demet, I told you!" There was a man there too, forty-something, who seemed the sort Dr. Mehta had in mind when he initially subjected me to his suspicious questions, who would spit out the pill if you didn't watch him swallow it.

When I got my first EEG Dr. Mehta and his assistant *ooh-ed* and *ah-ed*, saying the amplitude of my brainwaves was extremely impressive. They had never seen such amplitude! But what did this mean? Was this good? Once Dr. Mehta as he drew my blood declared: "Frankly, I am a racist!" I tried to explain to him the faultiness of his thinking, but realized that in India, the caste systems effectively assumed racism. Another day I realized his views on women were no more progressive when in his precise Indian-accented English he declared, "Tele-*phone!* Tele-*graph!* Tell a *voo*-man!"

Ed Tuttle

I had not been at Carbide long when I met Ed Tuttle, a tall and thin man of thirty-one with wire-rimmed glasses and a goatee, one of two in-house graphic designers. He was a husband and the father of a two-year-old girl and sometimes brought bits of text for me to proofread, which I sometimes returned to him in his office, where we might chat for a moment. Once we spoke a bit about faith and I realized he took the Bible seriously.

Eventually we had lunch, after which we had lunch rather regularly in the huge half-empty cafeteria. Ed often brought the conversation around to spiritual issues and I was not entirely averse to this, but as we talked I realized I didn't know much about the Bible at all. If he referred to something involving angels or demons, I would blanch and question how he could believe such things. But Ed humbly and impressively stood his ground, saying that Scripture was clear that these things were real. Then he might show me an instance in his Bible or tell me an anecdote from his or a friend's personal experience with such creatures, and I would nod, half-believing and half-disbelieving. Ed attended an Episcopal church in Waterbury and I suppose this made me reckon him safe, because most of the sophisticated and well-born Yalies I knew were Episcopalians and didn't seem to believe much of anything. Still, Ed was different.

During this time I met another character named Warren, a gigantically obese typesetter who could scarcely walk. He was well-groomed, with badly pockmarked skin and striking, distinctively American blue eyes, as one sees in photos of American pioneers or cowboys—and during our lunches he would fix me in his somehow sad and imploring gaze and tell me about something called Mindspring, a company or para-company or philosophical movement whose praises he perpetually sang. They had meetings and were "going places," but I never really understood what they were. He insistently pressed me to come to a meeting, which began to give me the creeps. I would have preferred to go to a church service with Ed, although I was hardly interested in that either. But at least I had some idea what that might entail. Mindspring sounded almost like a New-Age cult, which I eventually understood that it was, and Warren's glassy-eyed adherence to its vague and "universal" principles contrasted dramatically with Ed's down-to-earth and rather peaceful confidence. But I wasn't buying from either of them. Still, I continued having lunch with one or the other.

My relationship with Clarissa had come to a strange pass. I was now in Connecticut and felt odd rages of jealousy over her, which often boiled over into rage at myself, coupled with the blackest depression I had ever known. But it was all part of the same foul stew. When I saw her, a weekend here, a weekend there, all was well, but apart from her I fell again into that terrible slough of despond, which for me, was quickly becoming an endlessly self-contained and lightless abyss, a perfect hermetically sealed hell with no exit. What was I doing? Who was I? And what was the meaning of it all, or was there none?

Amidst this misery I continued commuting along the highway to that ghastly meta-building in the woods and each morning I sat in long patches of bumper-to-bumper traffic on the interstate, listening to the local FM station whose DJ brilliantly impersonated everyone from Elvis to Jimmy Swaggart. The station played a variety of classic rock music mixed in with contemporary hits.

I was bothered by the DJ's mocking of Jimmy Swaggart, whom I'd watched on TV now and again, mostly out of curiosity, but I always hated kicking someone when he was down, just as I could never abide burning bugs under magnifying glasses or exploding frogs with M-80s. The man had sinned and confessed his sin. Must we mock him endlessly too? Was that our way of saying everyone who talks about God is a phony and we are heroes for condemning them? I sat in the traffic, thinking about this and about my own problems, and wondered what caused this traffic and whether some infinitely long equation could explain it as it pulsed along in its fits and starts, like corpuscles in an artery. What did this merge from Route 7 do, and how was that affected by the upcoming hill, since hills always seemed to cause a slowdown, and so on and so on, twirling and twizzling these thoughts around and around until I found myself getting off Exit One and heading up to my day-prison in the woods.

During my first months back in Danbury my brother lived there, too. Usually this was a good thing, but we had our moments. One night after dinner, probably to escape, I decided I wanted to go to the Route 6 Mall to one of those abbreviated Waldenbooks bookstores a few stores down from the Marshalls where I had met George Duncan a thousand years before. I persuaded my brother to drive me, but along the way we got into such an argument that by the time we reached the parking lot he either kicked me out of the car or I got out and stormed off. We exchanged salted words and my brother peeled out, stranding me in the middle of the endless parking lot, at which point, of course, it began to rain.

But I was too angry to let the rain bother me, and calmly began walking toward the bookstore. I would browse for a while, wait out the rain, and was so angry I would be only too happy to walk the long journey home, though it entailed stepping over rusted guardrails and walking along an ill-lit highway in the dark. I walked into the bookstore, dripping as nonchalantly as I could, and eventually found my way to the self-help section, which in the autumn of 1987 included no book as ferociously as it did L. Ron Hubbard's volcanically sheathed paperback opus, *Dianetics*. It had been on the bestseller lists since gigantic palm fronds had rippled in the warm breezes of the Mesozoic Epoch—and in my straits, I picked it up to see what all the hoopla might be about. If ever I was desperately searching for the meaning of life I was doing so now. The book struck me immediately as confusing, impenetrable as a computer code, almost. But I was at my wits' end standing in that bookstore that night, in that no-man's-land strip mall, waiting for the rain outside to stop, waiting for God, for anyone, to send me an answer to my pain and confusion.

In the meantime, God sent something else. Down the aisle of books I saw my mother, waiting for me to notice her. She had her car keys in her hand and had evidently driven here to get me after talking with my furious brother. I was surprised she had found me. Neither she nor my brother knew where in the vast shopping center I might be. And I was thankful. But I would purchase the book first. And then we got in the car and drove home.

Since my brother and I had graduated from college my parents had taken over the large upstairs room that used to be my brother's and mine. So he slept in the guest room downstairs and I took the smaller attic room where my grandmother always stayed when she was with us. And there on the bed I proceeded to read. But it was very tough going, so tough that I am reminded of how when the Three Stooges are trying to chew something unchewable they eventually start working their jaws with their own hands, trying to help it along. I had gotten through many tough books over the years. I had even forced my way through such ghastly contemporary "meta-fiction" as John Barth's *Giles Goat-Boy*. Surely I could hack my way through this thick tangle and would break into a clearing eventually. I pressed on with my mental machete, my forearms growing wearier with each stroke through the mumbo-jumbo, but I had never read anything as awful as this pinched and confused pseudo-philosophy. It spoke of engrams and "clearing" and it read, truth be told, like something composed by insects. And yet I wanted something to believe in. Obviously. Else I'd never have bought this unprecedently irritating volume. There must be an answer to my troubles. But before I collapsed, teeth clenched and machete still in hand, I had not found it, nor even the promise of it. So I set the book down and went to sleep.

Thus my miserable life continued, with the daily morning commute along the clogged interstate listening to FM radio. I was struck at the number of people doing what I was then doing, and wondered how many man hours were spent in such traffic listening to inane morning radio across the infinite miles in hundreds of American cities, and I wondered how much ozone was destroyed and how many heart attacks prepared, and how many souls slowly lost. Here we were on this bright day, bumping along as the carbon monoxide ascended to the heavens and the molecules of insoluble fat clung one by one to the walls of arteries, accumulating silently as we stared glassy-eyed at the bumper ahead, the silver lodestar by which we navigated, and I can now almost see, too, the glorious souls of these travelers unravelling, wisp by ethereal wisp, like cotton candy being unmade, ungathering, unspooling into the cold, empty cosmos. Was I one of these people dying a little bit more every day? Was this the true end of my life, meaning that I had failed to find meaning, but had found what the grim joke carved into the wall at Yale said, that the search was a joke, that there was no meaning, and the larger joke was that we all somehow had enough on the ball to see that there was no meaning, which made it less a joke than a nightmare?

But as I drove I was yet hoping this wasn't true, so much so I found myself listening to lyrics. The Grateful Dead then had a hit called "Touch of Grey," which I loved, whose chorus said, "I will get by … I will survive" and I willed this to apply to myself in one of those confused prayers to the universe that amounts to nothing more than a wish, really, but I know now that God hears even those, seeing who we are and where we are, and I know he saw me then and heard my heart's longing. But at the time I didn't know it. I only hoped through a glass darkly and drove on.

Larry David

I don't remember how it came about, but somehow my pal Chris Noël and I were invited to read some of our humor at an event in Manhattan. Also reading would be the humorist Bill Franzen, who was the husband of our favorite *New Yorker* cartoonist, Roz Chast, who would herself be there! My

friend Monica arranged for her friend Larry David to come. He was struggling to succeed at that time, and who could predict that in a mere two years he would become the wildly successful co-creator of *Seinfeld*? My friend Charis Conn was there too, who, most of all the friends I had ever had, believed in my talents and in me. She was a senior editor at *Harper's Magazine* and had written some of the most brilliant fiction I'd ever read, and

Charis Conn, circa 2010

seeing her there that night made me so happy.

I read the two pieces I had published in *The Atlantic*, and then Chris Noël or I read the piece we had written together, about the man who created sculptures from meat, titled "Universität Meat." When the whole thing was over I was thrilled to meet Roz Chast, and then to have my friend Monica introduce her friend Larry, and to hear him say how much he loved what I had done and how "no one" was doing anything like what I was doing. It was true that by then Woody Allen had mostly stopped writing such pieces, which were in the tradition of Robert Benchley and S.J. Perelman, and the *New Yorker* had by this point gotten so "cool" that they thought genuinely funny jokes beneath them, unless written by Woody Allen himself, who might be grandfathered in. Larry suggested we get together, which we did, soon becoming friends.

I went to a dinner party at his apartment and the man who some years in the future would become famous as the "real Kramer" popped in to borrow something. Nor did I know that my friend Monica would be the basis for Elaine, complete with a famous gloomy writer dad and memories of working at a "Fat Camp." I looked at Larry's bookshelves and was thrilled to see that he had a copy of Ring Lardner's short stories, which he said he loved as I did.

One afternoon he took me to a book party at the Friars Club, where we hobnobbed with his friends Richard Belzer and Gilbert Gottfried, even then wearing his semi-frozen grimace. Larry thought so much of me that he connected me with his manager and future wife Laurie Lennard, who encouraged me to write sketches she could submit to *SNL* and to the *It's Garry Shandling's Show*. Not only did Laurie manage Larry, but also one of my favorite comedians, Chris Elliot—the son of Bob Elliot and his beautiful wife, Ray Goulding—who was then famous for his ultra-goofy sketches on *David Letterman*. Could I be far from noisily smashing the glass ceiling that kept Greek-German-Americans out of the comedy elites? But that wasn't to be, because whatever journey I was on to find the meaning of life would end up carrying me in another direction, one I certainly would not have chosen and did not choose.

Ed once said something to me that I didn't know quite how to take. "Ask God to show himself to you," he said. What puzzled me about it was the idea that I wasn't sure if God was there, so if I were to ask him to show himself to me, to whom would I be talking? I might just be talking to the oxygen and nitrogen in the atmosphere. But I was in enough pain during this period that I would sometimes be running in the cow pasture near my parents' home— where I had wandered and ridden my bike as a kid, and had gathered wildflowers in the fall of 1972—and coming to the top of a hill, it felt very natural to do just that. So I would pause and in my pain do the very thing that at other times seemed simply silly, and said, "OK, God, if you are there, and you can hear me, please give me some proof that you're there." And I'd look up at the sky and hope to get a sign, but never did.

Drogaris Funeral

But in the vast patches of nothingness that year, there were bits of punctuation that helped me make syntactical sense of the whole. Chief among them, like an exclamation point standing at attention amidst the ash-gray blather, was the funeral of my godfather, Nick Drogaris. The news came as a particular blow, because none of us had known he was sick. My Nouna Effie had decided to keep it quiet, so we hadn't heard from the Drogarises for some time, and before we thought to call them, we got Effie's phone call.

So one afternoon my father and mother and I, like an adolescent in the backseat, drove to Old Saybrook, on the Connecticut shore. The death of someone we love cannot help but force us to think about the big questions. I remember wondering about whether there is life after death and where my godfather was, if anywhere. His son, Anthony, whom I had known since we were infants, was adamantly indifferent to such things, but I wondered if the death of his father would make him reconsider them. At some point that day I spoke to him about something I had read regarding a life-after-death experience, but he politely waved it off.

I had heard that Mr. Vlastos might be at the funeral. Since I hadn't seen him in four and a half years, which at that time seemed an eternity, I was excited that I might see him and sure enough there he sat, amiably distracted as ever, in the front row. Seeing him was like seeing a celebrity, so I went over and said hello, but he hardly seemed to know me. In fact it was clear he didn't, and I was mystified and disappointed. He really had meant something to me. But he was old and tired and I didn't want to be a burden to him.[1]

---

[1] Not many years later I read with horror in the *New Yorker* what had eventually befallen him. A young ethnic woman had met him in a laundromat and told him her woes. He befriended her and before it was all over married her and signed hundreds of thousands of dollars over to her and her partner before they both—with an overdose of medicine—murdered him.

My godparents avoided the Greek Orthodox church, though of course they were married in it and a few years later consented to be my godparents. But christenings are for Greeks as much cultural events as anything. And of course when death occurs, people often revert to tradition. So for the funeral, Effie had indeed called a local Greek Orthodox priest, but when she said her husband's body would be cremated, the priest said he could not perform the funeral as the Orthodox, for not inconsiderable reasons, do not countenance cremation. So Effie opened the phone book and found someone else.

I was never before particularly appreciative of the effulgent beauty of most Greek Orthodox churches, but the pastel-colored chapel of this funeral home on the Post Road could remedy this. When the pastor hired for the ceremony—or to give the eulogy—began speaking, it became clear from his mispronunciation of my godfather's name and from his tone and the traffic pile-up of cliches that we were not in for any oration that would take its cues from Demosthenes or Saint John Chrysostom.

There were no references to Jesus or God, although at one point he said, "the psalmist writes ..." which seemed theologically vague enough. As he spoke I imagined a slideshow of bereavement cards with misty waterfalls and rainbows that would make anyone sensitive to the real beauty of life want to kill themselves. Unless you knew beforehand that this man would be your eulogist. He repeatedly mispronounced my godfather's name and each time, wincing spidered almost visibly like a lightning bolt through the seated mourners.

I think what bothered me—since I didn't know what I believed myself—was that the ceremony tried to split the difference between whether there was a God or wasn't, and in doing so drained everything of dignity. It was as when Jesus says he can handle heat and cold, but what is lukewarm he spits from his mouth. I guess I sensed the hypocrisy of this approach. If something is true, go with it, despite what some might think. And if it's not true, face the bleakness of that, since that's the reality we all need to face. Is it that when the chips are down is it simply too hard for people to face that bleakness, so they hypocritically borrow what they can from such faiths as might be tolerated? In any event, I was disgusted and infuriated at the charade. He had been such a good man—such a model husband and father—and this was at least unworthy of his memory.

On the ride home with my parents I railed at what I had observed, which made me think of our own church growing up, where despite everything there was nonetheless something similar at play, the sense that we weren't absolutely sure whether any of it were true and so were hedging our bets. We would shout over and over and over some of the most glorious words in human history, *"Christos Anesti!"* ("Jesus is Risen!")—but often with a strangely detached sullenness, as if we knew we couldn't know whether it were literally true, but weren't quite willing to say it wasn't either. So I sputtered at my poor parents and at the air itself, perhaps because I didn't know what I believed but was angry not to be getting more guidance from those who claimed to know what they did, or perhaps because I myself didn't know whether it was possible to know and didn't know what to do about that.

Around this time I got into a long conversation with Ed Tuttle, and at one point said something that betrayed where I stood. I think I was trying to figure out whether I should marry Clarissa, and said something like, "If there is a God, and I am definitely banking on the fact there is, then getting married is the right thing to do." Ed might easily have seen that I sort of wanted to believe and was leaning in that direction, but instead he stopped me right there in the underground parking lot where we were standing, having returned from lunch, and said: "Eric, I'm not sure you know God the way you could know him." Of course for Ed, banking on his existence wasn't at all the same as actually believing in Him, in knowing him personally, which for him was the whole point, and he felt the need then and there to make that clear. But I was taken aback by what he said, and when I returned to my miserable little cubicle, I found myself angry. *How on earth did he know* one could know God? It was just not possible to know as he seemed to claim it was, and if it were, I was sure I couldn't see any way forward to how that could happen, so I was stuck and I knew it and I resented the idea that there wasn't a damn thing I could do about it except kid myself, which I refused to do.

Over the weeks and months Ed continued to be my friend and talk about God. One day he came by my cubicle and handed me an index card with a Scripture verse he had written on it:

For I know the plans I have for you,
saith the Lord. Plans not to harm you,
but to give you hope and a future.
You will seek me and find me when
you seek me with all your heart.
—Jeremiah 29

I politely pinned this to the bulletin board in front of me and over the days and weeks following I considered the words. Eventually the logic of them got to me. If this God, whom I feared following—lest he embarrass me and turn me into a religious fanatic and ruin my life—was himself saying he did not mean to harm me, but to give me "hope and a future," then perhaps my reluctance in accepting him was not only wrong, but foolish. He seemed to be trying to put me at ease, to say that if I only knew him as he was I would trust him, knowing he wanted to bless me, not harm me. But how to know?

Around this time I picked up a book by M. Scott Peck, the Harvard psychiatrist who had written the monstrously popular *The Road Less Traveled*. But this one was titled *People of the Lie*, written before the other, and dealing with the concept of human evil. He discussed his experiences as a psychiatrist with people who evidenced something that, to him, seemed inexplicable in traditional psychological terms, something he came to see as genuine evil, as something infinitely sicker than any other psychological sickness, as something of a different order, whose vileness was to him palpable and horrifying. There was a chapter on the massacre at My Lai, about group evil, and he ended the book with some descriptions of exorcisms he attended, which I found completely fascinating and disturbingly believable. I'll never forget his description of someone's face horribly contorted into a heavy-lidded, reptilian mask.

As when I had seen *The Exorcist* eight years earlier, I intuited that if there really were such a thing as this kind of supernatural evil, then surely there had to be a God. But the idea struck me with a power it never had before.

Being in the environment of aggressive secularism at Yale and in Manhattan, I was also very concerned whether being a Christian made intellectual sense, and whether there were Christians with intellectual credibility, and whether I would look foolish believing in such things. Of course Christians like that were everywhere, but I hadn't met any. I had only just encountered M. Scott Peck, but around this time I stumbled upon Thomas Merton, who had been a Columbia University graduate with literary ambitions who converted to faith and even became a monk. I read his book *The Seven Storey Mountain,* telling his story, becoming slightly less worried about intellectual respectability. For goodness' sake, Leo Tolstoy was a Christian. So I began reading Tolstoy. But is this how we make our life decisions? It was a large part of how I did. But it was also less than the whole story.

Christians often talk about grace, and how it is God who chooses us, and not we who choose him. So for me it was as though my intellectual barriers and objections were not so much barriers to faith as barriers to my being able to see my true situation, meaning barriers to seeing across the vast abyss separating me from God. When each of these barriers was removed, like brushwood, as they seemed to be, day by day and week by week, and month by month, I was more and more able to see clearly across the vast abyss to God, whom I could not reach. But when at last I could see him across that abyss, I realized that although I could not reach him I could beckon to him to reach toward me. Wasn't that the point, that we cannot reach him across the vast abyss, but that he can reach us, but won't unless we want him to?

And so my life went on like this, with sputterings of hopelessness amidst the hope; and hope amidst the hopelessness. One day that spring I was driving to Union Carbide listening to the radio when Robert Plant's song "Heaven Knows" came on just about the time I was pulling onto the serpentine roads inside the building complex. As I pulled into a parking space I lingered to let the song finish. Over the weeks it had been in the Top 40, I had heard it a few times and had let myself wonder whether the universe was speaking to me through it, whether there was a Heaven and whether Heaven really did know about me, down here below the clouds, with my thoughts and hopes and dreams and fears. What if God really were real and really did know me? I couldn't imagine that was possible, but what if it were? And so as the song wound down and I prepared to exit the grim little vehicle into the grim vastness of this building I said to myself, "OK, if this song is on the radio when I turn it back on eight hours from now, I will know God is real." How many times in my life had I done something like that? And almost always I would forget about it five minutes later, which was exactly the right thing to do, since I didn't need evidence that God didn't exist and it was just as well I trudged on through life without having constant confirmations of it.

My days at Carbide were still unpleasant, but somehow I had gotten used to them, as I suppose most people get used to all kinds of things. Such is the hard reality of life for most of us and it seems a mercy that we do get used to things that were at first quite intolerable. But at least now I knew some of the people I worked with and liked many of them and joked with them. Bob Dube was a typesetter in his fifties with a pencil mustache who had been working there forever, and who had a distinctly Danburian way of speaking and a sly sense of humor that appealed to me. He sometimes seemed somewhat defeated by life, but never entirely so. I could tell that he actually loved his wife—"my wild Irish rose!" he called her—and one day he told me that his son, who was then a teenager, had at age twelve lost both his arms at the elbows in a ghastly train accident. But he seemed so proud of his son, who nonetheless worked on cars "with those hooks" that it moved me. And I eventually felt flattered that this hard-working soul should take a liking to me and say things I found funny.

And then there was Coré, who replaced the previous proofreader, a large woman who did copyediting whenever there was no proofreading, which was often. Coré had been in my class in high school, but I had never known her, although we had some mutual friends. She seemed a bit on the druggy side of things and I was as far from that in high school as one could be. But she had also been part of the same charismatic Christian community that George Duncan had been involved with, and which I had a few times attended. She was very clearly no longer on that theological page and almost cringed when Ed Tuttle came around, having by now adopted something of a sneering Southwestern hipster attitude, reveling in figures like Billie Holiday and Patsy Cline and Tom Waits. But we came to appreciate each other and become good friends, and sometimes discussed what it was that repulsed us about the world of "born-again" Christians.

And there were others, like Rudy, a friendly older black man in the graphics department who dressed very preppily, with horn rims, and a revolving bunch of crazies who came and went. Down the hall was an attractive but downright screwy Italian-American woman named Barbara, whom both of us hung around with sometimes. She was the proverbial scream. All she had to do was tell a story in her hard-edged Bronx accent and we would howl, as when she related a family affair featuring a cousin who for reasons that eluded us had to wear "rubber hands" instead of his real ones, and that weekend he had placed them on the radiator, of course feeling no pain, and they melted.

Ed was away for many weeks that spring, removing the evangelistic heat that I inevitably felt when he was around. He seemed to have a bad case of what was then called Epstein-Barr virus, although no one was ever clear what it was. But I knew he continued praying for me, and my thoughts about the existence of God continued, in their fashion.

At the end of the day in which I had that morning been listening to Robert Plant's "Heaven Knows" I got in my car to drive home and turned on the radio and Robert Plant's song "Heaven Knows" came on immediately. It took a few seconds for me to remember, but then suddenly I did remember that eight hours before—having utterly forgotten since—I had said, "If this song is on when I come back into this car I will know that Heaven does know and that God is real." And of course I sat there listening to the song and was flabbergasted. I simply didn't know what to do. The odds of such a coincidence were not in my favor and I goggled at the idea of it and then put the car in gear and drove along the serpentine roads that wound me out of the building, but as I did so I went almost crazy, incredulous that this really could have happened, that the very thing I had "prayed" or "wished" or "hoped" eight hours earlier and had completely forgotten about could really have come true. But I knew that it had, that God was real and that he knew me, that he had heard my cry and wanted to show me that he really did know me and care about me. Suddenly I was simply wild with the idea of it, that what I had hoped but didn't dare believe really was true, and I remember as I drove I was shouting to God from the inside of the car, though I don't remember what. But stranger than that song being on after I had asked for that sign was the fact that by the time I got home I had almost forgotten about the whole thing, and by the next day I had indeed forgotten about it. Was it that I couldn't allow myself to believe it? Or just that I needed more than that to change my life? And even if I were ready to change my life "for God," what did that mean? I had no idea.

CHAPTER THIRTY-FOUR

The Golden Fish

M y usual escapes from what I perceived as my parents' dourness would take me to New York City, where I would visit any of various friends. One weekend in June, I visited Kenny Doroshow, staying in his apartment Friday night and planning to go to my cousin John's wedding the following morning. I'd there meet my parents and brother, who were coming in from Connecticut. The wedding would be in the Greek Orthodox Cathedral, where my parents had been married twenty-nine years before. But my mother called me at Kenny's apartment to say Theo Takis had just had a bad stroke and was in a coma. This was devastating news, especially as my cousin was marrying the next day. Would they cancel the wedding? My mother said so many people had come from out of town that they would go through with it. But what a horrific development. And so the following day I went to my cousin's wedding, where all most people could do was think of my comatose uncle. We were really too sad to celebrate, but went through the motions as best we could. I remember that at the altar my sweet cousin John had tears in his eyes, which broke my heart.

On Monday, back at Union Carbide, I told Ed of these developments, and he told me that he'd be praying for my uncle. In fact, later that day he told me that a whole bunch of people from his church were praying for my uncle. This staggered me. I could hardly believe that total strangers could be praying for my uncle, and it moved me deeply in two ways: first that these Christians could be so extraordinarily kind as to pray for the uncle of someone they had never met; and second, that these people actually believed prayer could work, that it was real. I realized they weren't merely getting in touch with themselves or with the energy force within themselves, but were actually praying to someone outside themselves and beyond themselves, asking him to do something, so it wasn't in the realm of vague spirituality, with the idea of perhaps harmonizing one's "energy" with that of the universe, but had an actual and a linear and a causative and a distinctly personal feel to it, as though God was a person. He might have existed before time and outside of time and might have existed before he spoke the universe into being and he might have an intelligence of billions of human beings—but he was a person nonetheless. So we could talk to him. Perhaps because there was an object to the prayer that meant so much to me, I was more inclined to believe in it. My uncle's life was at stake, so suddenly my heart and mind were engaged. This, I think, is how God pulled me from unbelief into belief. It was a deep shift in my understanding of everything, and in me, too.

After work I went home, and because it was a hot day in June we went across the street to our neighbor's pool after supper. While we were there I excitedly told my parents that my friend, Ed, was praying for Theo Takis, and said we should pray too. I was enthused about praying in a way I simply never had been. Suddenly I had real hope. But amazingly to me, my parents were not interested. It seemed too painful for them to hope like that, as though it would only make things worse. But at the time this infuriated me. We were supposed to be Christians. They had forced me to go to church all those years, and now when I suggested we pray for my uncle they behaved as though it was almost foolish to hope too much. Of course in their defense, if you never see prayer work, the thought of it really can be painful, as though you are only digging at a wound and making it worse. But I was upset they had batted away my enthusiasm.

The following day I returned to Union Carbide, and this time when I met Ed Tuttle he asked me if I'd like to find some time to pray for my uncle with him. I said yes, and shortly thereafter we found an empty conference room and went in and shut the door. We sat on chairs, facing each other, and Ed bowed his head and closed his eyes, and I followed suit. Then Ed began praying for my uncle and for the doctors and for everything that could be prayed for. I had never done anything like this in my life, but with my uncle's life on the line, I wasn't going to let myself be embarrassed. And so I let Ed pray and keep praying. But as he did so, something quite extraordinary happened. As I sat there with my eyes shut, listening to him, I felt I had suddenly stumbled upon a hidden geography, as though Ed, with a few words, had opened a portal into another world, or as though with the mere invocation of the name of Jesus, he had with a fiery sword slit a hole in the air around us and it flapped aside like canvas and we felt and smelled the breeze of Heaven coming through it from another dimension. Somehow I felt this, though not in any powerfully mystical way, but it was as though while my body was in a beige, fluorescent conference room in the gray heart of corporate America, my soul nonetheless through this prayer had reached up, like Jack poking his head through the clouds at the top of the beanstalk, and I for the first time in my life breathed a bracing draught of Heaven's super-blue, perfectly innocent air. I was not supernaturally transported to another realm, but I nonetheless could somehow feel the reality of the dimension we were touching with that prayer. It seemed to me not just to be words but to have a reality to it, as though Ed had through his faith and this prayer opened the door to something beyond us, though I had never felt it or known it before now.

Then Ed closed the prayer in Jesus's name, and I opened my eyes. But it was startling suddenly to be fully back in the room, as though I'd rappelled down the beanstalk a little too quickly. But as I sat there now I knew that something really had happened. But what?

Every day Ed asked how my uncle was doing, and I began to pray now, too. I don't know what possessed me to leap in, as it were, to believe that I was actually talking to God, but sometimes it is the object, the goal, that moves the athlete across the field, and this was the case here. I just wanted my uncle to get better and if prayer to "God" could affect that, I was certainly willing to do it. But one day I got home from work and my mother told me that Theo

Takis had died. I was sad to hear it, and could hardly believe it. But for some reason I was not disappointed in the prayers that had not been answered as I had hoped. For some reason I believed they had been heard, though of course not with the answer we had hoped for, but their inability to produce the results I wanted did not anger me or put me off God. It was as if for some reason over the last weeks God had become real enough to me that I trusted him, even if he hadn't done what I had begged him to do.

The following Monday was my twenty-fifth birthday and my father's sixty-first, and it was the day we buried my uncle. The funeral was in the cathedral where a week earlier my cousin had been married. How my heart went out to him, whose love for his father had always been so obvious and touching. I remember that when I saw my uncle's body in the church I felt clearly that he was not there. It seemed clearer to me than anything that he was someplace else, and that this was only the body he had left behind. For some reason the priest asked me if I would read the Psalms in the background while people came to the coffin, and I was happy for something to do. But this was the first time I had ever read the psalms, near my uncle's body as the mourners filed past.

After the ceremony my brother and I drove to the cemetery across the Hudson in Nyack. We arrived early and found the grave site, next to which lounged the two lanky black grave-diggers who had just finished the job and who seemed like a pair of characters from a nineteenth-century American novel. One of them had actual holes through his front teeth; I was for some reason happy to speak with them, suddenly caring deeply for them. My brother and I talked with them until the hearse and everyone else arrived, and after the ceremony we drove to a local restaurant with some of the family and some friends. I didn't exactly realize it then, but twenty-five years to the day before, my father had welcomed me into the world, and now he was bidding his eldest and his dear brother goodbye. In the restaurant I sat next to Father Bob Stephanopoulos—the father of George—who for many years was the chief priest of the cathedral. We spoke briefly of spiritual things, as they were so much on my mind, though I do not remember the details. Something was happening to me, but I wasn't sure where it would lead.

That week in Danbury, life continued. It was a very hot summer, perhaps the hottest and most humid in memory. I many nights went with my parents across the street to the neighbor's pool. Looking back, it seems that God had surreptitiously established a beachhead in my soul and was now laboring to take the high ground, and in a few nights would do just that. I don't remember exactly which night it was, but it was just a few days after we buried my Theo Takis, a few days after my birthday and my father's. On that night I had a dream unlike any I had ever had before, and unlike any I have had since.

The Dream

In the dream I was ice fishing on Candlewood Lake in Danbury. I have a vague memory that John Tomanio and his father were with me; and in the dream it was a glorious winter day, sunny and bright and cold. And as I was standing there on the ice I remember looking down into the hole we had chopped in it, and seeing a fish, a pike or a pickerel, and it was sticking its snout out of the hole, so to speak, as though waiting for me to reach down and pull it out. It goes without saying that in the history of ice fishing, such things do not happen. But in the dream it was very real, and so when I saw the fish I reached down and lifted it up by the gill—because you don't dare lip-land fish like pike or pickerel, whose teeth are many and sharp—and then I stood and proudly held it up in the sunlight to show it off, and to get a good look at it myself.

It was a large fish, much larger than you would normally catch in Candlewood, and had the typical green and bronze coloring of its species. But as I held it up into the bright winter sunlight it seemed to take on a distinctly golden color—and then suddenly in the dream I realized that it did not merely look golden. No. It really was golden. I realized that it was an actual golden fish, a living fish that was made of gold, and yet entirely alive, like something out of a fairy tale.

And in the bright sunlight shining off the ice and the snow and under the brilliantly clear super-blue sky I beheld it, this golden fish that was alive, and as I beheld it a tremendous joy welled up inside me, inside my dream, inside my sleep. Because suddenly in that moment I knew that this golden fish I was holding up was no mere fish, but was what my father had told me about when we saw the chrome fish on the backs of cars in the seventies. This was that fish, was **IXTHYS**—*Iesous Christos Theon Yios Sotir*—Jesus Christ the Son of God our Savior. I knew in the dream—with a new kind of knowing I knew was from God himself—that the living golden fish I held in my hands and had simply lifted out of the water was Jesus, the Christ who had come into our world to die.

And right there in the dream I realized that God was speaking to me, that he was essentially one-upping me with my own symbol system, through symbols I alone would understand and did understand. I knew this was the metaphorical lake through whose frozen conscious surface I had wanted to chop, to find the water which was for me Jung's proverbial collective unconscious, which was the divine. But God in the dream had seen my metaphor and had raised me, so to speak. It was as if he were saying, "You thought you were searching for inert water, for an impersonal god-ness of which you were yourself a part—but I want to give you not mere water, but a living creature, a Golden Fish who is my son, your savior, Jesus Christ. Receive him." And there in the dream I did.

In fact I remember holding the fish with both arms as though I were hugging him, holding him to my breast, and in doing this I knew that he had come to me and I would never be alone again, that he was mine; and in the dream I was filled with joy, the kind of joy I had never had in my life. I knew then that I had found what I had always been searching for—or rather, that he had found me. And so I really had found truth, and the truth I had found was that Truth was a person, was Jesus, and I knew that truth or Truth could never be reduced to anything less, any more than light could be reduced to either particles or to waves without ceasing to be light. So as I held him who was Truth in my arms in the dream I knew it was over, my search for the meaning of life. I would spend the rest of my life figuring out what it meant in deeper and more detailed ways, but what I had been looking for and didn't know I could find I had found, just as those bumper stickers had said. I found it. In this fairytale-dream-come-true

I had found the Well at the World's End, from which we drink the living water that makes us never thirst again.

And so in the dream I held God in my arms and knew that he loved me. He had come here to die, had come from the other side of the door in my grandmother's dream when she brought my grandfather to Heaven. So I was standing there on the white, frozen lake, with the sky as blue as blue can be, and maybe bluer, and the winter sun shining as brightly as it ever shone, and my heart was bursting with joy, because I knew then for sure that this was real and that he would never leave me nor forsake me—no never—not even at the end of the world.

CHAPTER THIRTY-FIVE

As I Lay Dying

My Savior is a fish.

I Am Born Again, Etc.

The next day at Union Carbide I couldn't wait to see Ed, and I told him about my dream, but without going into too much interpretive detail. "What do you think it means?" he asked me.

"I know exactly what it means," I replied. And then I said what at any time before that day I would have cringed to hear, much less say myself. But I did not cringe. "It means I've accepted Jesus." And in the instant in which I said this I was filled with the same joy I had had in the dream itself. It bloomed inside me right there as I spoke to him, and I knew then that there was nothing temporary about this. I had been as they say born anew, born again, born "from above." I was what the Bible calls a new creation. What was I to make of it? And yet I knew it. I before had held the whole question of God at some arm's length, but was now suddenly running toward him without fear. I had suddenly become what I had previously feared and was unabashedly and unashamedly a follower of Jesus. I knew most of my friends would be horrified.

I have often said that what happened to me was like going to sleep single and waking up married. I had nothing to do with it and yet I was unable to pretend it hadn't happened or wasn't real. And since I was unconscious when it happened I couldn't take any credit for it. That would be like Lazarus taking credit for his own resurrection from the tomb. It was not him "exercising his faith" and believing Jesus could raise him from the dead that helped get him up from the slab because we know he was a rotting corpse who had no faith to exercise. Spiritually speaking we are all of us rotting corpses. We have no spiritual life and are spiritually dead. We are not sick, but dead. And only God who is life itself can resurrect us by giving us his life, which he gave via the cross and resurrection. So with his eternal life in us, we become alive eternally. In his death and resurrection, Death itself has died forever, and we can live forever. I could not contain my joy at last to know that this was all really true.

From there things get blurry. Sorting out the chronology and events of the first few weeks of my new faith are difficult. Thinking back to the first moments after one was born again is something like thinking back to the first months after one was physically born. It's not easy to recall somehow.[1]

I spent that weekend in New Canaan, Connecticut, with my old friend David Johnson. I remember reading a book I found in his mother's library by the English author John Stott, titled *Basic Christianity*. It was a simple apologia for the Christian faith, written in Stott's wonderfully precise style, and I gobbled it up. It was as if my heart, having made the leap o'er the fabled broomstick was now pulling my brain over to join it, something it has been doing ever since.

But I was generally out of my head for joy, knowing I had just begun a great adventure. A few days after my conversion Ed Tuttle asked if I wanted to hear someone speak in Fishkill, over the Connecticut border. The speaker had a local television show in which he declaimed his particular take on end-time prophecies. Only weeks before I had considered him a well-meaning but voluble crank, but now I was a Jesus believer and he was too, so I couldn't wait to hear what he had to say, not caring how screwy it might sound. Ed and I went to a crummy room in a Ramada Inn and the man began speechifying about the European

---

[1] In one Bugs Bunny cartoon he asks a bulldog chasing him when he was born, and the bulldog replies: "Duh, I dunno. I was pretty young den."

Union and the Beast with ten horns, saying whoever became the head of the EU must surely be the Antichrist, but he delivered it all in a funny way, as if it weren't the end of the world or anything, which, of course, ironically, it was, if he was correct. And there in the room with me were the crazies I had spent years avoiding, the brush-cut rubes who didn't know Marcel Proust from Marcel Marceau. For the first time I saw that these folks might know something my Yale friends didn't, and what they knew was more important. And whatever they didn't know didn't mean a damn thing compared to that. I had been shown the reality behind the curtain, and God seemed to be elbowing me at the hilarity of it, because it was all simultaneously the funniest and truest thing in the universe.

It was just a few days later that my newfound faith began to manifest itself in very practical ways. For one thing, knowing God had now come to live inside me, I happily surrendered to him in all things, so that when I next saw Clarissa I told her what happened and said that I could no longer be physically intimate. My feelings for God were so strong that that was suddenly simply impossible. Of course it must have been difficult and confusing to hear such a thing, but I felt I had no choice in saying it. Another way my faith manifested itself practically was in my moving from my parents' house to my friend David Johnson's, who lived in New Canaan. I needed space from my poor parents, who probably now found me more trying than ever, so for the next three months with David's generous permission I slept on a canvas army cot in a three-and-a-half by seven-foot alcove in his third-floor apartment, with my worldly belongings shoved under the cot, so that my first months in the Kingdom had something of a bootcamp flavor to them.

One evening David found me reading a book and asked me what it was. If I had replied *Ivanhoe* or *1066 and All That* or *Two Years Before the Mast* or *archie & mehitabel* he would have been thrilled and a fascinating conversation would have ensued, but when I said I was reading the Bible—as matter-of-factly as possible—his face dropped. "Oh," he said. My poor friends would not have an easy time with my strange transformation. I soon after had dinner with my friend Sam on the Upper East Side when I shared, as gingerly as I could, what had happened, and he didn't take it well. One minute we were having a calm conversation and the next he believed I was consigning him to Hell, which I certainly hadn't, but who can deny these subjects are as rife with misunderstanding on both sides as any in the world?

Many of my Yale friends heard that I had flipped my wig, such that my mere presence now made them squirm. But anyone claiming to have found God somehow inevitably represents a threat to much that we hold dear, and avoiding them is often the only sane course. I vividly remember feeling this way myself, so how could I judge my friends for it now? Not that it didn't hurt, but what could I do? And what of my family, who in their midst now had a maniac constantly talking of Jesus and the Bible, as though they had raised me as some kind of atheist? And what about the Greeks who would think I had left their great and historic church for some shallow Protestant fad designed to break my heart?

Some friends like Chris Noël and Kenny Doroshow—and Charis Conn, to whom I dedicate this book—were generously accepting of my newfound faith, even though they didn't share it; but they were somehow fascinated, which is why we were always such good friends. They were intellectually curious and had something childlike about them, in the best sense. But for some others I had become their worst nightmare. I was one of them in every way, but had suddenly been transformed into someone monstrous whom they must for their own emotional health and social standing avoid. And so it was in this strange way, no longer so welcome in my previous circles, that I somehow became a fish out of water once more. But now, of course, it would be different and was different, because now I enjoyed the company of that Golden Fish of Fishes who had come out of the water for me—and who in doing so promised me that I could now in part and one day fully and forever return with him to that happiest medium for which I had been created in the first place; so that I was truly no longer a fish out of water at all, and would never again be one. No, never. World without end. *Amen.*

Epilogue

Two weeks after my dream I decided to see Scorsese's hugely controversial film *The Last Temptation of Christ*, although I was not privy to the important objections many Christians had to it. I had been a Scorsese fan since *Raging Bull* and figured anything by him was worth seeing, so I went to Manhattan to see it with my friend Ken Doroshow. But when we approached the Ziegfeld on 54th Street, I saw I had underestimated things. The line snaked all the way back to Sixth Avenue and 55th, and there were protestors everywhere. Some seemed Christlike in their protest, singing hymns and praying, but others were less pacific, which embarrassed me in the presence of my friend, who was Jewish and knew I had recently become serious about my faith. "You are going to Hell!" one of the protestors howled at me, glaring at me through thick-lensed, heavy-framed nerd glasses, as though out of central casting, a living caricature of someone whose moralistic view of the world forced him to damn me for seeing this movie.

To be fair however, the movie was a cinematic catastrophe, and a theological horror. When Harvey Keitel as Judas spoke in a tough-guy Brooklyn accent, there were titters and stifled guffaws. And then, when Willem Dafoe as a conflicted, mealy-mouthed Jesus was tempted in the desert, Satan at one point became a kindly-looking lion—who suddenly spoke in Harvey's Brooklyn voice, provoking horse laughs. It was almost camp. But the crucifixion scene I found powerfully moving. It has to be one of the best ever put on the screen and brought tears to my eyes.

The weeks of that summer went along and every day I spent time with Ed Tuttle, who answered my questions, suggested books, and simply showed me what it was to follow Jesus. But I knew I needed to find a church. The journey with God is meant in some sense to be a communal one, and the Bible says we are not to "neglect the gathering together of the brethren." So Ed suggested I check out St. Paul's church in Darien, just a few miles from where I was staying with David, and that Sunday I went to a service.

The church was situated down in a grove of trees immediately south of the Merritt Parkway. It was architecturally typical of what passed for contemporary in the mid-sixties, which is to say ugly. But that morning a great pink-and-white-striped tent was set up on the lawn, and the service was held there. The rector was Terry Fullam, whose son had been married there the day before and they had left the tent up. So the first service of my new life was under a wedding tent. It was one of those gorgeous September mornings that itself seems to be a promise of how wonderful the future is going to be. The preacher was Mark Browne, a thirty-five-year-old Texan with horn-rimmed glasses. His was the first "evangelical" sermon I ever heard. Interestingly enough, he spoke about the movie I had just seen, explaining that the problem with Scorsese's movie—and with Nikos Kazantzakis's book, on which it was based—was that it depicted a Christ who was as broken and sinful as we are, making him not the savior of the world, but someone who is therefore theologically self-contradictory and fatally confused.

I found at St. Paul's a true community of friends who sustained me for years, and the preaching was so spectacular I often went to both the morning and evening services. I had never sung to God before, and the worship was so moving that I sometimes wept. I had never understood what worship was, and remembered when my good friend Elizabeth at Yale told me of her boyfriend's sister's conversion, how the sister said she loved "to worship," at which Elizabeth made a face that communicated the lunacy of it to both of us, and made us howl. What could someone mean by that? And here I was now, one of those people.

A few months later St. Paul's put on a conference in Ridgefield, and I went. At the end of one session a man in his eighties from Texas hugged me. "My brother!" he said. I had never had a grandfather, so to have this old man hug me and say that to me, who was sixty years his junior, really got to me.

The conference was led by Father Fullam, assisted by Reverend Peter Church, and Mr. Lee Buck, who had been a top executive with Arthur Andersen before his conversion but who now was a lay evangelist, which term I found awkward. In the course of the conference Lee Buck told us fascinating stories, one of which involved casting a demon out of a girl. It was unembellished and detailed and credible. Why hadn't I heard stories like this before? Jesus cast out demons and His disciples did too. Who had insisted we must take these stories as metaphors and why had anyone bought that? I would hear many such stories over the next few years, and almost every time I thought, *Why haven't I heard this before?* Why did we pretend we somehow knew these things weren't happening and had probably never happened when there was so much evidence to the contrary?

In a recent book, my friend Greg Laurie carefully documents how Steve McQueen in his last years became an ardent Jesus-follower and churchgoer who wanted to use his fame to share Jesus with the world, but who fell ill before he could, and who literally died holding Billy Graham's own Bible in his hands. How had the world never heard of this before?

I came to see that a kind of secular filter has developed over the last fifty years or so, and the mass media have largely—sometimes scandalously—ignored some of the most amazing stories of our time, principally because they tend to be uncomfortable talking about anything touching on faith—sometimes because of an embarrassing ignorance of theological matters, and other times for fear of how it will be perceived by their preponderantly secular colleagues. But as a result, most Americans have missed some tremendously important things about the reality and role of faith in history and culture.

It was only because of my book on William Wilberforce that I discovered it was almost exclusively serious Christians who launched the abolitionist movements in Europe and America. But I have discovered much more along similar lines, such as the fact that civil rights leaders such as Jackie Robinson and Rosa Parks were devoutly Christian, and that their heroic faith played the central role in their achievements. The film *42* about Robinson's life omits this, and the otherwise excellent Johnny Cash biopic *Walk the Line* also bizarrely omits the central fact of Cash's life: that it was his "born-again" experience with Jesus—and the strong faith of his wife, June—that pulled him out of the living hell of drug abuse and made him the man he eventually became, and who often played at Billy Graham crusades as a way of being public about his transformation. I was also stunned to learn that minutes after Apollo 11 landed, Buzz Aldrin took communion on the moon and read the words of Jesus aloud in the Lunar Module, which I eventually had the privilege of discussing with him.

During these same first months of my newfound faith I began reading books to fill in the holes in my thinking. My heart was lightyears ahead of my mind and there was much upon which to catch up. I read an extraordinary book by F.F. Bruce titled *The New Testament Documents: Are they Reliable?* I read a book titled *Evidence That Demands a Verdict.* I read books by David Wilkerson and by Smith Wigglesworth and by Watchman Nee. And of course I read C.S. Lewis and Dietrich Bonhoeffer, whose *The Cost of Discipleship* Ed Tuttle gave me one day, neither of us then dreaming that I would one day write a biography of the great martyr. At some point I found the writings of Malcolm Muggeridge and G.K. Chesterton's *Orthodoxy* and Chuck Colson's *Loving God,* shocked to learn in its pages that Solzhenitsyn had found God in the Soviet Gulag. And then I read my favorite book, *Chance or the Dance?* by Thomas Howard, whom I had the inestimable privilege of meeting at Lewis's college in Oxford, and eventually calling my friend.

And what more shall I say? I do not have time to tell about Peter Kreeft's books and Alice von Hildebrand's and Corrie ten Boom's and Richard Wurmbrand's and Os Guinness's and Tim Keller's and John Lennox's and Hugh Ross's and Rosaria Butterfield's and John Rankin's. Why had I never heard of these books or people before? Why hadn't we read C.S. Lewis at Yale and why didn't everyone in every English department in the country know they should teach that sublimest of all books—*Perelandra*—alongside

Paradise Lost? What was wrong with the world and how could the world be *that* wrong?

Tomorrow

The rest of the story—and the many stories—of what happened to me after my dream in 1988 must be told in another book. But the paragraph-long version is that I miraculously got a job writing for a children's book company called Rabbit Ears, during which time God miraculously spoke to me about my future and miraculously led me to end my long and difficult relationship, and then through the miraculous words of a friend comforted me during that heartbreaking experience; and then gave me the strength to withstand twenty years of Chronic Fatigue Syndrome and depression and serious financial struggles, and in the midst of that time miraculously spoke to me about a friend's death via a Romanian fairytale, and then miraculously spoke to me about my Uncle Othon's death and about my future with my father's homeland, and miraculously showed me what he could do in the life of someone I had thought past redemption; and he also led me to my wife, and miraculously spoke to me about her in a dream, and later miraculously spoke to me about her in a movie theater, and then miraculously spoke to me about how we were to be engaged, and then miraculously fulfilled what he had spoken to me about it; and miraculously told me my wife and I would have a child and miraculously spoke to me about 9/11 and miraculously spoke to me about my financial difficulties and miraculously spoke to me about my future through a huge snapping turtle in Central Park and miraculously spoke to me about writing my biography of William Wilberforce and then miraculously spoke to me about writing my book about Dietrich Bonhoeffer and about my future with my mother's homeland. It is important to be clear that not in any of these instances have I used the word "miraculously" lightly. But as I say, the details must wait for another book.

This is therefore only the first part of my story, ending with my crossing the starting line of my life with God. I hope more than anything that it encourages you in your own search for the meaning of life, which I have come to believe is itself a part of the meaning of life.

But having told these stories of my younger life, I close this volume with the last stanzas of Milton's "Lycidas."

Thus sang the uncouth swain to th' oaks and rills,
While the still morn went out with sandals grey;
He touched the tender stops of various quills,
With eager thought warbling his Doric lay:
And now the sun had stretched out all the hills,
And now was dropped into the western bay.
At last he rose, and twitched his mantle blue:
Tomorrow to fresh woods, and pastures new.

Appendix

Swimming to My Father

ERIC METAXAS

I was seven years old and couldn't swim,
but my father made me swim to him.
I was over my head in Peconic Bay
and while I swam he backed away.
To me it seemed a nasty trick.
"Keep your fingers closed and kick!"
he said and didn't seem to see my fear,
but praised me slowly drawing near.
I still can see his giddy face
and feel his wet and warm embrace.
Right now I see him standing there:
He's young and strong with dark brown hair.
Where could that strength and youth now be?
I think he lent them both to me.
He lent a bit of each that day.
What's good is good to give away.
I also have his giddy glee
when now my daughter swims to me.

At the Last Wedding

ERIC METAXAS

If wind were blue
rushing like water through treetops,
through knee-grasses,
If I could more than glimpse it
on a scattering of trees, a primary blueness
streaking from the southwest.
Now the sky descends like a stream pouring
through the clouds, raw and original blue
rushing down to sweep across the face of its brother.
Along white sea cliffs,
through temples ruined surging,
the verb of life flows up the peopled mount
To the altar, waiting.
Lift the veil.
See at last the crystal wind;
the kiss, as deed embraces intention;
reality and appearance spinning
arm in arm in arm.
I unpurse a laughing stream of blue,
cutting through the haze to an opening,
in through the rock, bursting blue again.

The Little Black Boy

WILLIAM BLAKE

My mother bore me in the southern wild,
And I am black, but O! my soul is white;
White as an angel is the English child:
But I am black as if bereav'd of light.
My mother taught me underneath a tree
And sitting down before the heat of day,
She took me on her lap and kissed me,
And pointing to the east began to say.
Look on the rising sun: there God does live
And gives his light, and gives his heat away.
And flowers and trees and beasts and men receive
Comfort in morning joy in the noonday.
And we are put on earth a little space,
That we may learn to bear the beams of love,
And these black bodies and this sun-burnt face
Is but a cloud, and like a shady grove.
For when our souls have learn'd the heat to bear
The cloud will vanish we shall hear his voice.
Saying: come out from the grove my love & care,
And round my golden tent like lambs rejoice.
Thus did my mother say and kissed me,
And thus I say to little English boy.
When I from black and he from white cloud free,
And round the tent of God like lambs we joy:
Ill shade him from the heat till he can bear,
To lean in joy upon our fathers knee.
And then I'll stand and stroke his silver hair,
And be like him and he will then love me.